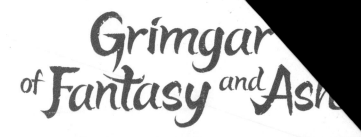

Grimgar
of Fantasy and Ash

I

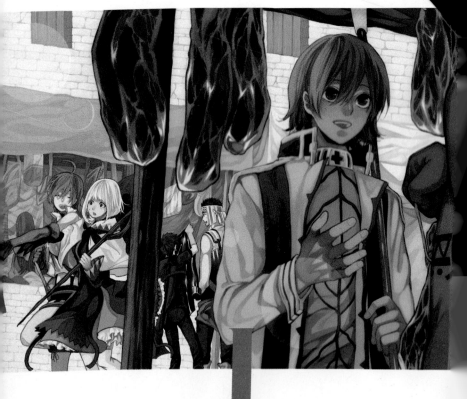

LEVEL.1

ORIGINAL STORY
Ao Jyumonji

ART
Mutsumi Okubashi

CHARACTER DESIGN
Eiri Shirai

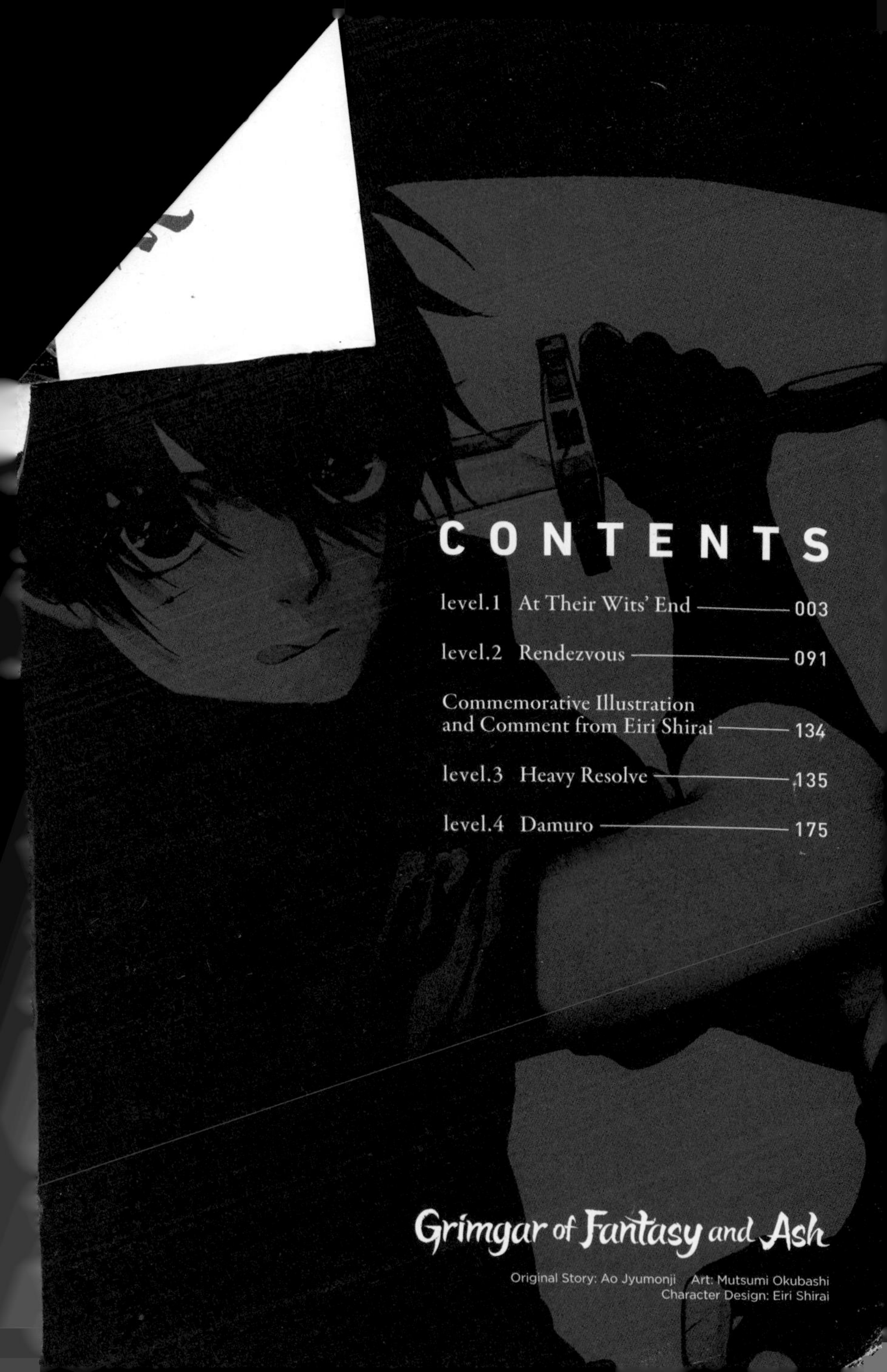

CONTENTS

Grimgar of Fantasy and Ash

Original Story: Ao Jyumonji Art: Mutsumi Okubashi
Character Design: Eiri Shirai

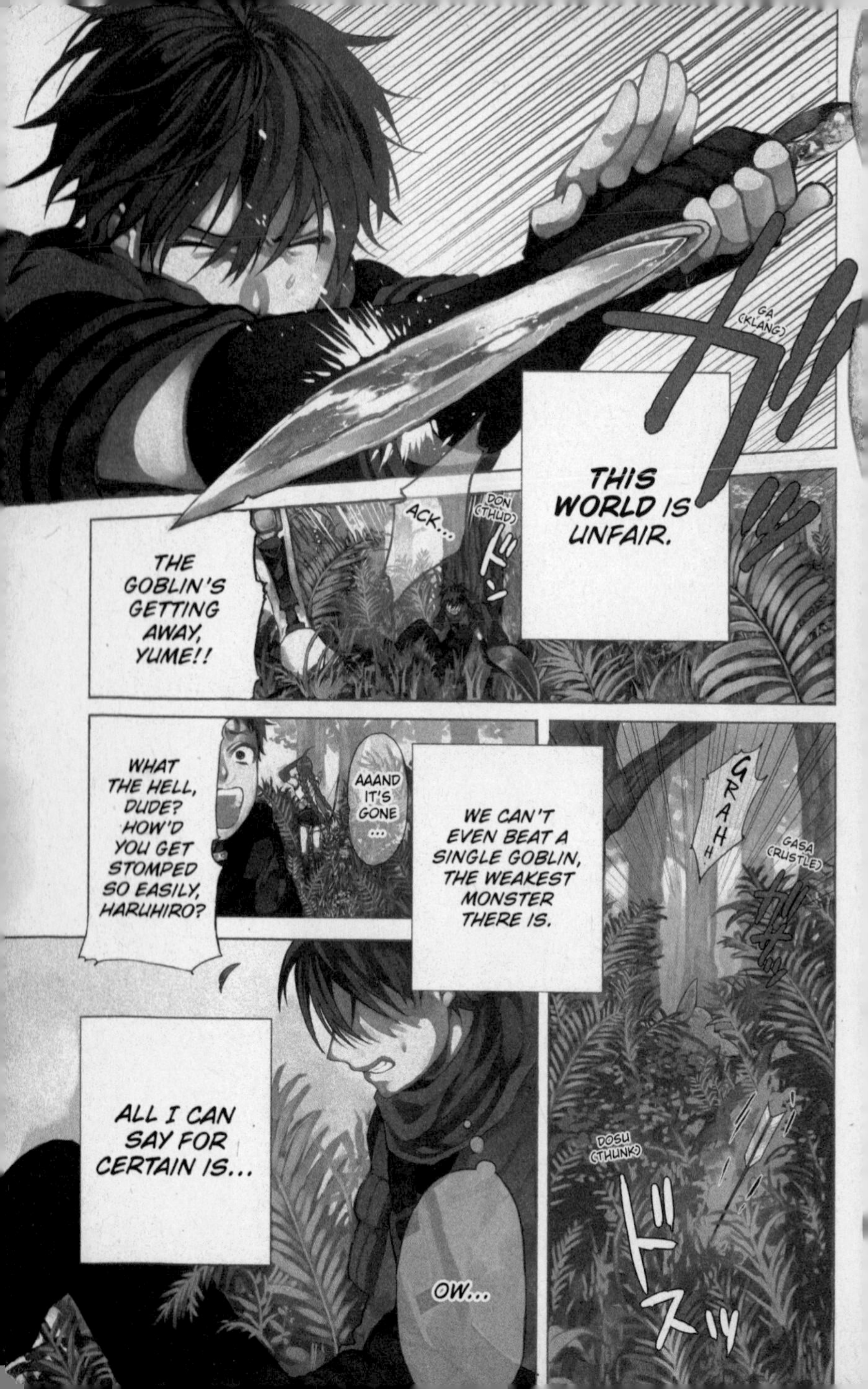
GA (KLANG)
THIS WORLD IS UNFAIR.
ACK...
DON (THUD)
THE GOBLIN'S GETTING AWAY, YUME!!
GRAHH
GASA (RUSTLE)
DOSU (THUNK)
WE CAN'T EVEN BEAT A SINGLE GOBLIN, THE WEAKEST MONSTER THERE IS.
AAAND IT'S GONE...
WHAT THE HELL, DUDE? HOW'D YOU GET STOMPED SO EASILY, HARUHIRO?
ALL I CAN SAY FOR CERTAIN IS...
OW...

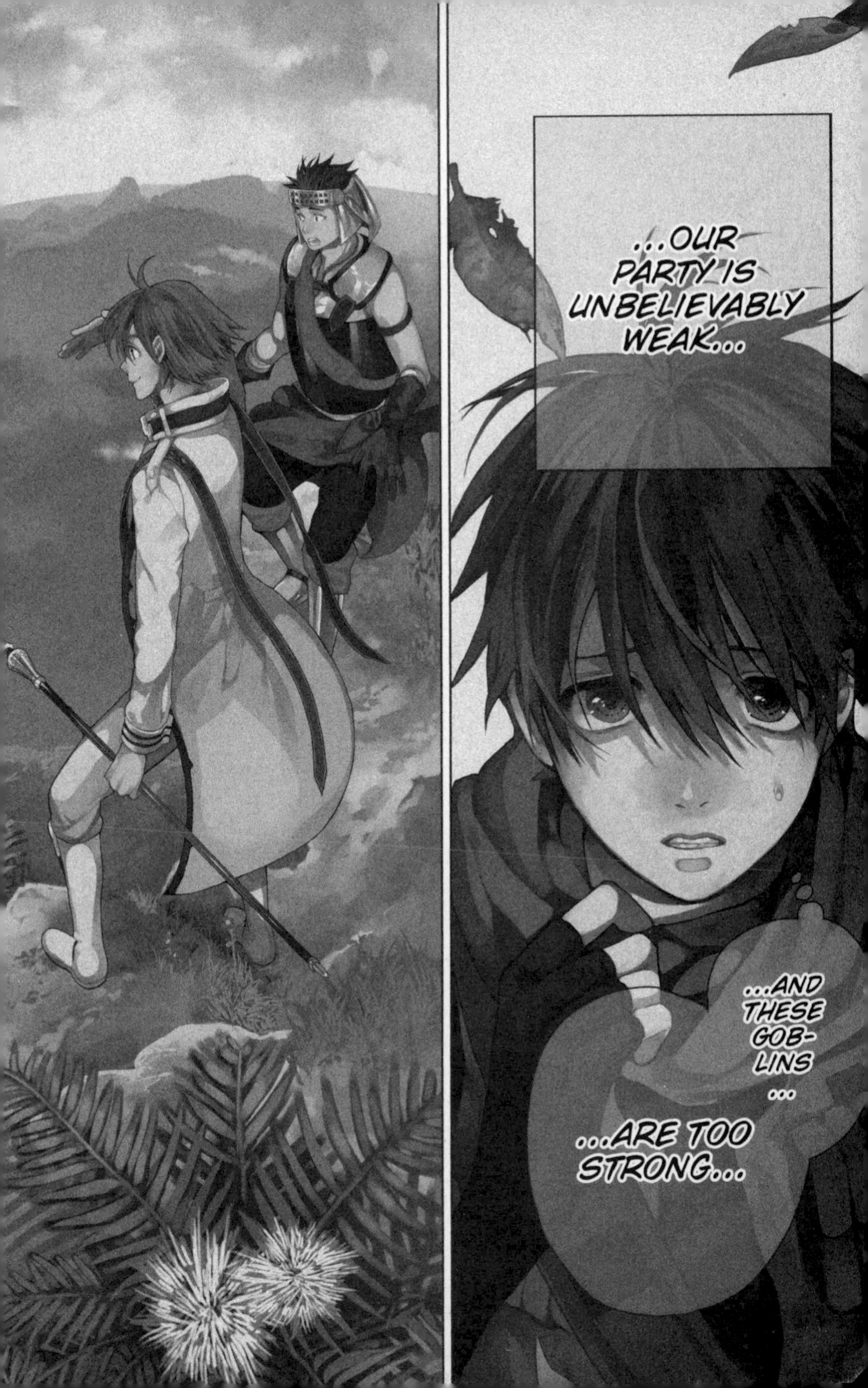
...OUR PARTY IS UNBELIEVABLY WEAK...
...AND THESE GOB-LINS ...
...ARE TOO STRONG...

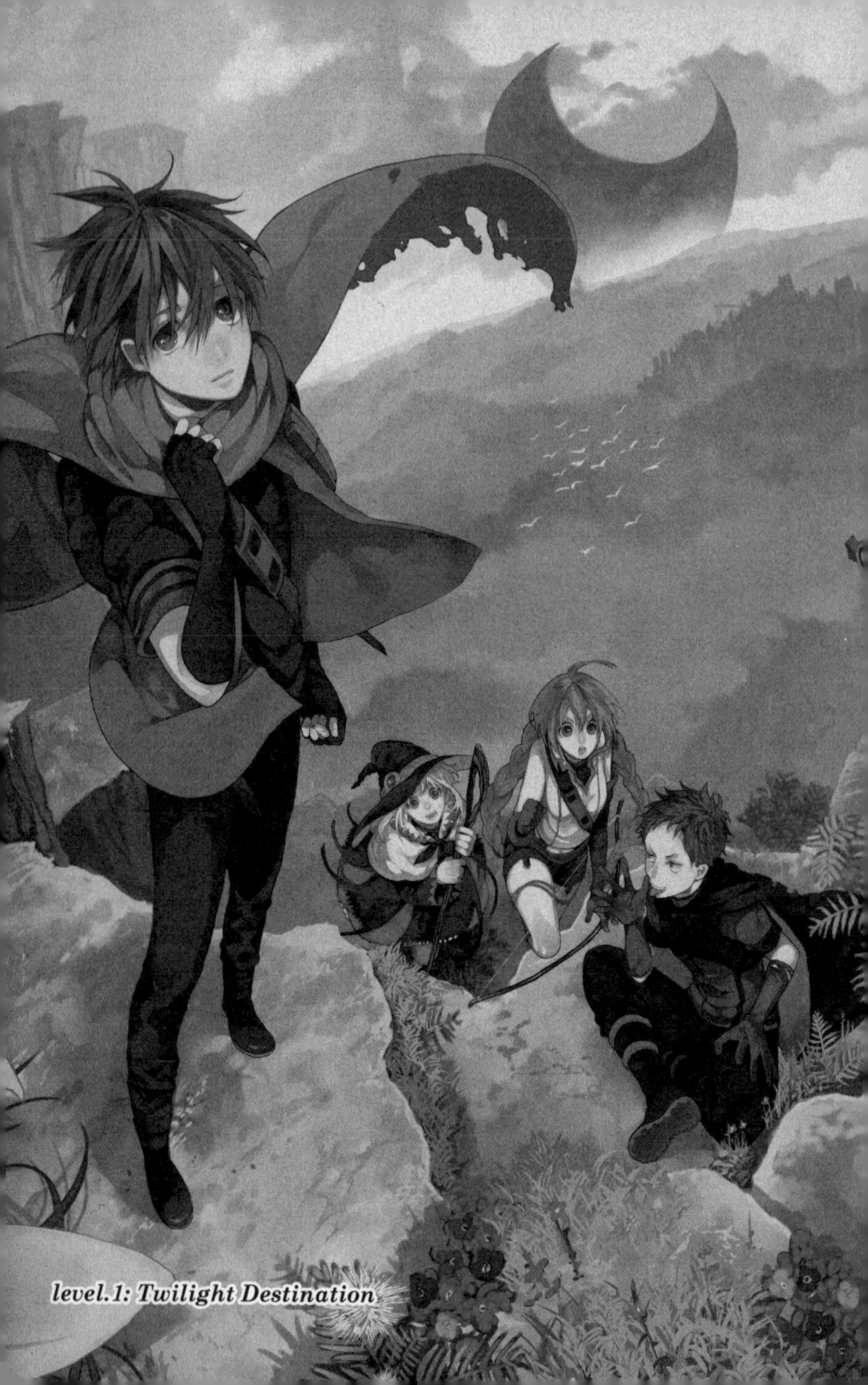
level.1: Twilight Destination

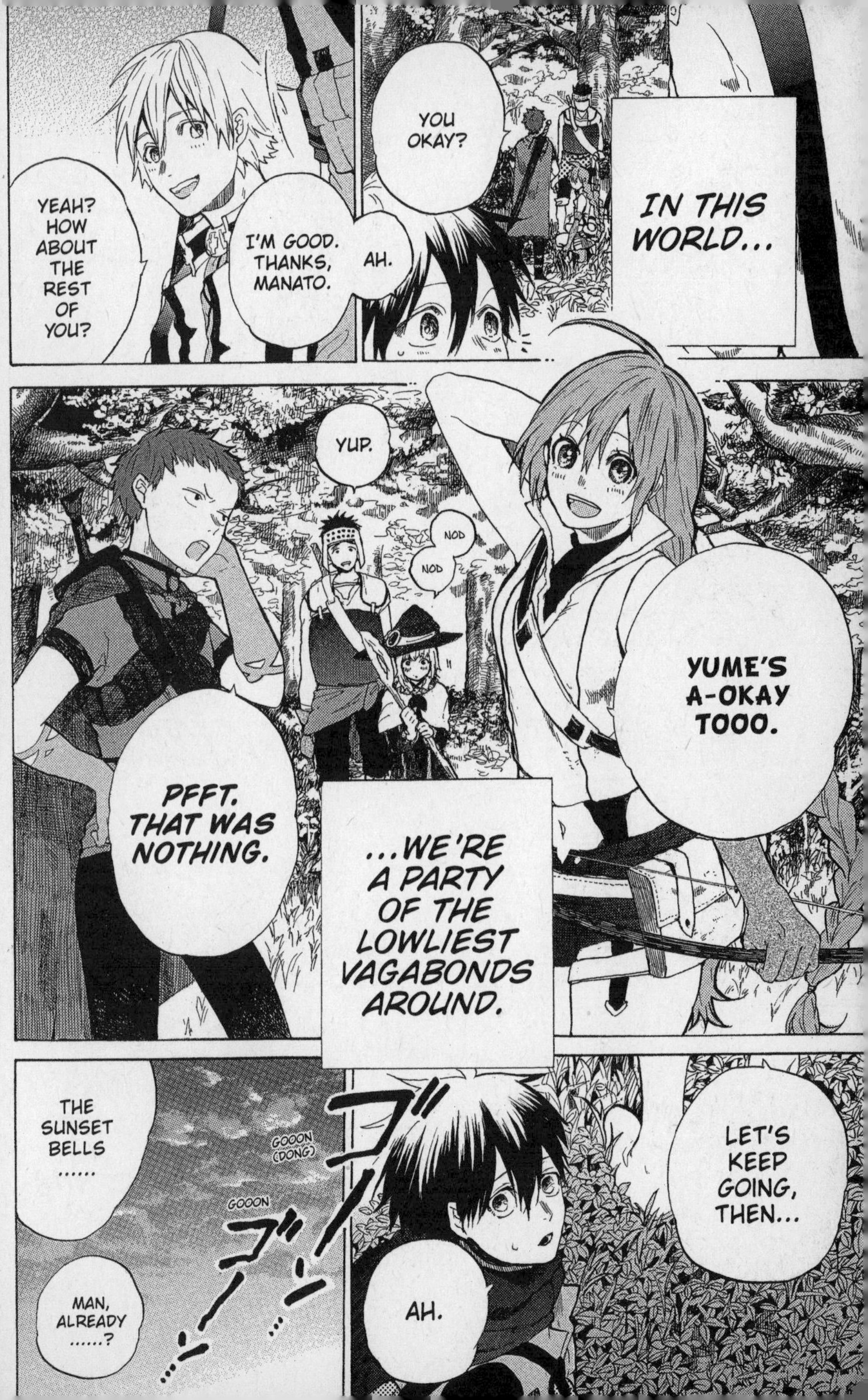
IN THIS WORLD...
YOU OKAY?
AH.
I'M GOOD. THANKS, MANATO.
YEAH? HOW ABOUT THE REST OF YOU?
YUME'S A-OKAY TOOO.
YUP.
NOD
NOD
PFFT. THAT WAS NOTHING.
...WE'RE A PARTY OF THE LOWLIEST VAGABONDS AROUND.
LET'S KEEP GOING, THEN...
AH.
GOOON (DONG)
GOOON
THE SUNSET BELLS......
MAN, ALREADY......?

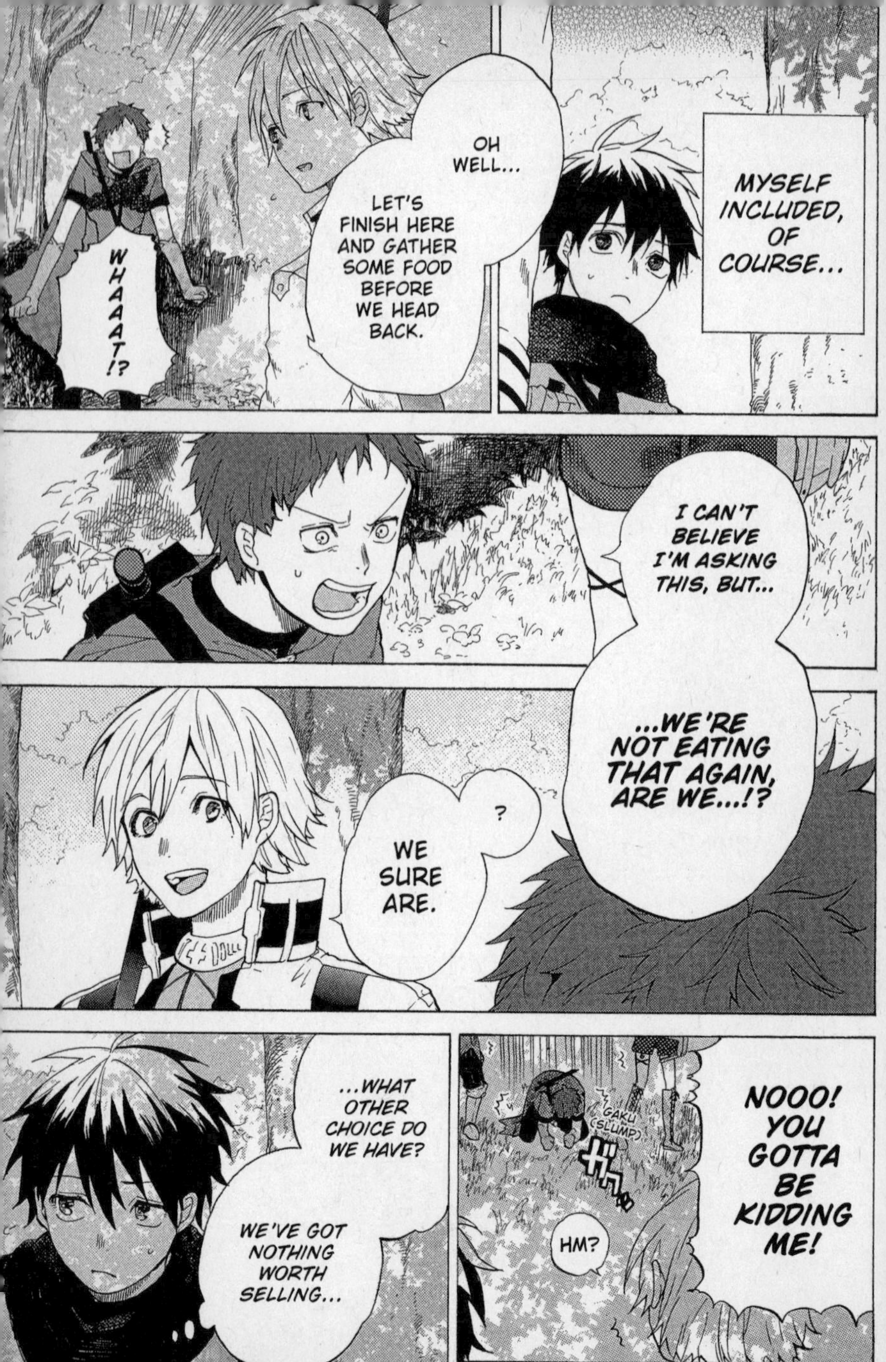
MYSELF INCLUDED, OF COURSE...
OH WELL...
LET'S FINISH HERE AND GATHER SOME FOOD BEFORE WE HEAD BACK.
WHAAAAT!?
I CAN'T BELIEVE I'M ASKING THIS, BUT...
...WE'RE NOT EATING THAT AGAIN, ARE WE...!?
?
WE SURE ARE.
NOOO! YOU GOTTA BE KIDDING ME!
GAKU (SLUMP)
HM?
...WHAT OTHER CHOICE DO WE HAVE?
WE'VE GOT NOTHING WORTH SELLING...

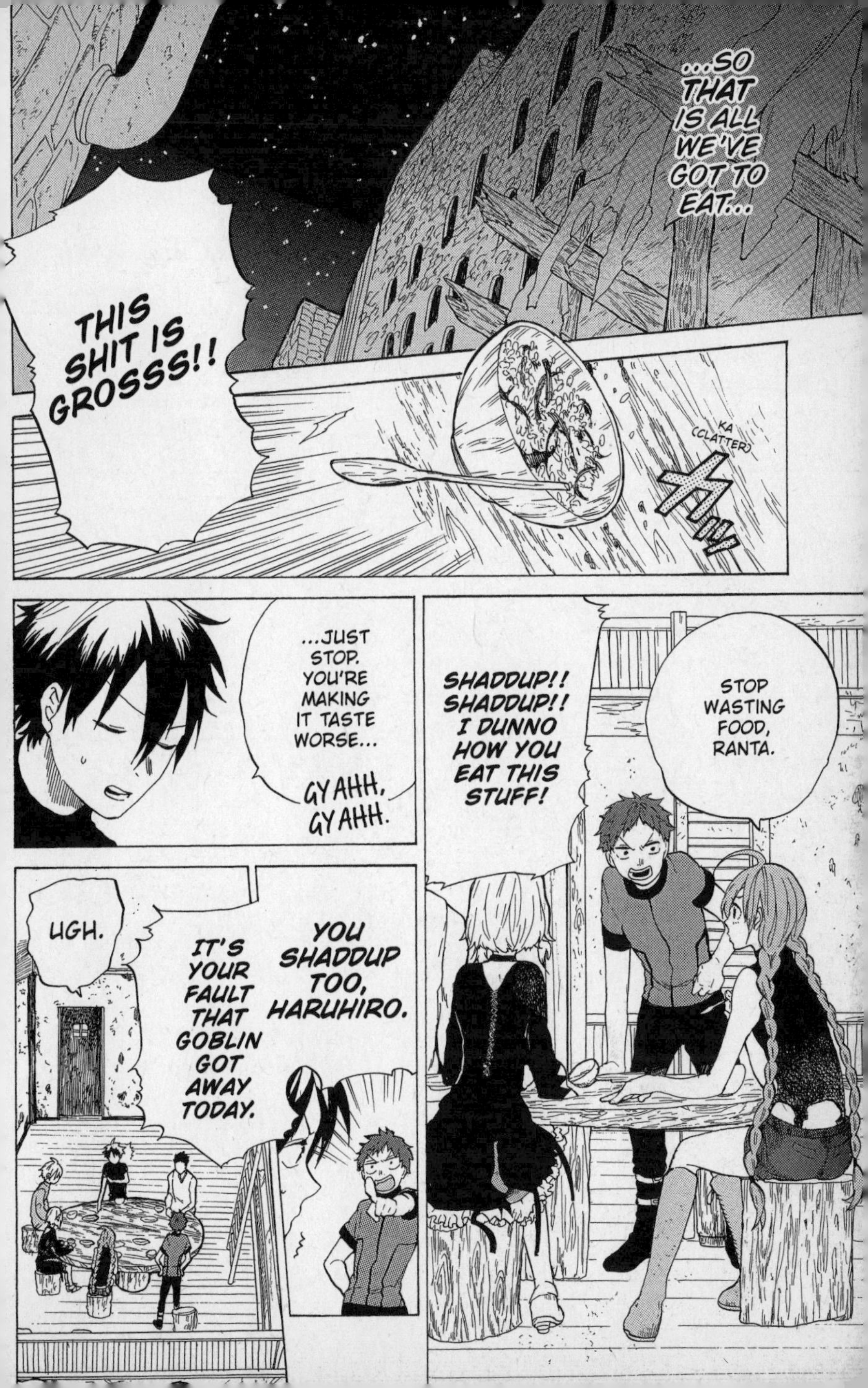
...SO THAT IS ALL WE'VE GOT TO EAT...
THIS SHIT IS GROSSS!!
KA (CLATTER)
STOP WASTING FOOD, RANTA.
SHADDUP!! SHADDUP!! I DUNNO HOW YOU EAT THIS STUFF!
...JUST STOP. YOU'RE MAKING IT TASTE WORSE...
GYAHH, GYAHH.
YOU SHADDUP TOO, HARUHIRO.
IT'S YOUR FAULT THAT GOBLIN GOT AWAY TODAY.
UGH.

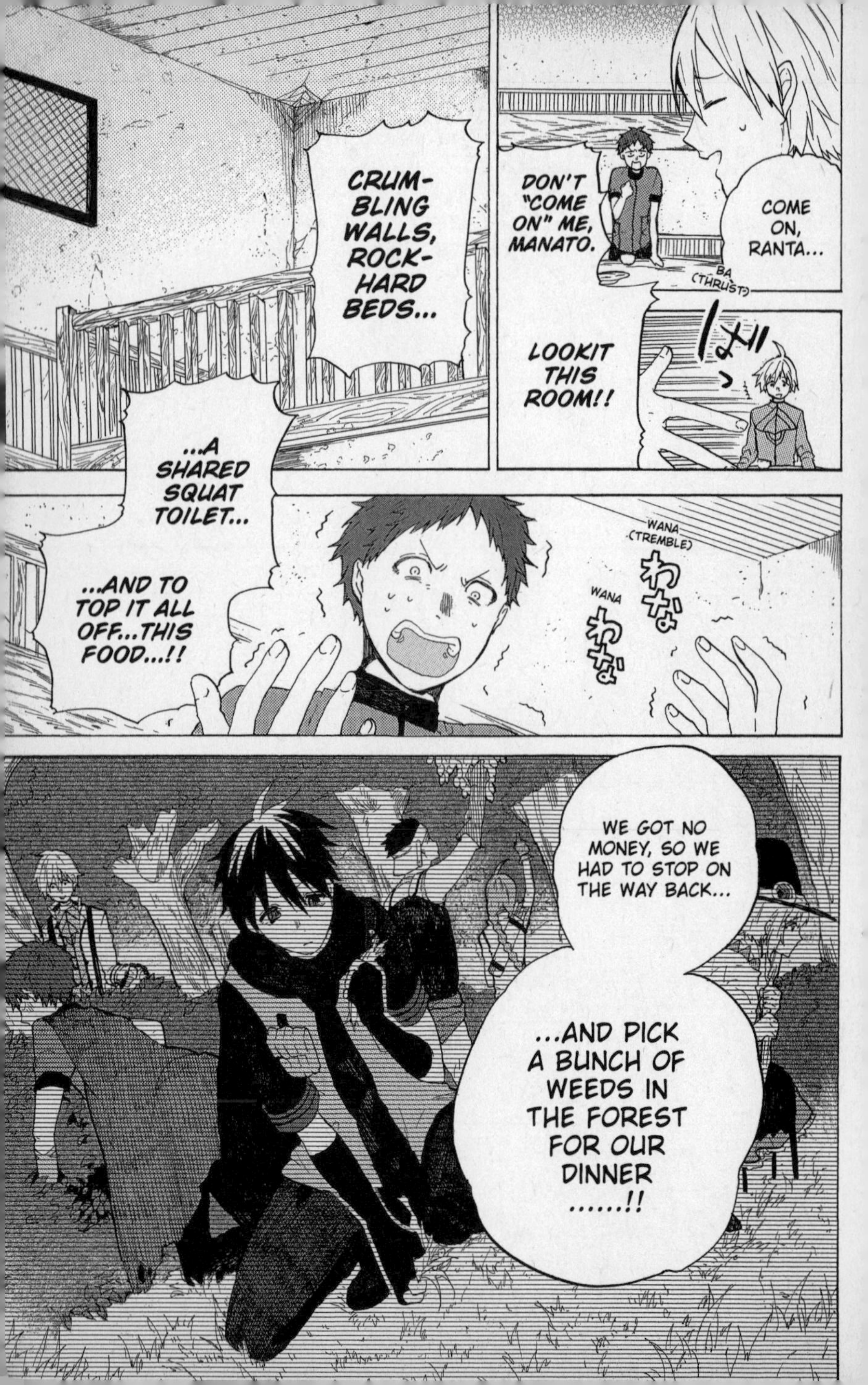
COME ON, RANTA...
DON'T "COME ON" ME, MANATO.
BA (THRUST)
ぱッ
LOOKIT THIS ROOM!!
CRUM-BLING WALLS, ROCK-HARD BEDS...
...A SHARED SQUAT TOILET...
WANA (TREMBLE)
わな
WANA
わな
...AND TO TOP IT ALL OFF...THIS FOOD...!!
WE GOT NO MONEY, SO WE HAD TO STOP ON THE WAY BACK...
...AND PICK A BUNCH OF WEEDS IN THE FOREST FOR OUR DINNER ......!!

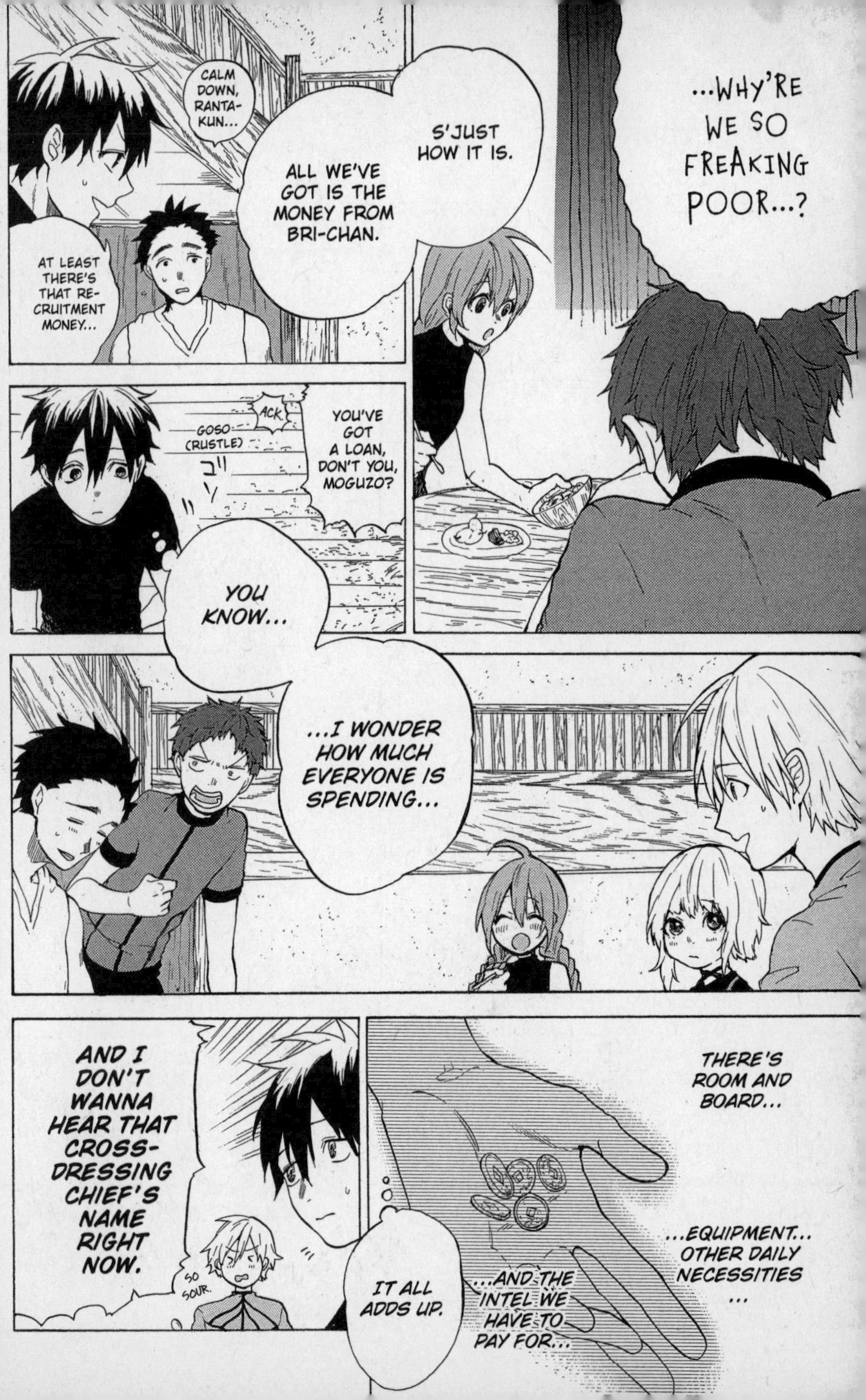

...WHY'RE WE SO FREAKING POOR...?
S'JUST HOW IT IS. ALL WE'VE GOT IS THE MONEY FROM BRI-CHAN.
CALM DOWN, RANTA-KUN...
AT LEAST THERE'S THAT RE-CRUITMENT MONEY...
ACK
GOSO (RUSTLE)
ゴソ
YOU'VE GOT A LOAN, DON'T YOU, MOGUZO?
YOU KNOW...
...I WONDER HOW MUCH EVERYONE IS SPENDING...
THERE'S ROOM AND BOARD...
...EQUIPMENT... OTHER DAILY NECESSITIES...
...AND THE INTEL WE HAVE TO PAY FOR...
IT ALL ADDS UP.
AND I DON'T WANNA HEAR THAT CROSS-DRESSING CHIEF'S NAME RIGHT NOW.
SO SOUR.

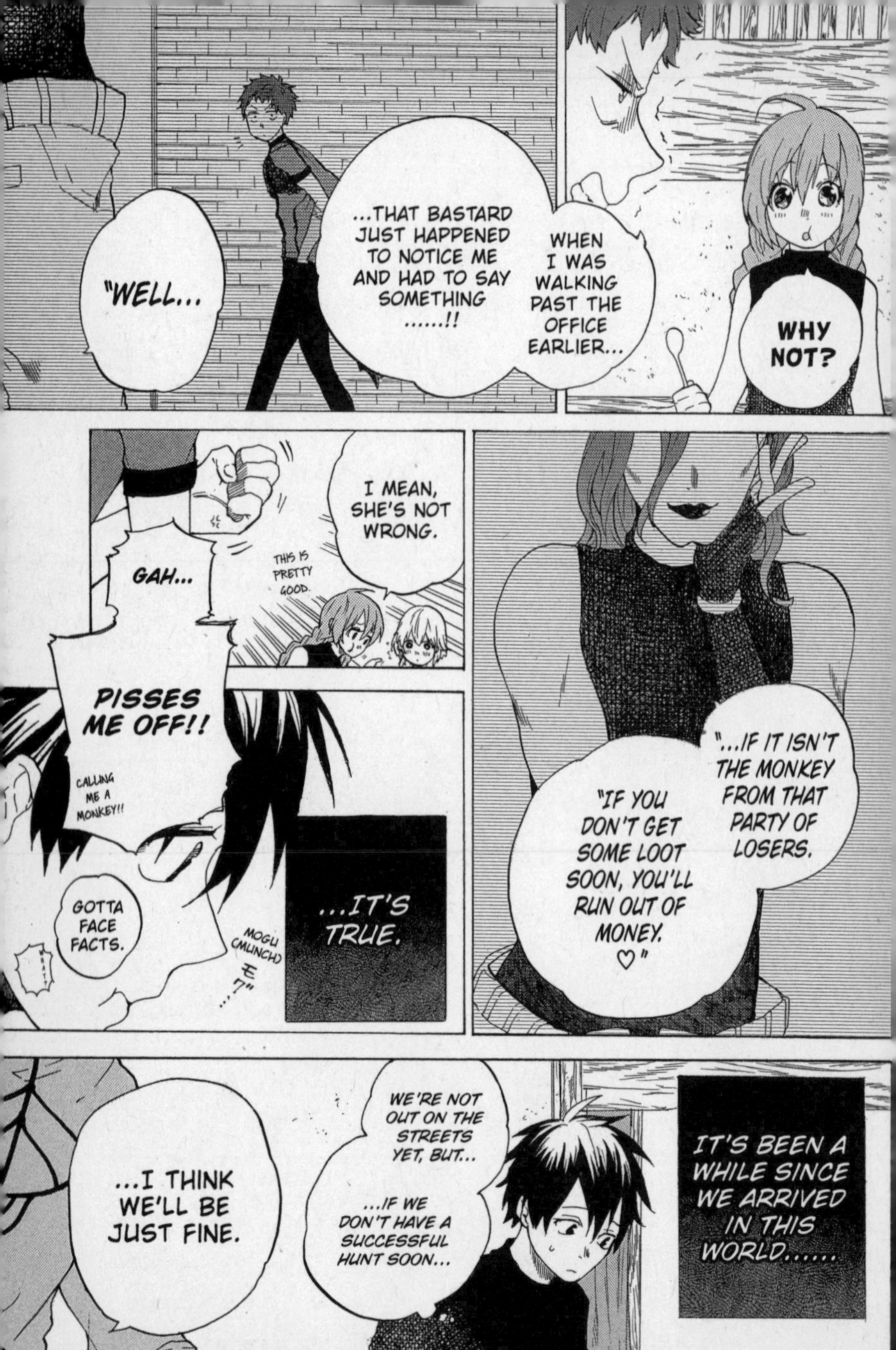
WHY NOT?
WHEN I WAS WALKING PAST THE OFFICE EARLIER...
...THAT BASTARD JUST HAPPENED TO NOTICE ME AND HAD TO SAY SOMETHING ......!!
"WELL...
"...IF IT ISN'T THE MONKEY FROM THAT PARTY OF LOSERS.
"IF YOU DON'T GET SOME LOOT SOON, YOU'LL RUN OUT OF MONEY. ♡"
I MEAN, SHE'S NOT WRONG.
THIS IS PRETTY GOOD.
GAH...
PISSES ME OFF!!
CALLING ME A MONKEY!!
...IT'S TRUE.
MOGU (MUNCH)
GOTTA FACE FACTS.
IT'S BEEN A WHILE SINCE WE ARRIVED IN THIS WORLD......
WE'RE NOT OUT ON THE STREETS YET, BUT...
...IF WE DON'T HAVE A SUCCESSFUL HUNT SOON...
...I THINK WE'LL BE JUST FINE.

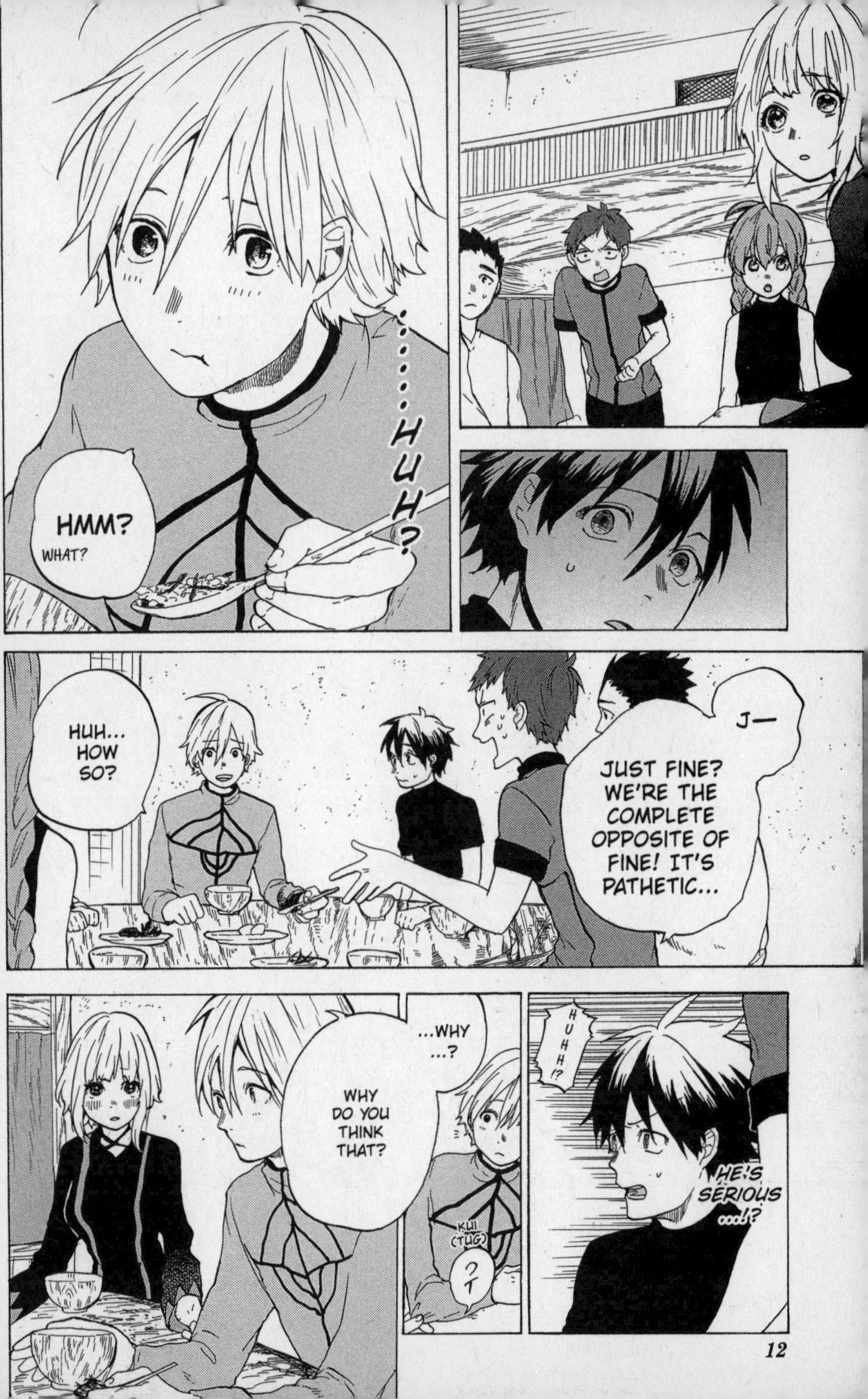
......HUH?
HMM? WHAT?
J— JUST FINE? WE'RE THE COMPLETE OPPOSITE OF FINE! IT'S PATHETIC...
HUH... HOW SO?
HUHH!?
HE'S SERIOUS...!?
...WHY ...?
KUI (TUG)
クイ
WHY DO YOU THINK THAT?

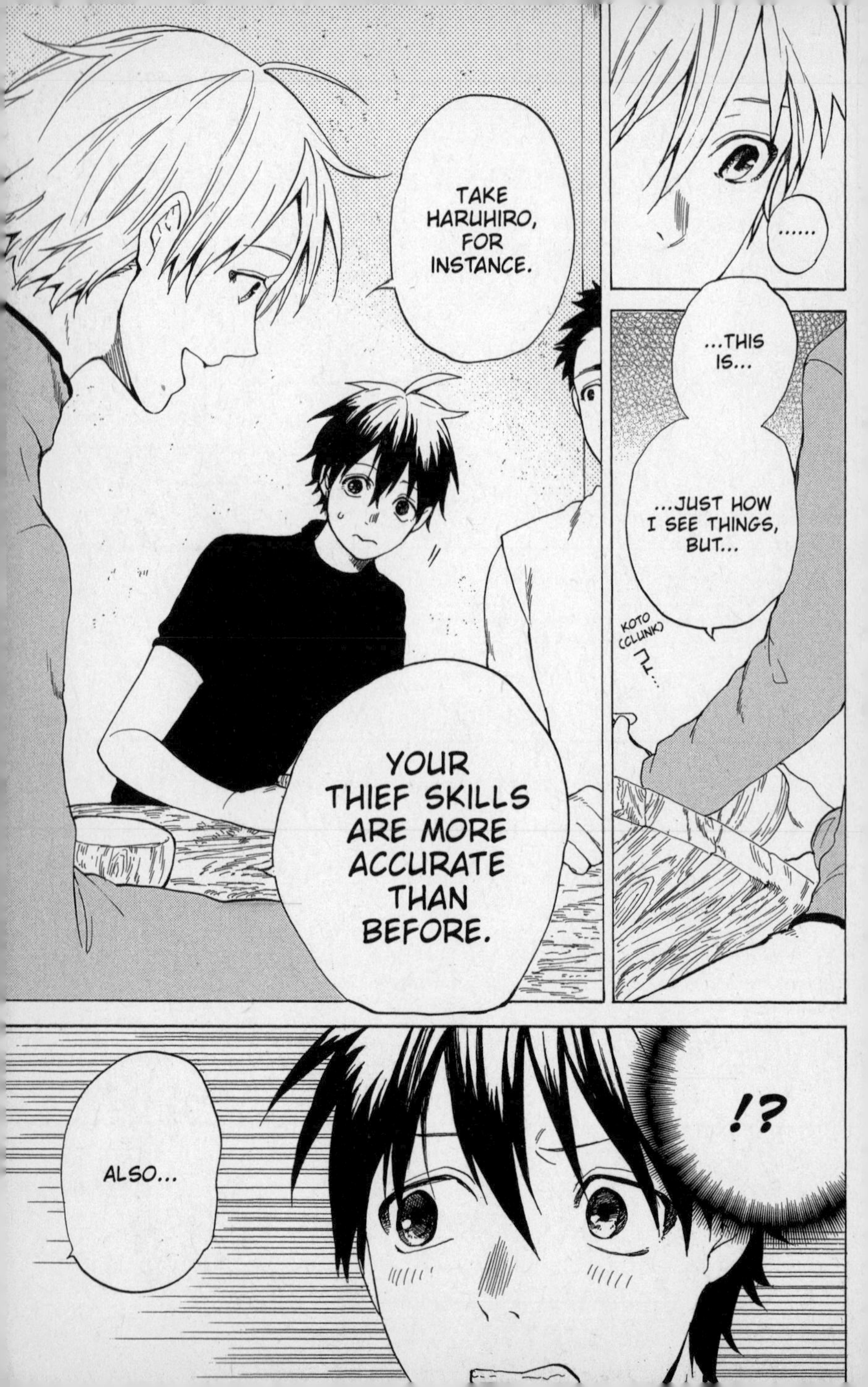
......
...THIS IS...
...JUST HOW I SEE THINGS, BUT...
KOTO (CLUNK)
TAKE HARUHIRO, FOR INSTANCE.
YOUR THIEF SKILLS ARE MORE ACCURATE THAN BEFORE.
!?
ALSO...

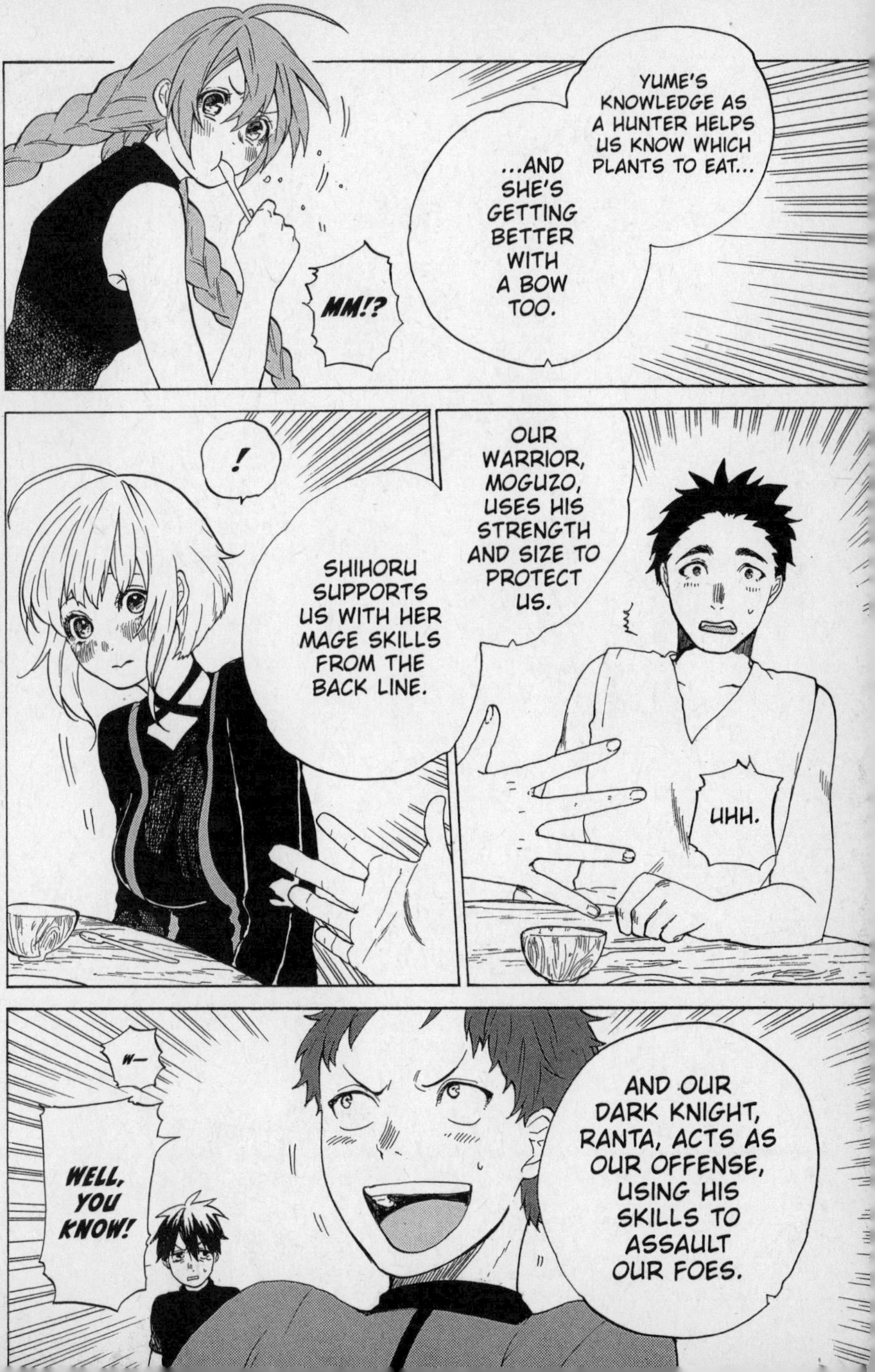
YUME'S KNOWLEDGE AS A HUNTER HELPS US KNOW WHICH PLANTS TO EAT...
...AND SHE'S GETTING BETTER WITH A BOW TOO.
MM!?
OUR WARRIOR, MOGUZO, USES HIS STRENGTH AND SIZE TO PROTECT US.
UHH.
!
SHIHORU SUPPORTS US WITH HER MAGE SKILLS FROM THE BACK LINE.
AND OUR DARK KNIGHT, RANTA, ACTS AS OUR OFFENSE, USING HIS SKILLS TO ASSAULT OUR FOES.
W—
WELL, YOU KNOW!

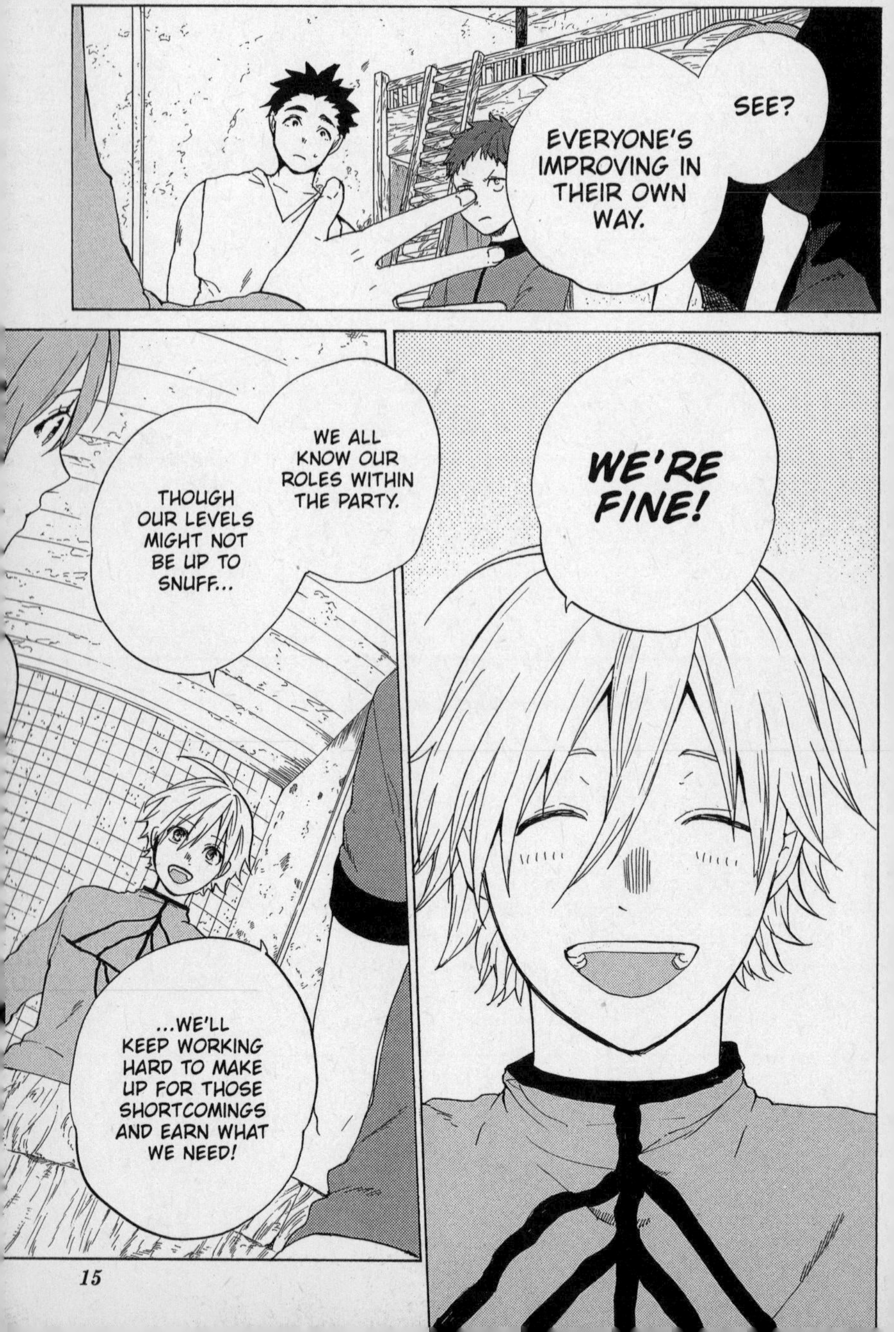
SEE?
EVERYONE'S IMPROVING IN THEIR OWN WAY.
WE'RE FINE!
WE ALL KNOW OUR ROLES WITHIN THE PARTY.
THOUGH OUR LEVELS MIGHT NOT BE UP TO SNUFF...
...WE'LL KEEP WORKING HARD TO MAKE UP FOR THOSE SHORTCOMINGS AND EARN WHAT WE NEED!

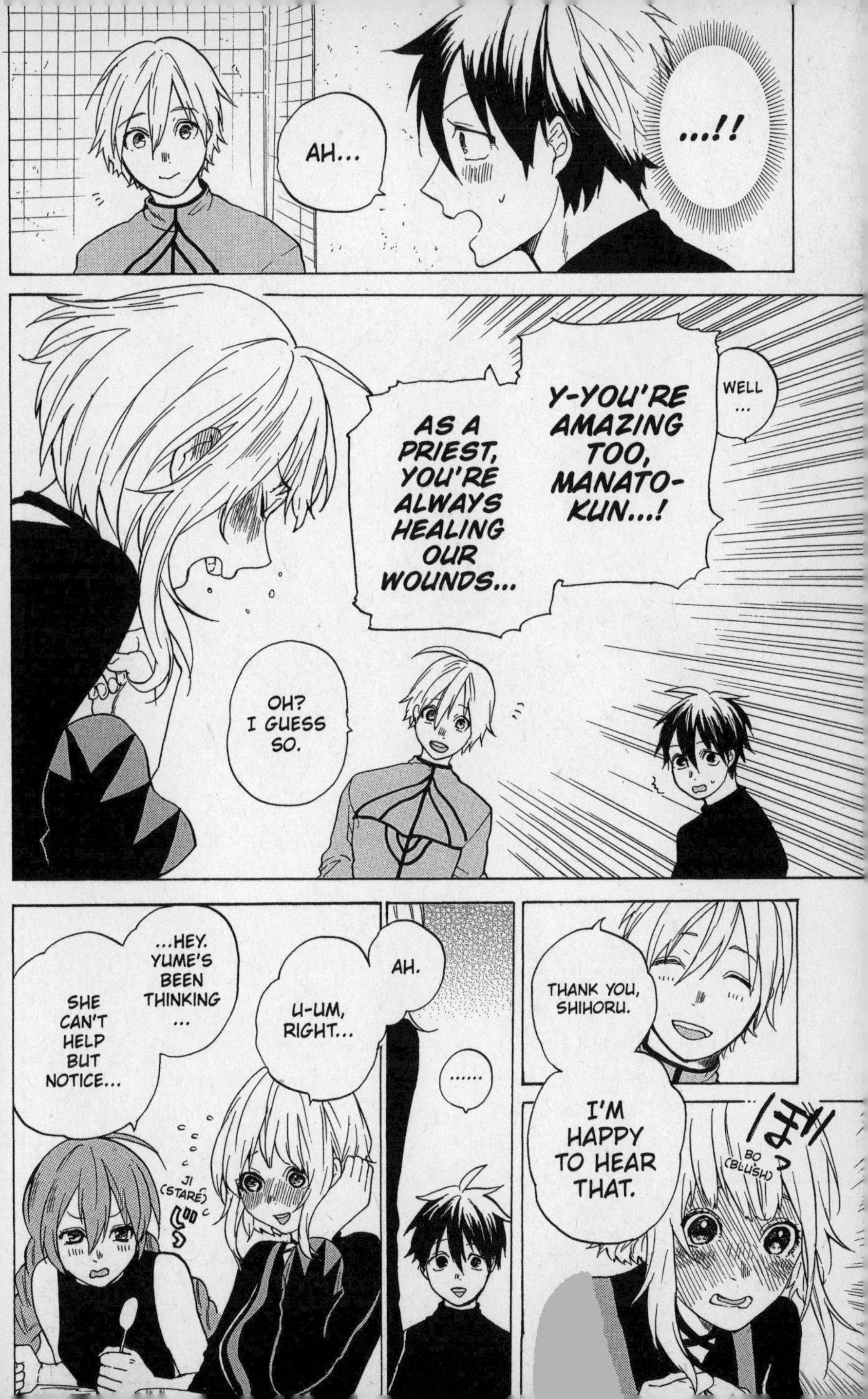

...!!
AH...
WELL ...
Y-YOU'RE AMAZING TOO, MANATO-KUN...!
AS A PRIEST, YOU'RE ALWAYS HEALING OUR WOUNDS...
OH? I GUESS SO.
THANK YOU, SHIHORU.
I'M HAPPY TO HEAR THAT.
BO (BLUSH)
AH.
......
U-UM, RIGHT...
...HEY. YUME'S BEEN THINKING ...
SHE CAN'T HELP BUT NOTICE...
JI (STARE)

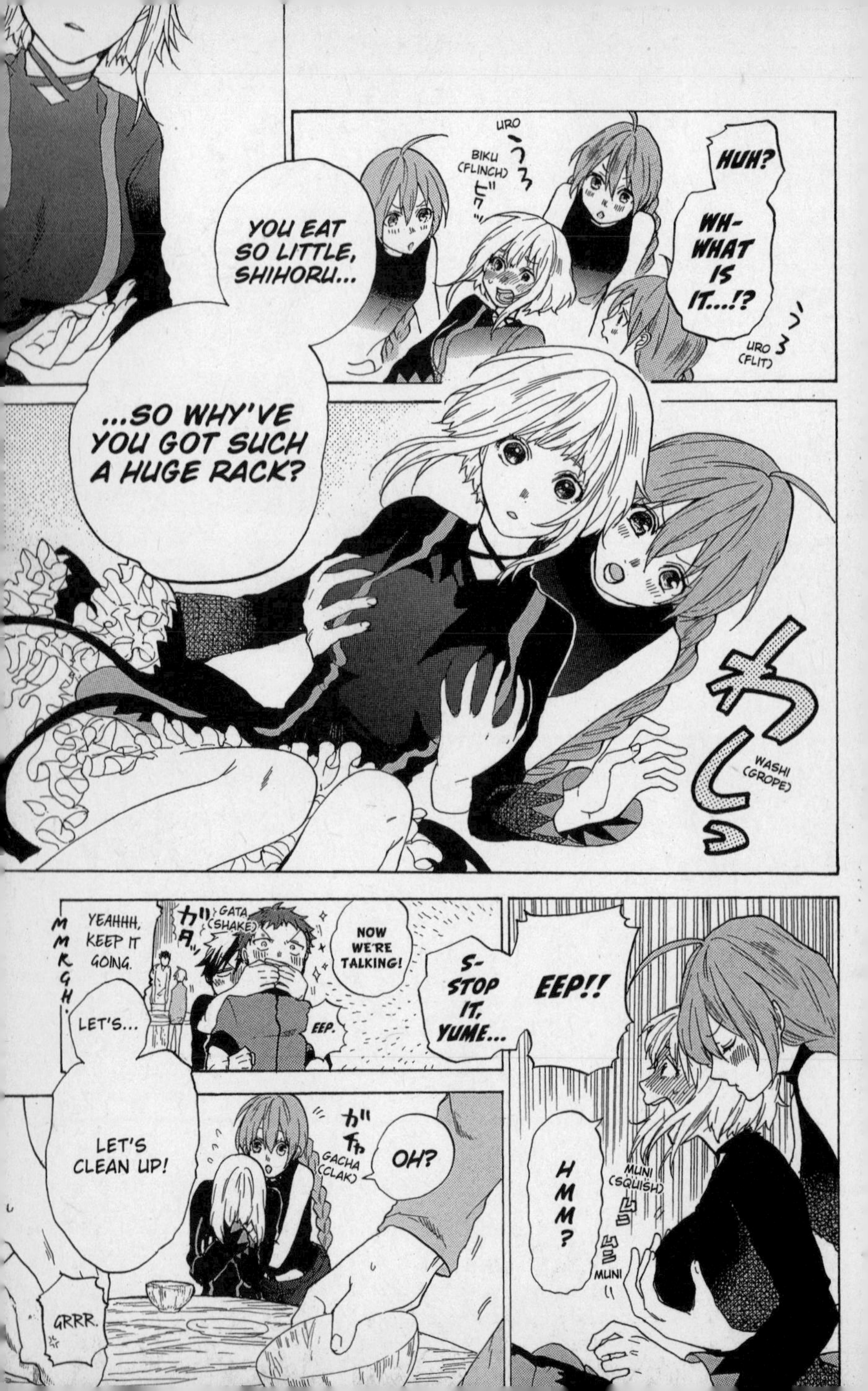
HUH?
WH-WHAT IS IT...!?
URO (FLIT)
URO
BIKU (FLINCH)
YOU EAT SO LITTLE, SHIHORU...
...SO WHY'VE YOU GOT SUCH A HUGE RACK?
WASHI (GROPE)
EEP!!
S-STOP IT, YUME...
HMM?
MUNI (SQUISH)
MUNI
NOW WE'RE TALKING!
GATA (SHAKE)
YEAHHH, KEEP IT GOING.
MMRGH.
EEP.
LET'S...
OH?
GACHA (CLAK)
LET'S CLEAN UP!
GRRR.

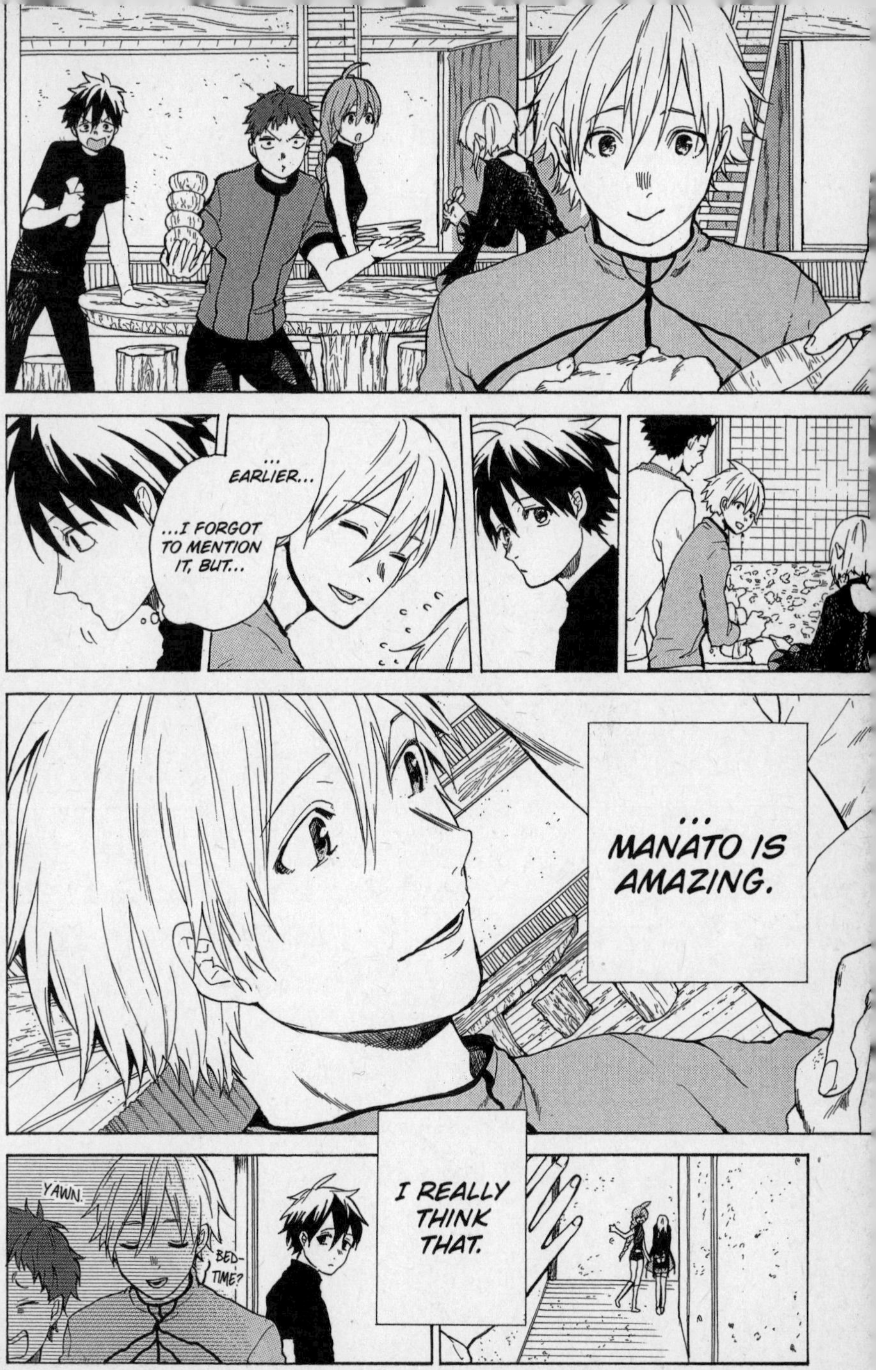
... EARLIER...
...I FORGOT TO MENTION IT, BUT...
... MANATO IS AMAZING.
I REALLY THINK THAT.
BED-TIME?
YAWN.

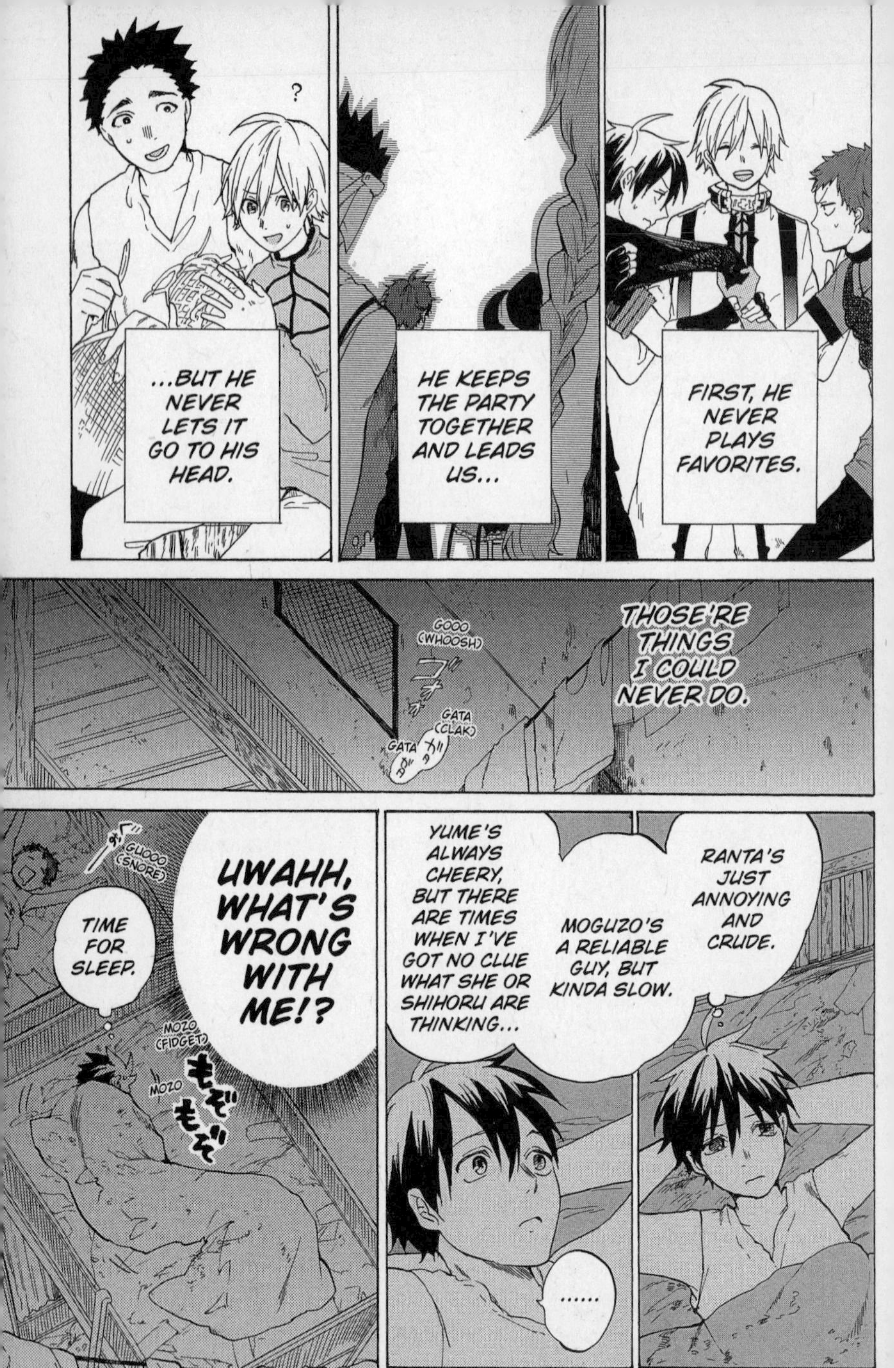
FIRST, HE NEVER PLAYS FAVORITES.
HE KEEPS THE PARTY TOGETHER AND LEADS US...
?
...BUT HE NEVER LETS IT GO TO HIS HEAD.
THOSE'RE THINGS I COULD NEVER DO.
GOOO (WHOOSH)
GATA (CLAK)
GATA
RANTA'S JUST ANNOYING AND CRUDE.
MOGUZO'S A RELIABLE GUY, BUT KINDA SLOW.
YUME'S ALWAYS CHEERY, BUT THERE ARE TIMES WHEN I'VE GOT NO CLUE WHAT SHE OR SHIHORU ARE THINKING...
......
UWAHH, WHAT'S WRONG WITH ME!?
GUOOO (SNORE)
TIME FOR SLEEP.
MOZO (FIDGET)
MOZO

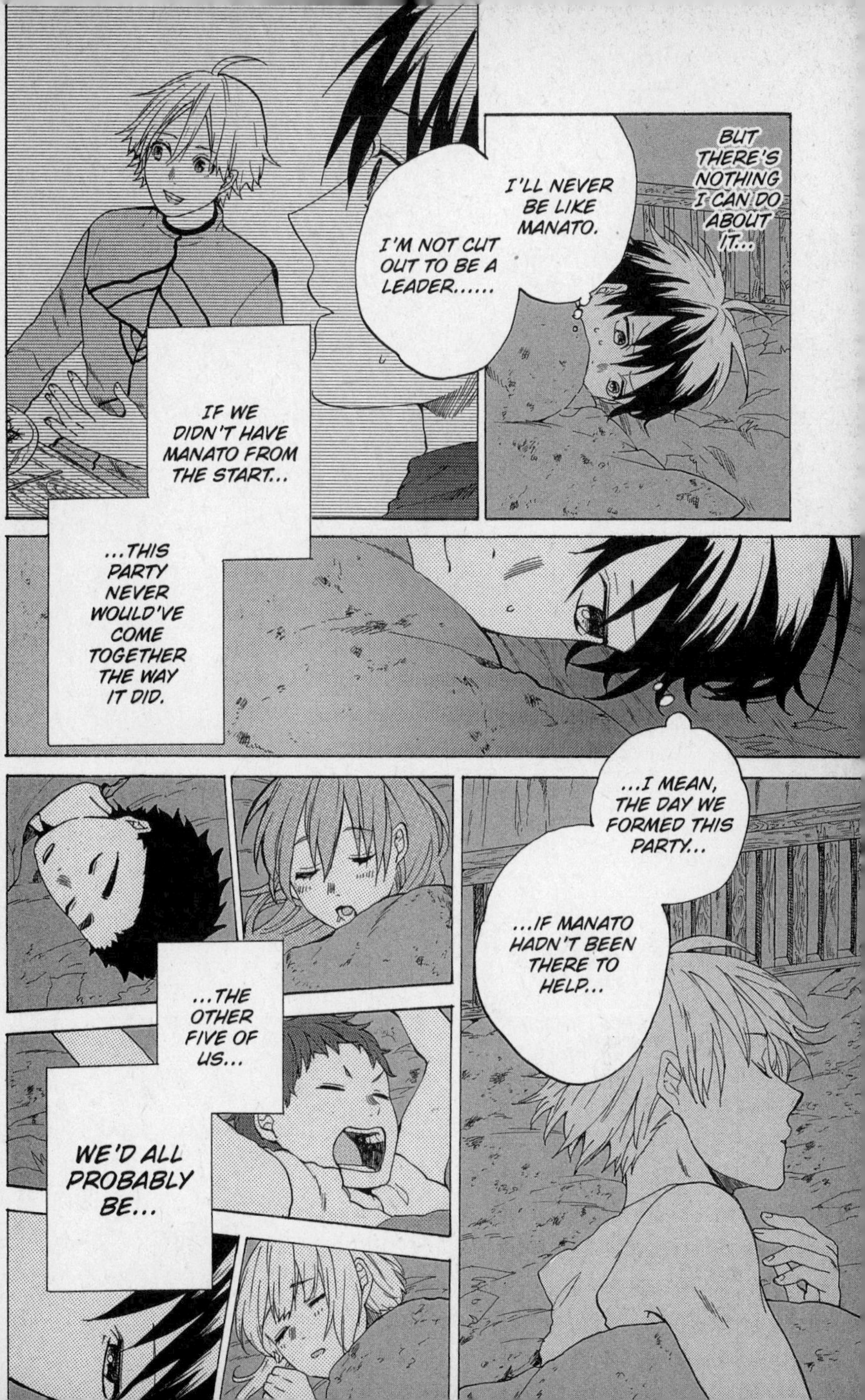
BUT THERE'S NOTHING I CAN DO ABOUT IT...
I'LL NEVER BE LIKE MANATO.
I'M NOT CUT OUT TO BE A LEADER......
IF WE DIDN'T HAVE MANATO FROM THE START...
...THIS PARTY NEVER WOULD'VE COME TOGETHER THE WAY IT DID.
...I MEAN, THE DAY WE FORMED THIS PARTY...
...IF MANATO HADN'T BEEN THERE TO HELP...
...THE OTHER FIVE OF US...
WE'D ALL PROBABLY BE...

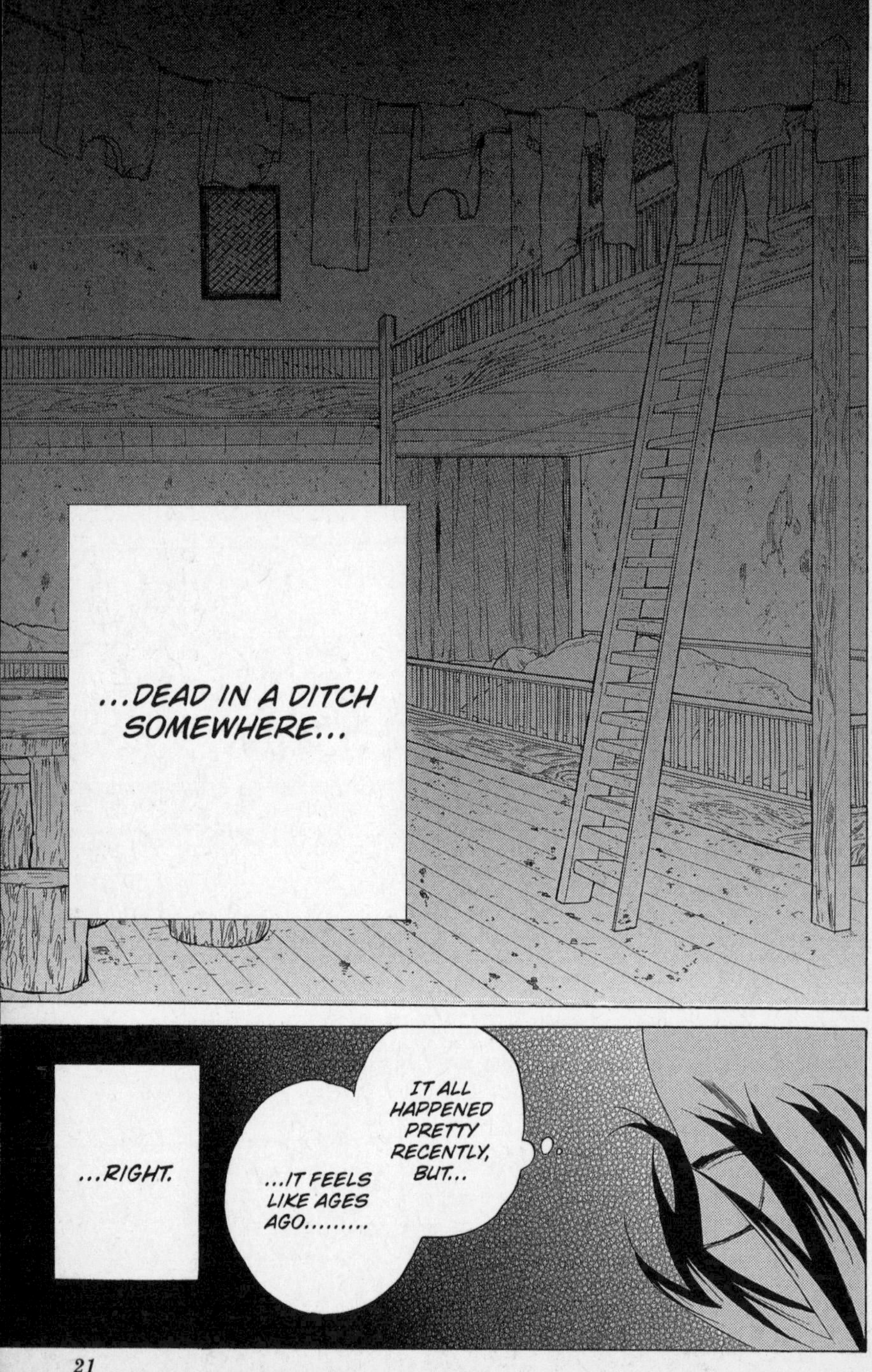
...DEAD IN A DITCH SOMEWHERE...
IT ALL HAPPENED PRETTY RECENTLY, BUT...
...IT FEELS LIKE AGES AGO.........
...RIGHT.

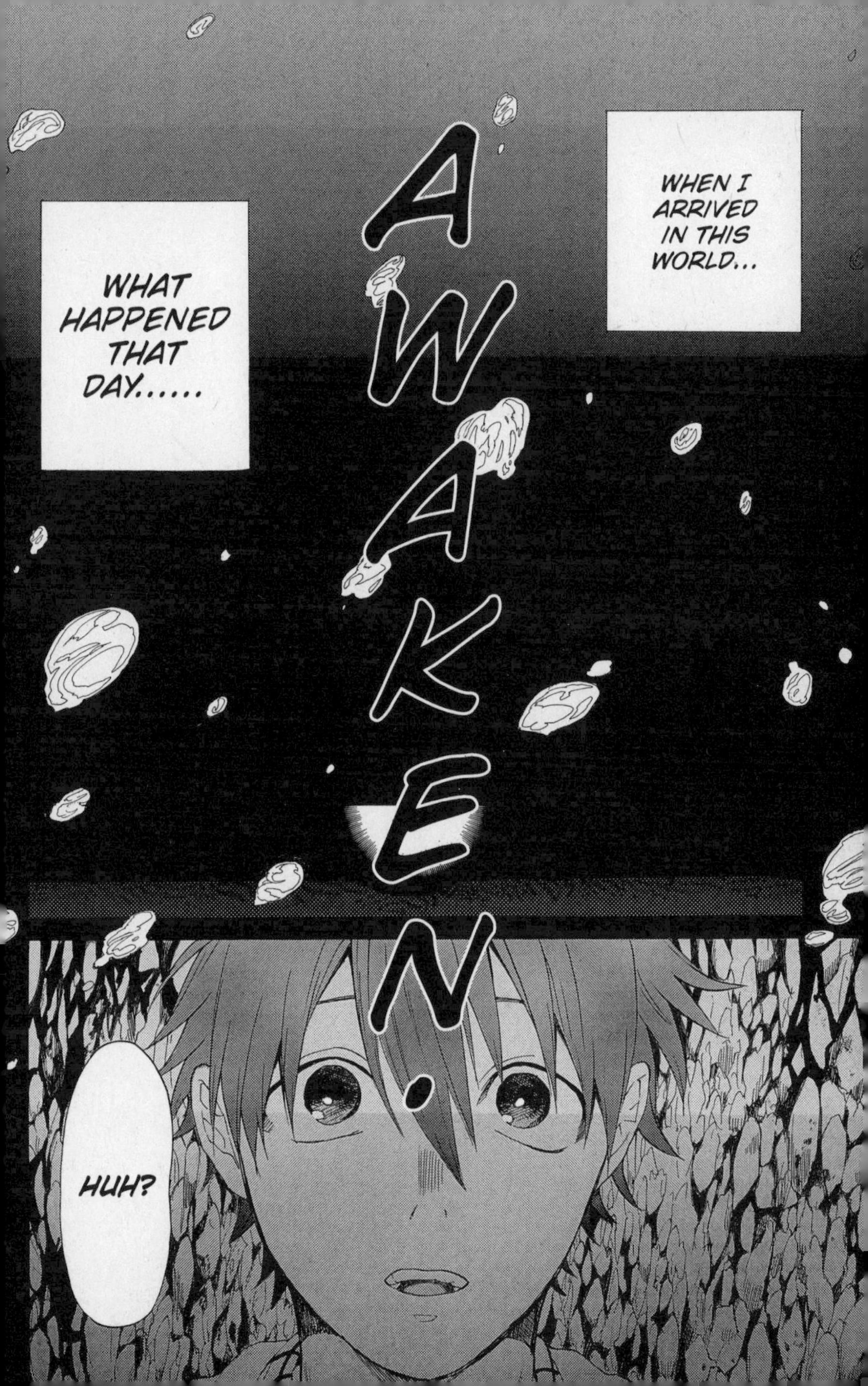
WHEN I ARRIVED IN THIS WORLD...
WHAT HAPPENED THAT DAY......
AWAKEN.
HUH?

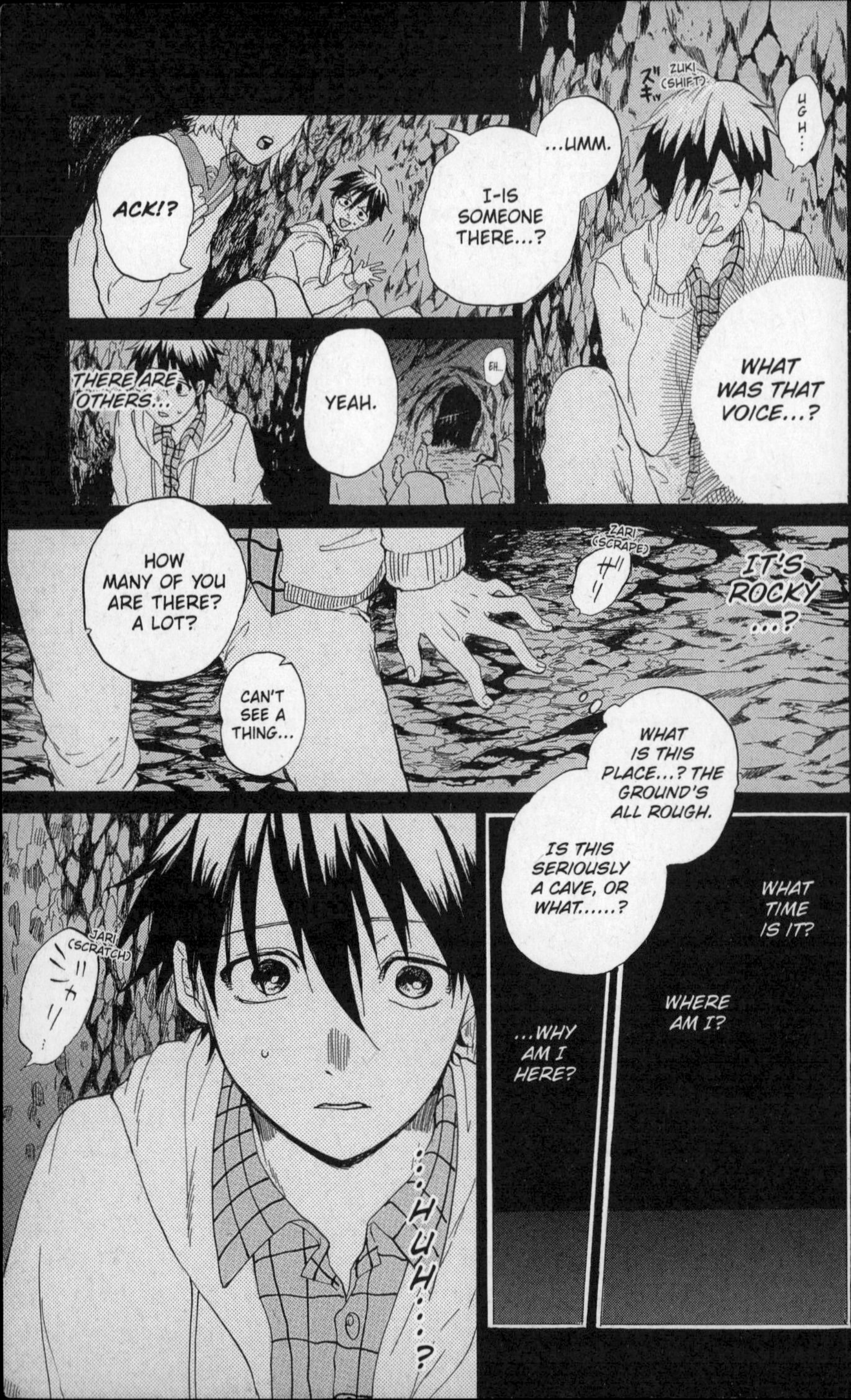
ズキッ
ZUKI (SHIFT)
UGH...
WHAT WAS THAT VOICE...?
...UMM.
I-IS SOMEONE THERE...?
ACK!?
EH...
YEAH.
THERE ARE OTHERS...
IT'S ROCKY...?
ZARI (SCRAPE)
ザリ
HOW MANY OF YOU ARE THERE? A LOT?
CAN'T SEE A THING...
WHAT IS THIS PLACE...? THE GROUND'S ALL ROUGH.
IS THIS SERIOUSLY A CAVE, OR WHAT......?
WHAT TIME IS IT?
WHERE AM I?
...WHY AM I HERE?
JARI (SCRATCH)
ジャリ...
...HUH...?

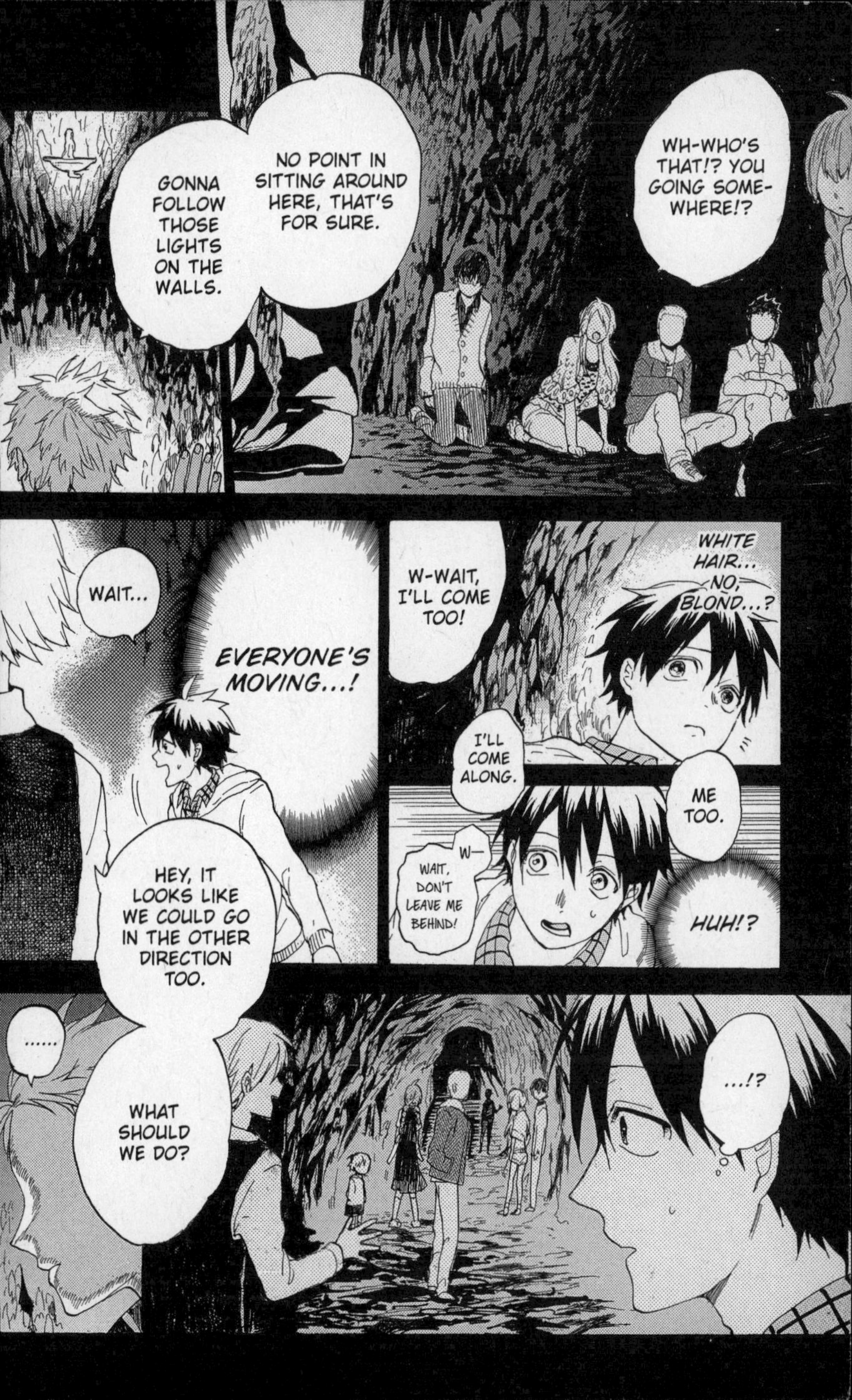
WH-WHO'S THAT!? YOU GOING SOME-WHERE!?
NO POINT IN SITTING AROUND HERE, THAT'S FOR SURE.
GONNA FOLLOW THOSE LIGHTS ON THE WALLS.
WHITE HAIR... NO, BLOND...?
W-WAIT, I'LL COME TOO!
ME TOO.
I'LL COME ALONG.
HUH!?
W— WAIT, DON'T LEAVE ME BEHIND!
EVERYONE'S MOVING...!
WAIT...
HEY, IT LOOKS LIKE WE COULD GO IN THE OTHER DIRECTION TOO.
...!?
WHAT SHOULD WE DO?
......

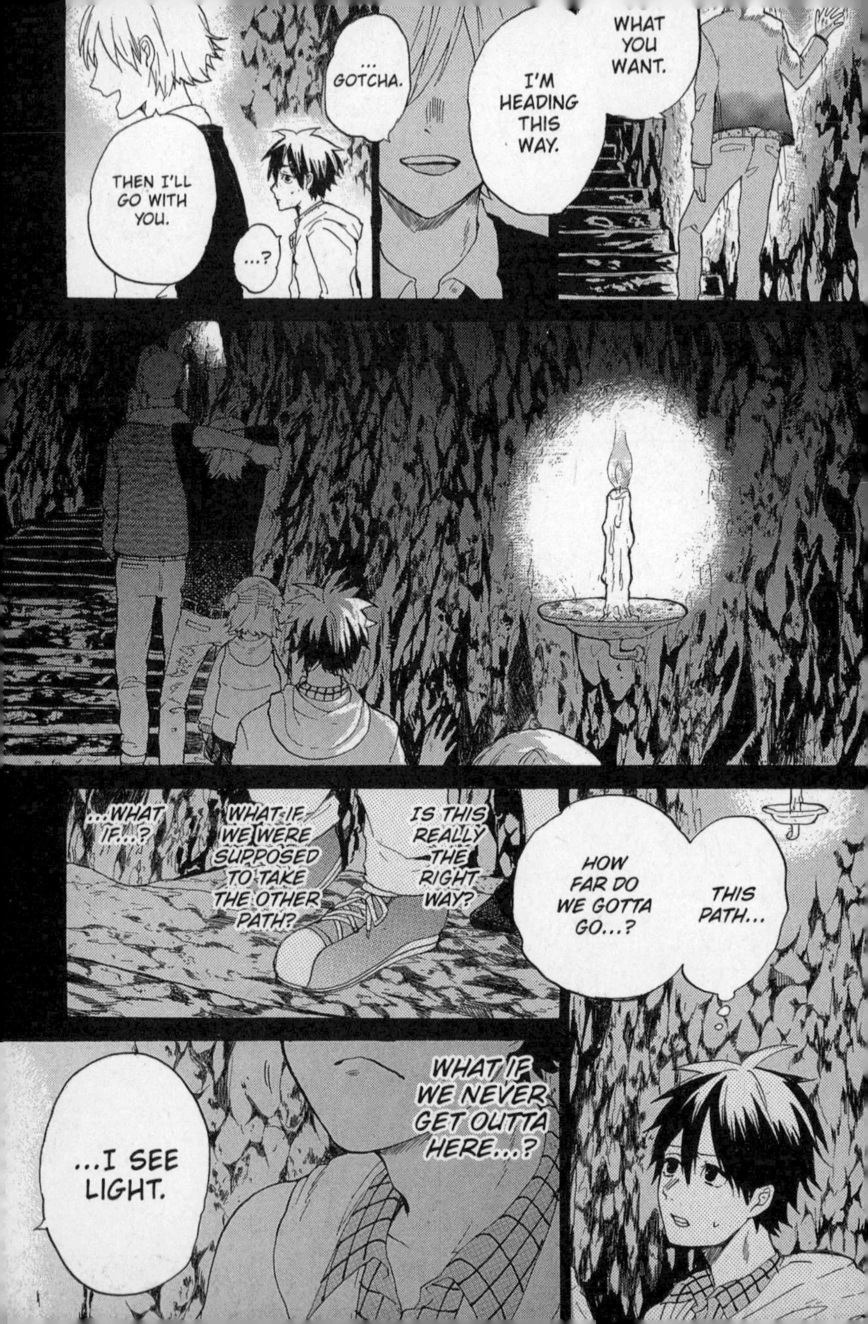
WHAT YOU WANT.
I'M HEADING THIS WAY.
... GOTCHA.
THEN I'LL GO WITH YOU.
...?
THIS PATH...
HOW FAR DO WE GOTTA GO...?
IS THIS REALLY THE RIGHT WAY?
WHAT IF WE WERE SUPPOSED TO TAKE THE OTHER PATH?
...WHAT IF...?
WHAT IF WE NEVER GET OUTTA HERE...?
...I SEE LIGHT.

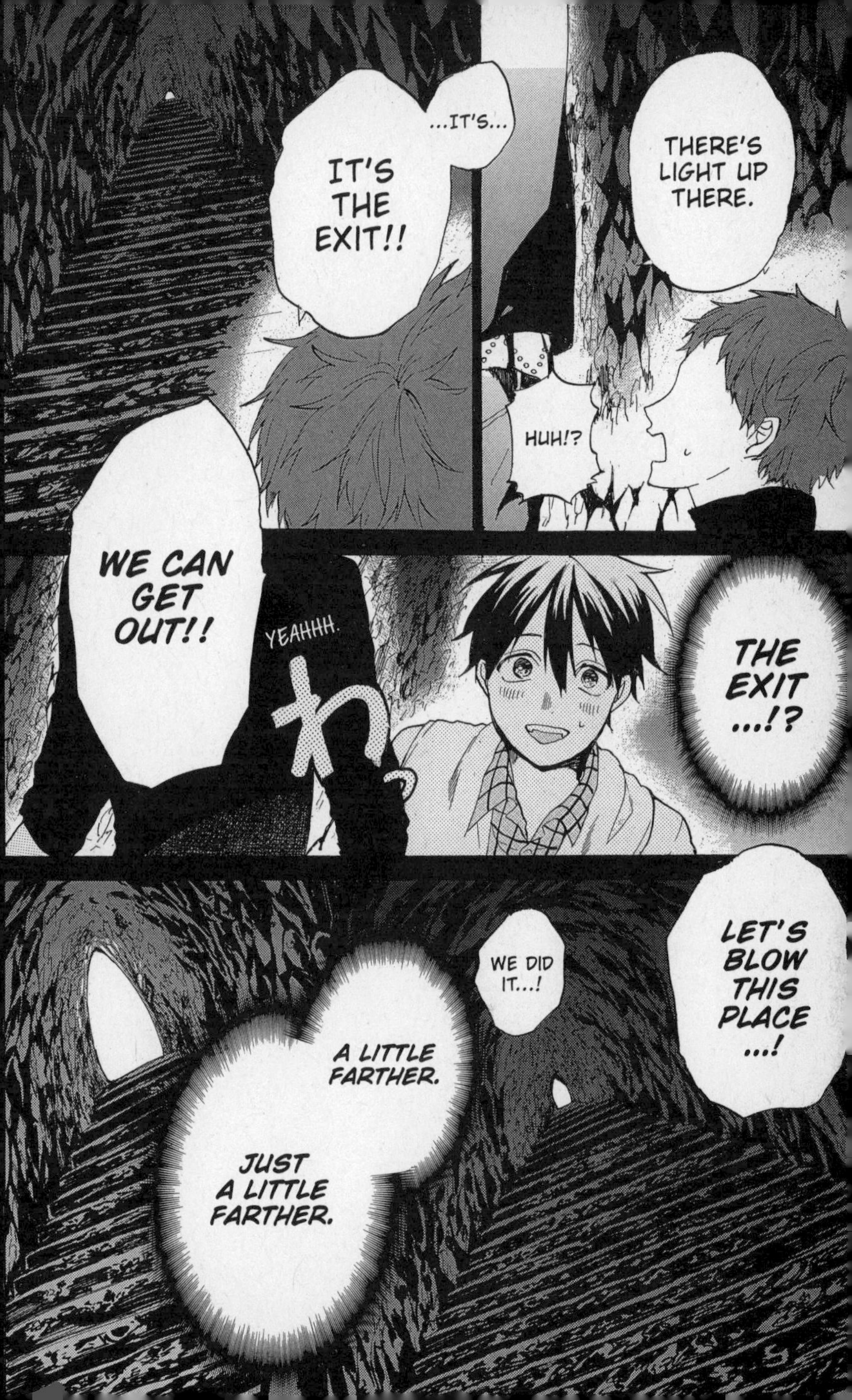
THERE'S LIGHT UP THERE.
HUH!?
...IT'S...
IT'S THE EXIT!!
THE EXIT ...!?
WE CAN GET OUT!!
YEAHHH.
LET'S BLOW THIS PLACE ...!
WE DID IT...!
A LITTLE FARTHER.
JUST A LITTLE FARTHER.

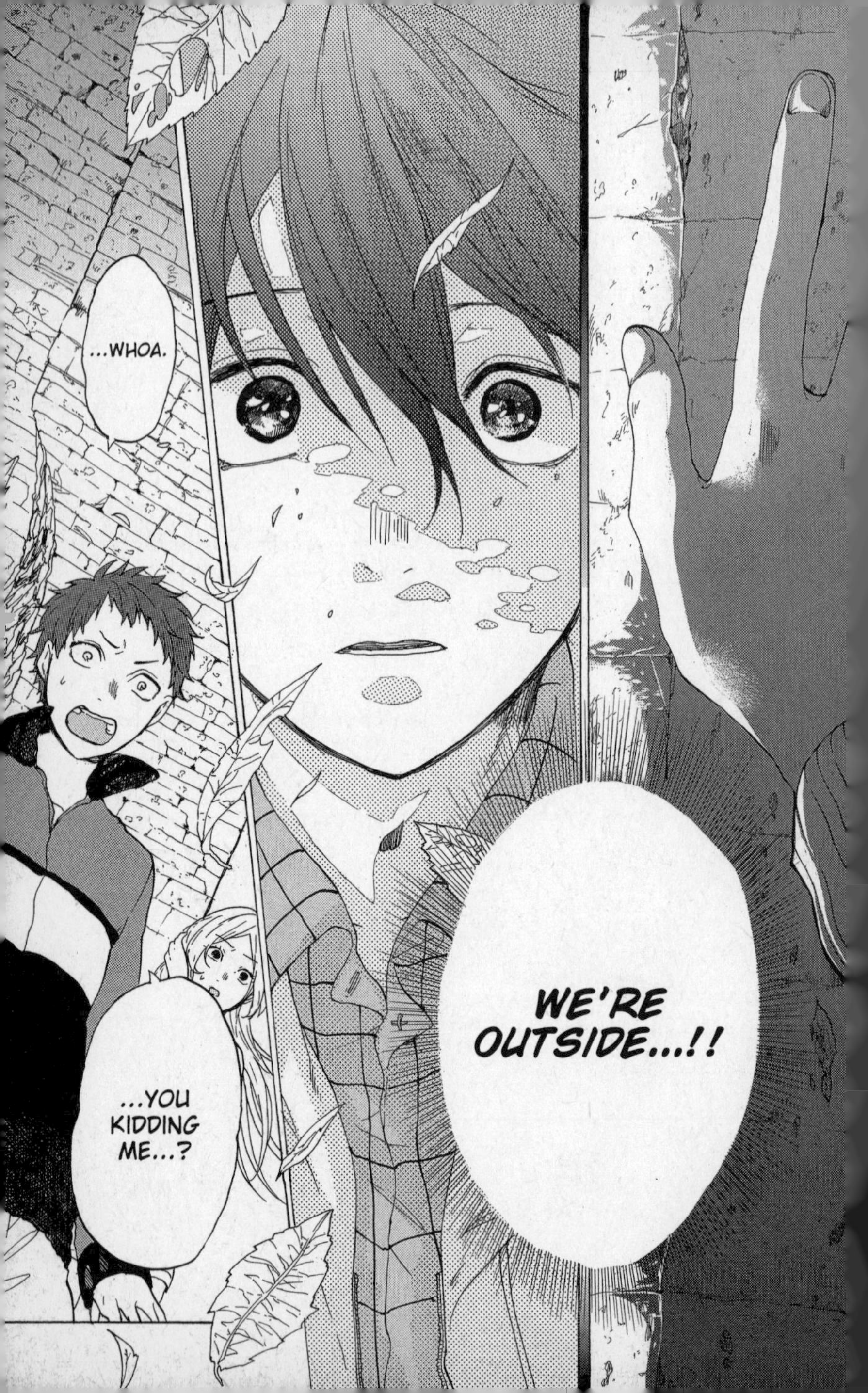
WE'RE OUTSIDE...!!
...WHOA.
...YOU KIDDING ME...?

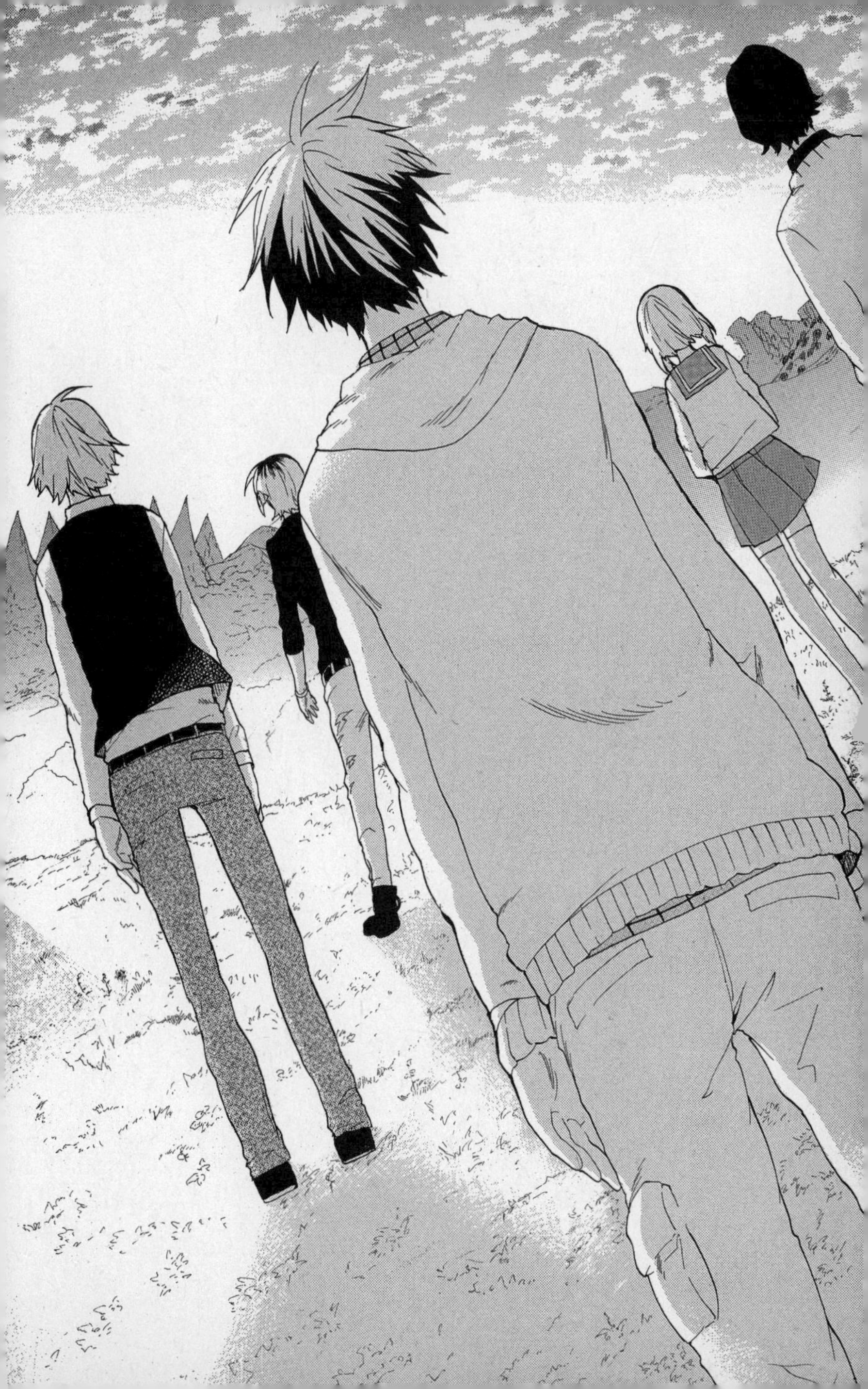

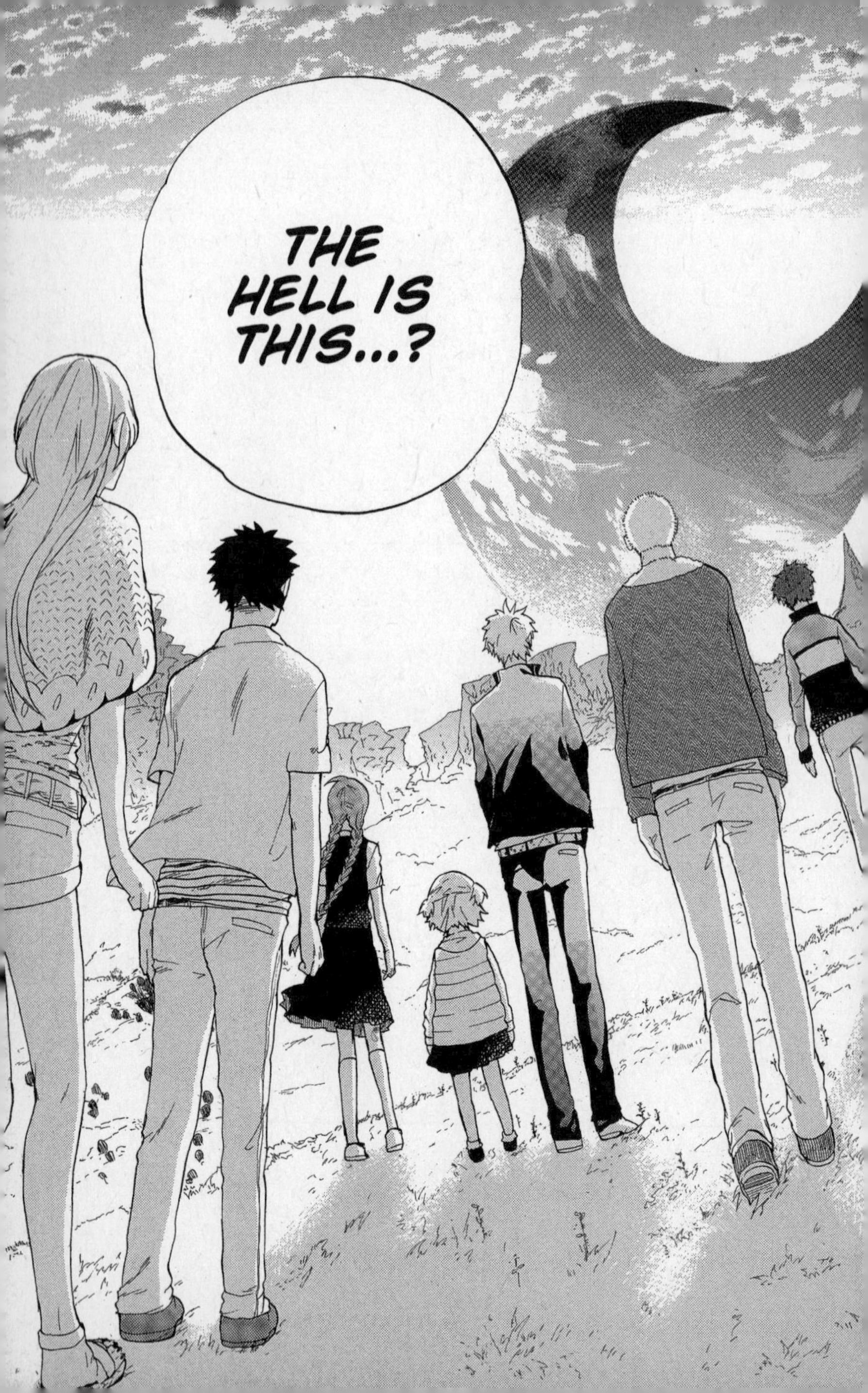
THE HELL IS THIS...?

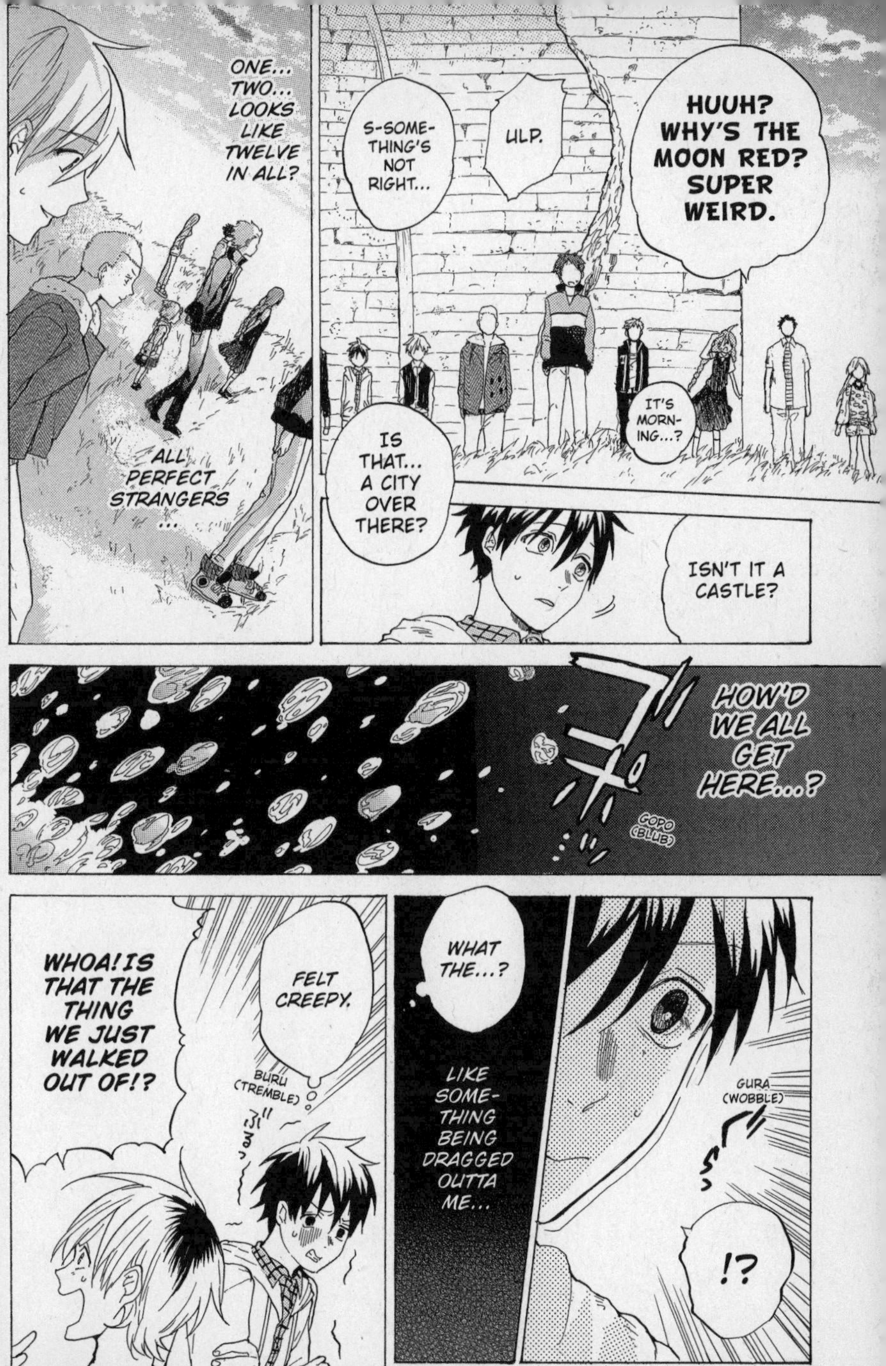
HUUH? WHY'S THE MOON RED? SUPER WEIRD.
ULP.
S-SOMETHING'S NOT RIGHT...
IT'S MORNING...?
IS THAT... A CITY OVER THERE?
ISN'T IT A CASTLE?
ONE... TWO... LOOKS LIKE TWELVE IN ALL?
ALL PERFECT STRANGERS...
HOW'D WE ALL GET HERE...?
GOPO (BLUB)
GURA (WOBBLE)
!?
WHAT THE...?
LIKE SOMETHING BEING DRAGGED OUTTA ME...
WHOA! IS THAT THE THING WE JUST WALKED OUT OF!?
FELT CREEPY.
BURU (TREMBLE)

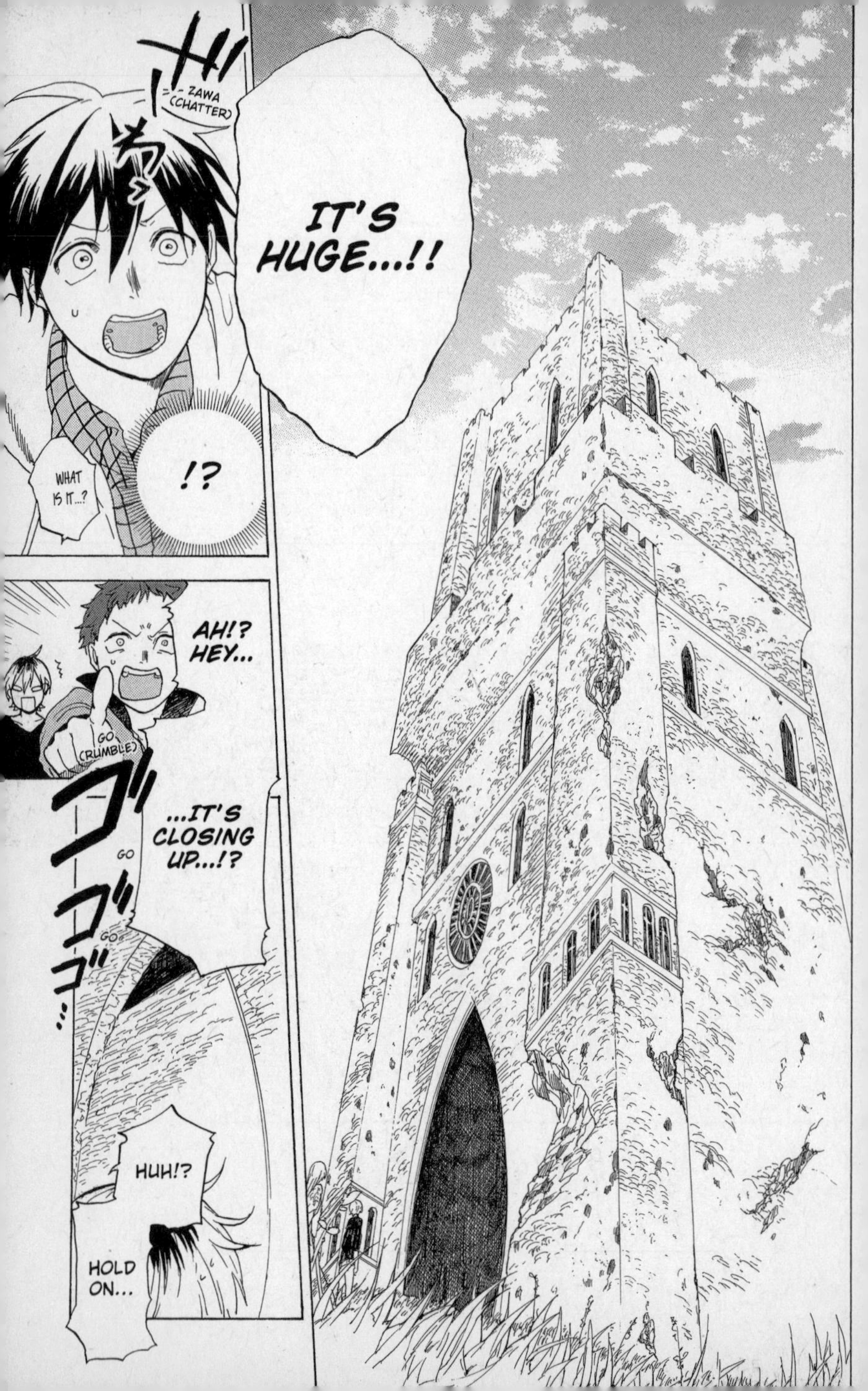
IT'S HUGE...!!
ZAWA (CHATTER)
!?
WHAT IS IT...?
AH!? HEY...
GO (RUMBLE)
...IT'S CLOSING UP...!?
GO
GO
HUH!?
HOLD ON...

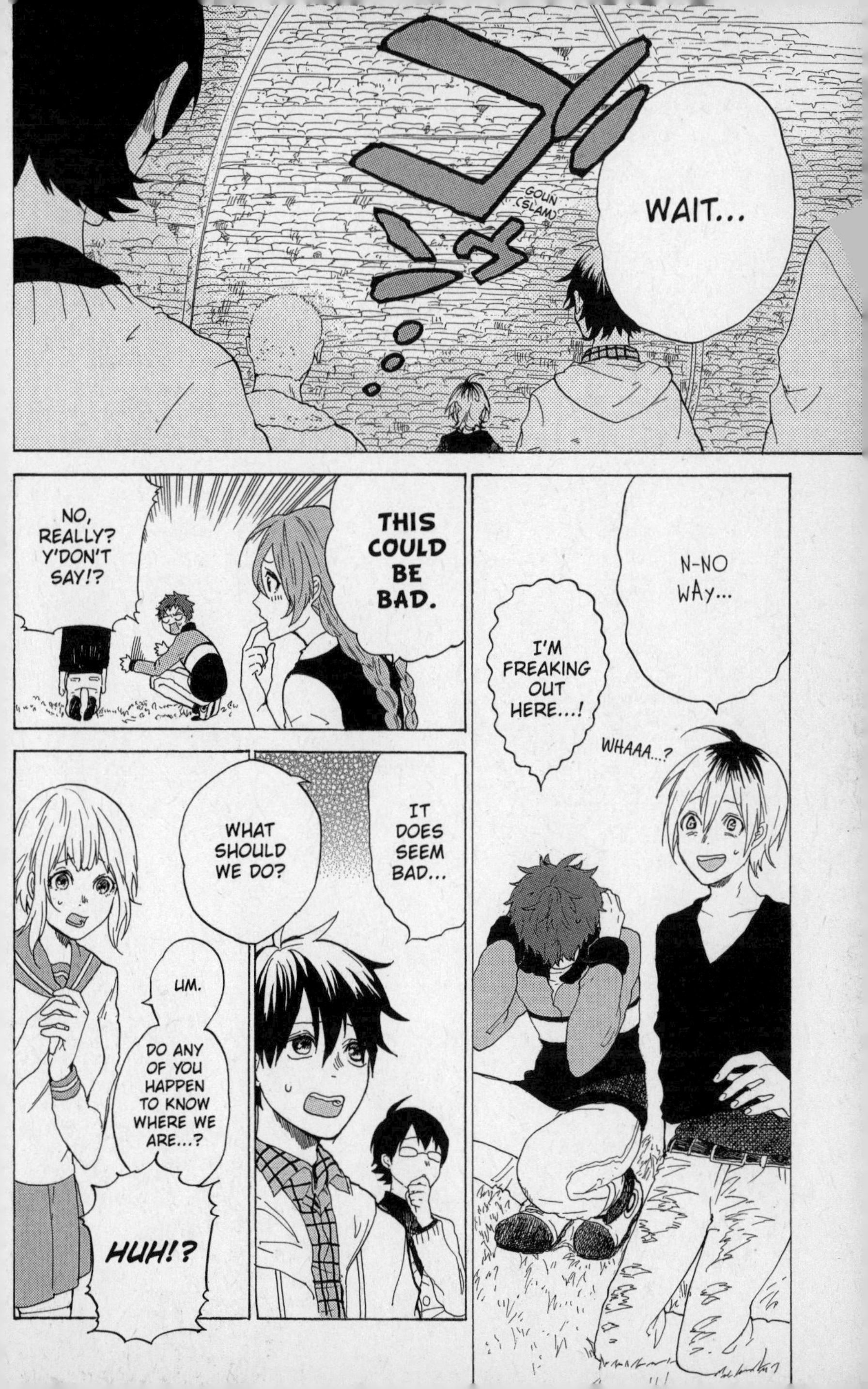
WAIT...
GOUN (SLAM)
N-NO WAY...
I'M FREAKING OUT HERE...!
WHAAA...?
THIS COULD BE BAD.
NO, REALLY? Y'DON'T SAY!?
IT DOES SEEM BAD...
WHAT SHOULD WE DO?
UM.
DO ANY OF YOU HAPPEN TO KNOW WHERE WE ARE...?
HUH!?

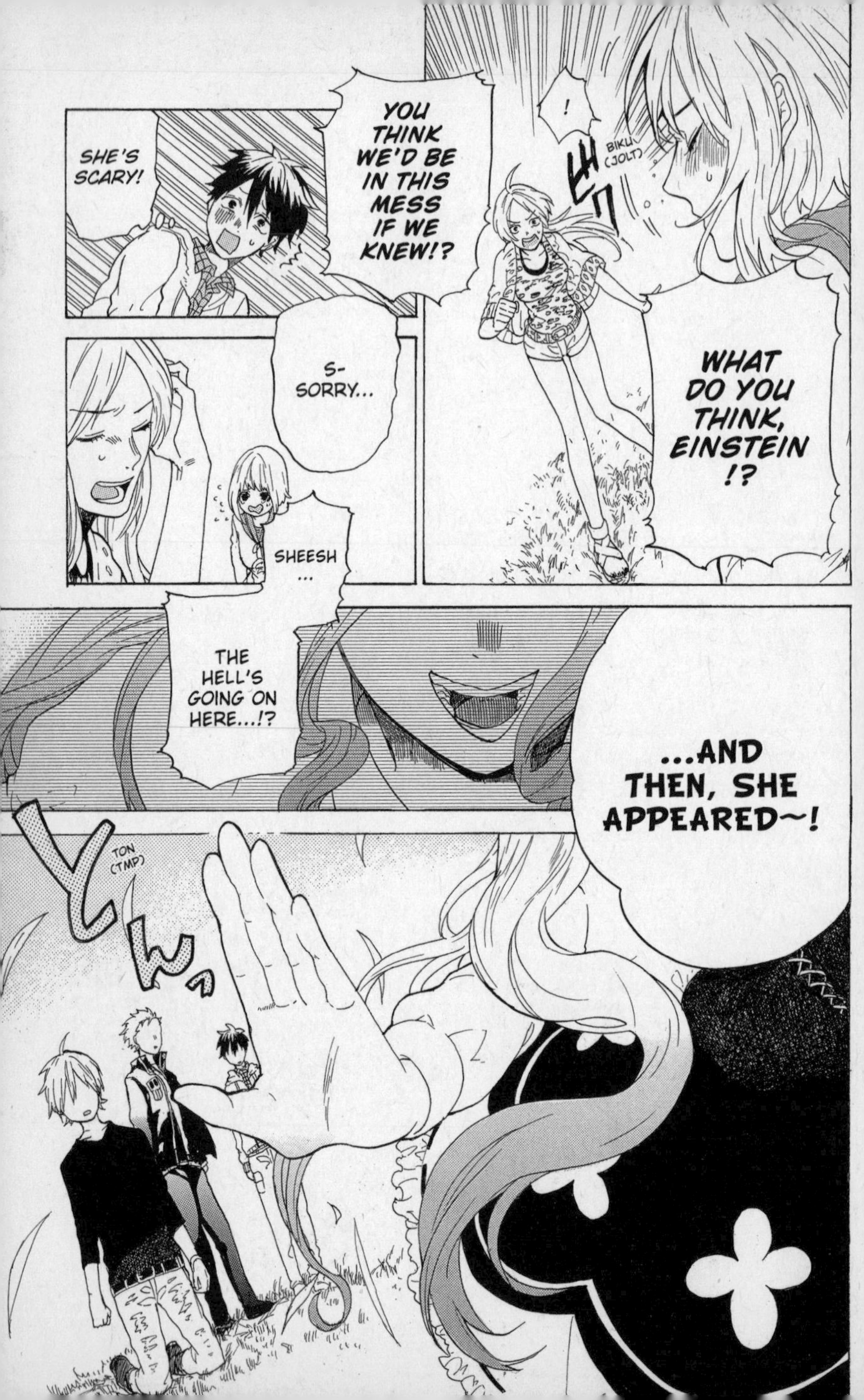
!
BIKU (JOLT)
WHAT DO YOU THINK, EINSTEIN!?
YOU THINK WE'D BE IN THIS MESS IF WE KNEW!?
SHE'S SCARY!
S-SORRY...
SHEESH...
THE HELL'S GOING ON HERE...!?
...AND THEN, SHE APPEARED~!
TON (TMP)

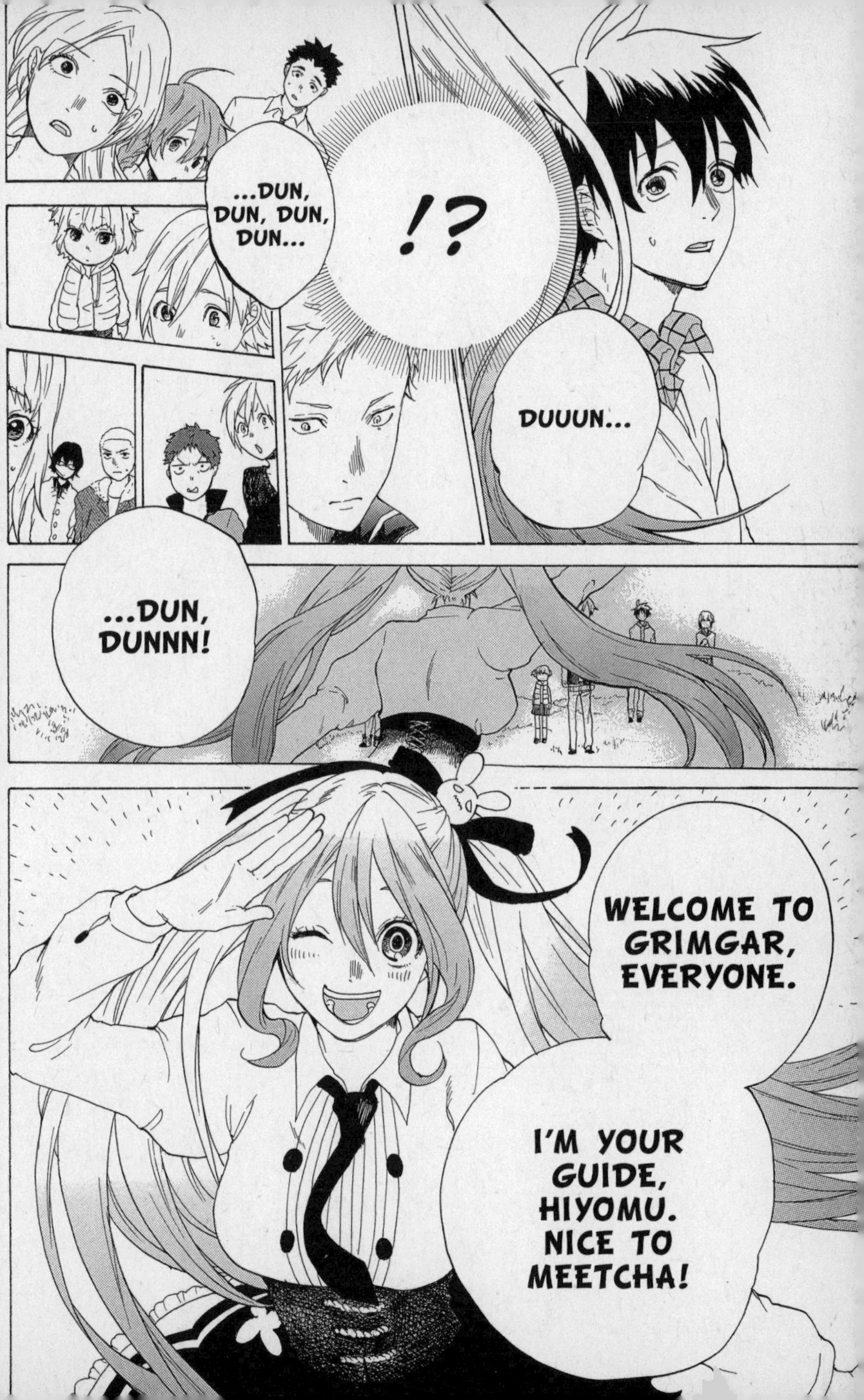
!?
DUUUN...
...DUN, DUN, DUN, DUN...
...DUN, DUNNN!
WELCOME TO GRIMGAR, EVERYONE.
I'M YOUR GUIDE, HIYOMU. NICE TO MEETCHA!

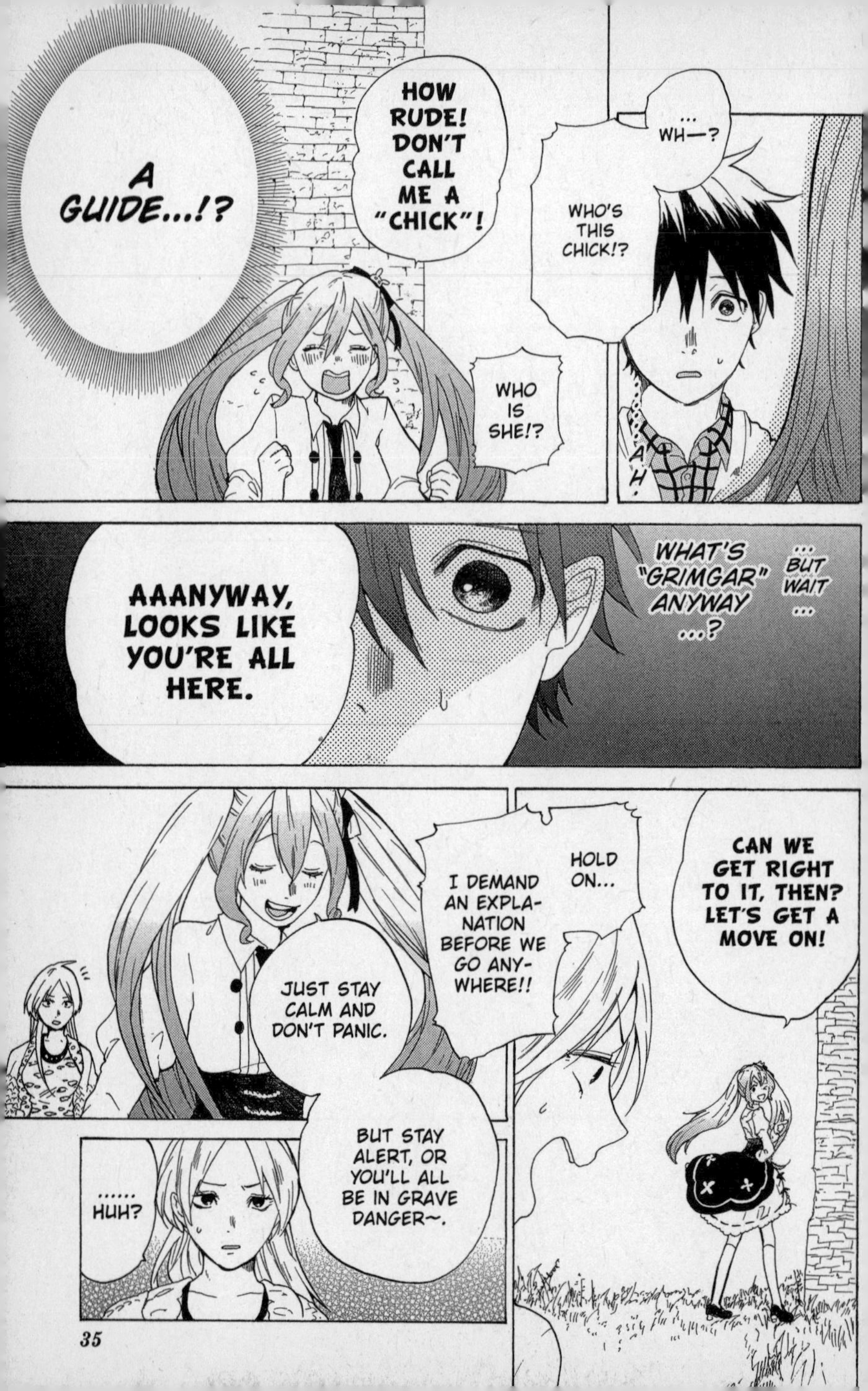
... WH—?
WHO'S THIS CHICK!?
AH!
HOW RUDE! DON'T CALL ME A "CHICK"!
WHO IS SHE!?
A GUIDE...!?
... BUT WAIT ...
WHAT'S "GRIMGAR" ANYWAY ...?
AAANYWAY, LOOKS LIKE YOU'RE ALL HERE.
CAN WE GET RIGHT TO IT, THEN? LET'S GET A MOVE ON!
HOLD ON...
I DEMAND AN EXPLA- NATION BEFORE WE GO ANY- WHERE!!
JUST STAY CALM AND DON'T PANIC.
BUT STAY ALERT, OR YOU'LL ALL BE IN GRAVE DANGER~.
...... HUH?

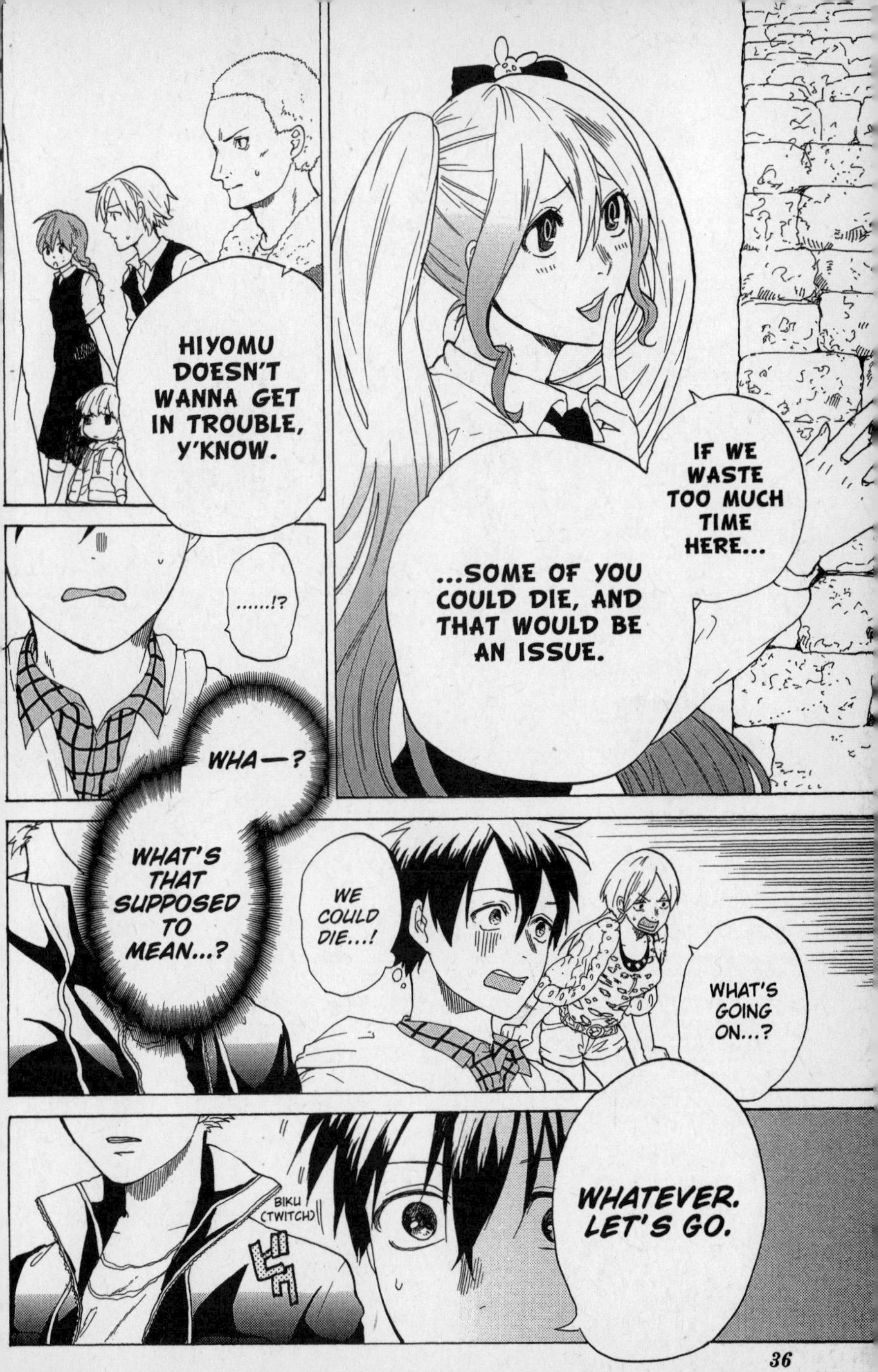
IF WE WASTE TOO MUCH TIME HERE...
...SOME OF YOU COULD DIE, AND THAT WOULD BE AN ISSUE.
HIYOMU DOESN'T WANNA GET IN TROUBLE, Y'KNOW.
......!?
WHA—?
WHAT'S THAT SUPPOSED TO MEAN...?
WHAT'S GOING ON...?
WE COULD DIE...!
WHATEVER. LET'S GO.
BIKU (TWITCH)

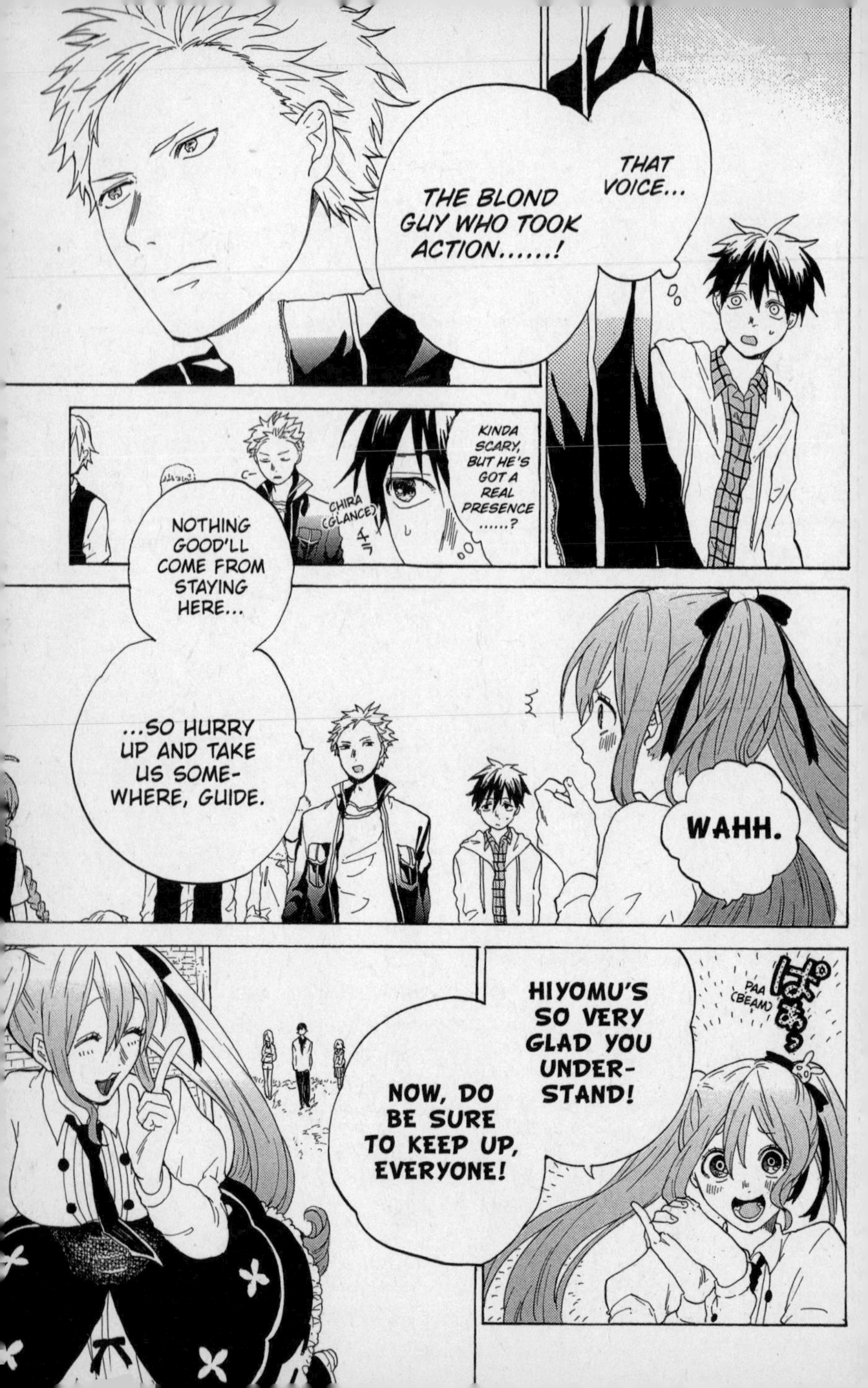
THAT VOICE...
THE BLOND GUY WHO TOOK ACTION......!
KINDA SCARY, BUT HE'S GOT A REAL PRESENCE......?
CHIRA (GLANCE)
NOTHING GOOD'LL COME FROM STAYING HERE...
...SO HURRY UP AND TAKE US SOME-WHERE, GUIDE.
WAHH.
PAA (BEAM)
HIYOMU'S SO VERY GLAD YOU UNDER-STAND!
NOW, DO BE SURE TO KEEP UP, EVERYONE!

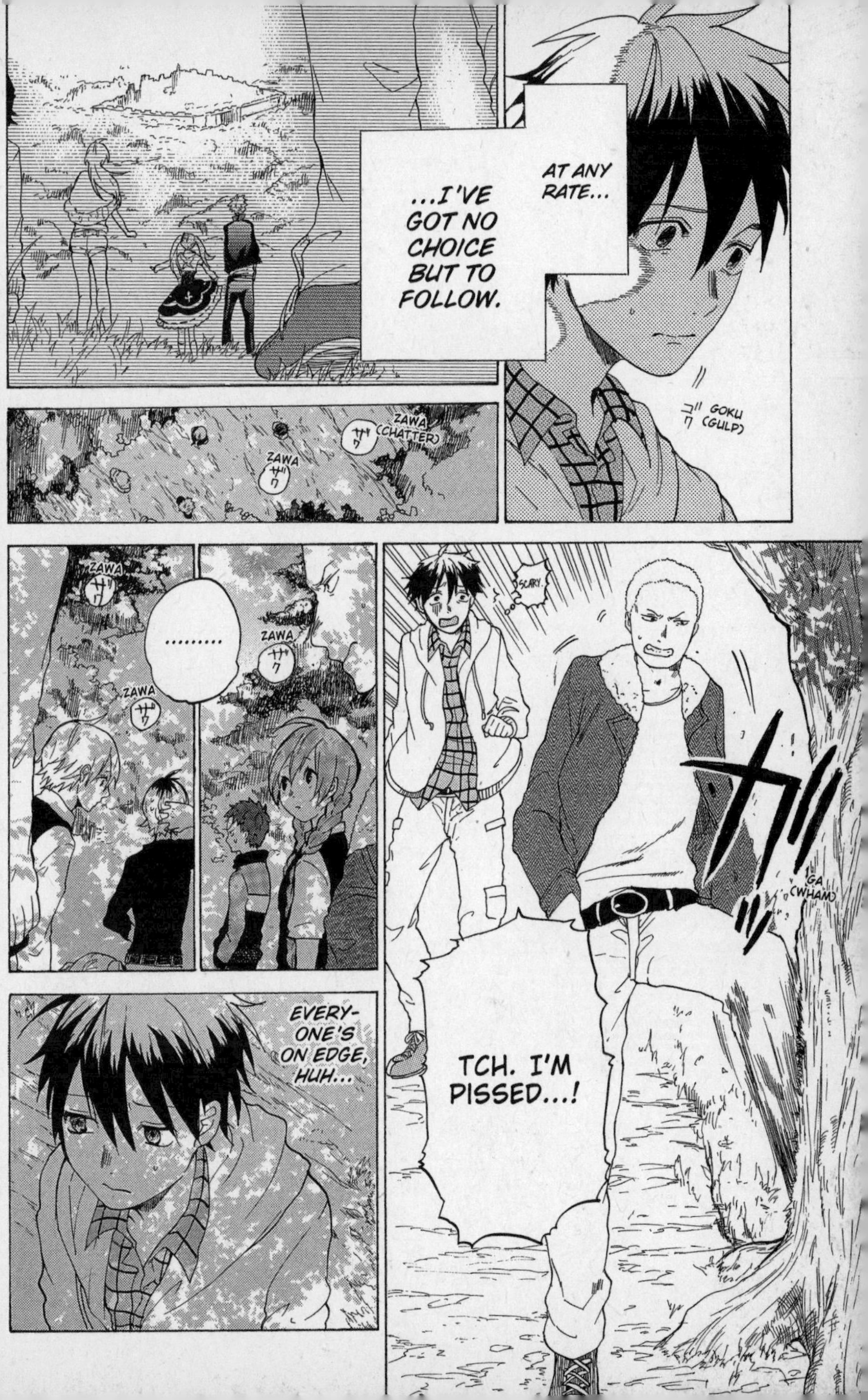

AT ANY RATE...
...I'VE GOT NO CHOICE BUT TO FOLLOW.
GOKU (GULP)
ZAWA (CHATTER)
ZAWA
SCARY.
TCH. I'M PISSED...!
GA (WHAM)
ZAWA
....
ZAWA
ZAWA
EVERY-ONE'S ON EDGE, HUH...

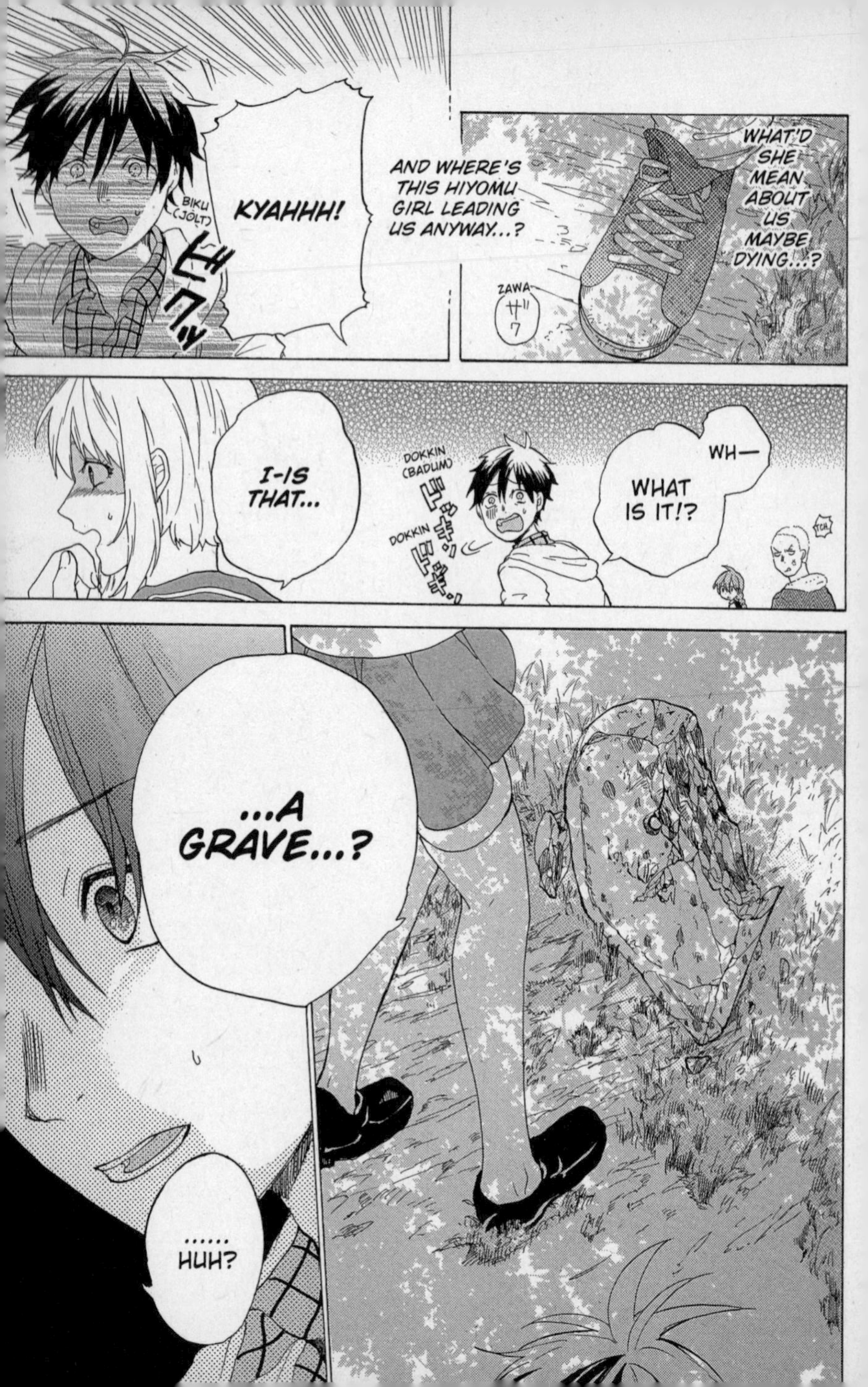
WHAT'D SHE MEAN ABOUT US MAYBE DYING...?
AND WHERE'S THIS HIYOMU GIRL LEADING US ANYWAY...?
ZAWA
ザワ
KYAHHH!
BIKU (JOLT)
ビクッ
WH—
WHAT IS IT!?
TCH
DOKKIN (BADUM)
DOKKIN
I-IS THAT...
...A GRAVE...?
......HUH?

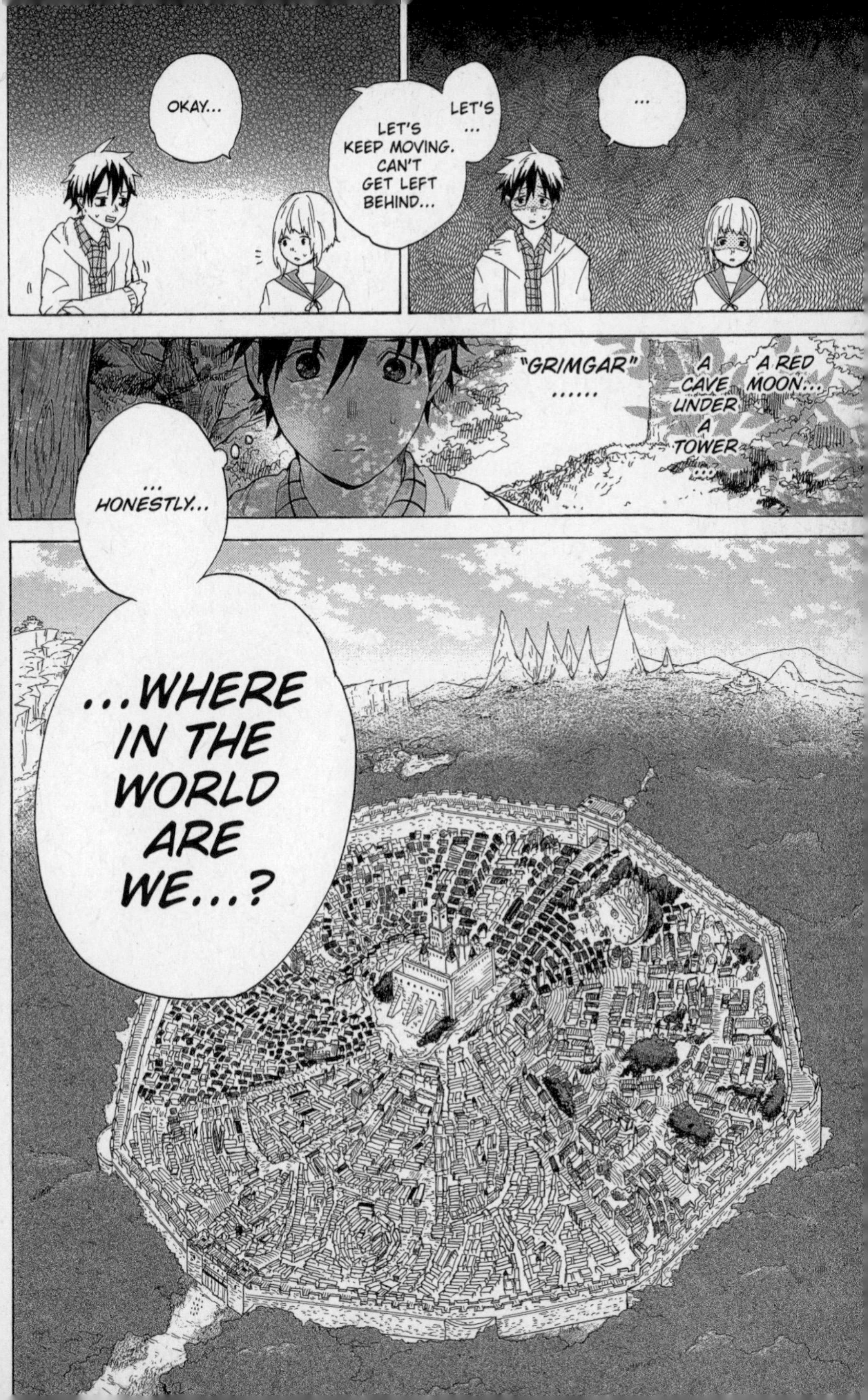
...
LET'S ...
LET'S KEEP MOVING. CAN'T GET LEFT BEHIND...
OKAY...
A RED MOON...
A CAVE UNDER A TOWER ...
"GRIMGAR" ......
... HONESTLY...
...WHERE IN THE WORLD ARE WE...?

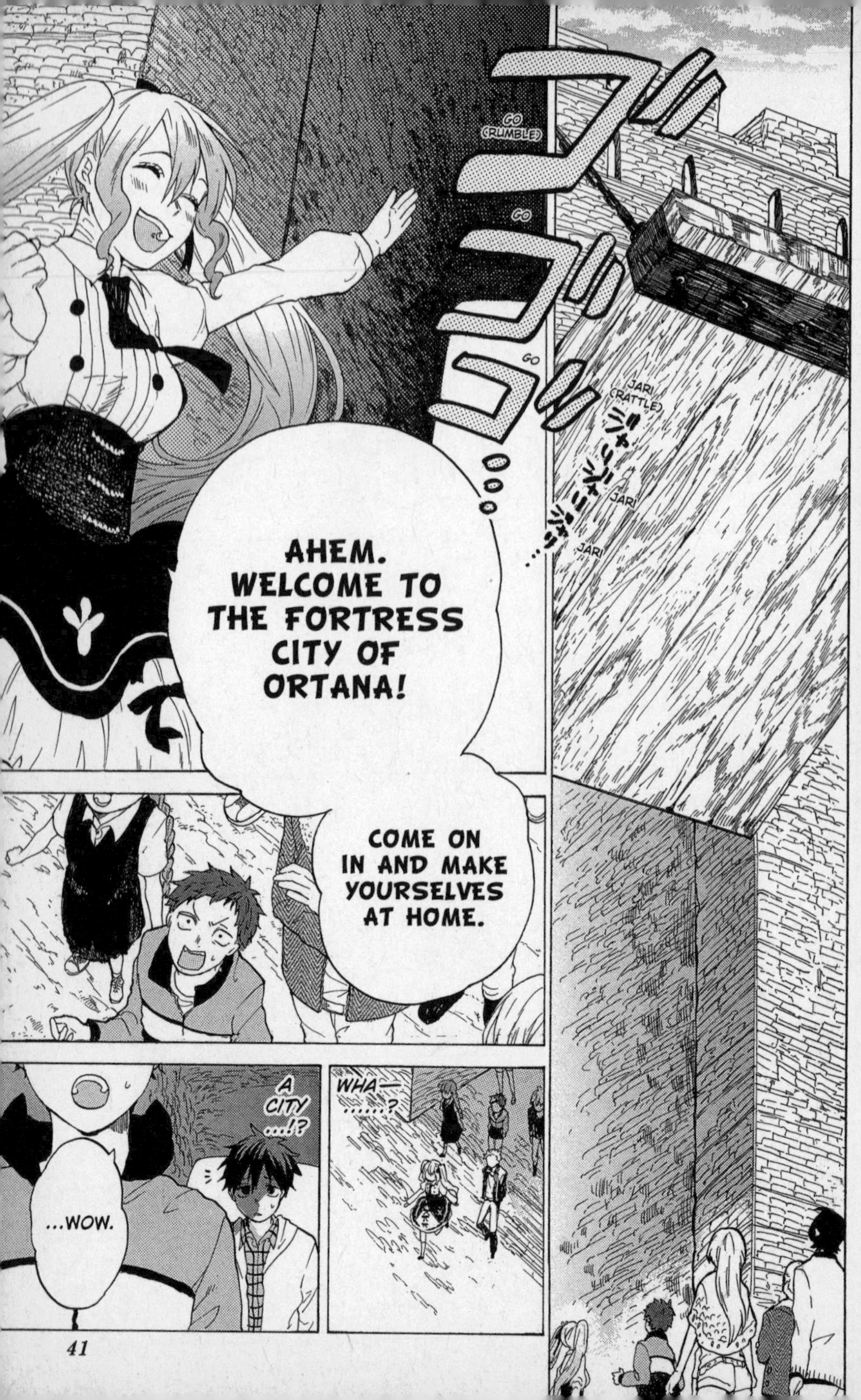
ゴゴゴゴ…
GO (RUMBLE)
GO
GO
ジャリジャリジャリ…
JARI (RATTLE)
JARI
JARI
AHEM. WELCOME TO THE FORTRESS CITY OF ORTANA!
COME ON IN AND MAKE YOURSELVES AT HOME.
WHA— ......?
A CITY ...!?
...WOW.

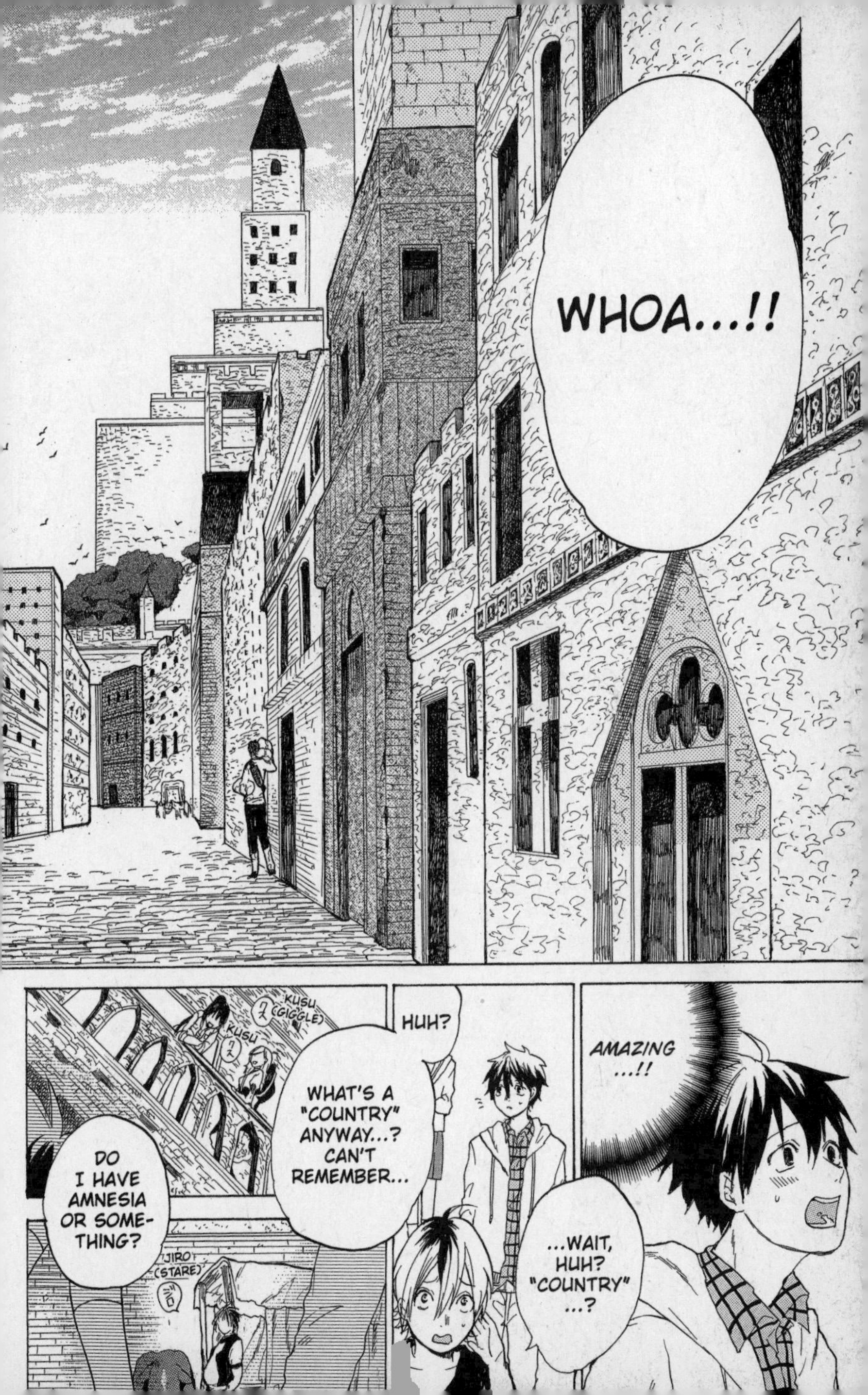
WHOA...!!
AMAZING ...!!
...WAIT, HUH? "COUNTRY" ...?
HUH?
WHAT'S A "COUNTRY" ANYWAY...? CAN'T REMEMBER...
DO I HAVE AMNESIA OR SOME-THING?
KUSU (GIGGLE)
KUSU
JIRO (STARE)

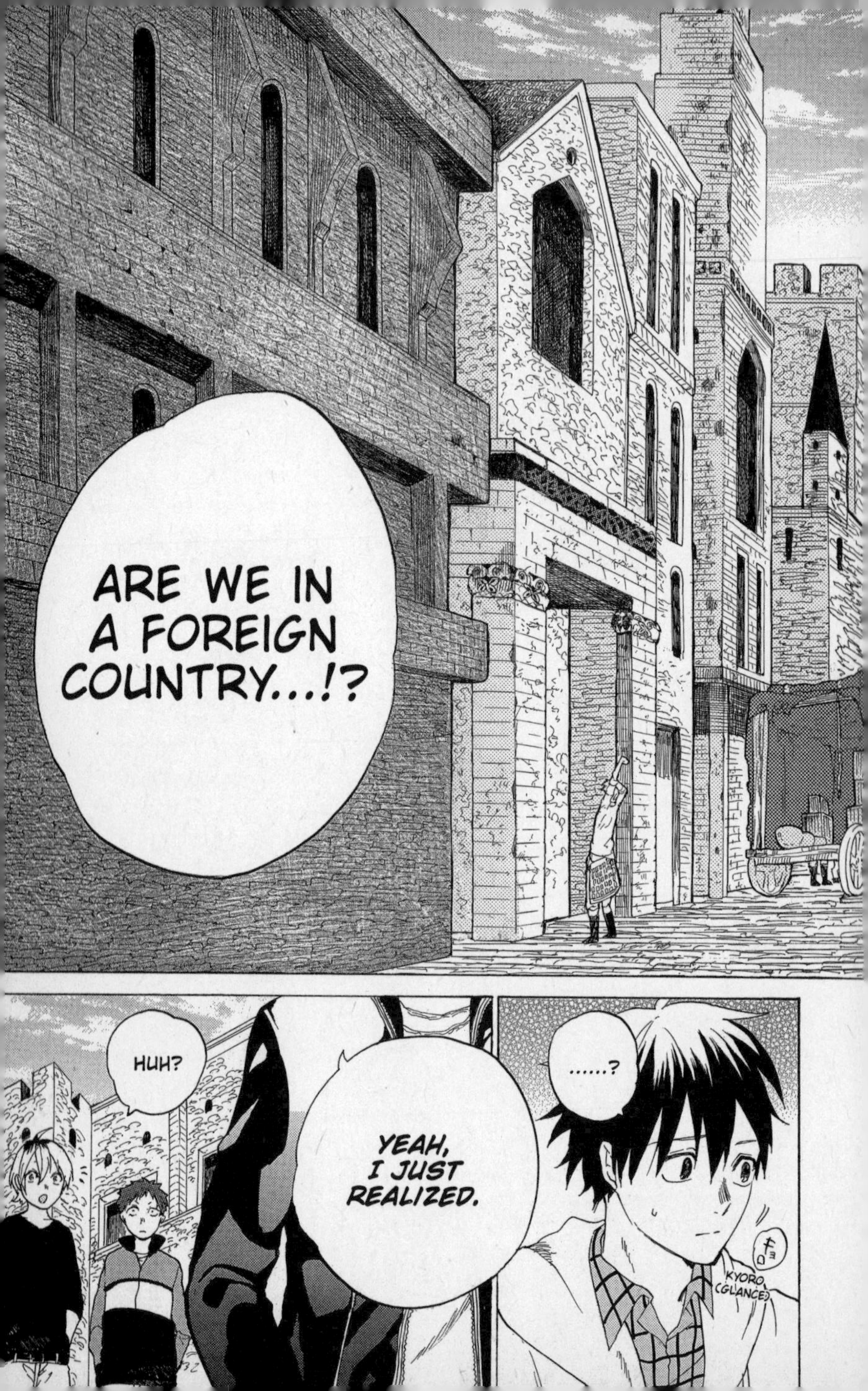
ARE WE IN A FOREIGN COUNTRY...!?
......?
KYORO (GLANCE)
HUH?
YEAH, I JUST REALIZED.

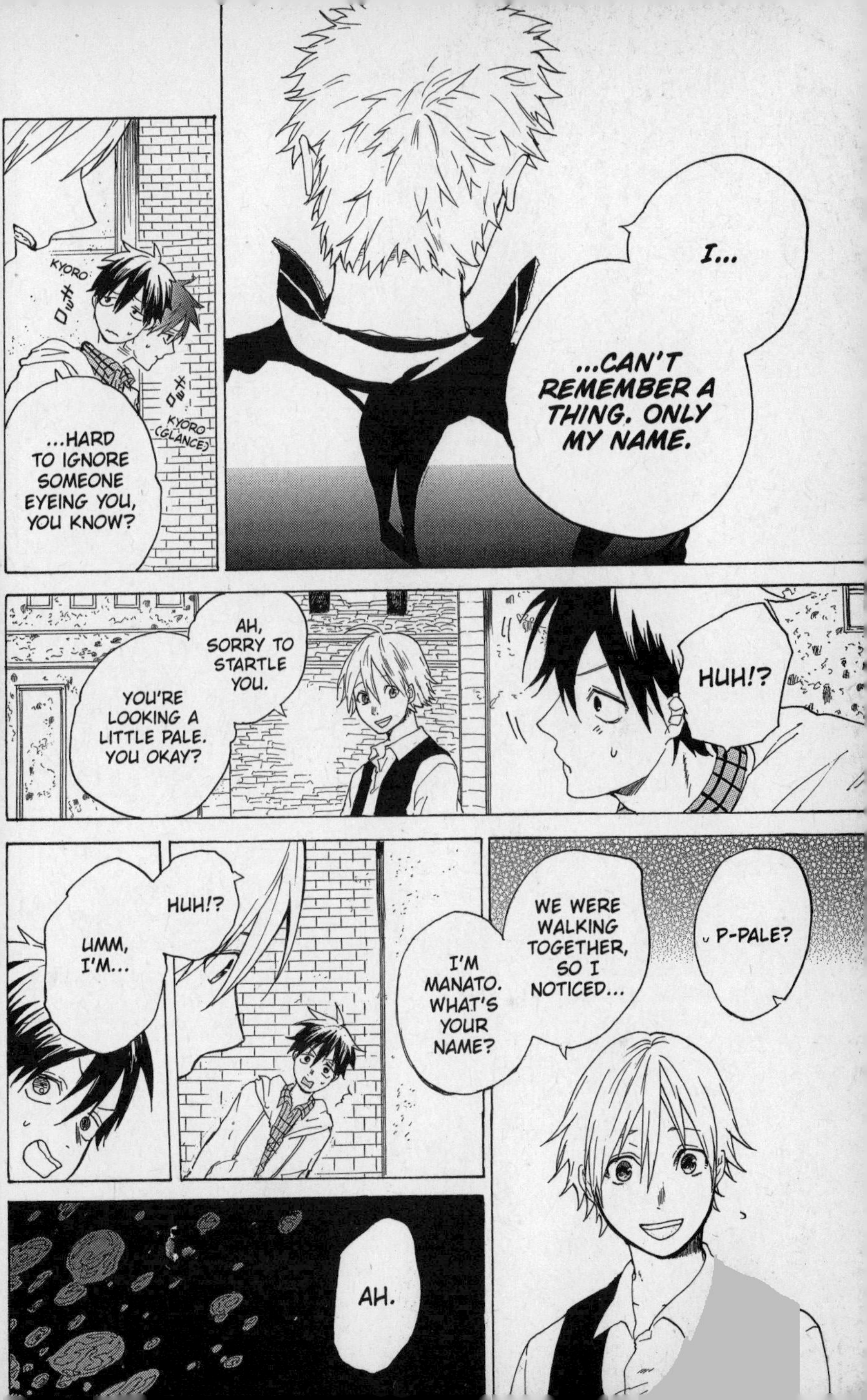
I...
...CAN'T REMEMBER A THING. ONLY MY NAME.
KYORO
キョロ
キョロ
KYORO (GLANCE)
...HARD TO IGNORE SOMEONE EYEING YOU, YOU KNOW?
HUH!?
AH, SORRY TO STARTLE YOU.
YOU'RE LOOKING A LITTLE PALE. YOU OKAY?
P-PALE?
WE WERE WALKING TOGETHER, SO I NOTICED...
I'M MANATO. WHAT'S YOUR NAME?
HUH!?
UMM, I'M...
AH.

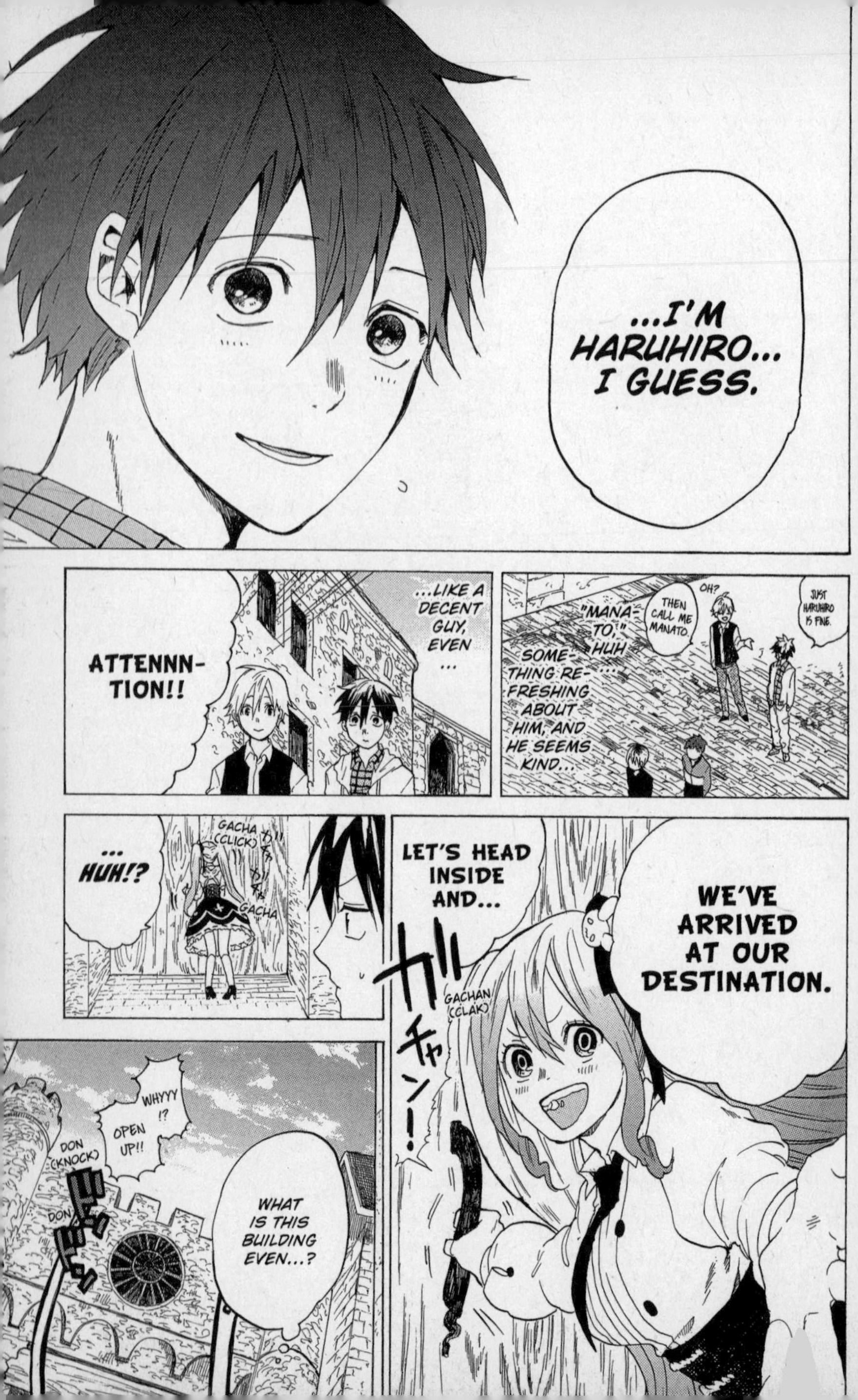

...I'M HARUHIRO... I GUESS.
JUST HARUHIRO IS FINE.
OH?
THEN CALL ME MANATO.
"MANATO," HUH...
SOMETHING REFRESHING ABOUT HIM, AND HE SEEMS KIND...
...LIKE A DECENT GUY, EVEN...
ATTENNNTION!!
WE'VE ARRIVED AT OUR DESTINATION.
LET'S HEAD INSIDE AND...
GACHAN (CLAK)
GACHA (CLICK)
...HUH!?
GACHA
WHYYY!?
OPEN UP!!
DON (KNOCK)
DON
WHAT IS THIS BUILDING EVEN...?

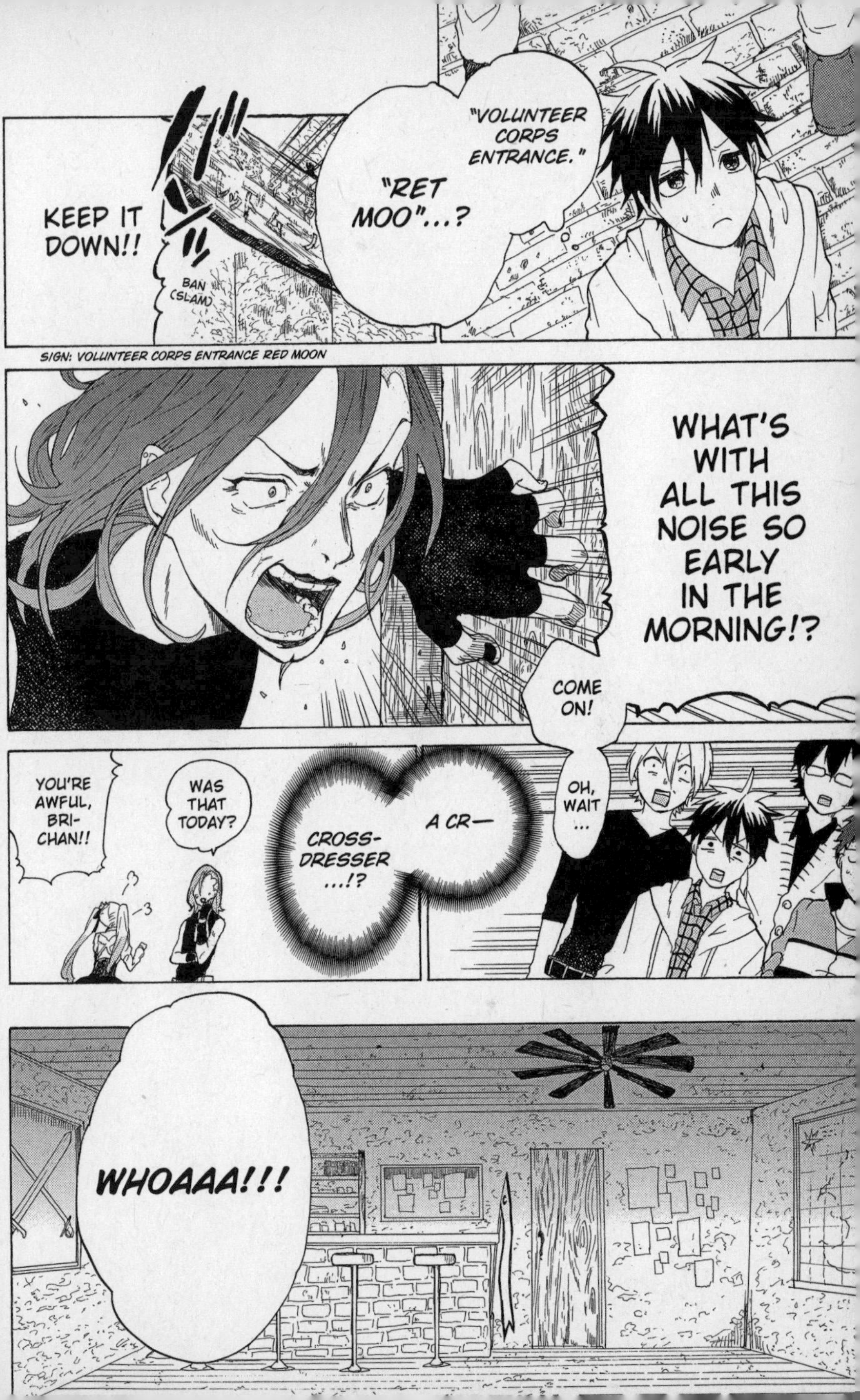
"VOLUNTEER CORPS ENTRANCE."
"RET MOO"...?
KEEP IT DOWN!!
BAN (SLAM)
SIGN: VOLUNTEER CORPS ENTRANCE RED MOON
WHAT'S WITH ALL THIS NOISE SO EARLY IN THE MORNING!?
COME ON!
OH, WAIT...
A CR—
CROSS-DRESSER...!?
WAS THAT TODAY?
YOU'RE AWFUL, BRI-CHAN!!
WHOAAA!!!

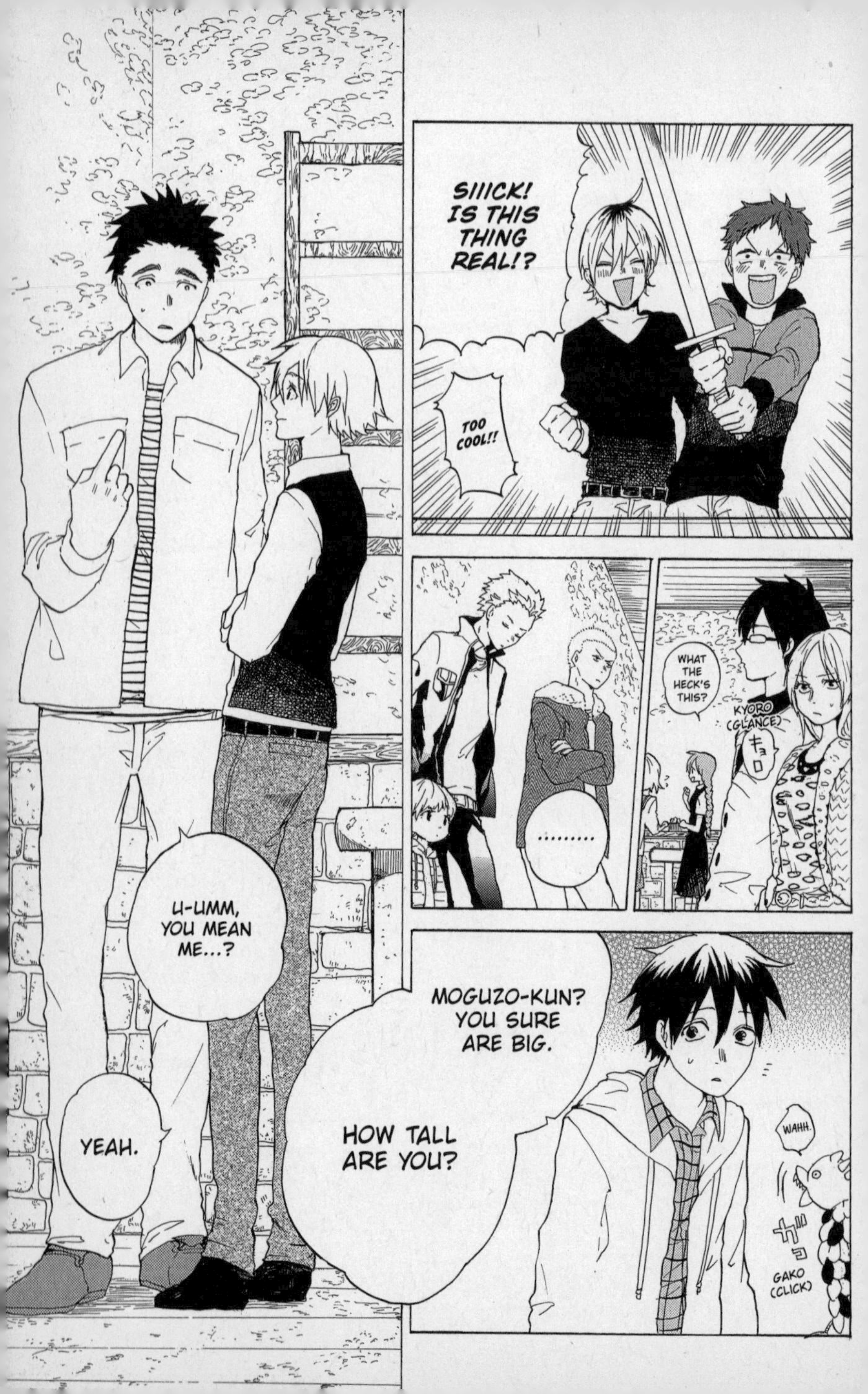
SIIICK! IS THIS THING REAL!?
TOO COOL!!
WHAT THE HECK'S THIS?
KYORO (GLANCE)
キョロ
....
MOGUZO-KUN? YOU SURE ARE BIG.
HOW TALL ARE YOU?
WAHH.
ガコ
GAKO (CLICK)
U-UMM, YOU MEAN ME...?
YEAH.

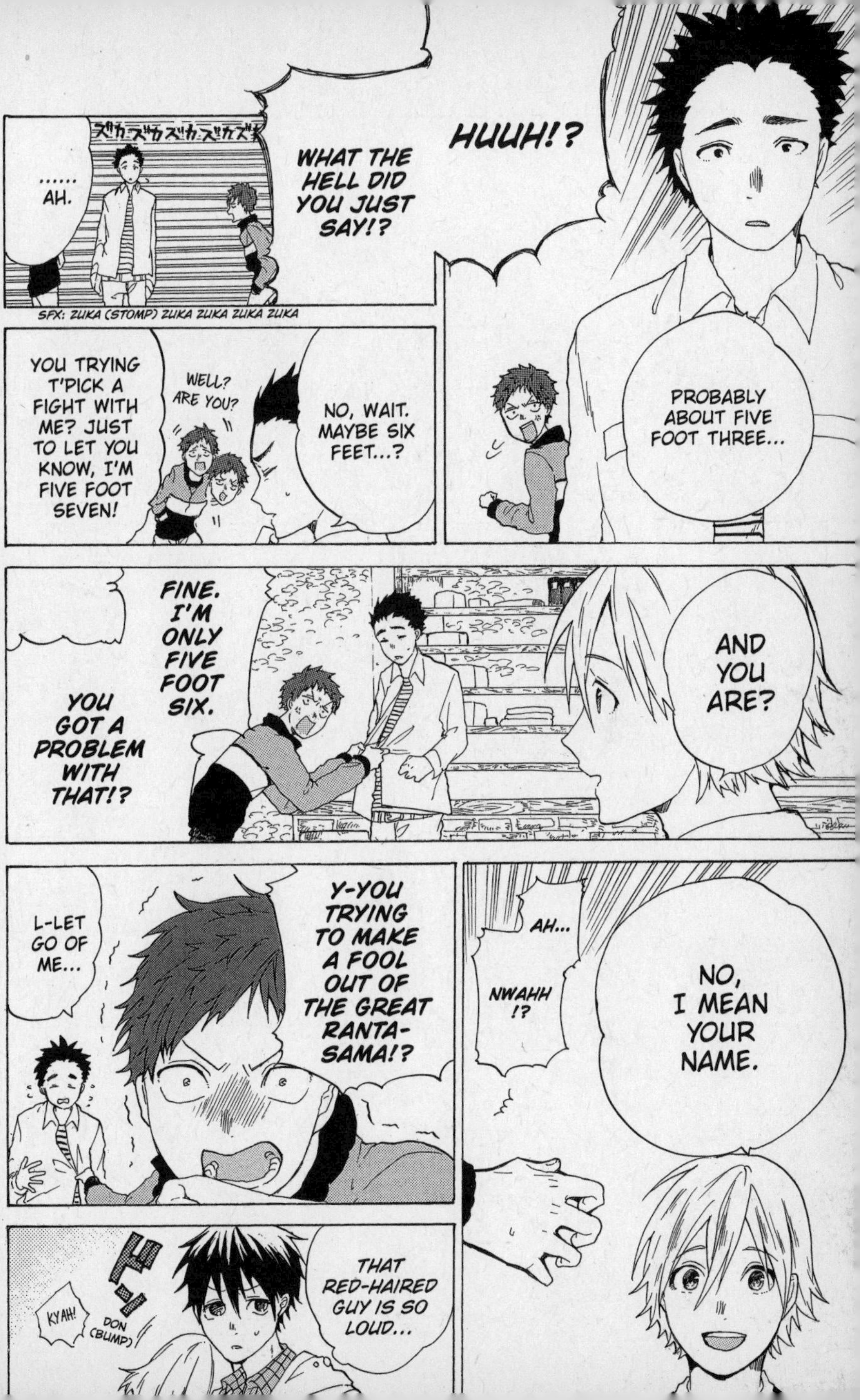
HUUH!?
WHAT THE HELL DID YOU JUST SAY!?
PROBABLY ABOUT FIVE FOOT THREE...
...... AH.
SFX: ZUKA (STOMP) ZUKA ZUKA ZUKA ZUKA
NO, WAIT. MAYBE SIX FEET...?
WELL? ARE YOU?
YOU TRYING T'PICK A FIGHT WITH ME? JUST TO LET YOU KNOW, I'M FIVE FOOT SEVEN!
AND YOU ARE?
FINE. I'M ONLY FIVE FOOT SIX.
YOU GOT A PROBLEM WITH THAT!?
NO, I MEAN YOUR NAME.
AH...
NWAHH !?
Y-YOU TRYING TO MAKE A FOOL OUT OF THE GREAT RANTA-SAMA!?
L-LET GO OF ME...
THAT RED-HAIRED GUY IS SO LOUD...
DON (BUMP)
KYAH!

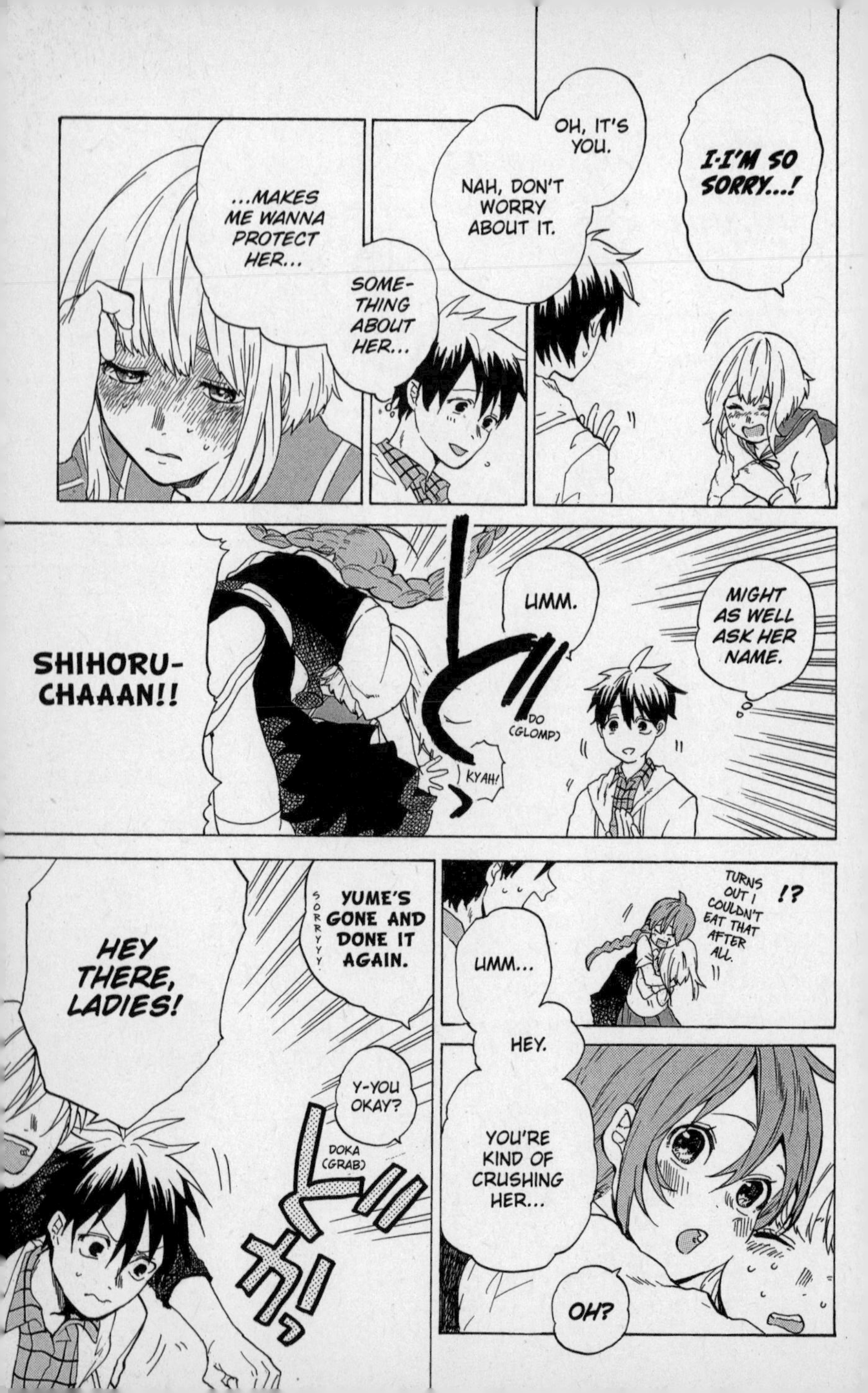
I-I'M SO SORRY...!
OH, IT'S YOU.
NAH, DON'T WORRY ABOUT IT.
SOME-THING ABOUT HER...
...MAKES ME WANNA PROTECT HER...
MIGHT AS WELL ASK HER NAME.
UMM.
DO (GLOMP)
KYAH!
SHIHORU-CHAAAN!!
!?
TURNS OUT I COULDN'T EAT THAT AFTER ALL.
UMM...
HEY.
YOU'RE KIND OF CRUSHING HER...
OH?
HEY THERE, LADIES!
YUME'S GONE AND DONE IT AGAIN.
SORRYYY.
Y-YOU OKAY?
DOKA (GRAB)

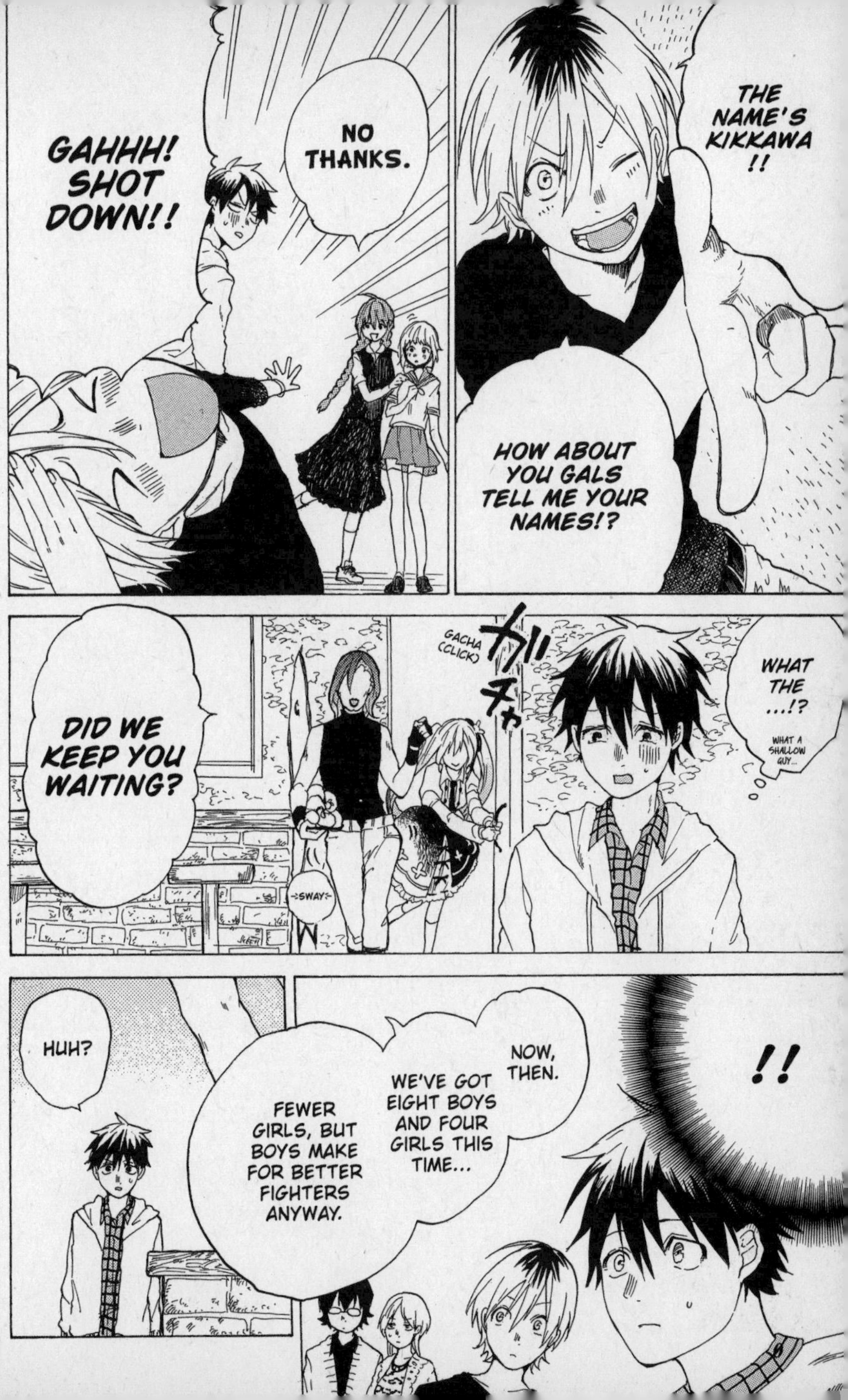

THE NAME'S KIKKAWA !!
HOW ABOUT YOU GALS TELL ME YOUR NAMES!?
NO THANKS.
GAHHH! SHOT DOWN!!
WHAT THE ...!?
WHAT A SHALLOW GUY...
GACHA (CLICK)
DID WE KEEP YOU WAITING?
SWAY
!!
NOW, THEN.
WE'VE GOT EIGHT BOYS AND FOUR GIRLS THIS TIME...
FEWER GIRLS, BUT BOYS MAKE FOR BETTER FIGHTERS ANYWAY.
HUH?

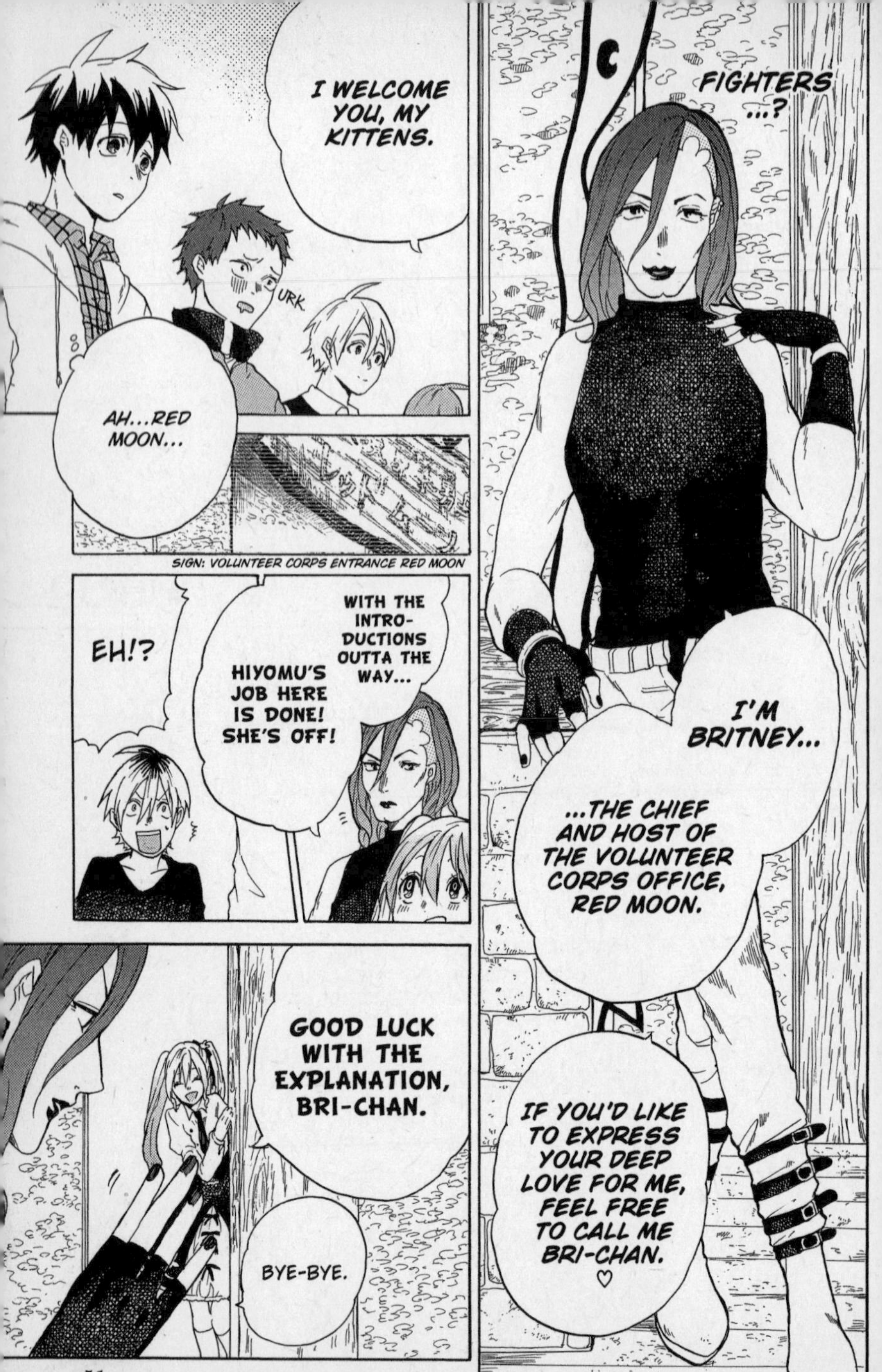
FIGHTERS ...?
I'M BRITNEY...
...THE CHIEF AND HOST OF THE VOLUNTEER CORPS OFFICE, RED MOON.
IF YOU'D LIKE TO EXPRESS YOUR DEEP LOVE FOR ME, FEEL FREE TO CALL ME BRI-CHAN. ♡
I WELCOME YOU, MY KITTENS.
URK.
AH...RED MOON...
SIGN: VOLUNTEER CORPS ENTRANCE RED MOON
WITH THE INTRODUCTIONS OUTTA THE WAY...
HIYOMU'S JOB HERE IS DONE! SHE'S OFF!
EH!?
GOOD LUCK WITH THE EXPLANATION, BRI-CHAN.
BYE-BYE.

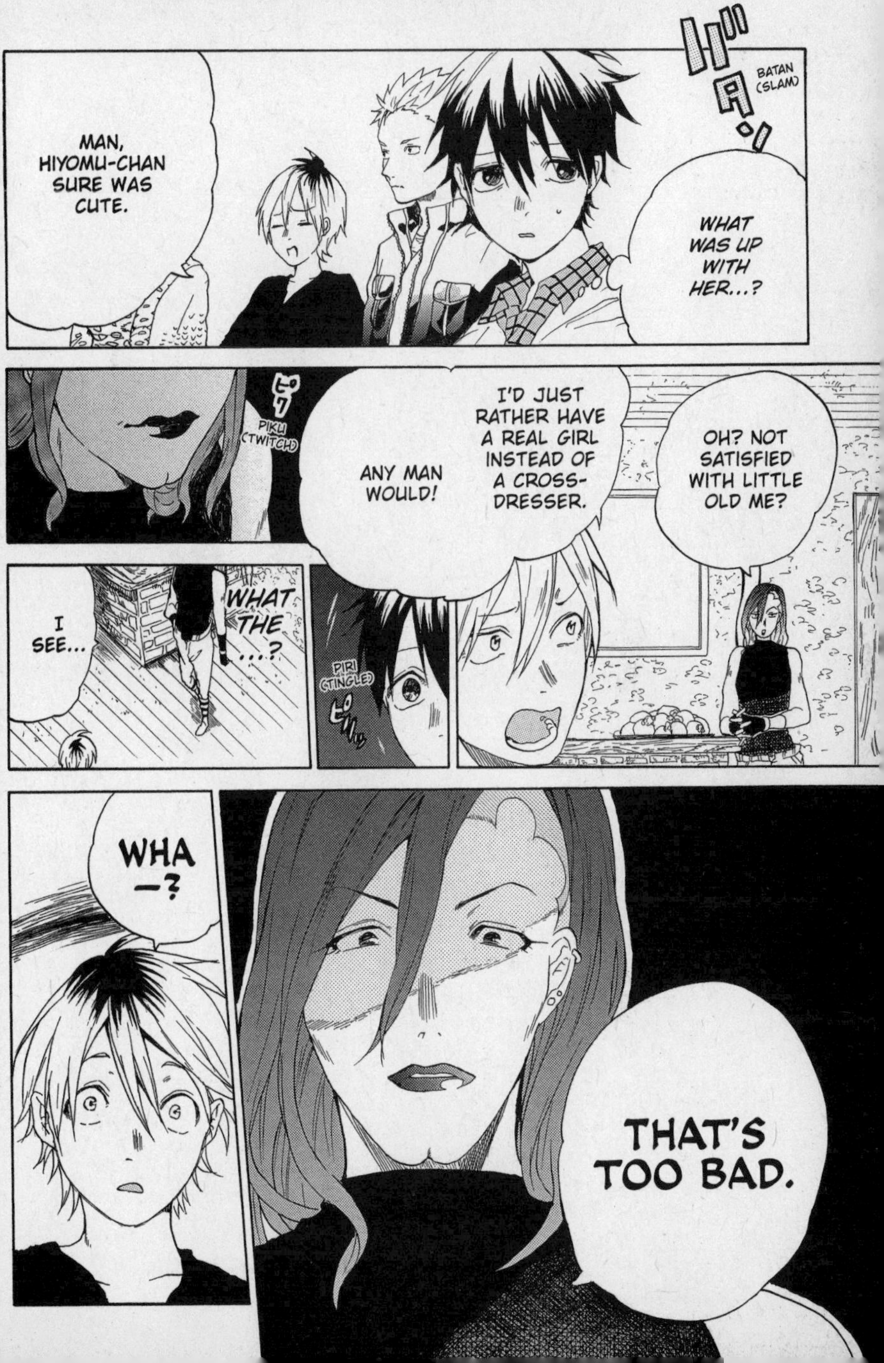
BATAN (SLAM)
WHAT WAS UP WITH HER...?
MAN, HIYOMU-CHAN SURE WAS CUTE.
OH? NOT SATISFIED WITH LITTLE OLD ME?
I'D JUST RATHER HAVE A REAL GIRL INSTEAD OF A CROSS-DRESSER.
ANY MAN WOULD!
PIKU (TWITCH)
PIRI (TINGLE)
WHAT THE ...?
I SEE...
THAT'S TOO BAD.
WHA —?

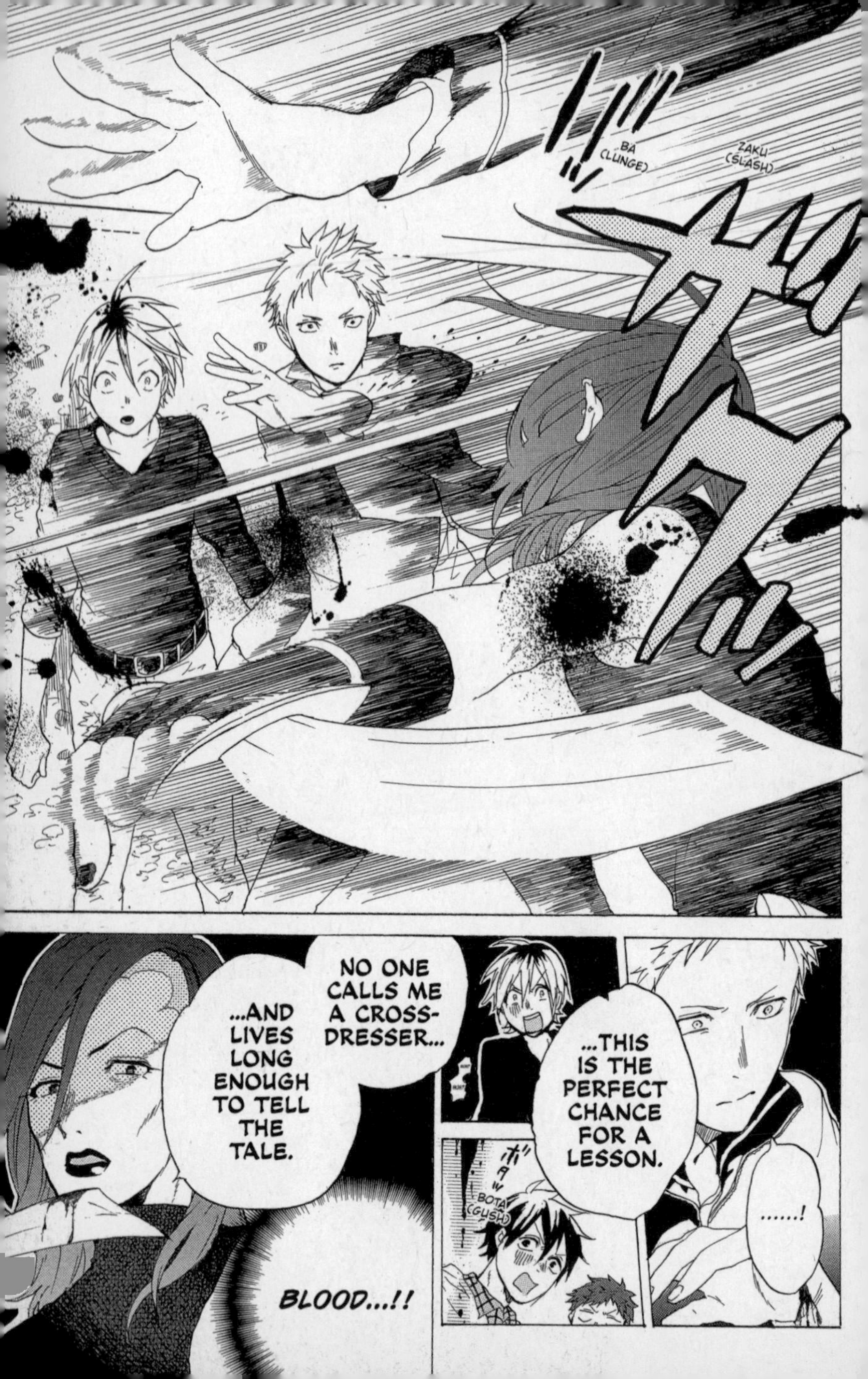
ZAKU
(SLASH)
BA
(LUNGE)
...THIS IS THE PERFECT CHANCE FOR A LESSON.
......!
BOTA
(GUSH)
NO ONE CALLS ME A CROSS-DRESSER...
...AND LIVES LONG ENOUGH TO TELL THE TALE.
BLOOD...!!

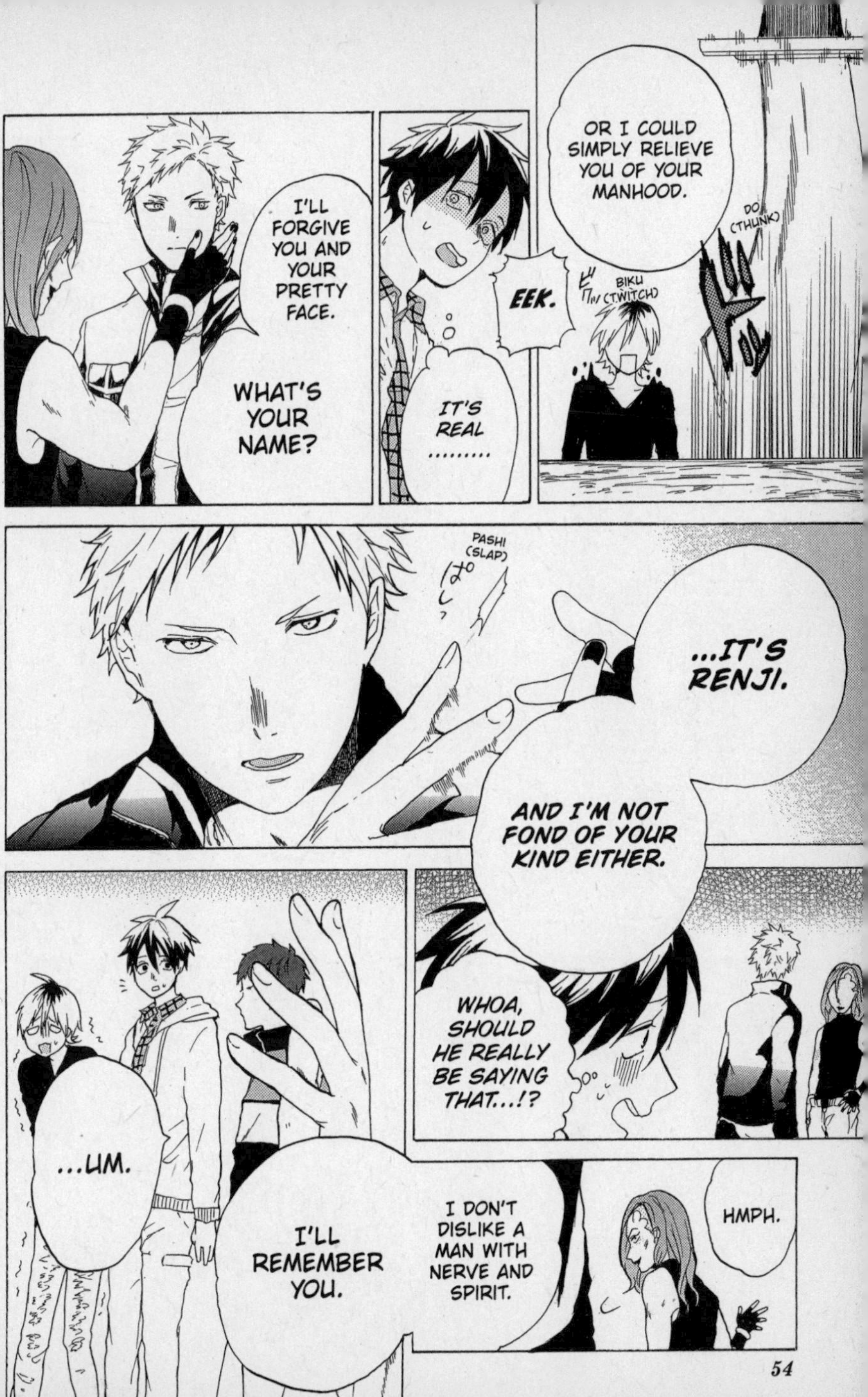
OR I COULD SIMPLY RELIEVE YOU OF YOUR MANHOOD.
DO (THUNK)
BIKU (TWITCH)
EEK.
IT'S REAL ....
I'LL FORGIVE YOU AND YOUR PRETTY FACE.
WHAT'S YOUR NAME?
PASHI (SLAP)
...IT'S RENJI.
AND I'M NOT FOND OF YOUR KIND EITHER.
WHOA, SHOULD HE REALLY BE SAYING THAT...!?
HMPH.
I DON'T DISLIKE A MAN WITH NERVE AND SPIRIT.
I'LL REMEMBER YOU.
...UM.

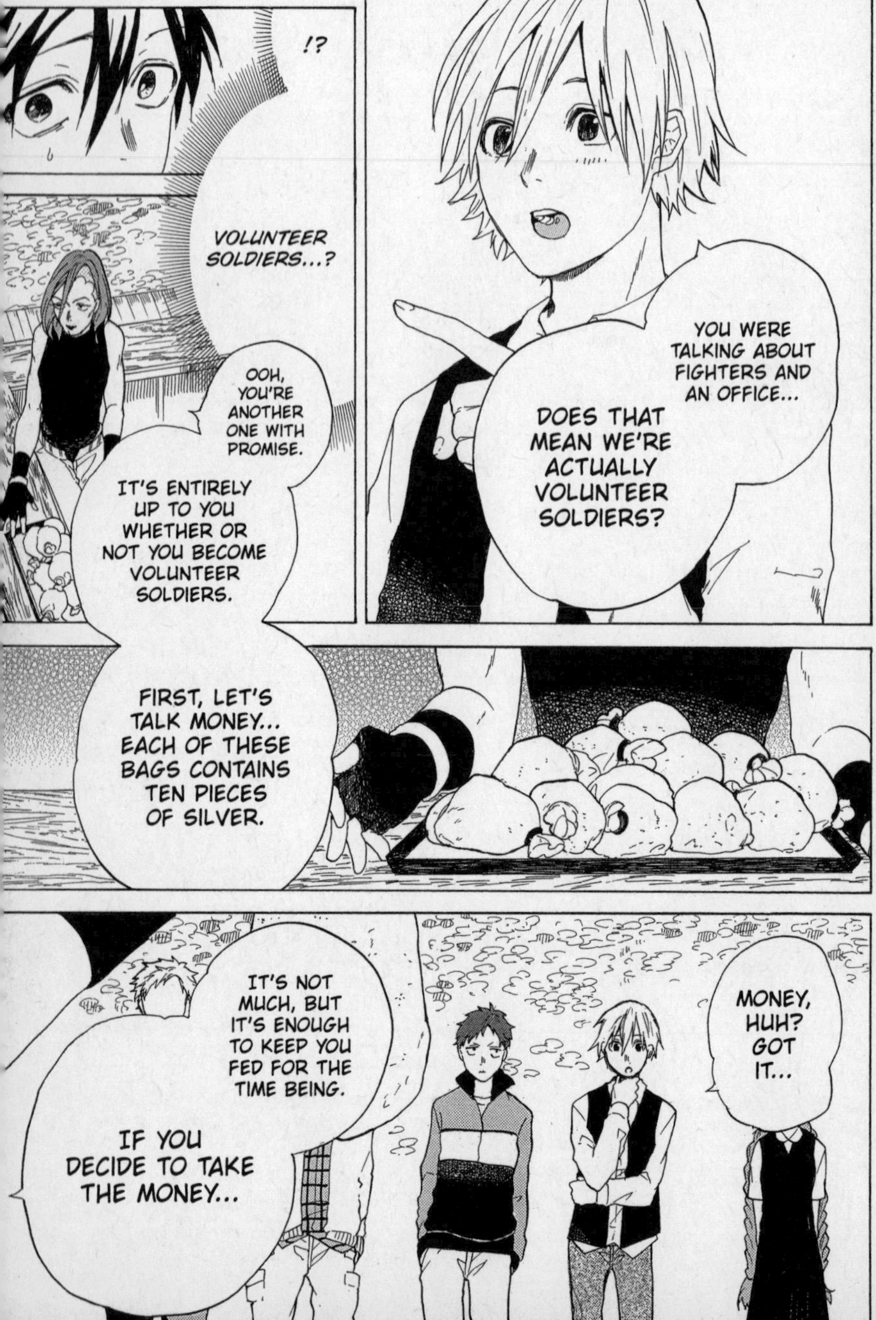
YOU WERE TALKING ABOUT FIGHTERS AND AN OFFICE...
DOES THAT MEAN WE'RE ACTUALLY VOLUNTEER SOLDIERS?
!?
VOLUNTEER SOLDIERS...?
OOH, YOU'RE ANOTHER ONE WITH PROMISE.
IT'S ENTIRELY UP TO YOU WHETHER OR NOT YOU BECOME VOLUNTEER SOLDIERS.
FIRST, LET'S TALK MONEY... EACH OF THESE BAGS CONTAINS TEN PIECES OF SILVER.
MONEY, HUH? GOT IT...
IT'S NOT MUCH, BUT IT'S ENOUGH TO KEEP YOU FED FOR THE TIME BEING.
IF YOU DECIDE TO TAKE THE MONEY...

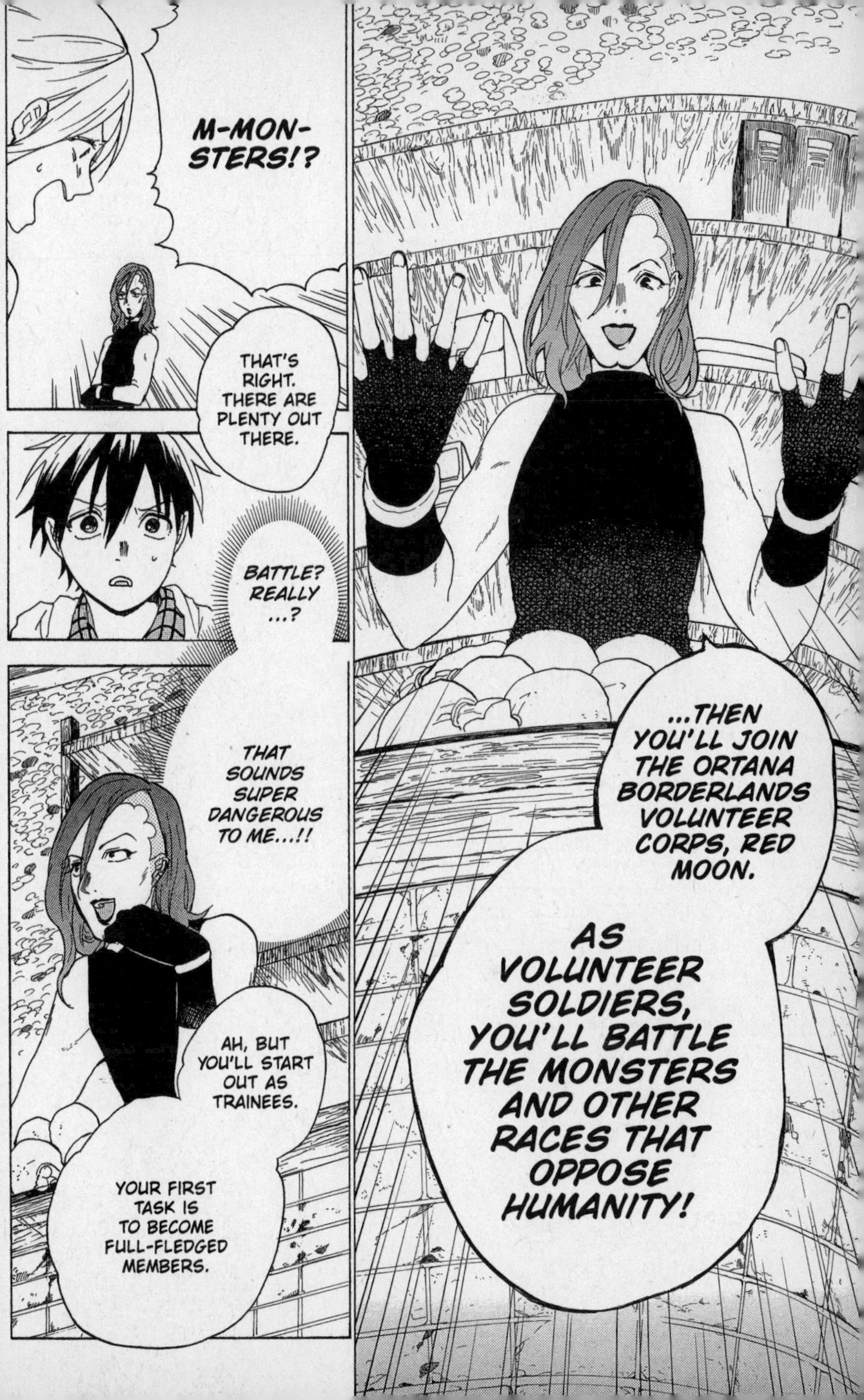
...THEN YOU'LL JOIN THE ORTANA BORDERLANDS VOLUNTEER CORPS, RED MOON.
AS VOLUNTEER SOLDIERS, YOU'LL BATTLE THE MONSTERS AND OTHER RACES THAT OPPOSE HUMANITY!
M-MONSTERS!?
THAT'S RIGHT. THERE ARE PLENTY OUT THERE.
BATTLE? REALLY ...?
THAT SOUNDS SUPER DANGEROUS TO ME...!!
AH, BUT YOU'LL START OUT AS TRAINEES.
YOUR FIRST TASK IS TO BECOME FULL-FLEDGED MEMBERS.

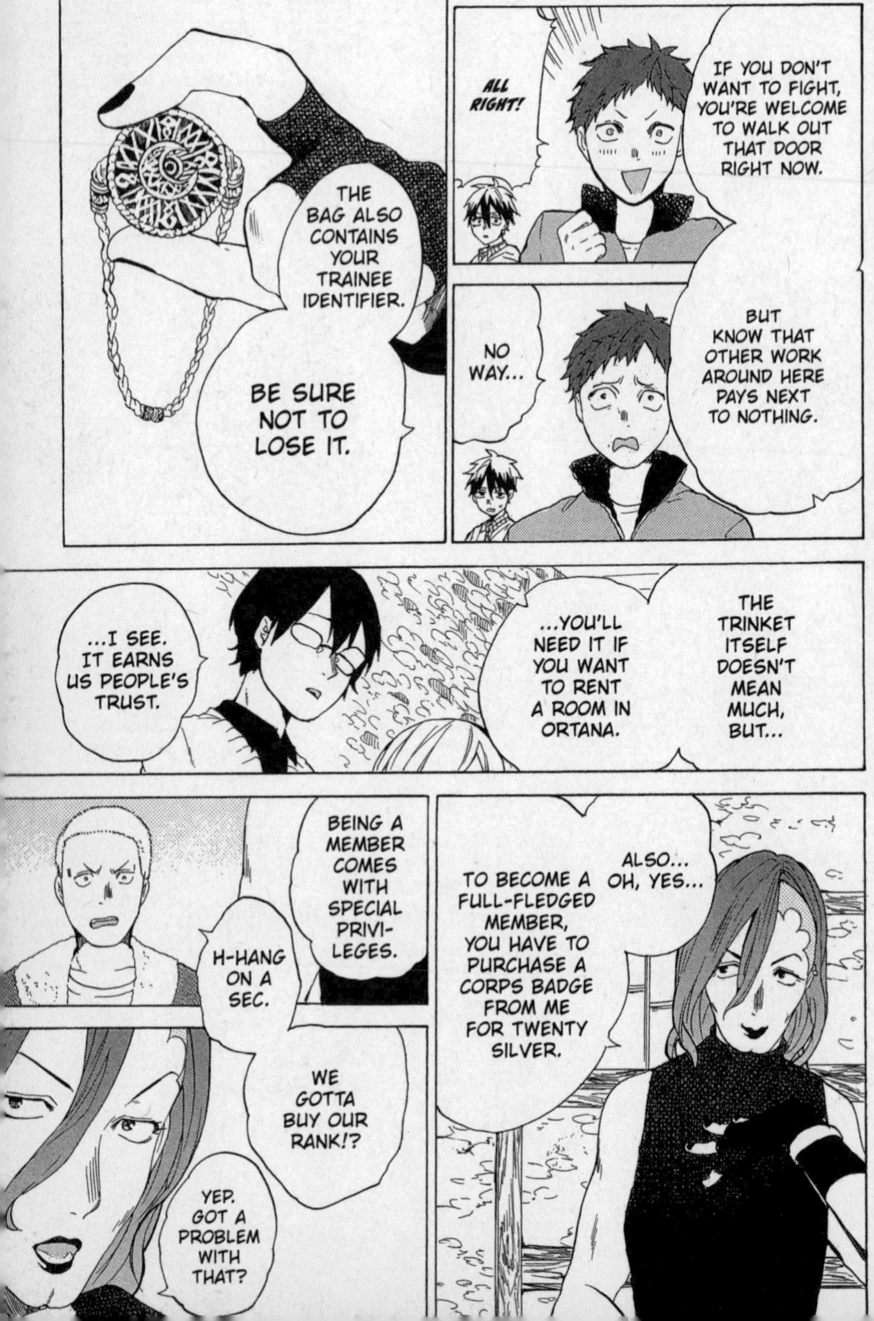
IF YOU DON'T WANT TO FIGHT, YOU'RE WELCOME TO WALK OUT THAT DOOR RIGHT NOW.
ALL RIGHT!
BUT KNOW THAT OTHER WORK AROUND HERE PAYS NEXT TO NOTHING.
NO WAY...
THE BAG ALSO CONTAINS YOUR TRAINEE IDENTIFIER.
BE SURE NOT TO LOSE IT.
THE TRINKET ITSELF DOESN'T MEAN MUCH, BUT...
...YOU'LL NEED IT IF YOU WANT TO RENT A ROOM IN ORTANA.
...I SEE. IT EARNS US PEOPLE'S TRUST.
ALSO... OH, YES...
TO BECOME A FULL-FLEDGED MEMBER, YOU HAVE TO PURCHASE A CORPS BADGE FROM ME FOR TWENTY SILVER.
BEING A MEMBER COMES WITH SPECIAL PRIVI-LEGES.
H-HANG ON A SEC.
WE GOTTA BUY OUR RANK!?
YEP. GOT A PROBLEM WITH THAT?

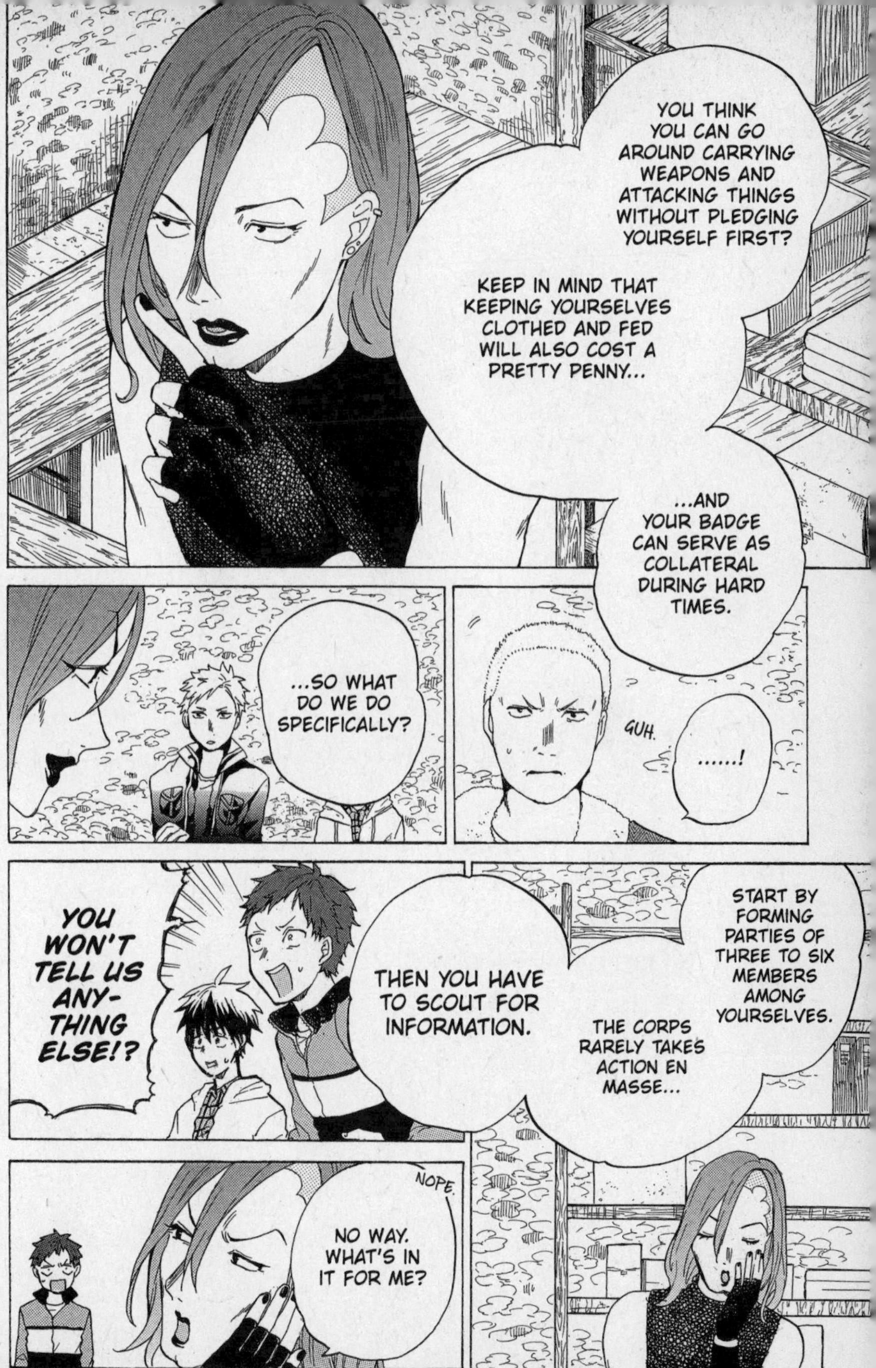
YOU THINK YOU CAN GO AROUND CARRYING WEAPONS AND ATTACKING THINGS WITHOUT PLEDGING YOURSELF FIRST?
KEEP IN MIND THAT KEEPING YOURSELVES CLOTHED AND FED WILL ALSO COST A PRETTY PENNY...
...AND YOUR BADGE CAN SERVE AS COLLATERAL DURING HARD TIMES.
GUH.
......!
...SO WHAT DO WE DO SPECIFICALLY?
START BY FORMING PARTIES OF THREE TO SIX MEMBERS AMONG YOURSELVES.
THE CORPS RARELY TAKES ACTION EN MASSE...
THEN YOU HAVE TO SCOUT FOR INFORMATION.
YOU WON'T TELL US ANY-THING ELSE!?
NOPE.
NO WAY. WHAT'S IN IT FOR ME?

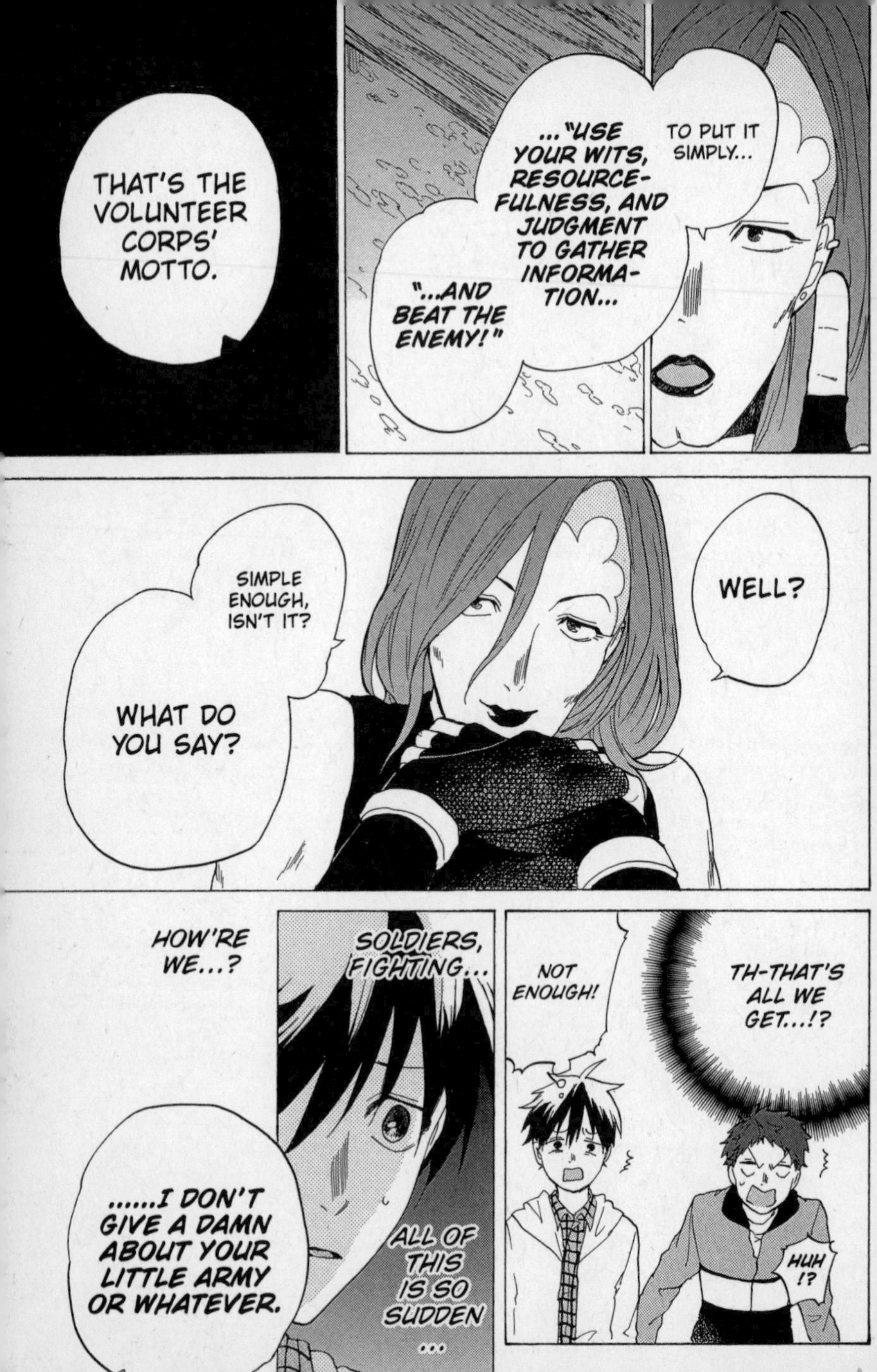
TO PUT IT SIMPLY...
..."USE YOUR WITS, RESOURCE-FULNESS, AND JUDGMENT TO GATHER INFORMA-TION...
"...AND BEAT THE ENEMY!"
THAT'S THE VOLUNTEER CORPS' MOTTO.
WELL?
SIMPLE ENOUGH, ISN'T IT?
WHAT DO YOU SAY?
TH-THAT'S ALL WE GET...!?
NOT ENOUGH!
HUH!?
SOLDIERS, FIGHTING...
HOW'RE WE...?
ALL OF THIS IS SO SUDDEN...
......I DON'T GIVE A DAMN ABOUT YOUR LITTLE ARMY OR WHATEVER.

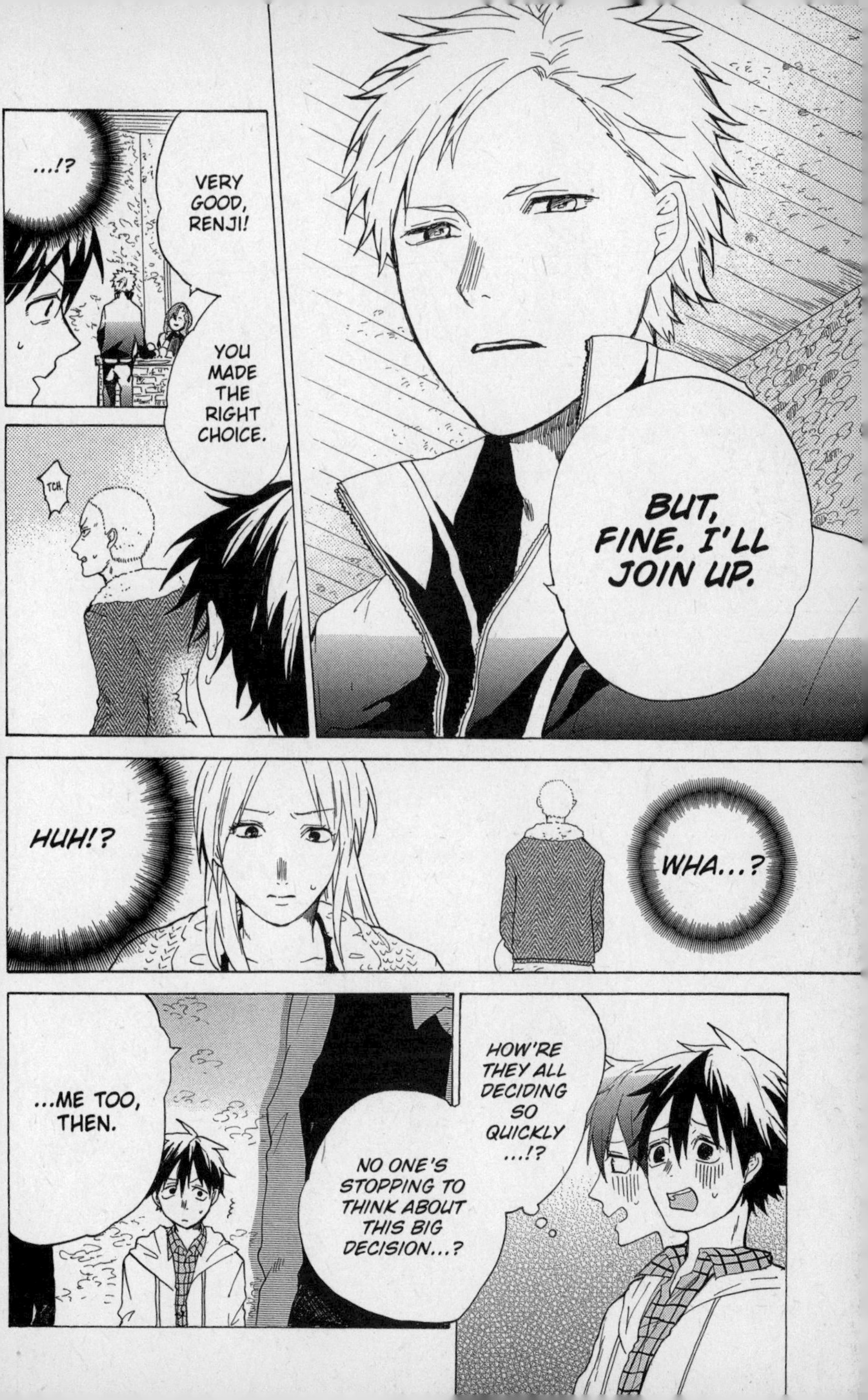
BUT, FINE. I'LL JOIN UP.
VERY GOOD, RENJI!
YOU MADE THE RIGHT CHOICE.
...!?
TCH.
WHA...?
HUH!?
HOW'RE THEY ALL DECIDING SO QUICKLY ...!?
NO ONE'S STOPPING TO THINK ABOUT THIS BIG DECISION...?
...ME TOO, THEN.

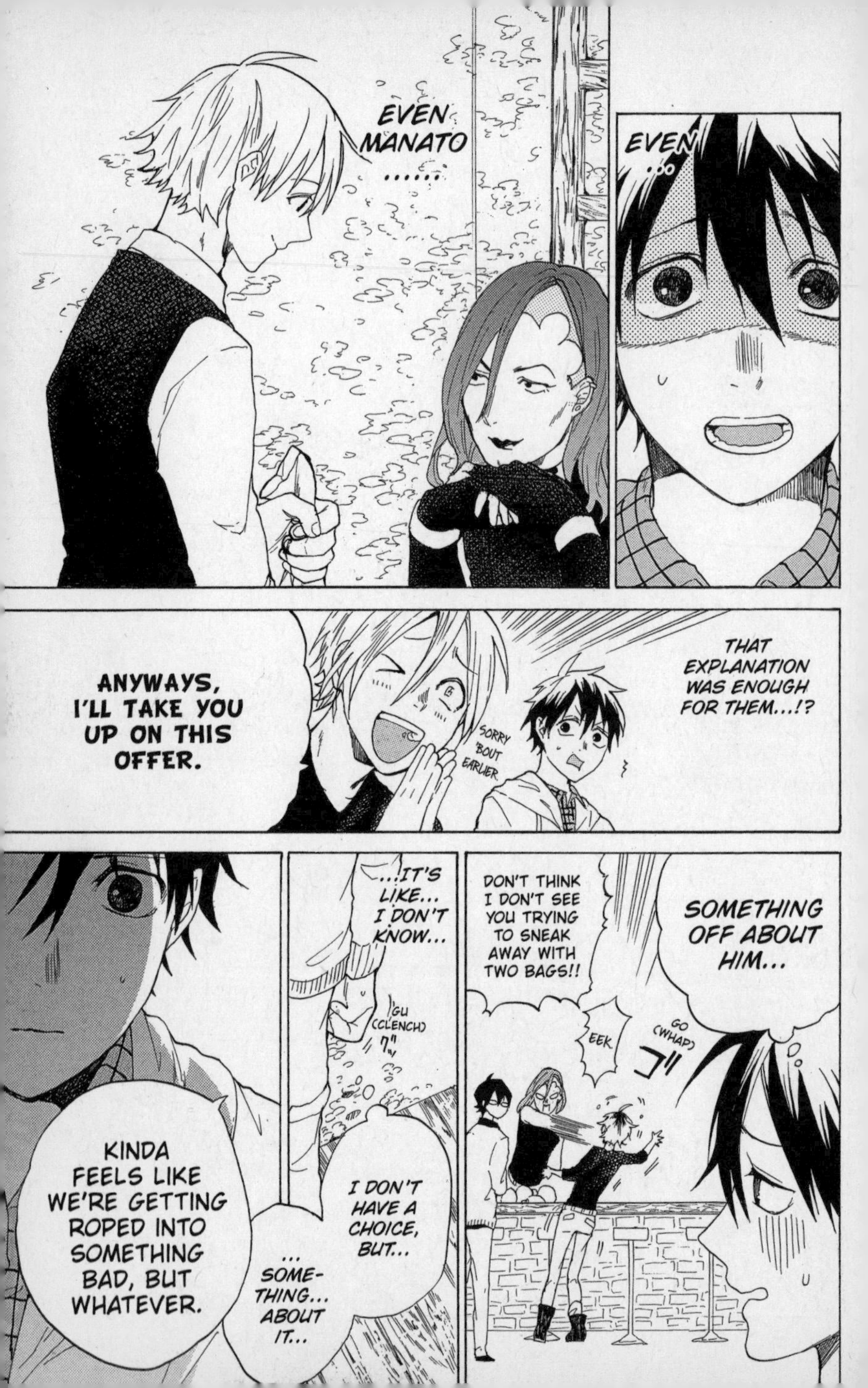
EVEN...
EVEN MANATO......
THAT EXPLANATION WAS ENOUGH FOR THEM...!?
SORRY 'BOUT EARLIER
ANYWAYS, I'LL TAKE YOU UP ON THIS OFFER.
SOMETHING OFF ABOUT HIM...
GO (WHAP)
EEK
DON'T THINK I DON'T SEE YOU TRYING TO SNEAK AWAY WITH TWO BAGS!!
...IT'S LIKE... I DON'T KNOW...
GU (CLENCH)
I DON'T HAVE A CHOICE, BUT...
...SOMETHING... ABOUT IT...
KINDA FEELS LIKE WE'RE GETTING ROPED INTO SOMETHING BAD, BUT WHATEVER.

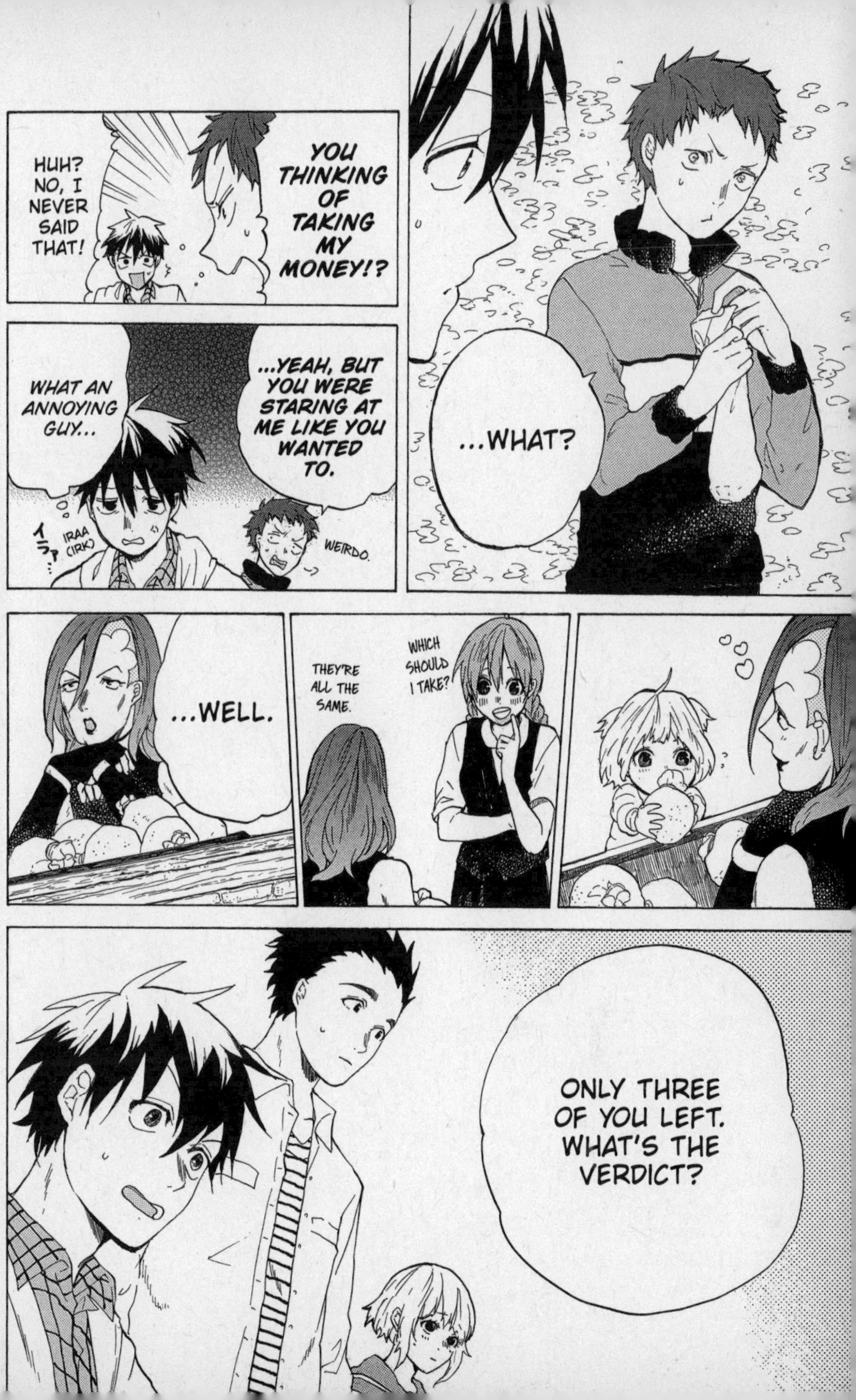
...WHAT?
YOU THINKING OF TAKING MY MONEY!?
HUH? NO, I NEVER SAID THAT!
...YEAH, BUT YOU WERE STARING AT ME LIKE YOU WANTED TO.
WEIRDO.
WHAT AN ANNOYING GUY...
IRAA (IRK)
WHICH SHOULD I TAKE?
THEY'RE ALL THE SAME.
...WELL.
ONLY THREE OF YOU LEFT. WHAT'S THE VERDICT?

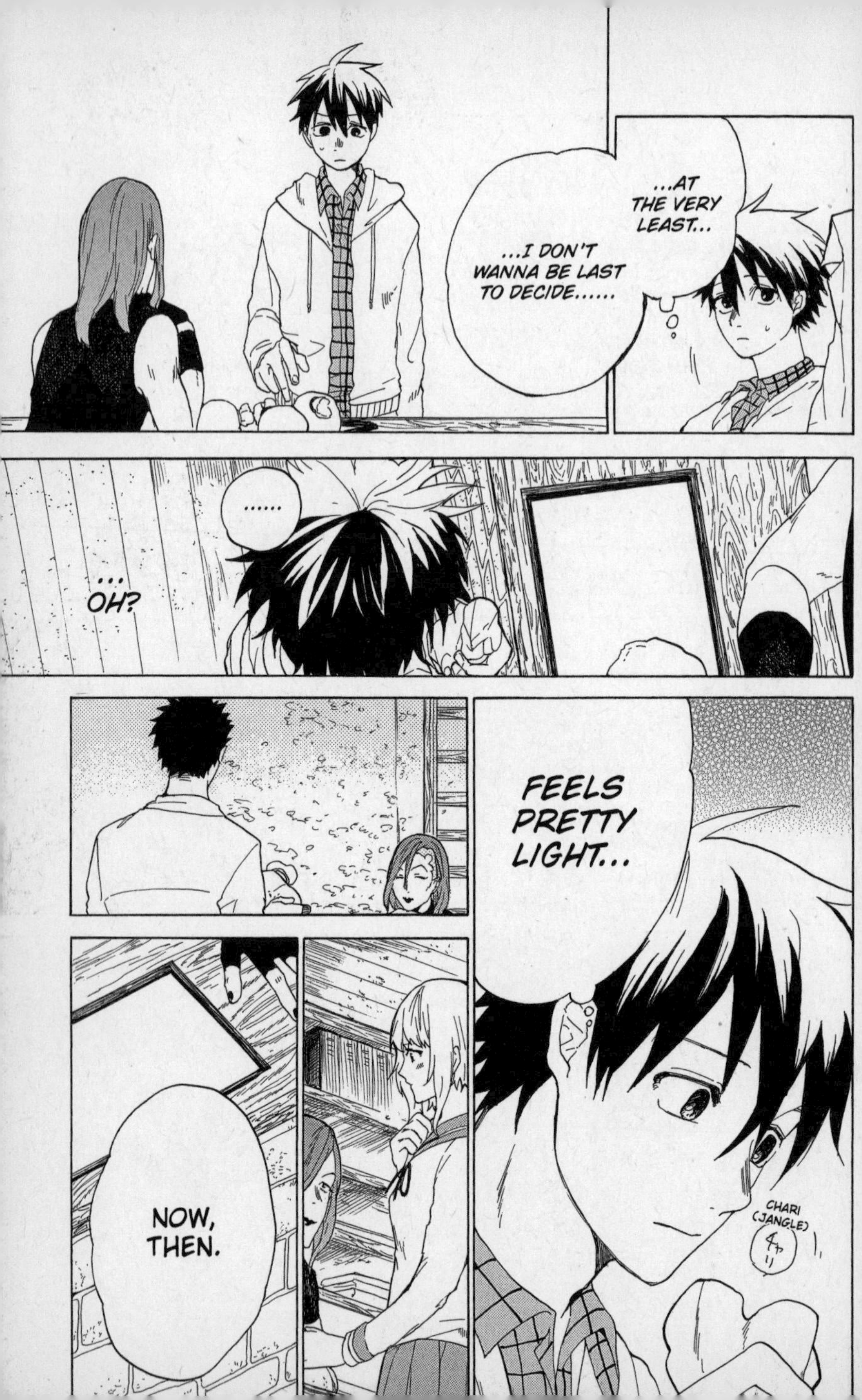
...AT THE VERY LEAST...
...I DON'T WANNA BE LAST TO DECIDE......
......
... OH?
FEELS PRETTY LIGHT...
CHARI (JANGLE)
NOW, THEN.

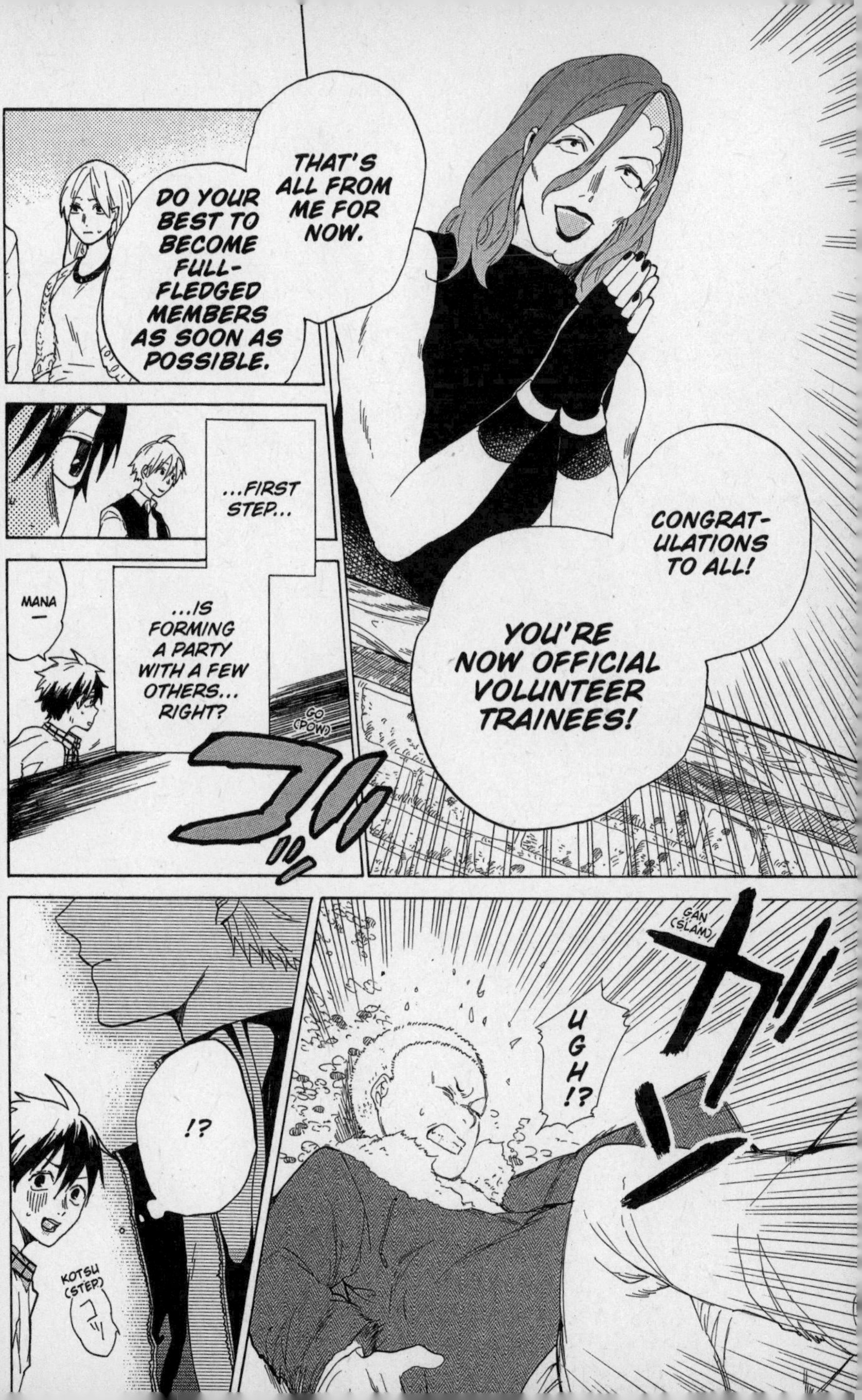
THAT'S ALL FROM ME FOR NOW.
DO YOUR BEST TO BECOME FULL-FLEDGED MEMBERS AS SOON AS POSSIBLE.
CONGRAT-ULATIONS TO ALL!
YOU'RE NOW OFFICIAL VOLUNTEER TRAINEES!
...FIRST STEP...
...IS FORMING A PARTY WITH A FEW OTHERS... RIGHT?
MANA—
GO (POW)
GAN (SLAM)
UGH!?
!?
KOTSU (STEP)

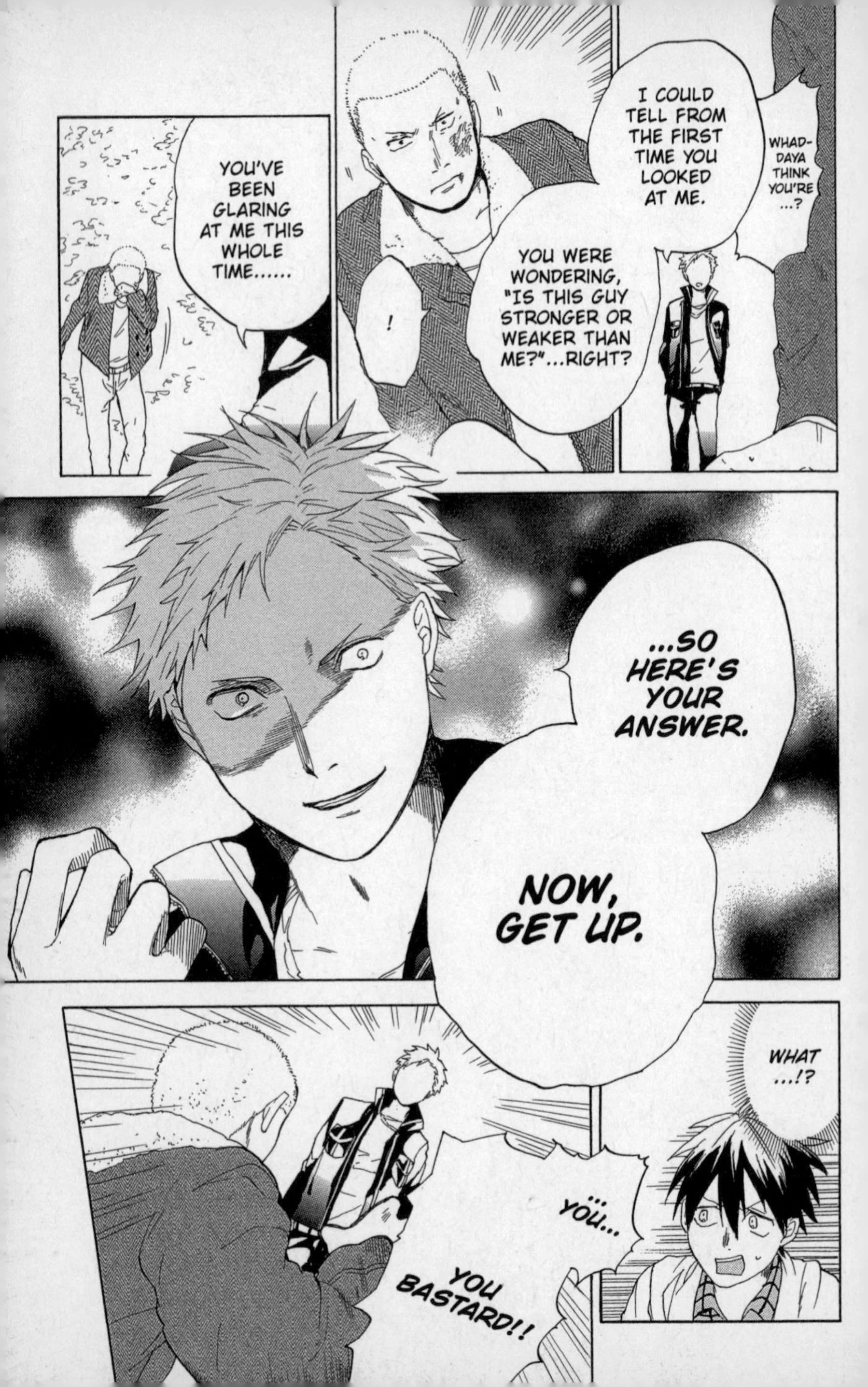
WHAD-DAYA THINK YOU'RE ...?
I COULD TELL FROM THE FIRST TIME YOU LOOKED AT ME.
YOU WERE WONDERING, "IS THIS GUY STRONGER OR WEAKER THAN ME?"...RIGHT?
!
YOU'VE BEEN GLARING AT ME THIS WHOLE TIME......
...SO HERE'S YOUR ANSWER.
NOW, GET UP.
WHAT ...!?
... YOU...
YOU BASTARD!!

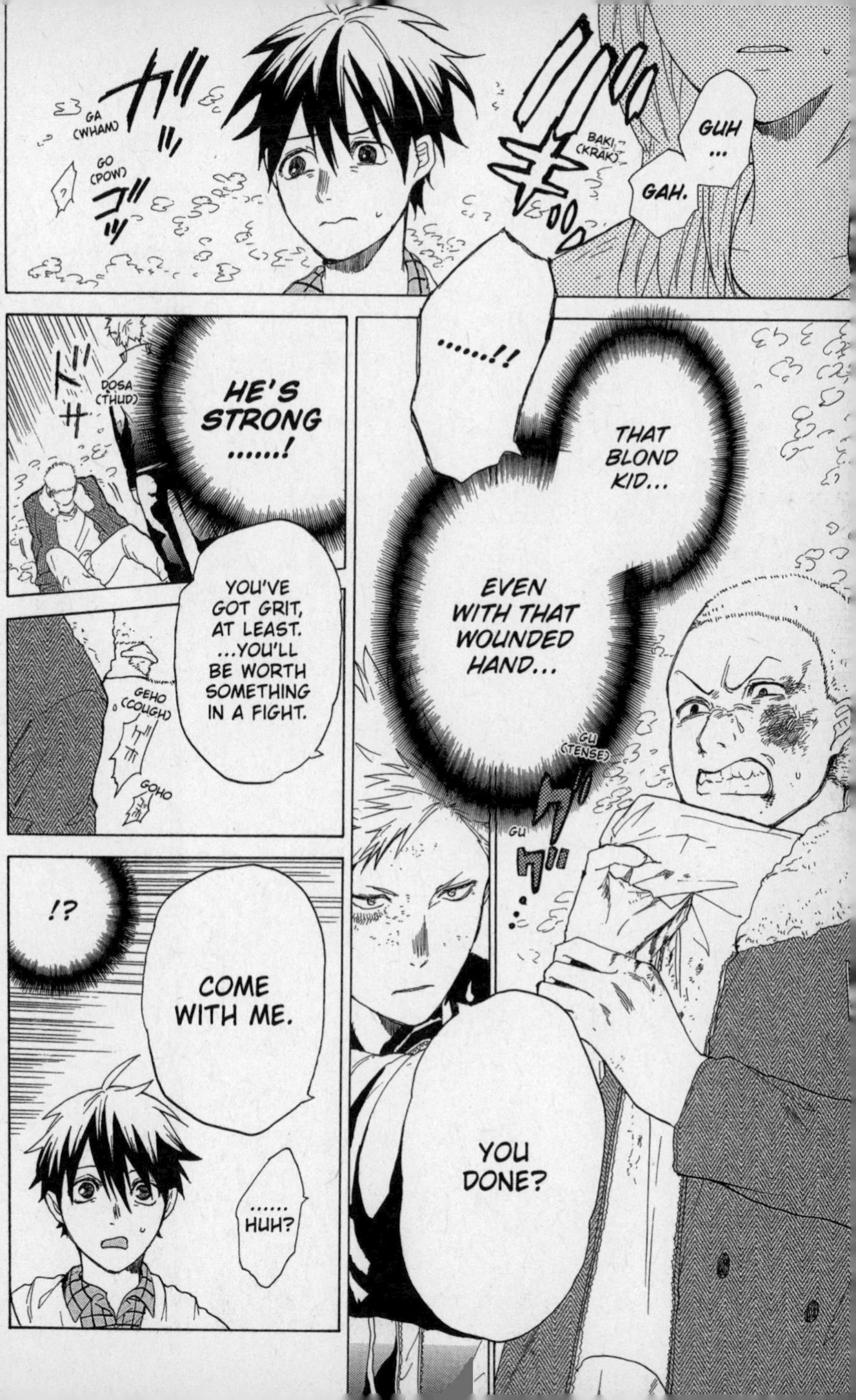

BAKI (KRAK)
GUH...
GAH.
GA (WHAM)
GO (POW)
......!!
THAT BLOND KID...
EVEN WITH THAT WOUNDED HAND...
GU (TENSE)
GU
YOU DONE?
DOSA (THUD)
HE'S STRONG......!
GEHO (COUGH)
GOHO
YOU'VE GOT GRIT, AT LEAST. ...YOU'LL BE WORTH SOMETHING IN A FIGHT.
!?
COME WITH ME.
......HUH?

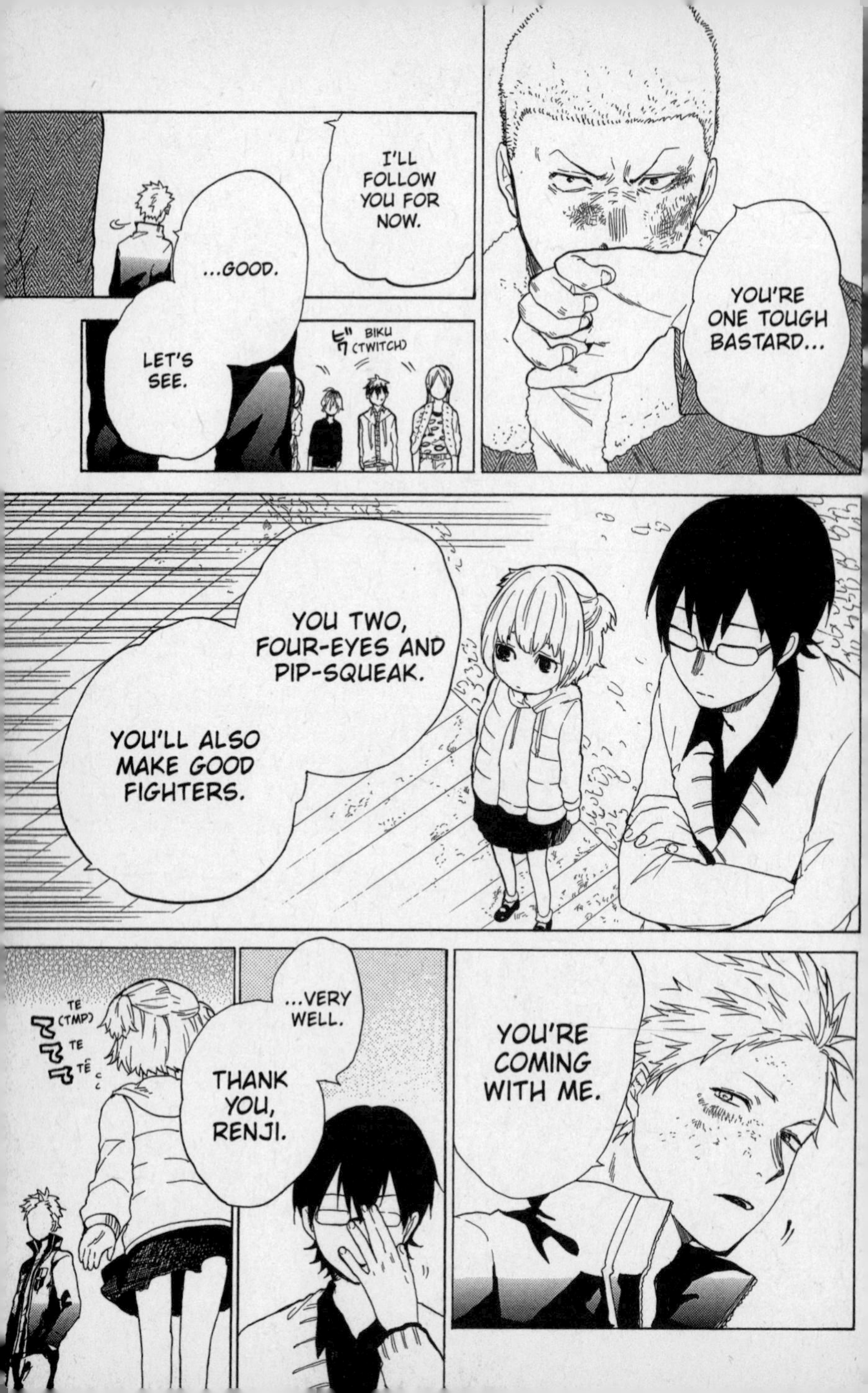
YOU'RE ONE TOUGH BASTARD...
I'LL FOLLOW YOU FOR NOW.
...GOOD.
LET'S SEE.
ビク BIKU (TWITCH)
YOU TWO, FOUR-EYES AND PIP-SQUEAK.
YOU'LL ALSO MAKE GOOD FIGHTERS.
YOU'RE COMING WITH ME.
...VERY WELL.
THANK YOU, RENJI.
TE (TMP)
TE
TE

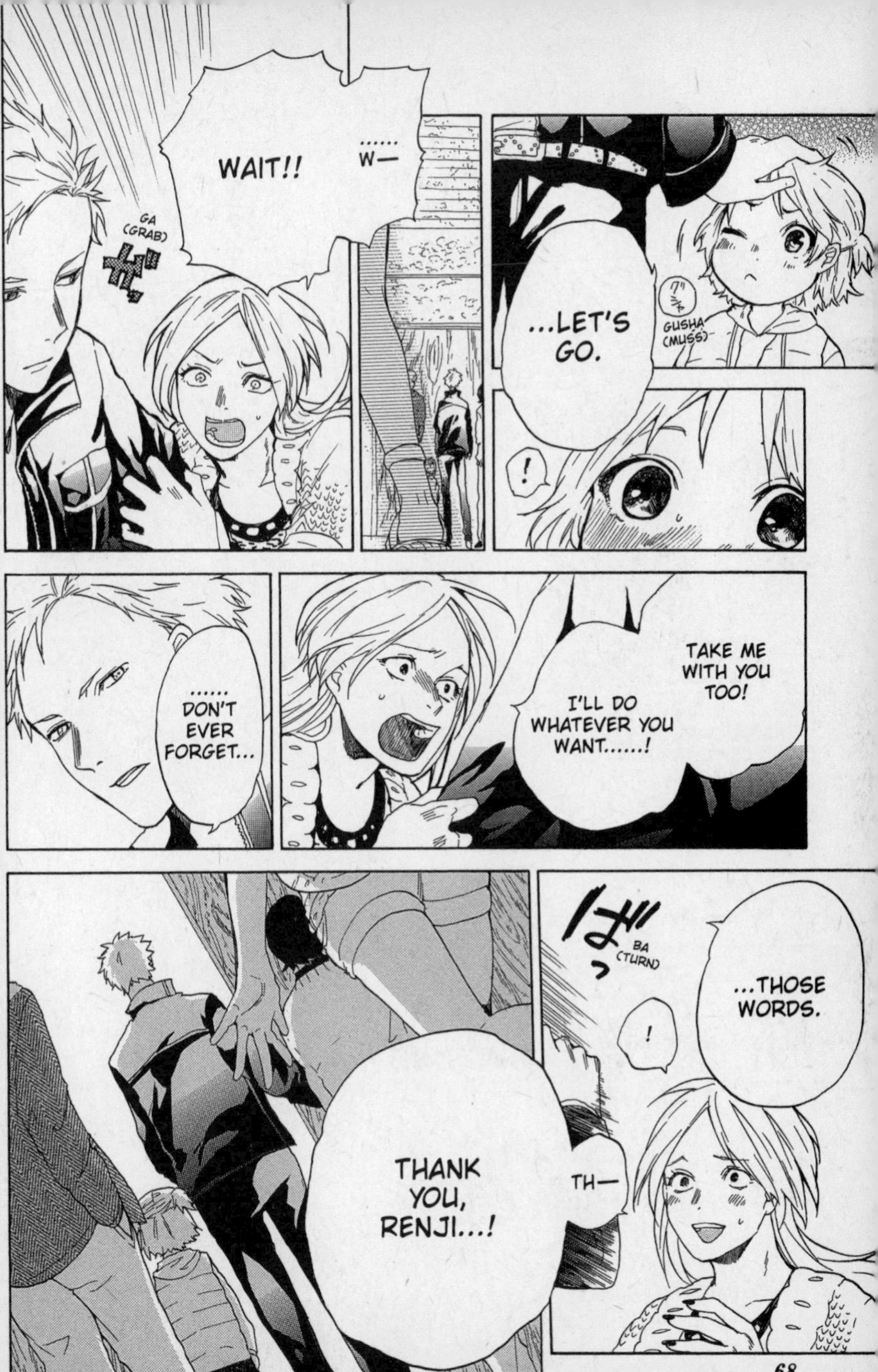
...LET'S GO.
GUSHA (MUSS)
!
...... W—
WAIT!!
GA (GRAB)
TAKE ME WITH YOU TOO!
I'LL DO WHATEVER YOU WANT......!
...... DON'T EVER FORGET...
BA (TURN)
...THOSE WORDS.
!
TH—
THANK YOU, RENJI...!

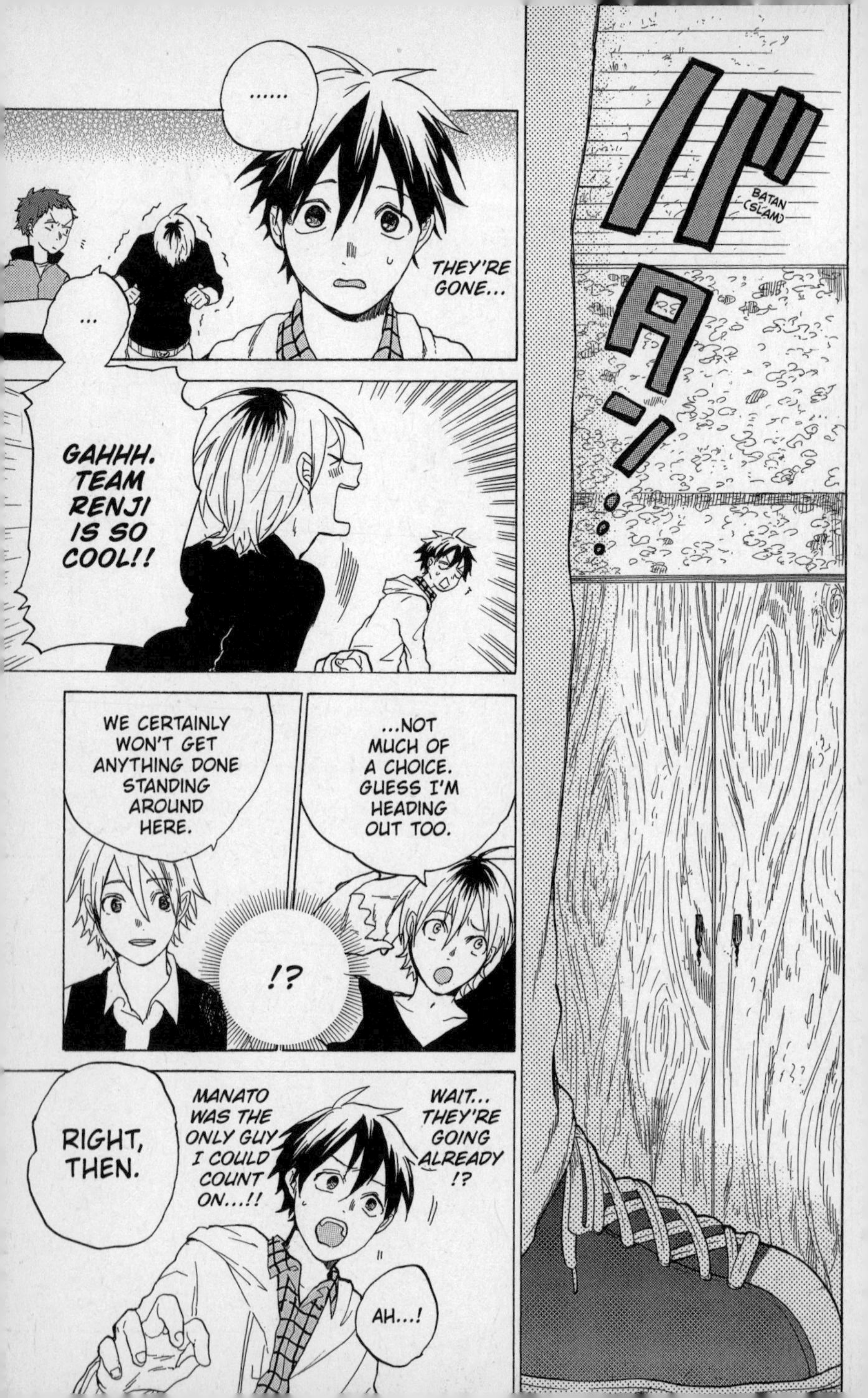
BATAN (SLAM)
......
THEY'RE GONE...
...
GAHHH. TEAM RENJI IS SO COOL!!
...NOT MUCH OF A CHOICE. GUESS I'M HEADING OUT TOO.
WE CERTAINLY WON'T GET ANYTHING DONE STANDING AROUND HERE.
!?
WAIT... THEY'RE GOING ALREADY!?
MANATO WAS THE ONLY GUY I COULD COUNT ON...!!
RIGHT, THEN.
AH...!

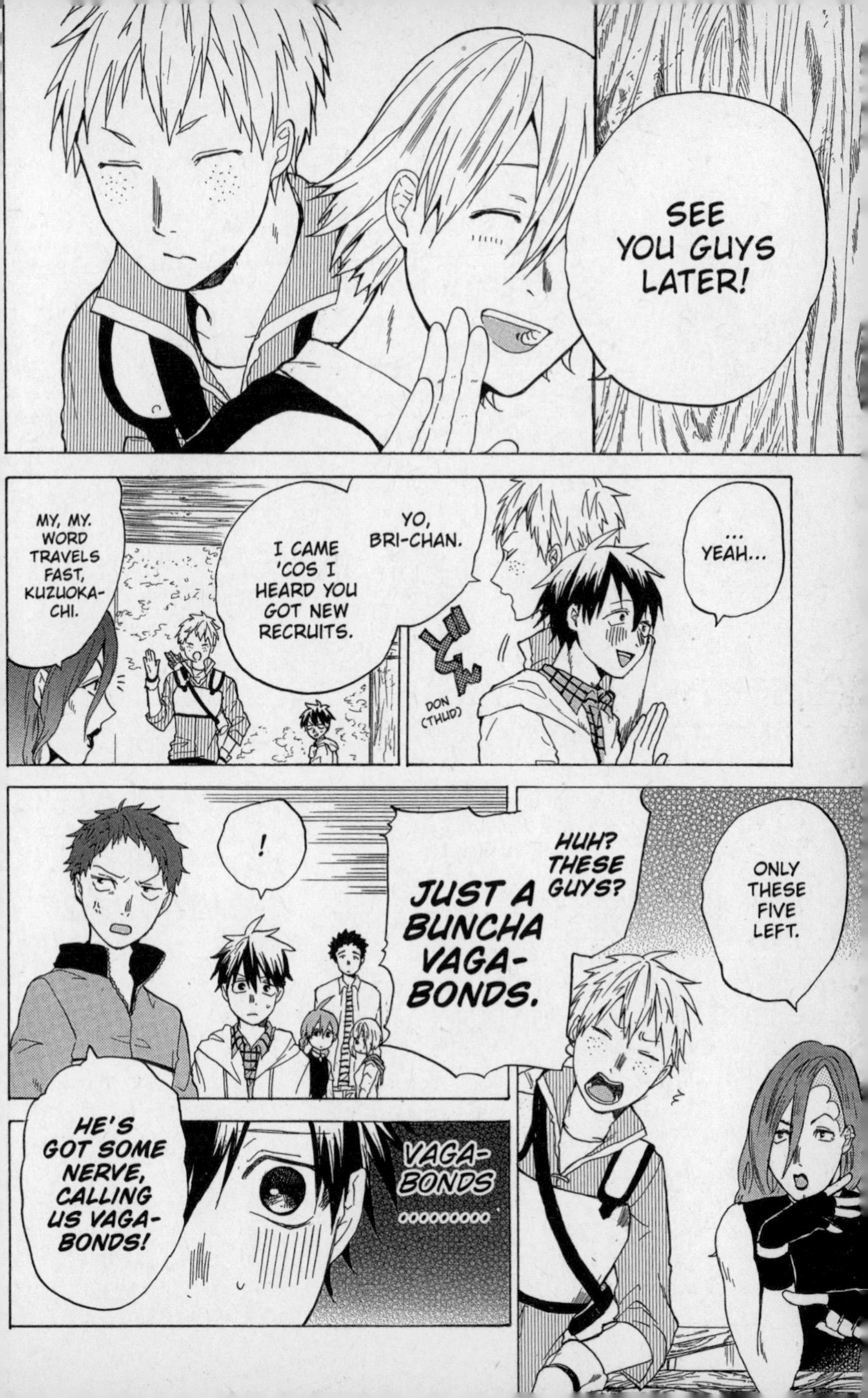
SEE YOU GUYS LATER!
...YEAH...
DON (THUD)
YO, BRI-CHAN.
I CAME 'COS I HEARD YOU GOT NEW RECRUITS.
MY, MY. WORD TRAVELS FAST, KUZUOKA-CHI.
ONLY THESE FIVE LEFT.
HUH? THESE GUYS?
JUST A BUNCHA VAGA-BONDS.
!
VAGA-BONDS OOOOOOOOO
HE'S GOT SOME NERVE, CALLING US VAGA-BONDS!

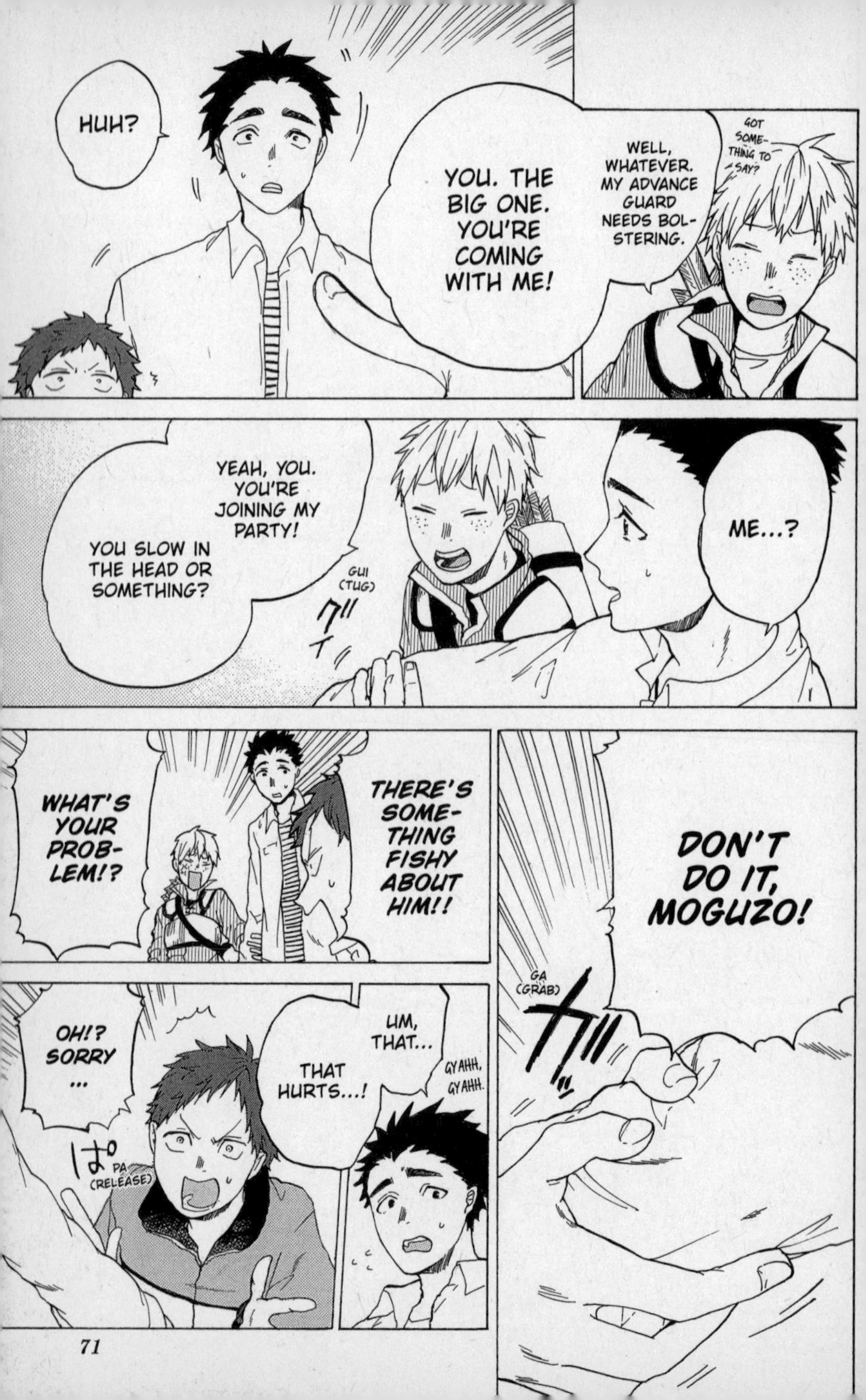
GOT SOME-THING TO SAY?
WELL, WHATEVER. MY ADVANCE GUARD NEEDS BOL-STERING.
YOU. THE BIG ONE. YOU'RE COMING WITH ME!
HUH?
ME...?
YEAH, YOU. YOU'RE JOINING MY PARTY!
YOU SLOW IN THE HEAD OR SOMETHING?
GUI (TUG)
グイ
DON'T DO IT, MOGUZO!
GA (GRAB)
ガッ
THERE'S SOME-THING FISHY ABOUT HIM!!
WHAT'S YOUR PROB-LEM!?
GYAHH, GYAHH.
UM, THAT...
THAT HURTS...!
OH!? SORRY ...
ぱ
PA (RELEASE)

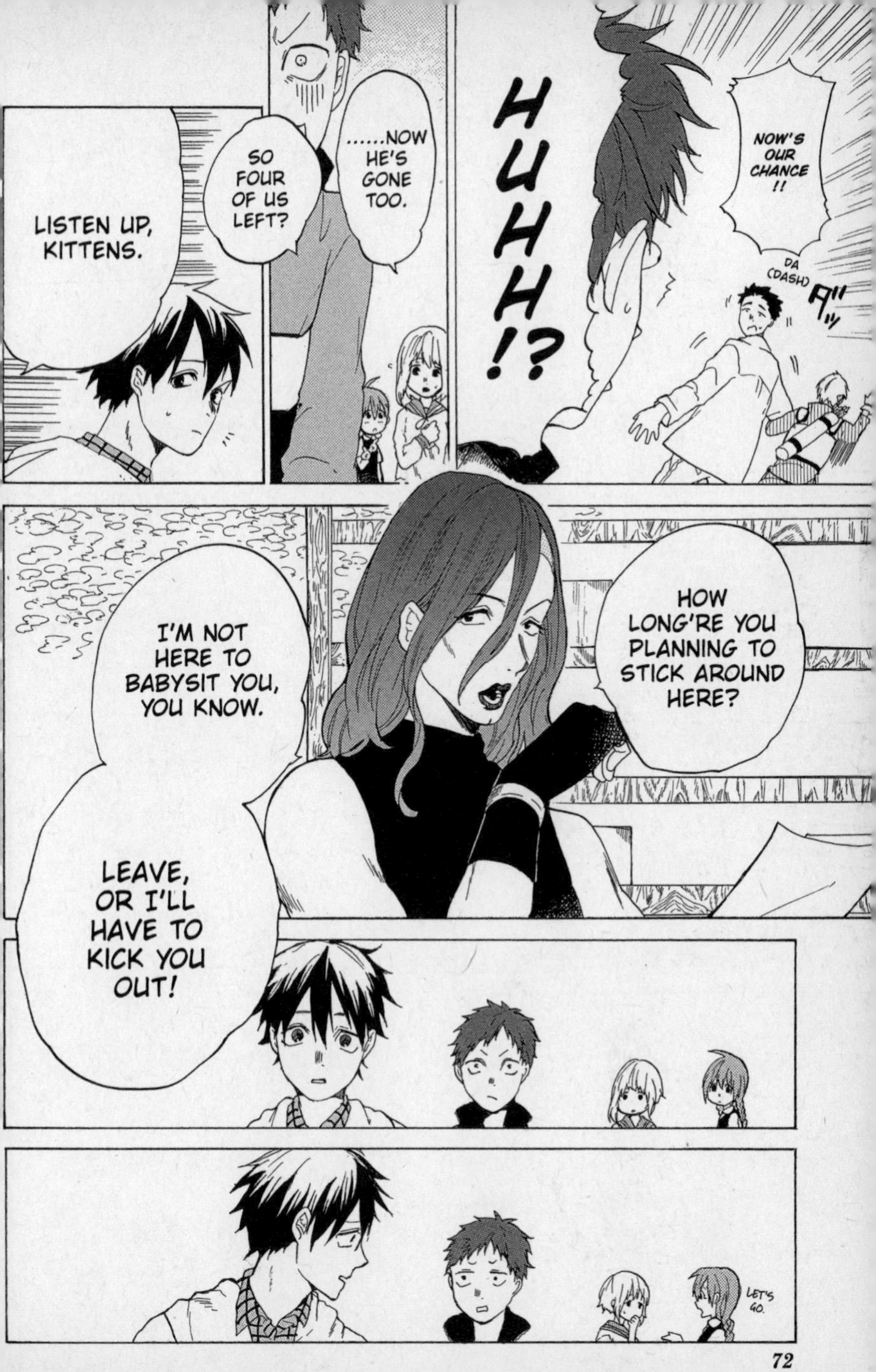
NOW'S OUR CHANCE !!
DA (DASH)
ダッ
HUHH!?
......NOW HE'S GONE TOO.
SO FOUR OF US LEFT?
LISTEN UP, KITTENS.
HOW LONG'RE YOU PLANNING TO STICK AROUND HERE?
I'M NOT HERE TO BABYSIT YOU, YOU KNOW.
LEAVE, OR I'LL HAVE TO KICK YOU OUT!
LET'S GO.

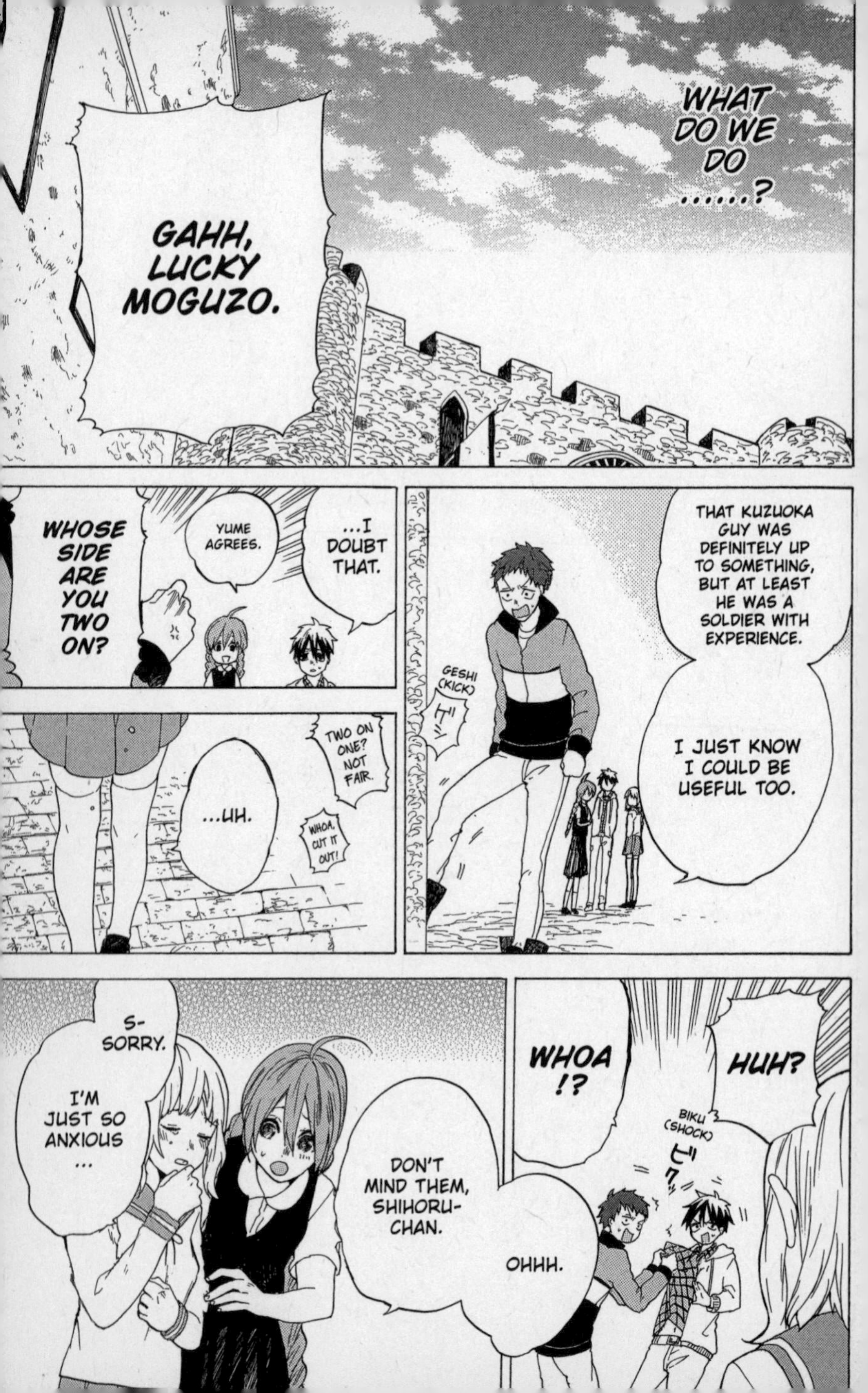

WHAT DO WE DO ......?
GAHH, LUCKY MOGUZO.
THAT KUZUOKA GUY WAS DEFINITELY UP TO SOMETHING, BUT AT LEAST HE WAS A SOLDIER WITH EXPERIENCE.
I JUST KNOW I COULD BE USEFUL TOO.
GESHI (KICK)
...I DOUBT THAT.
YUME AGREES.
WHOSE SIDE ARE YOU TWO ON?
TWO ON ONE? NOT FAIR.
WHOA, CUT IT OUT!
...UH.
HUH?
WHOA!?
BIKU (SHOCK)
OHHH.
DON'T MIND THEM, SHIHORU-CHAN.
S-SORRY.
I'M JUST SO ANXIOUS...

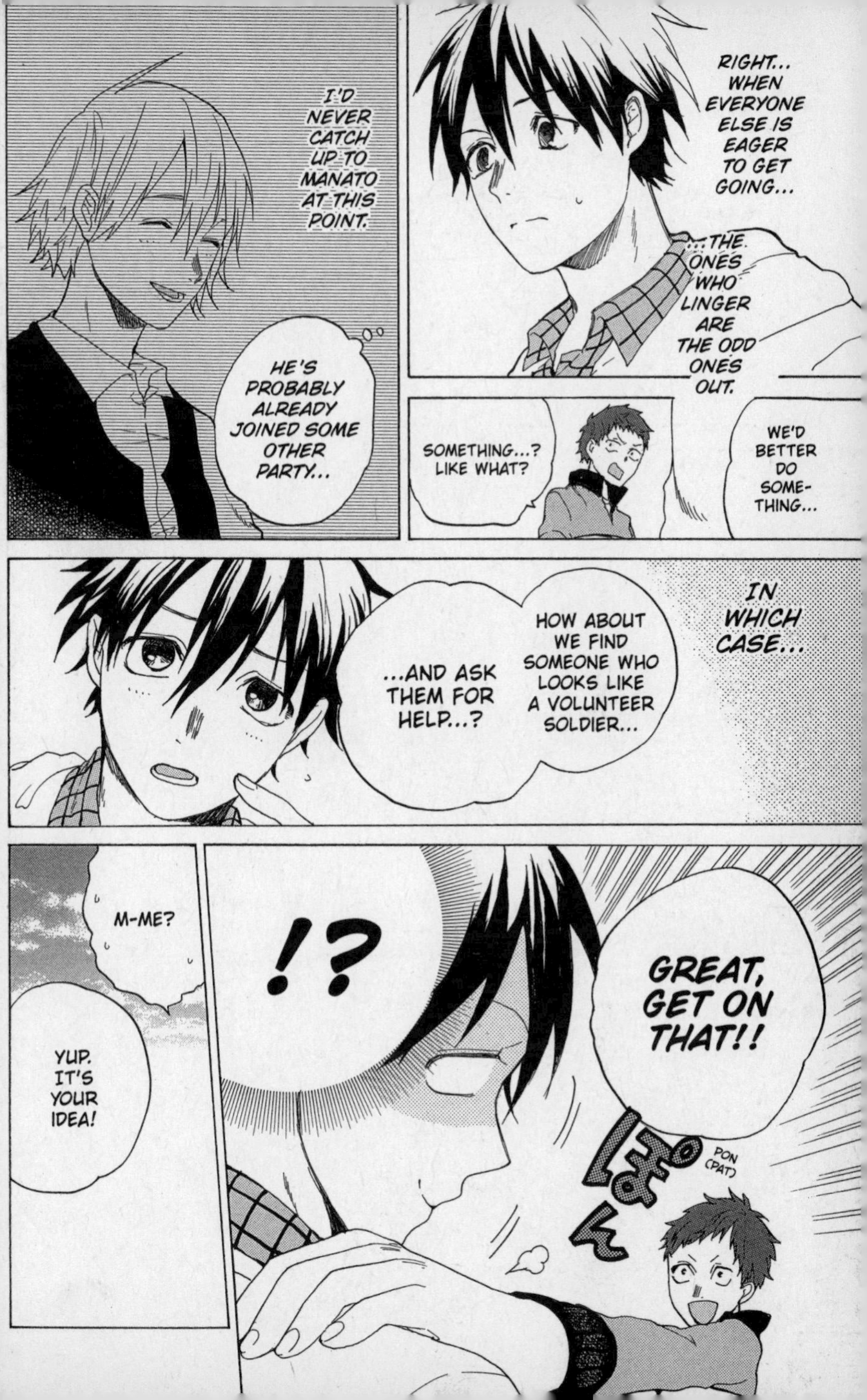
RIGHT... WHEN EVERYONE ELSE IS EAGER TO GET GOING...
...THE ONES WHO LINGER ARE THE ODD ONES OUT.
WE'D BETTER DO SOME-THING...
SOMETHING...? LIKE WHAT?
I'D NEVER CATCH UP TO MANATO AT THIS POINT.
HE'S PROBABLY ALREADY JOINED SOME OTHER PARTY...
IN WHICH CASE...
HOW ABOUT WE FIND SOMEONE WHO LOOKS LIKE A VOLUNTEER SOLDIER...
...AND ASK THEM FOR HELP...?
GREAT, GET ON THAT!!
ぽん
PON (PAT)
!?
M-ME?
YUP. IT'S YOUR IDEA!

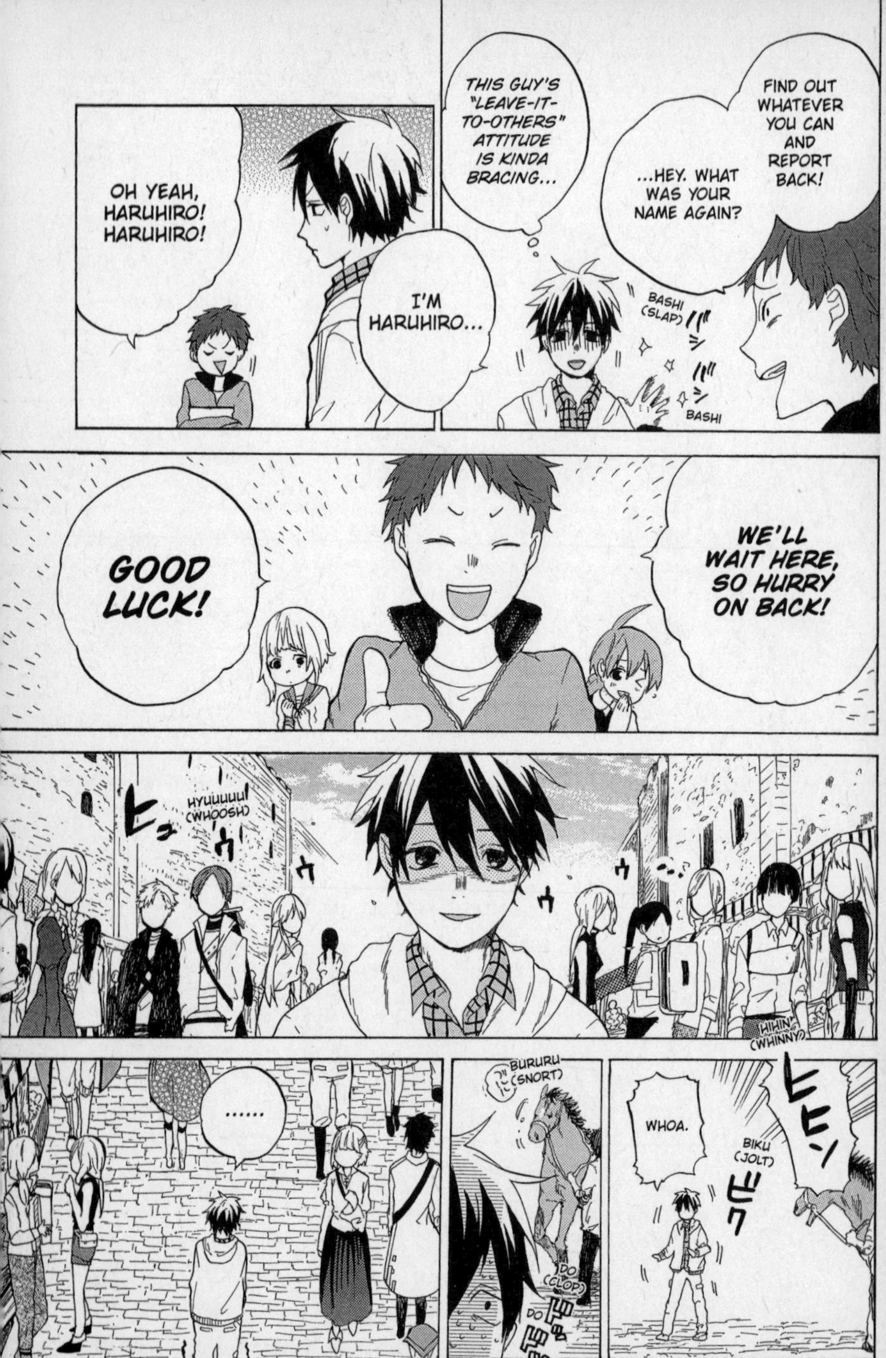
FIND OUT WHATEVER YOU CAN AND REPORT BACK!
...HEY. WHAT WAS YOUR NAME AGAIN?
BASHI (SLAP)
BASHI
THIS GUY'S "LEAVE-IT-TO-OTHERS" ATTITUDE IS KINDA BRACING...
I'M HARUHIRO...
OH YEAH, HARUHIRO! HARUHIRO!
WE'LL WAIT HERE, SO HURRY ON BACK!
GOOD LUCK!
HIHIN (WHINNY)
HYUUUUU! (WHOOSH)
WHOA.
BIKU (JOLT)
BURURU (SNORT)
DO (CLOP)
DO
......

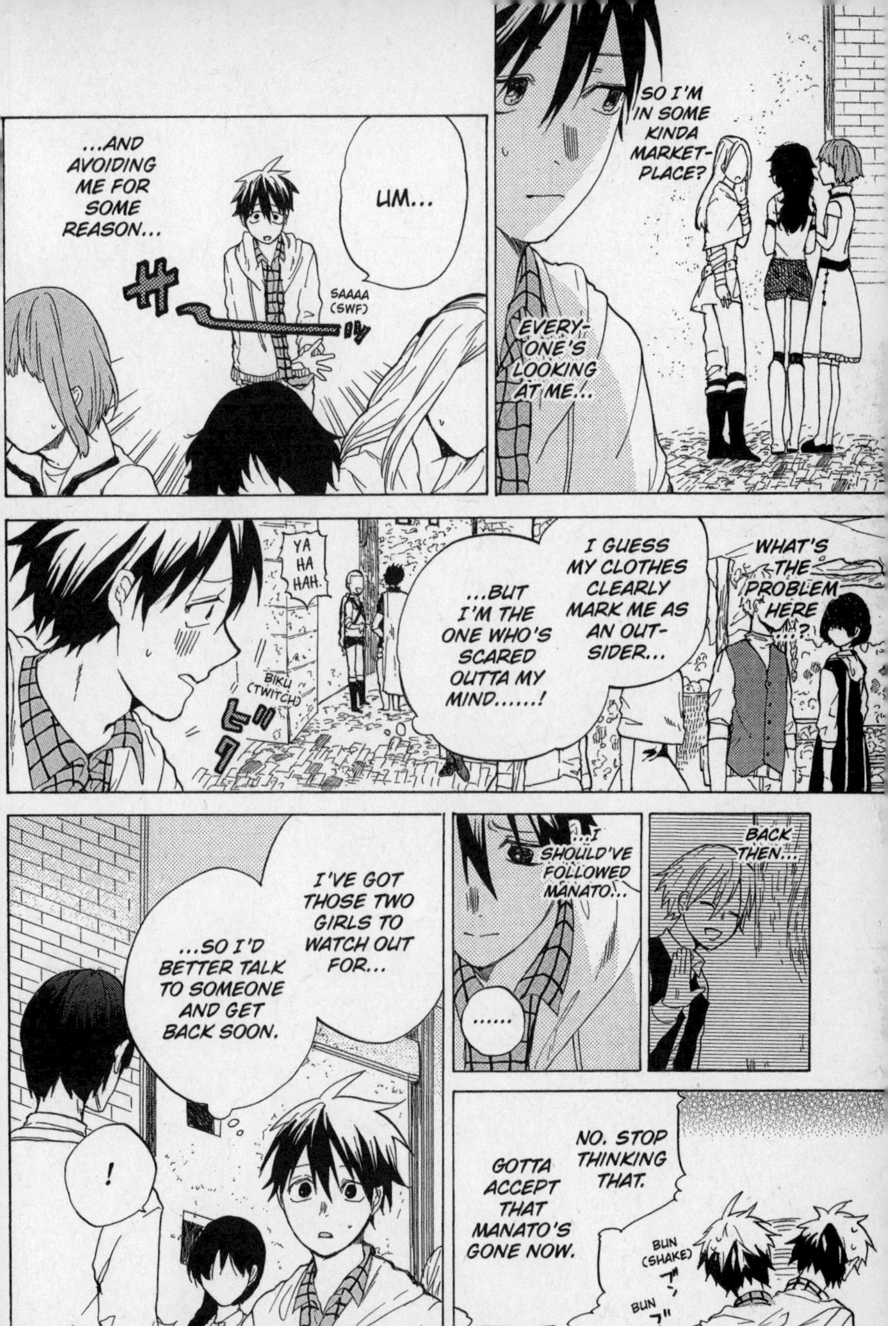
SO I'M IN SOME KINDA MARKET-PLACE?
EVERY-ONE'S LOOKING AT ME...
...AND AVOIDING ME FOR SOME REASON...
UM...
SAAAA (SWF)
WHAT'S THE PROBLEM HERE...?
I GUESS MY CLOTHES CLEARLY MARK ME AS AN OUT-SIDER...
...BUT I'M THE ONE WHO'S SCARED OUTTA MY MIND......!
YA HA HAH.
BIKU (TWITCH)
BACK THEN...
...I SHOULD'VE FOLLOWED MANATO...
......
NO. STOP THINKING THAT.
GOTTA ACCEPT THAT MANATO'S GONE NOW.
BUN (SHAKE)
BUN
I'VE GOT THOSE TWO GIRLS TO WATCH OUT FOR...
...SO I'D BETTER TALK TO SOMEONE AND GET BACK SOON.
!

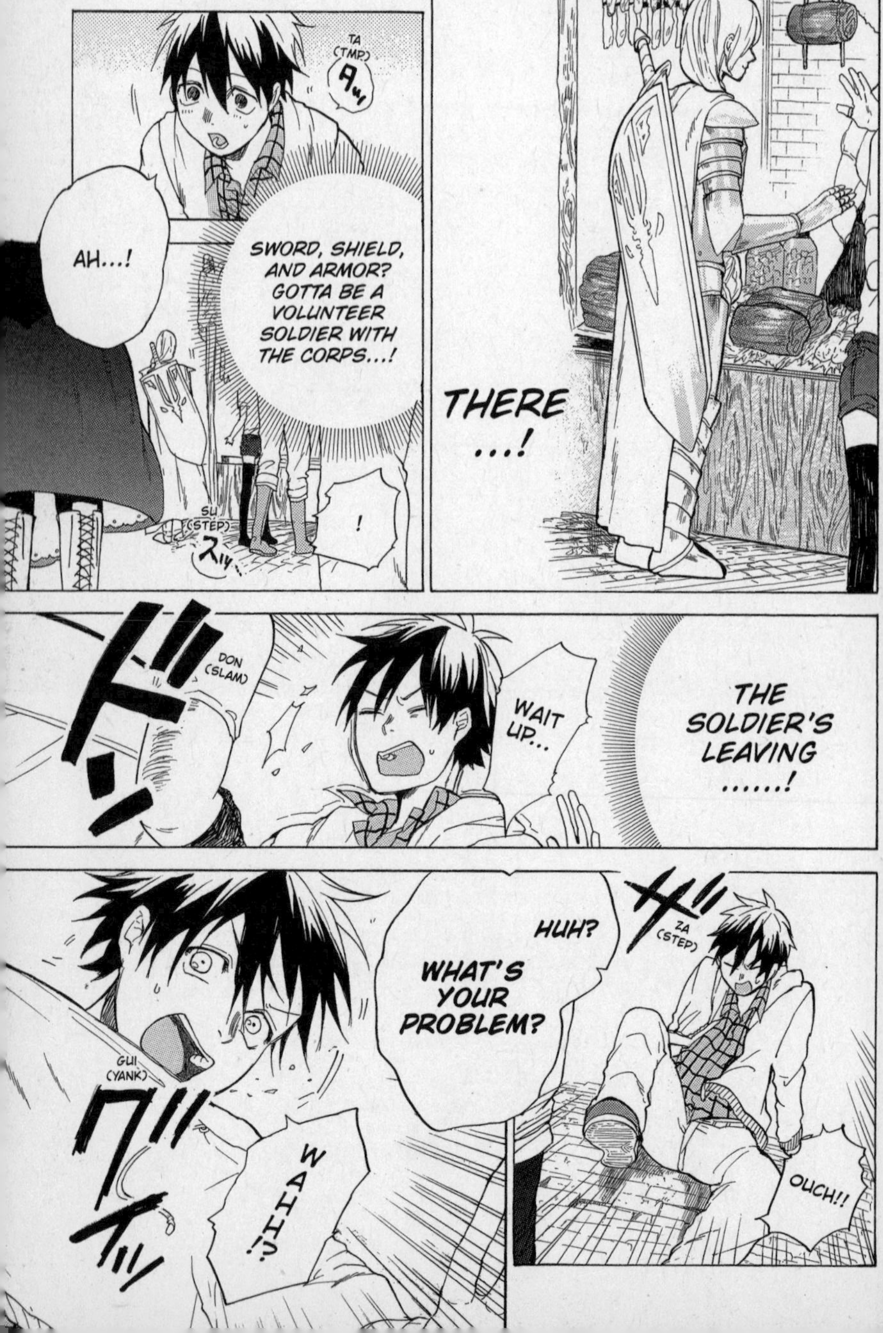
THERE ...!
TA (TMP)
タッ
SWORD, SHIELD, AND ARMOR? GOTTA BE A VOLUNTEER SOLDIER WITH THE CORPS...!
AH...!
!
SU (STEP)
スッ
THE SOLDIER'S LEAVING ......!
WAIT UP...
DON (SLAM)
ドン
ZA (STEP)
ザッ
OUCH!!
HUH?
WHAT'S YOUR PROBLEM?
GUI (YANK)
グイッ
WAHH!?

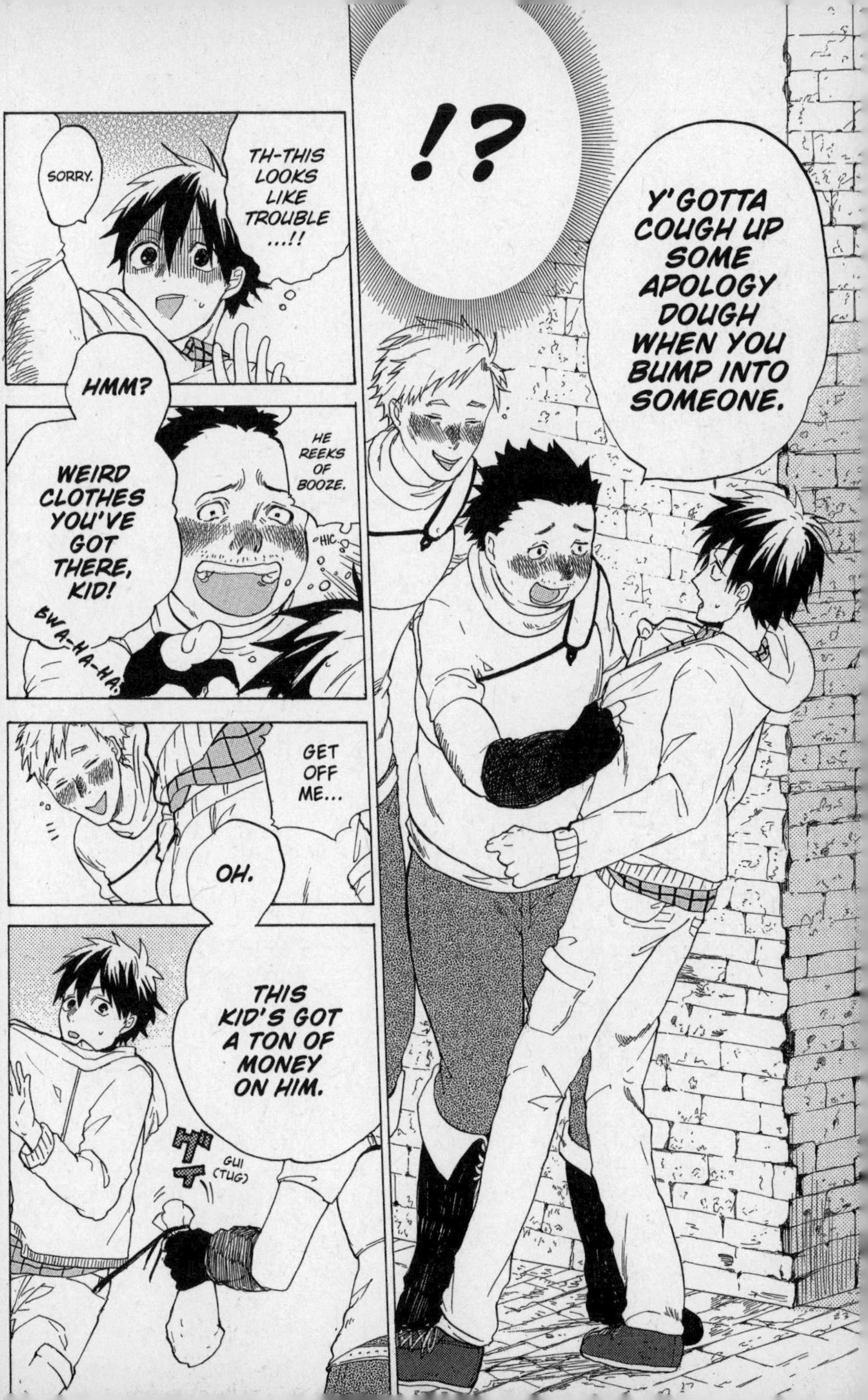
!?
Y'GOTTA COUGH UP SOME APOLOGY DOUGH WHEN YOU BUMP INTO SOMEONE.
TH-THIS LOOKS LIKE TROUBLE ...!!
SORRY.
HMM?
HE REEKS OF BOOZE.
HIC.
WEIRD CLOTHES YOU'VE GOT THERE, KID!
BWA-HA-HA
GET OFF ME...
OH.
THIS KID'S GOT A TON OF MONEY ON HIM.
GUI (TUG)

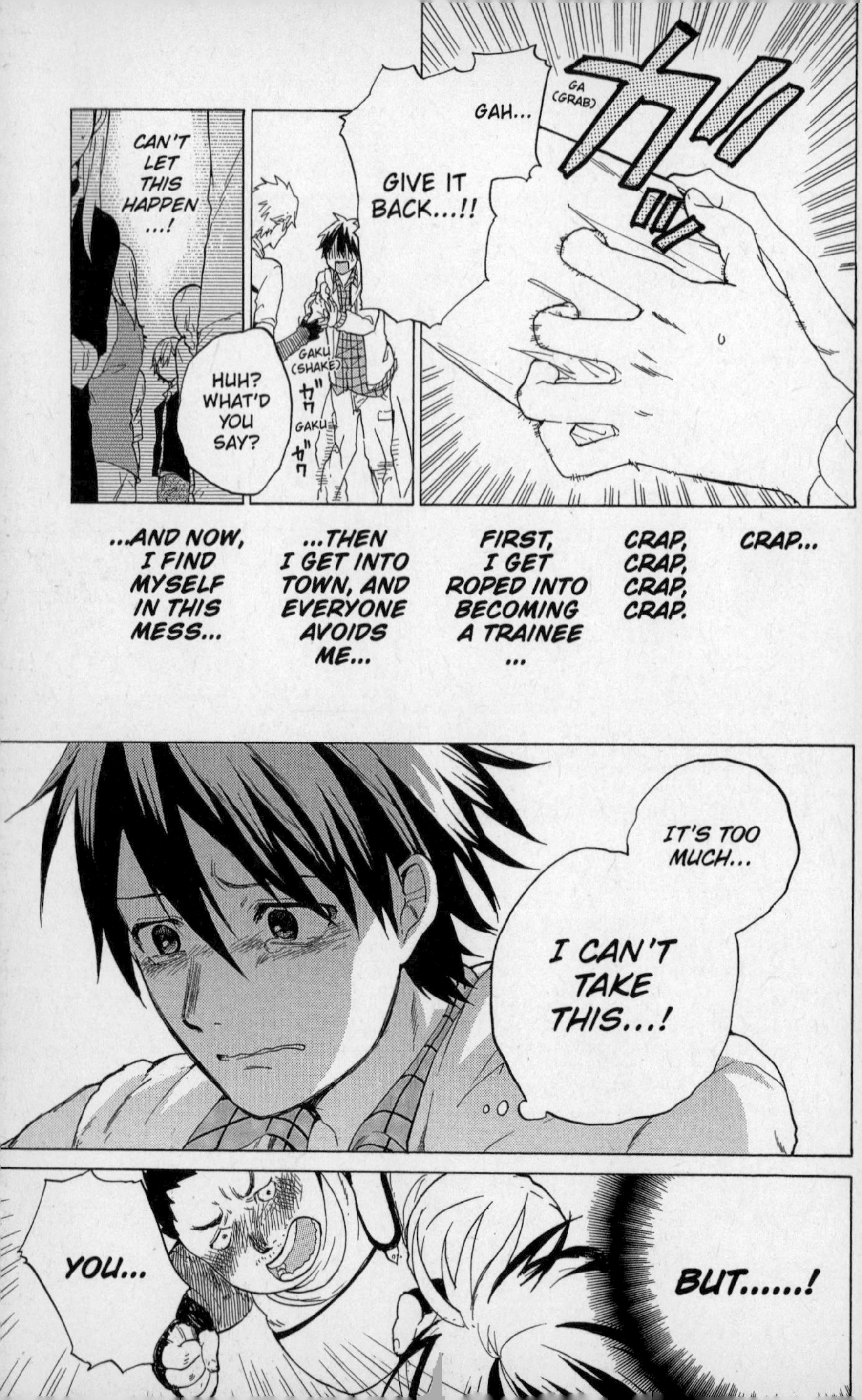
GA (GRAB)
GAH...
GIVE IT BACK...!!
GAKU (SHAKE)
GAKU
HUH? WHAT'D YOU SAY?
CAN'T LET THIS HAPPEN...!
CRAP...
CRAP, CRAP, CRAP, CRAP.
FIRST, I GET ROPED INTO BECOMING A TRAINEE...
...THEN I GET INTO TOWN, AND EVERYONE AVOIDS ME...
...AND NOW, I FIND MYSELF IN THIS MESS...
IT'S TOO MUCH...
I CAN'T TAKE THIS...!
BUT......!
YOU...

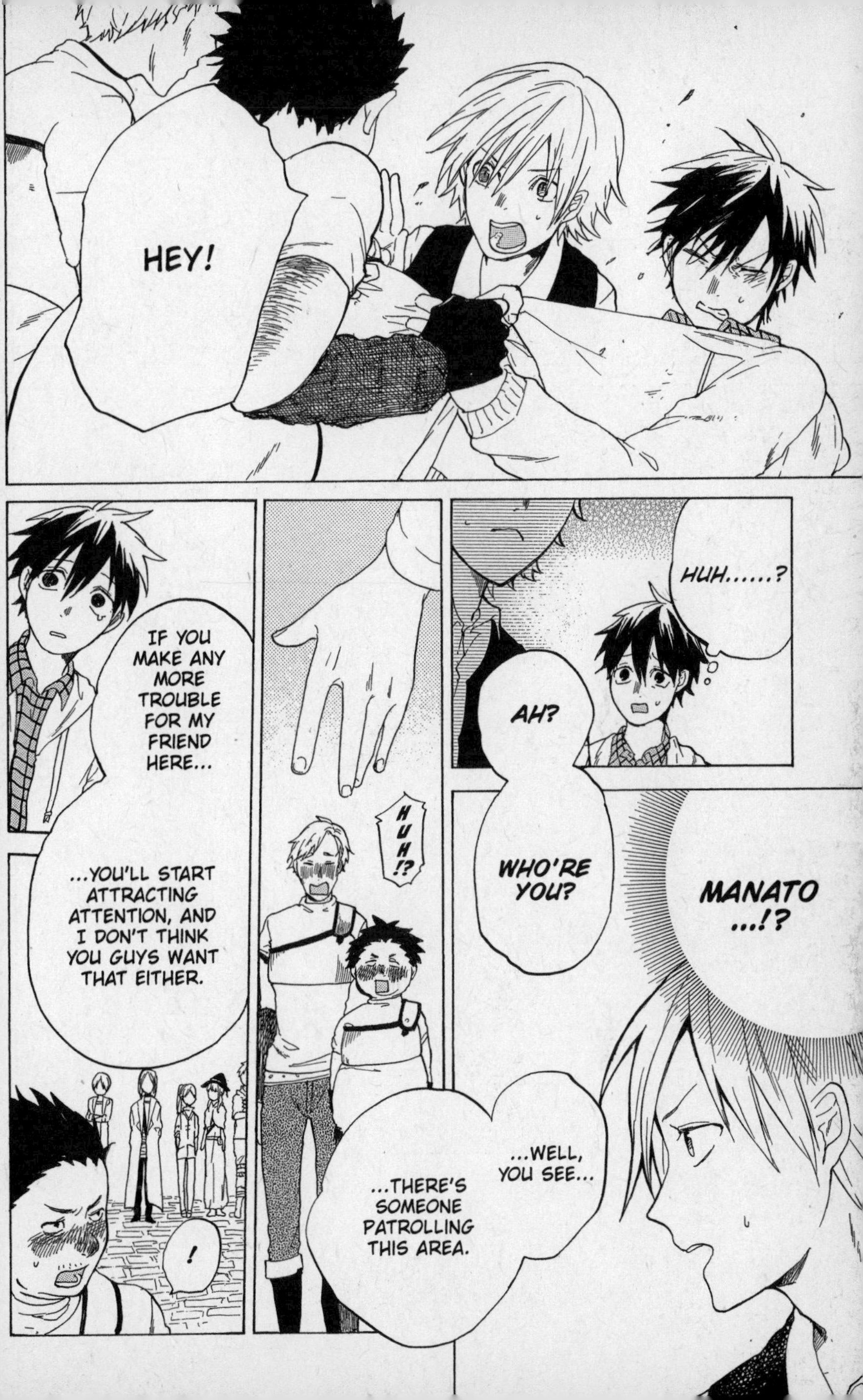
HEY!
HUH......?
AH?
MANATO ...!?
WHO'RE YOU?
...WELL, YOU SEE...
...THERE'S SOMEONE PATROLLING THIS AREA.
HUH!?
IF YOU MAKE ANY MORE TROUBLE FOR MY FRIEND HERE...
...YOU'LL START ATTRACTING ATTENTION, AND I DON'T THINK YOU GUYS WANT THAT EITHER.
!

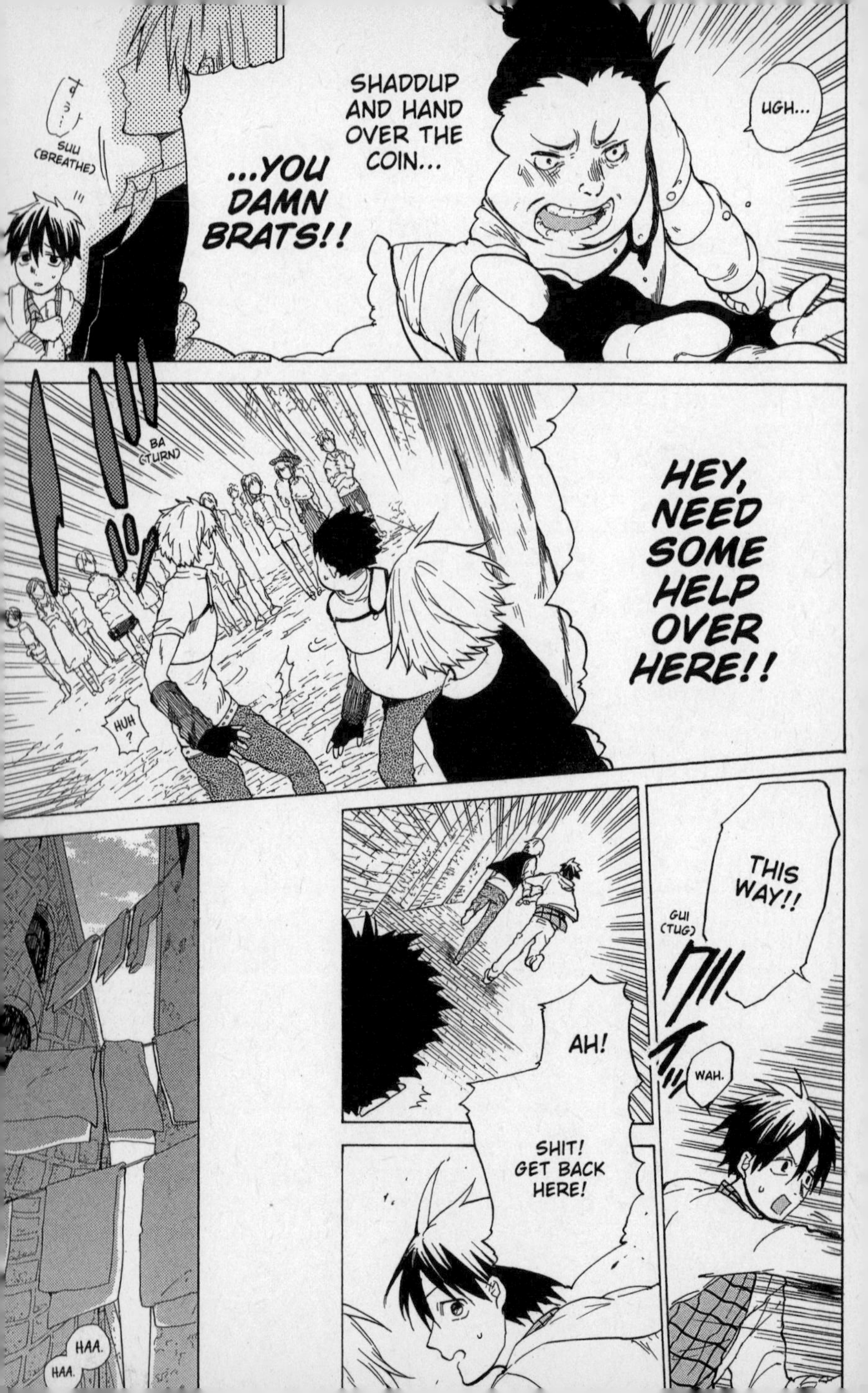
UGH...
SHADDUP AND HAND OVER THE COIN...
...YOU DAMN BRATS!!
すぅ…
SUU (BREATHE)
HEY, NEED SOME HELP OVER HERE!!
BA (TURN)
HUH?
THIS WAY!!
GUI (TUG)
WAH.
AH!
SHIT! GET BACK HERE!
HAA. HAA.

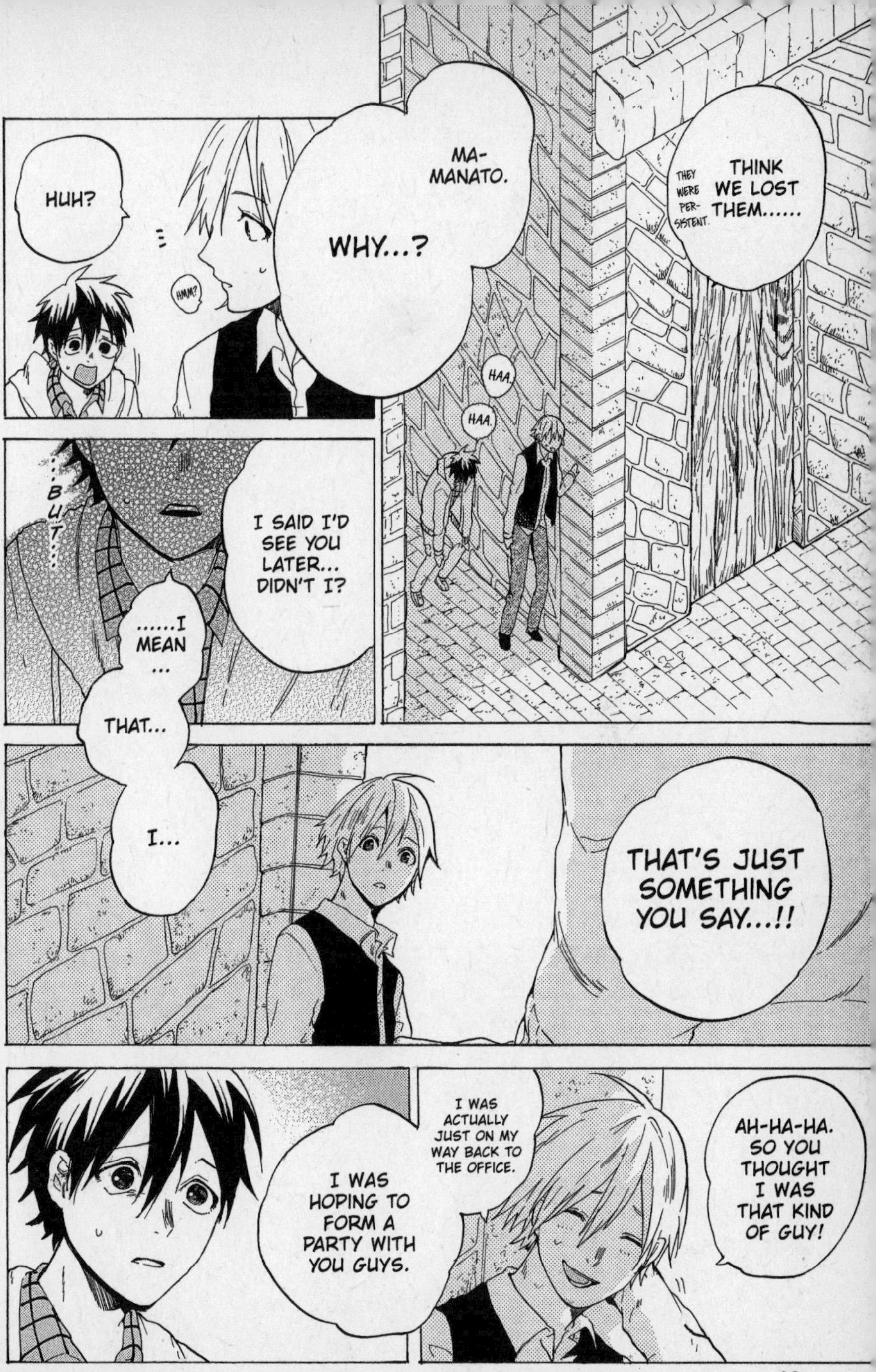
THINK WE LOST THEM......
THEY WERE PER-SISTENT.
MA-MANATO.
WHY...?
HAA.
HAA.
HMM?
HUH?
I SAID I'D SEE YOU LATER... DIDN'T I?
...BUT...
......I MEAN ...
THAT...
I...
THAT'S JUST SOMETHING YOU SAY...!!
AH-HA-HA. SO YOU THOUGHT I WAS THAT KIND OF GUY!
I WAS ACTUALLY JUST ON MY WAY BACK TO THE OFFICE.
I WAS HOPING TO FORM A PARTY WITH YOU GUYS.

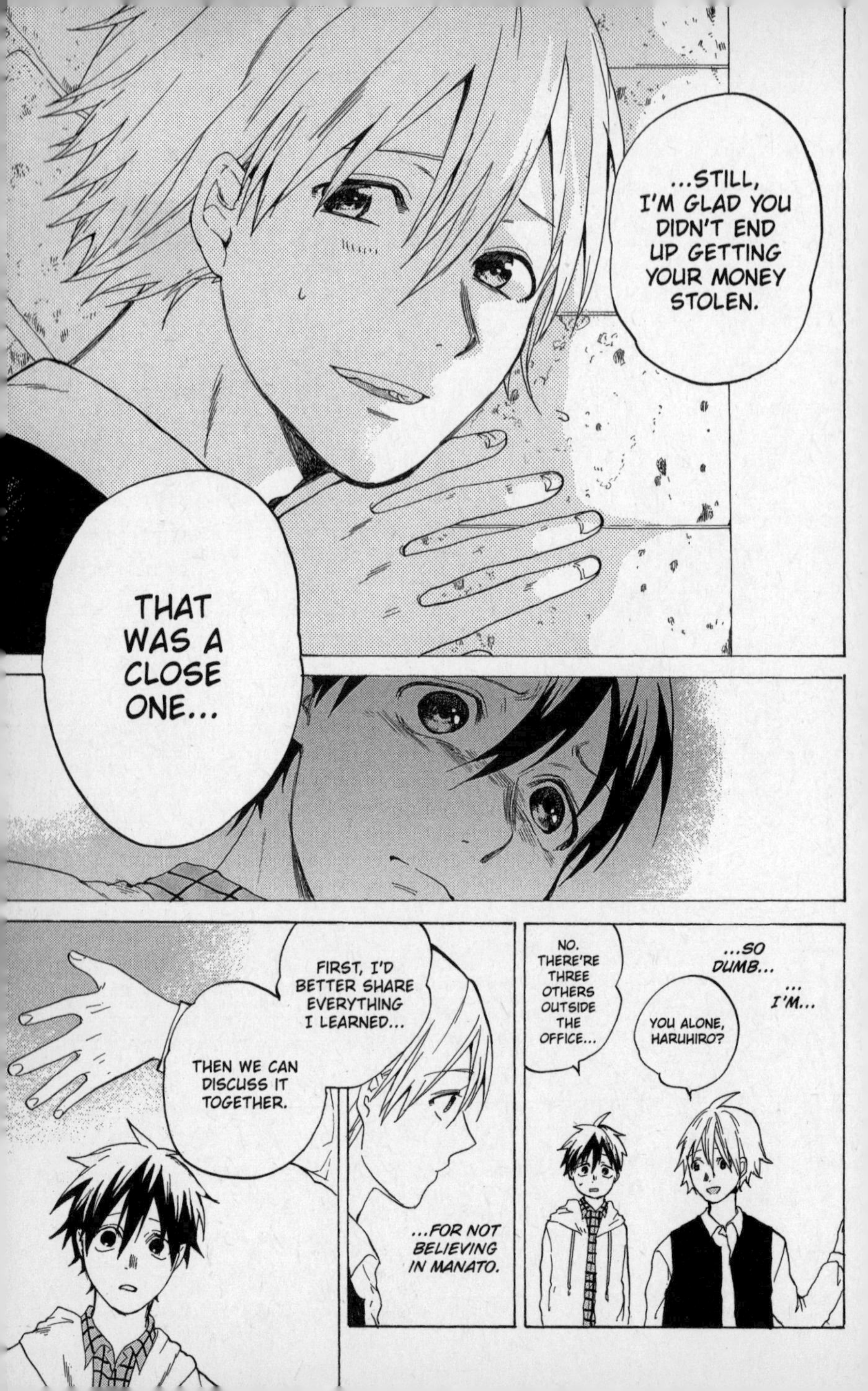
...STILL, I'M GLAD YOU DIDN'T END UP GETTING YOUR MONEY STOLEN.
THAT WAS A CLOSE ONE...
...I'M...
...SO DUMB...
YOU ALONE, HARUHIRO?
NO. THERE'RE THREE OTHERS OUTSIDE THE OFFICE...
FIRST, I'D BETTER SHARE EVERYTHING I LEARNED...
THEN WE CAN DISCUSS IT TOGETHER.
...FOR NOT BELIEVING IN MANATO.

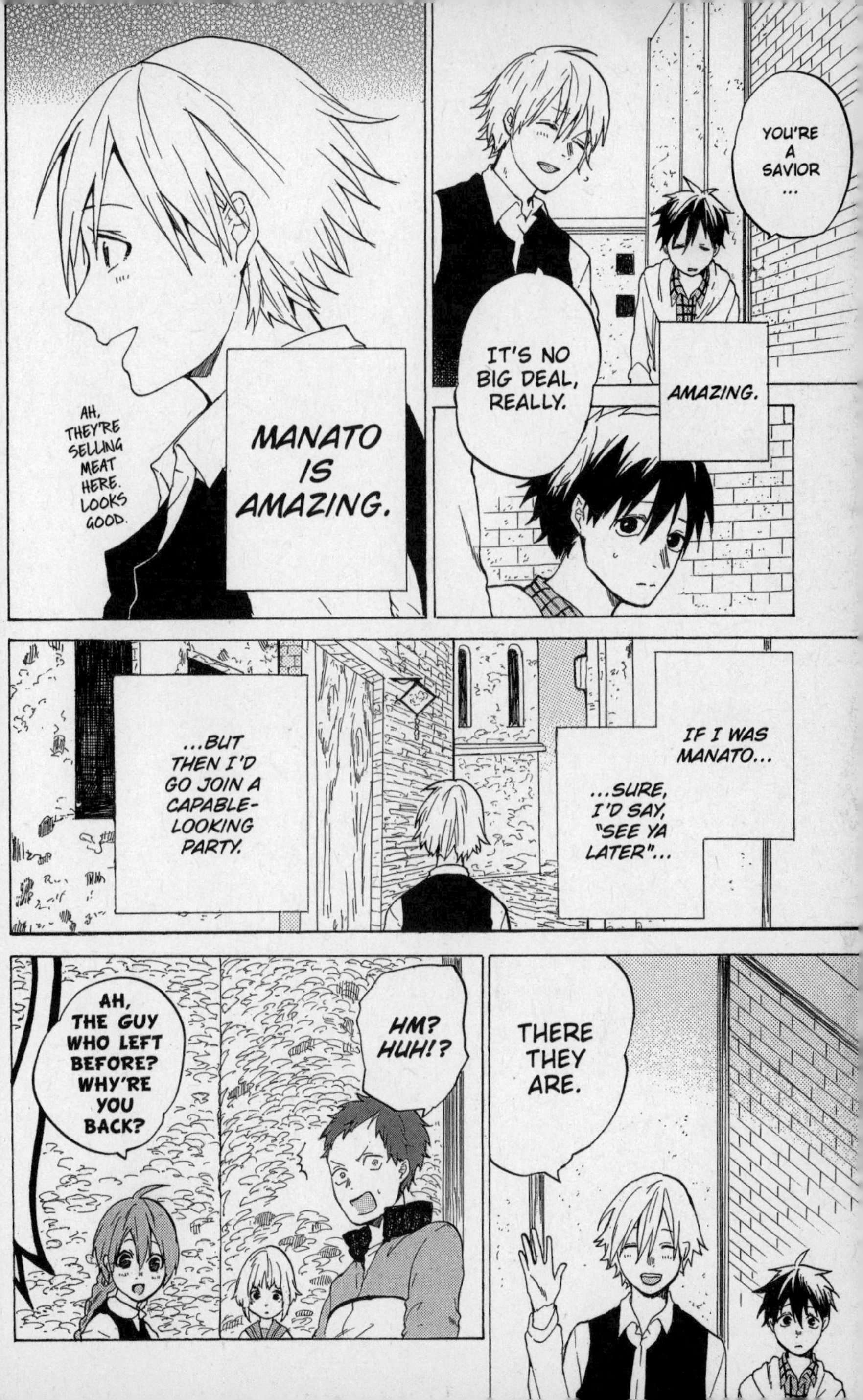
YOU'RE A SAVIOR ...
IT'S NO BIG DEAL, REALLY.
AMAZING.
MANATO IS AMAZING.
AH, THEY'RE SELLING MEAT HERE. LOOKS GOOD.
IF I WAS MANATO...
...SURE, I'D SAY, "SEE YA LATER"...
...BUT THEN I'D GO JOIN A CAPABLE-LOOKING PARTY.
THERE THEY ARE.
HM? HUH!?
AH, THE GUY WHO LEFT BEFORE? WHY'RE YOU BACK?

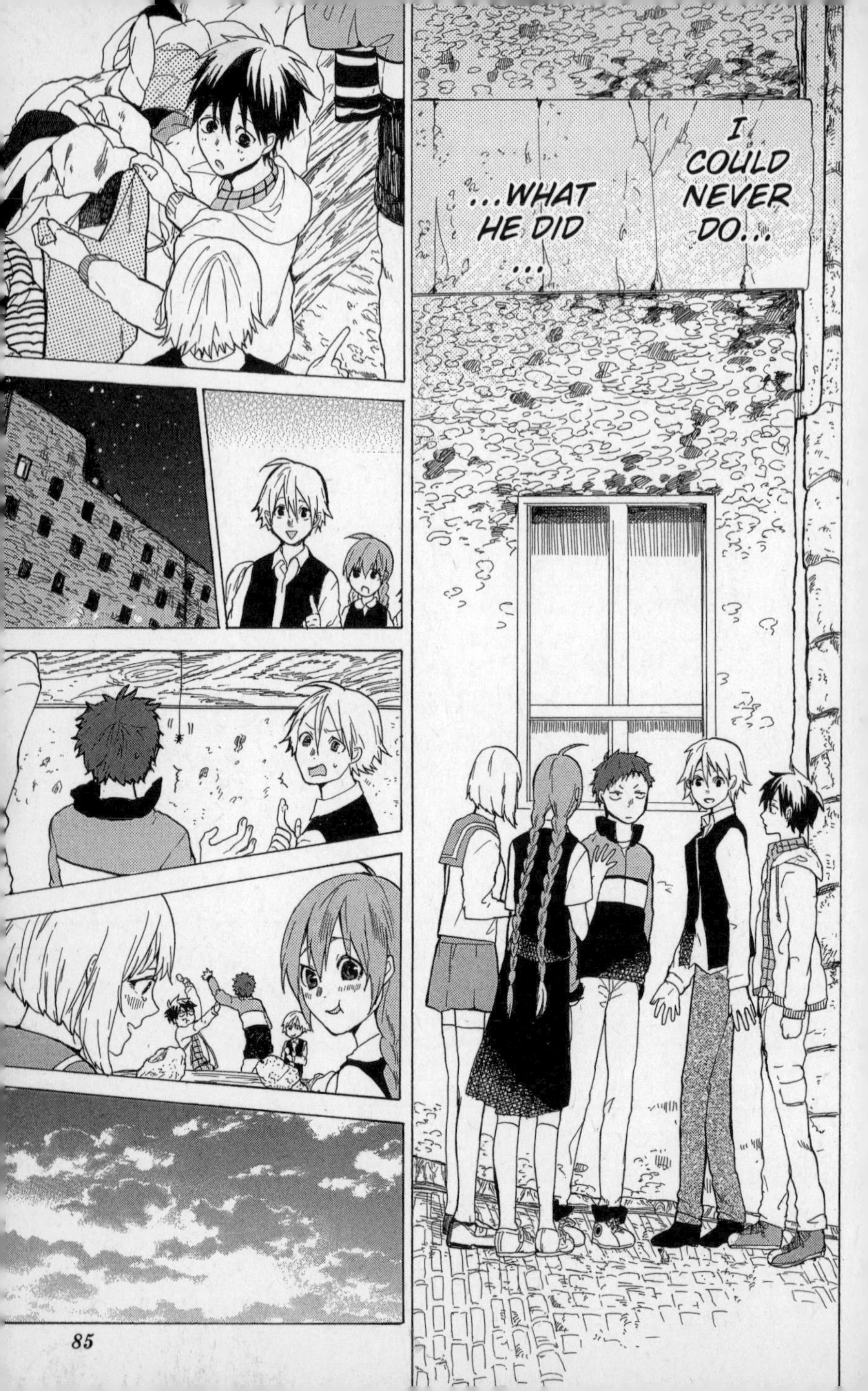
I COULD NEVER DO...
...WHAT HE DID
...

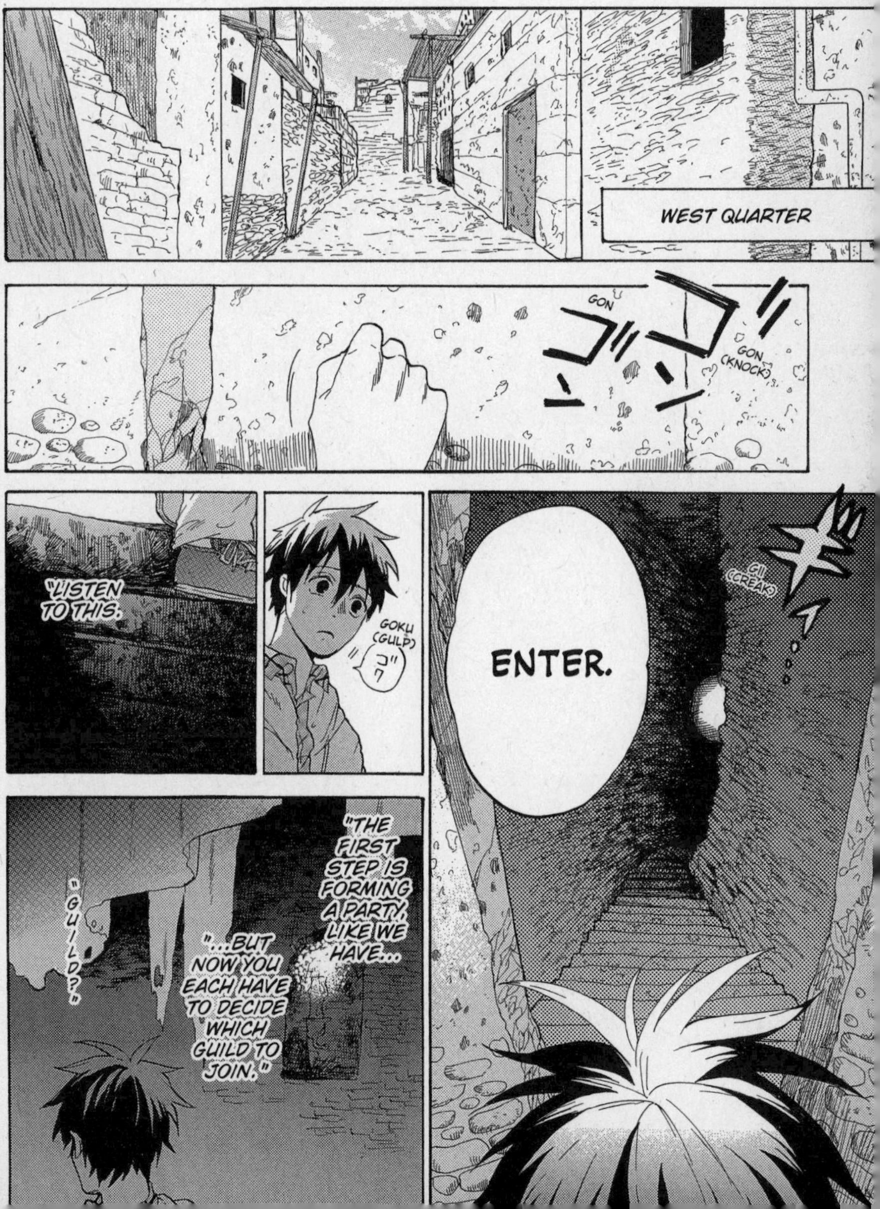
WEST QUARTER
GON
GON (KNOCK)
GII (CREAK)
ENTER.
GOKU (GULP)
"LISTEN TO THIS.
"THE FIRST STEP IS FORMING A PARTY, LIKE WE HAVE...
"...BUT NOW YOU EACH HAVE TO DECIDE WHICH GUILD TO JOIN."
"GUILD?"

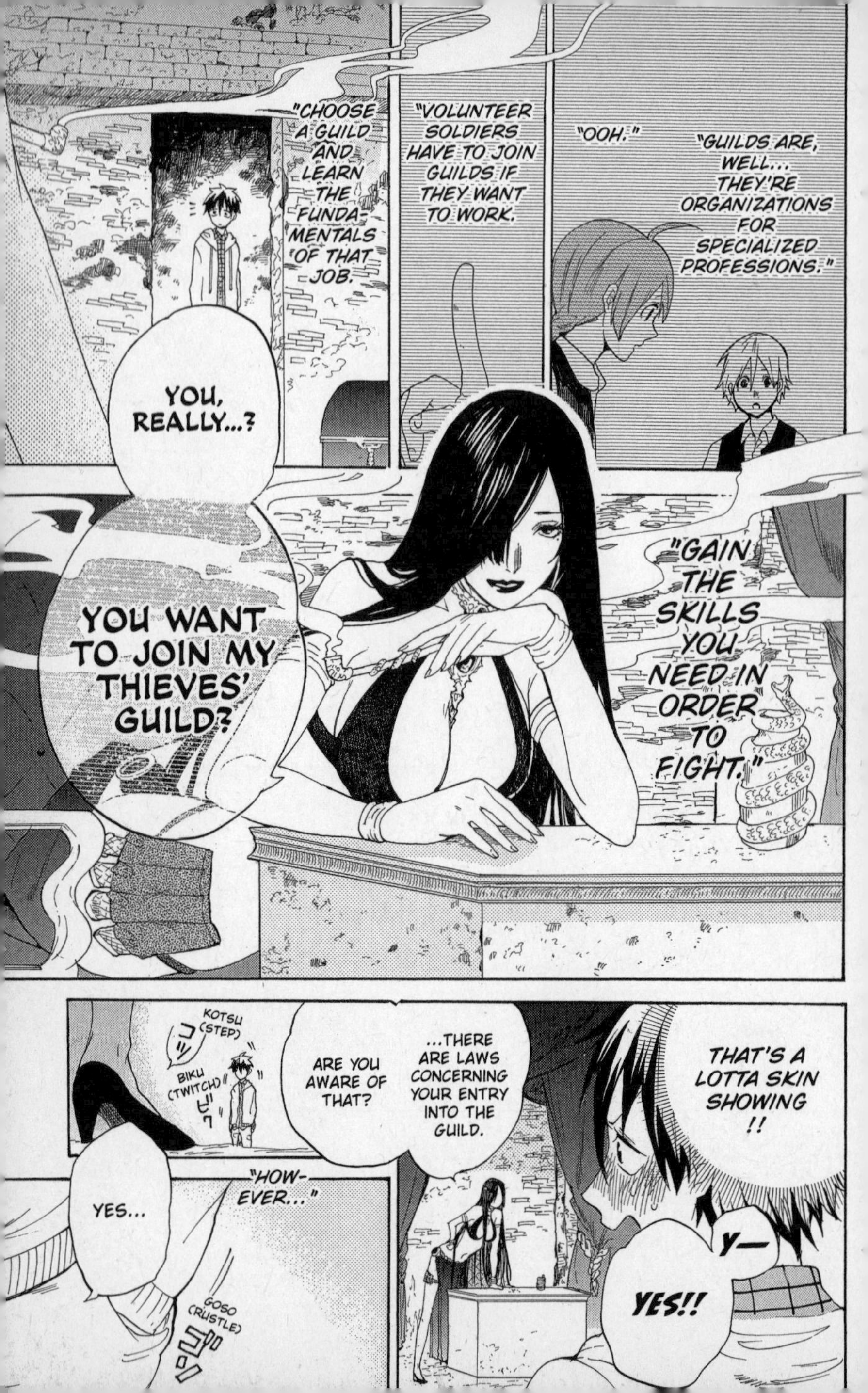
"GUILDS ARE, WELL... THEY'RE ORGANIZATIONS FOR SPECIALIZED PROFESSIONS."
"OOH."
"VOLUNTEER SOLDIERS HAVE TO JOIN GUILDS IF THEY WANT TO WORK.
"CHOOSE A GUILD AND LEARN THE FUNDAMENTALS OF THAT JOB.
"GAIN THE SKILLS YOU NEED IN ORDER TO FIGHT."
YOU, REALLY...?
YOU WANT TO JOIN MY THIEVES' GUILD?
THAT'S A LOTTA SKIN SHOWING!!
Y—
YES!!
...THERE ARE LAWS CONCERNING YOUR ENTRY INTO THE GUILD.
ARE YOU AWARE OF THAT?
KOTSU (STEP)
BIKU (TWITCH)
"HOW-EVER..."
YES...
GOSO (RUSTLE)

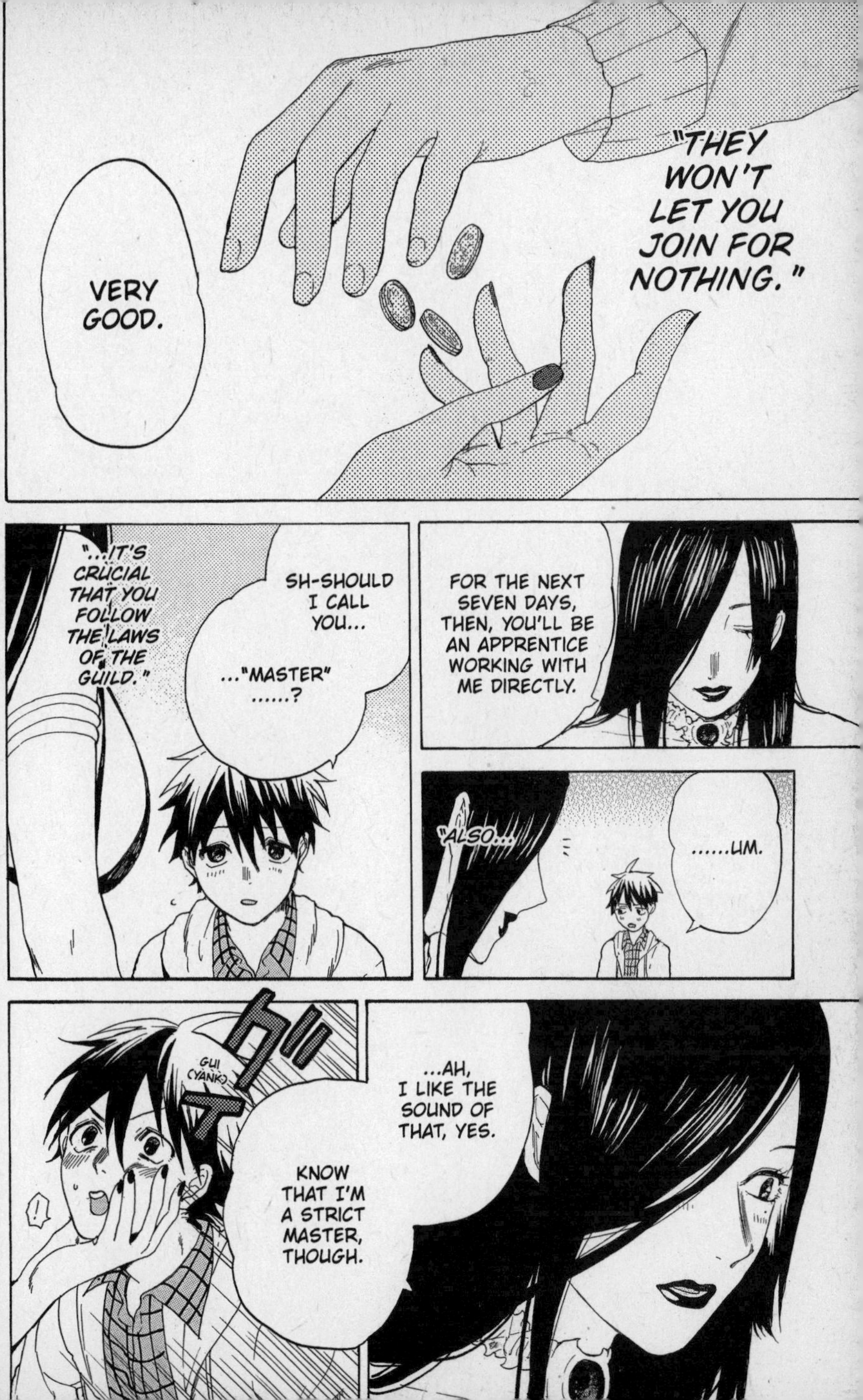
"THEY WON'T LET YOU JOIN FOR NOTHING."
VERY GOOD.
FOR THE NEXT SEVEN DAYS, THEN, YOU'LL BE AN APPRENTICE WORKING WITH ME DIRECTLY.
......UM.
"ALSO...
SH-SHOULD I CALL YOU...
..."MASTER" ......?
"...IT'S CRUCIAL THAT YOU FOLLOW THE LAWS OF THE GUILD."
...AH, I LIKE THE SOUND OF THAT, YES.
KNOW THAT I'M A STRICT MASTER, THOUGH.
GUI (YANK)
!

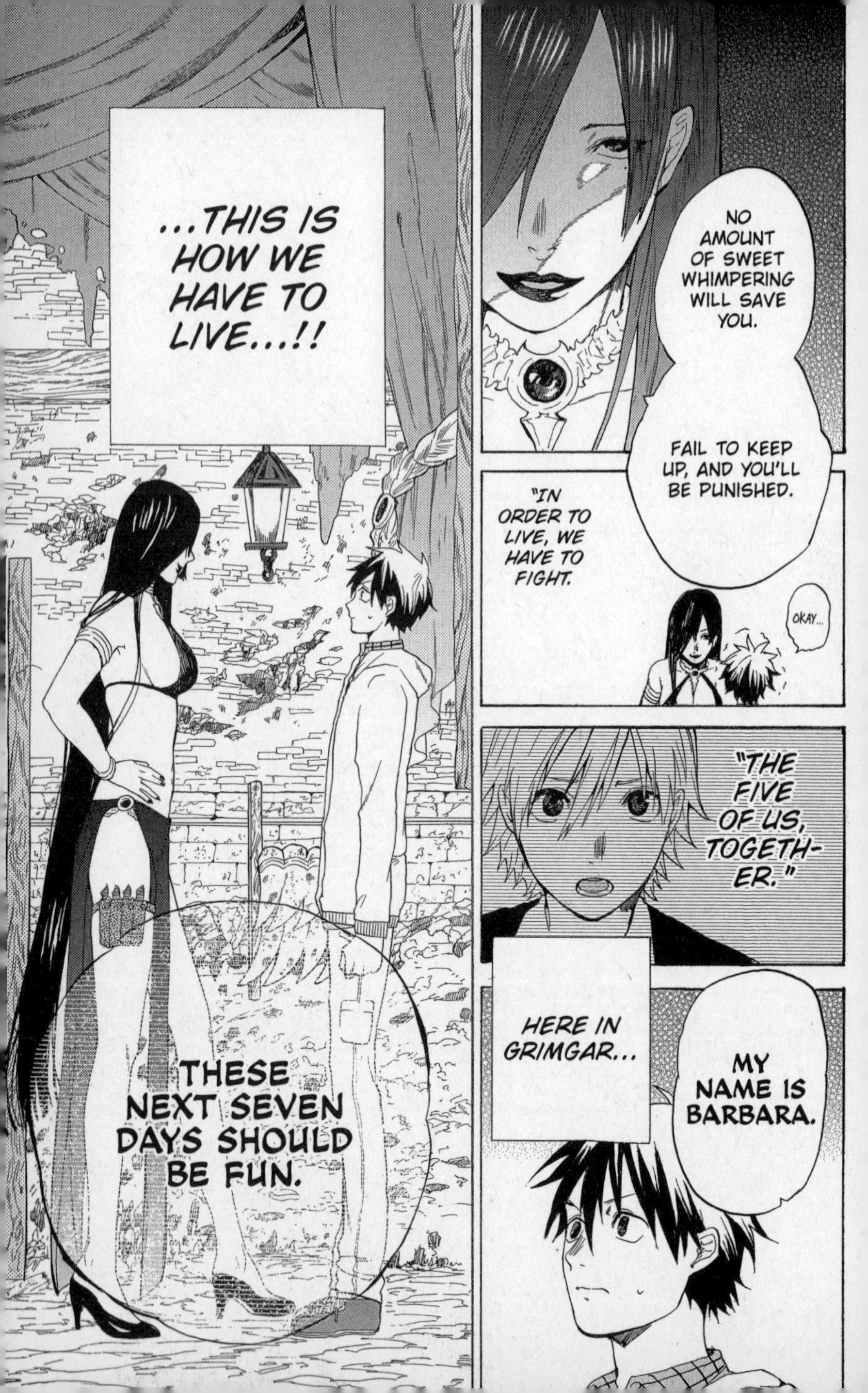
NO AMOUNT OF SWEET WHIMPERING WILL SAVE YOU.
FAIL TO KEEP UP, AND YOU'LL BE PUNISHED.
OKAY...
"IN ORDER TO LIVE, WE HAVE TO FIGHT.
"THE FIVE OF US, TOGETHER."
MY NAME IS BARBARA.
HERE IN GRIMGAR...
...THIS IS HOW WE HAVE TO LIVE...!!
THESE NEXT SEVEN DAYS SHOULD BE FUN.

level.2: Rendezvous

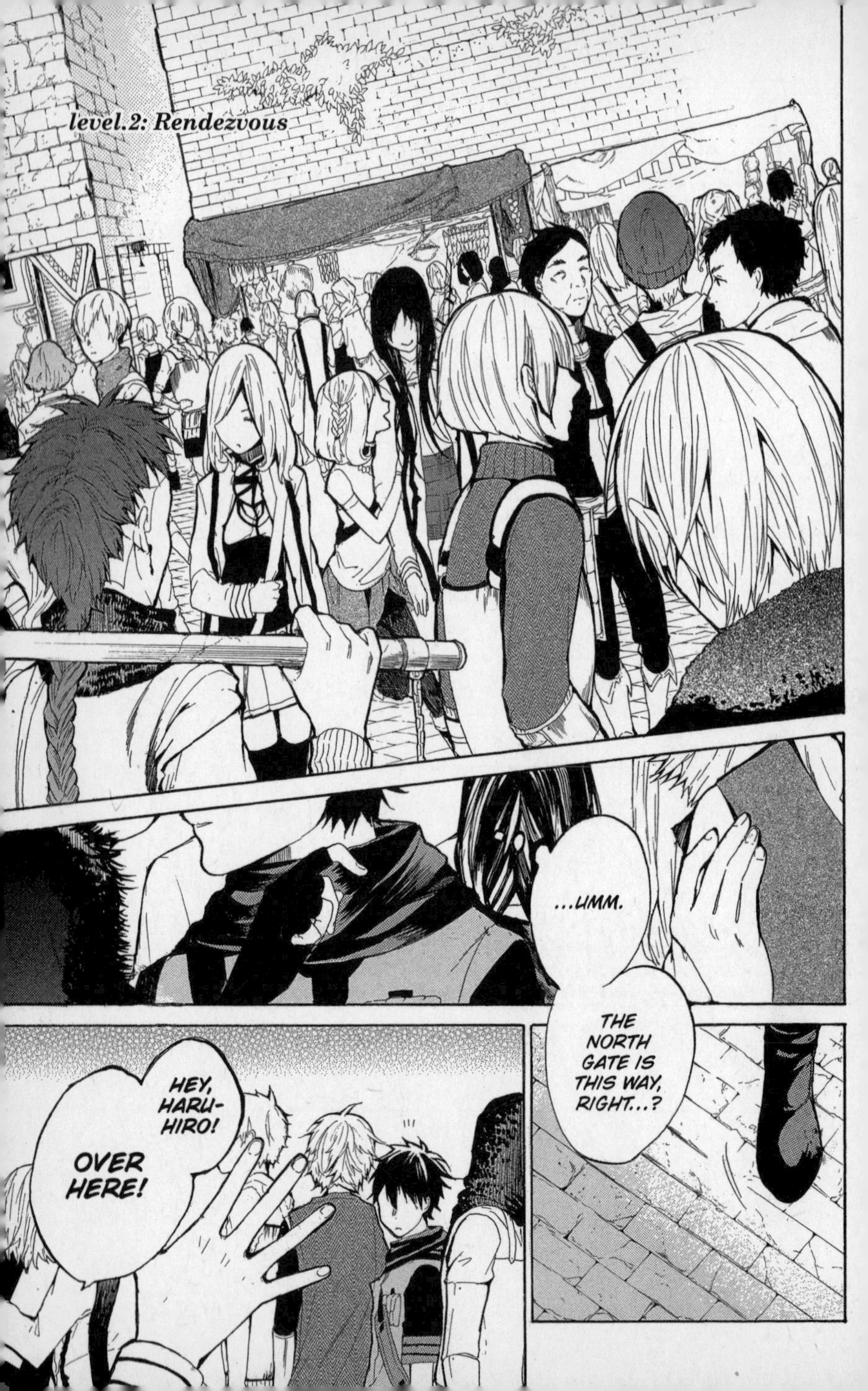
...UMM.
THE NORTH GATE IS THIS WAY, RIGHT...?
HEY, HARUHIRO!
OVER HERE!

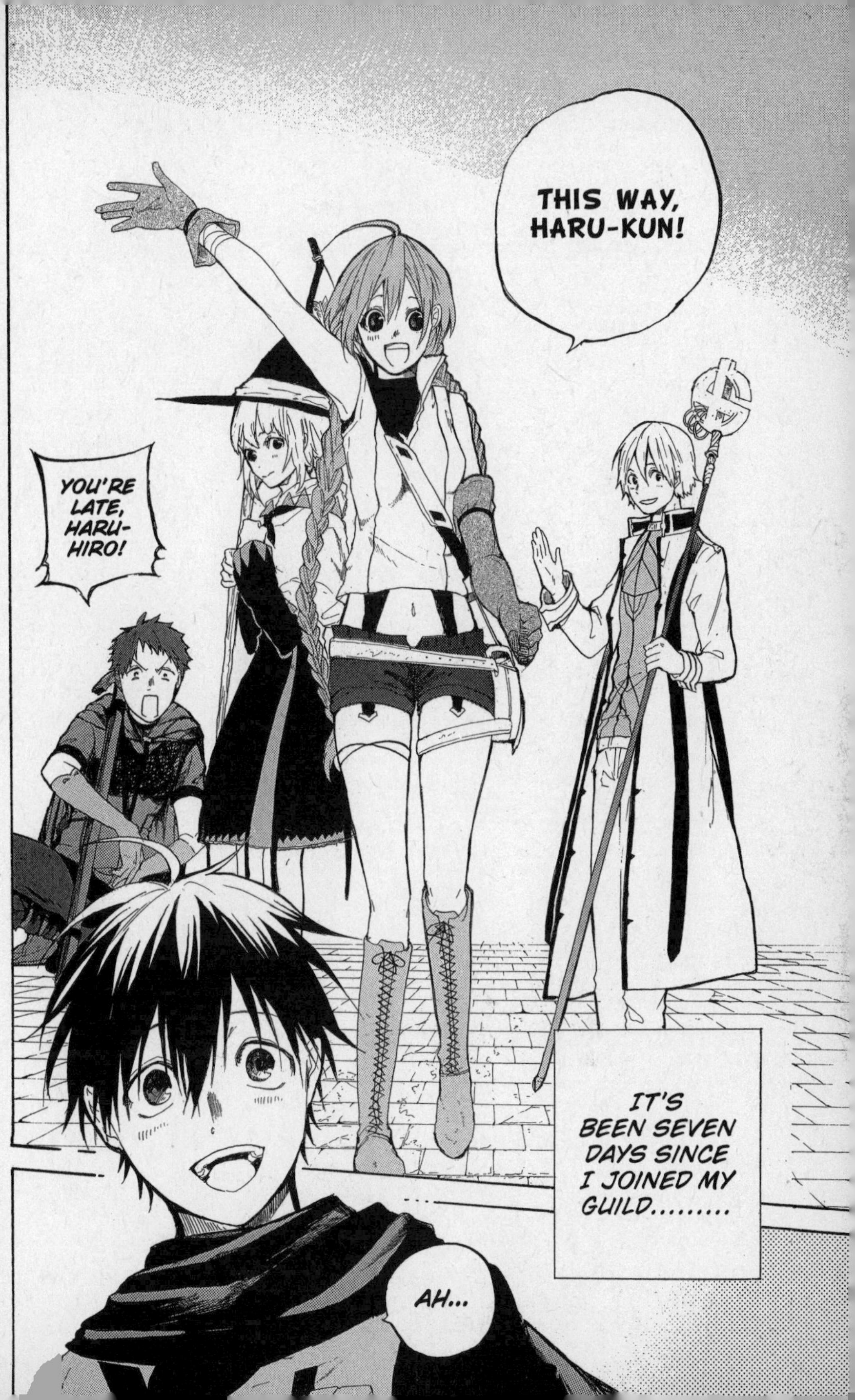
THIS WAY, HARU-KUN!
YOU'RE LATE, HARU-HIRO!
IT'S BEEN SEVEN DAYS SINCE I JOINED MY GUILD.........
AH...

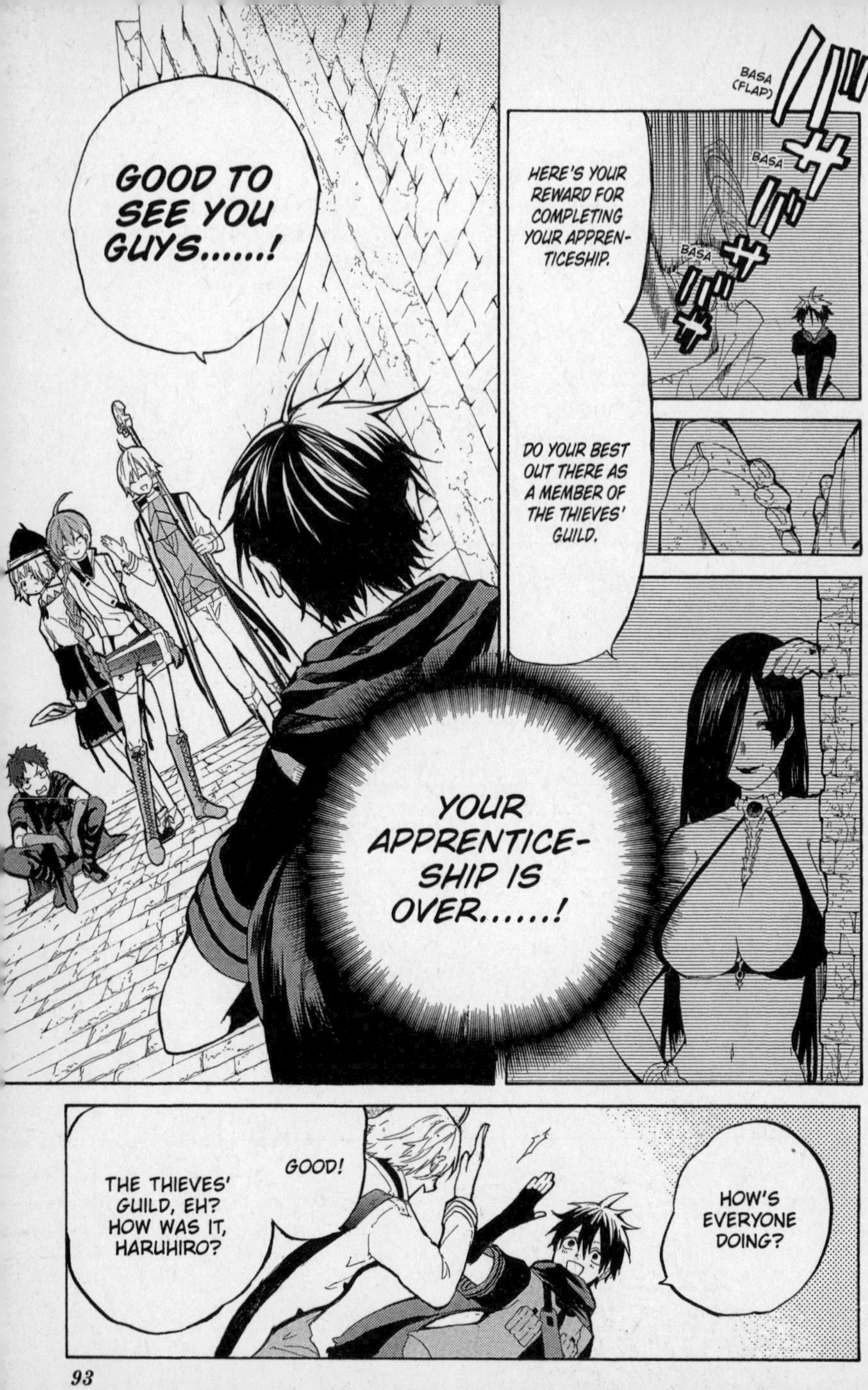
BASA (FLAP)
BASA
BASA
HERE'S YOUR REWARD FOR COMPLETING YOUR APPREN-TICESHIP.
DO YOUR BEST OUT THERE AS A MEMBER OF THE THIEVES' GUILD.
YOUR APPRENTICE-SHIP IS OVER......!
GOOD TO SEE YOU GUYS......!
HOW'S EVERYONE DOING?
GOOD!
THE THIEVES' GUILD, EH? HOW WAS IT, HARUHIRO?

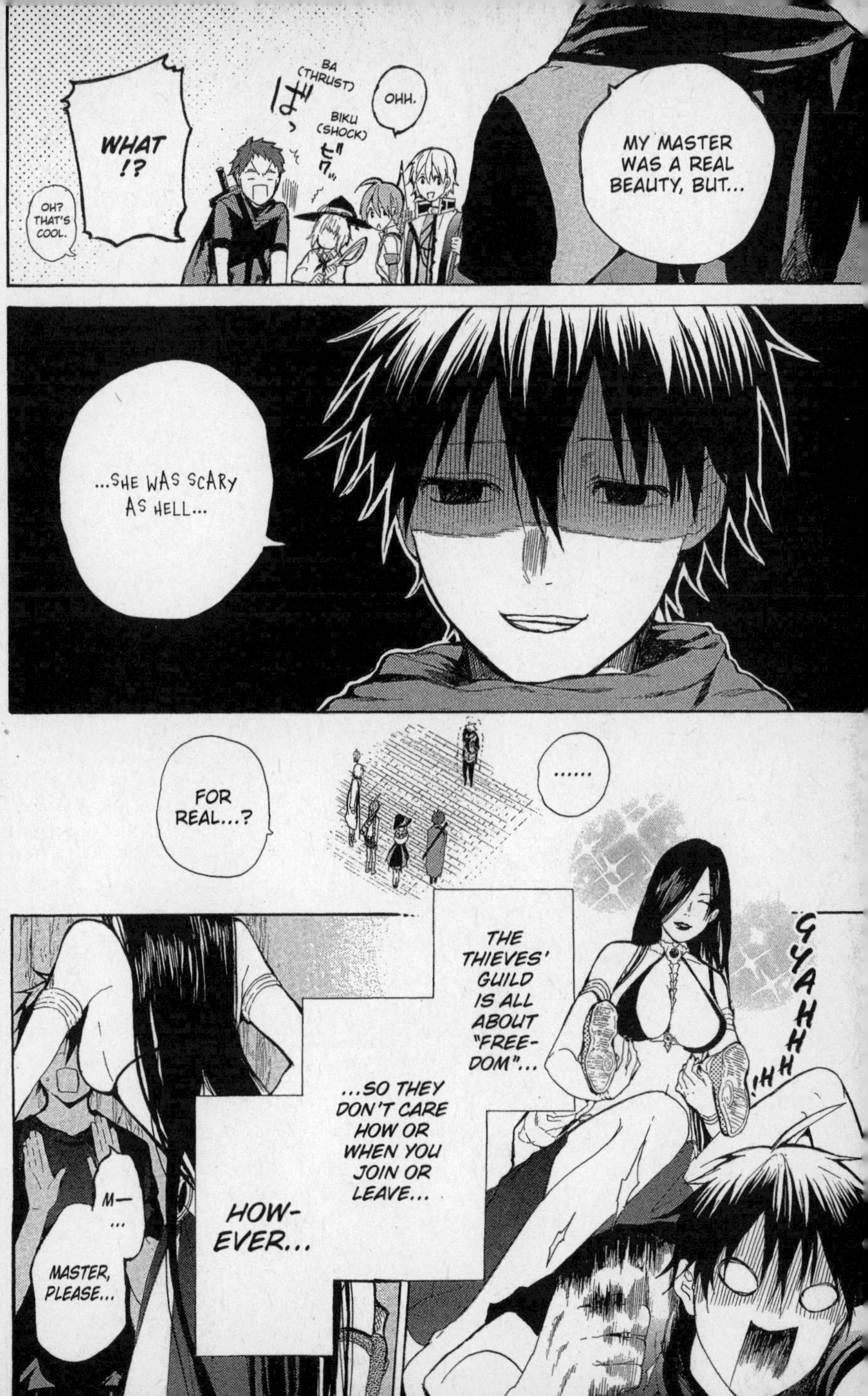
MY MASTER WAS A REAL BEAUTY, BUT...
OHH.
BA (THRUST)
ば
BIKU (SHOCK)
ビクッ
WHAT!?
OH? THAT'S COOL.
...SHE WAS SCARY AS HELL...
......
FOR REAL...?
THE THIEVES' GUILD IS ALL ABOUT "FREE-DOM"...
GYAHHHH!!
...SO THEY DON'T CARE HOW OR WHEN YOU JOIN OR LEAVE...
HOW-EVER...
M—... MASTER, PLEASE...

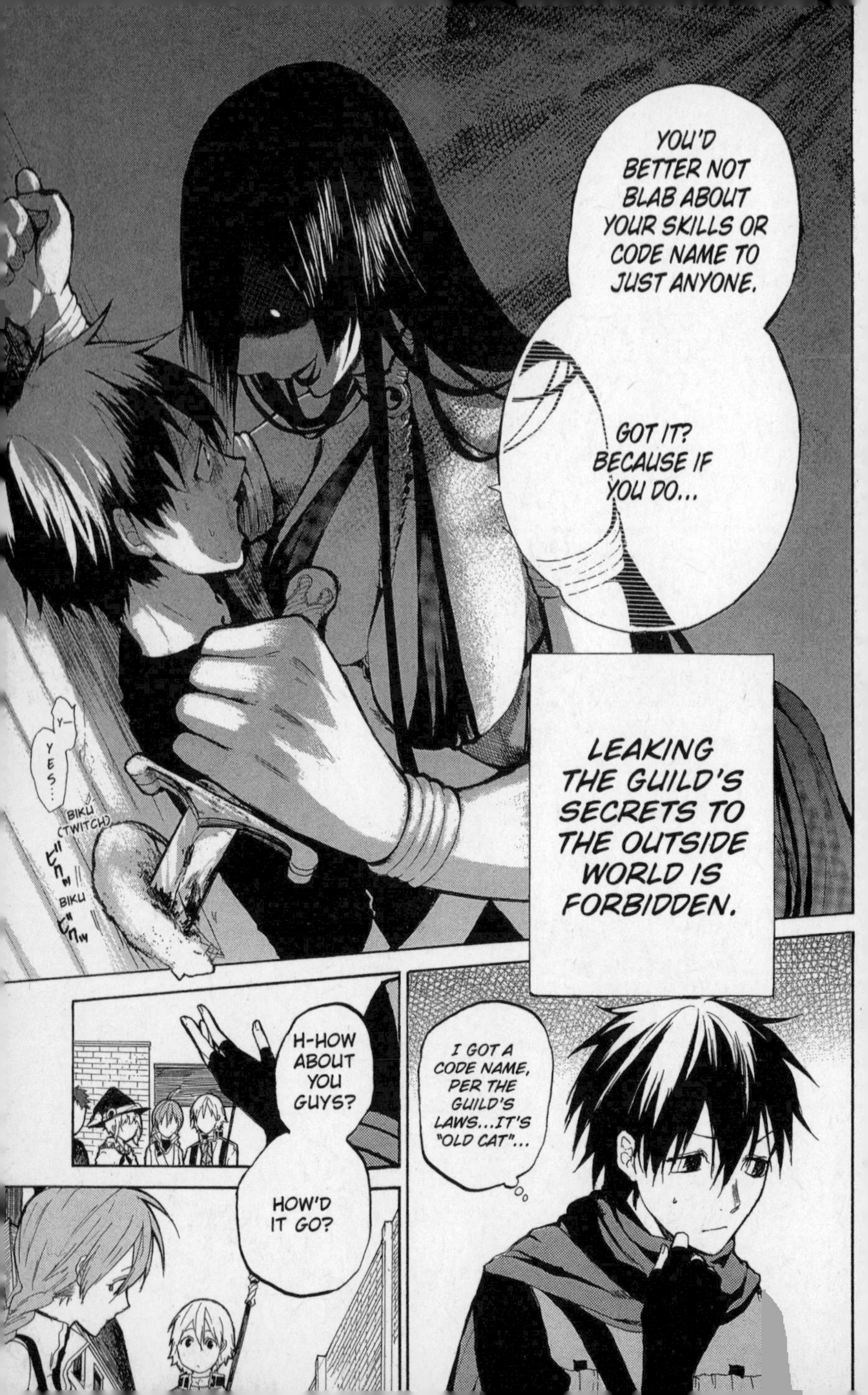
YOU'D BETTER NOT BLAB ABOUT YOUR SKILLS OR CODE NAME TO JUST ANYONE.
GOT IT? BECAUSE IF YOU DO...
Y— YES...
BIKU (TWITCH)
BIKU
LEAKING THE GUILD'S SECRETS TO THE OUTSIDE WORLD IS FORBIDDEN.
I GOT A CODE NAME, PER THE GUILD'S LAWS...IT'S "OLD CAT"...
H-HOW ABOUT YOU GUYS?
HOW'D IT GO?

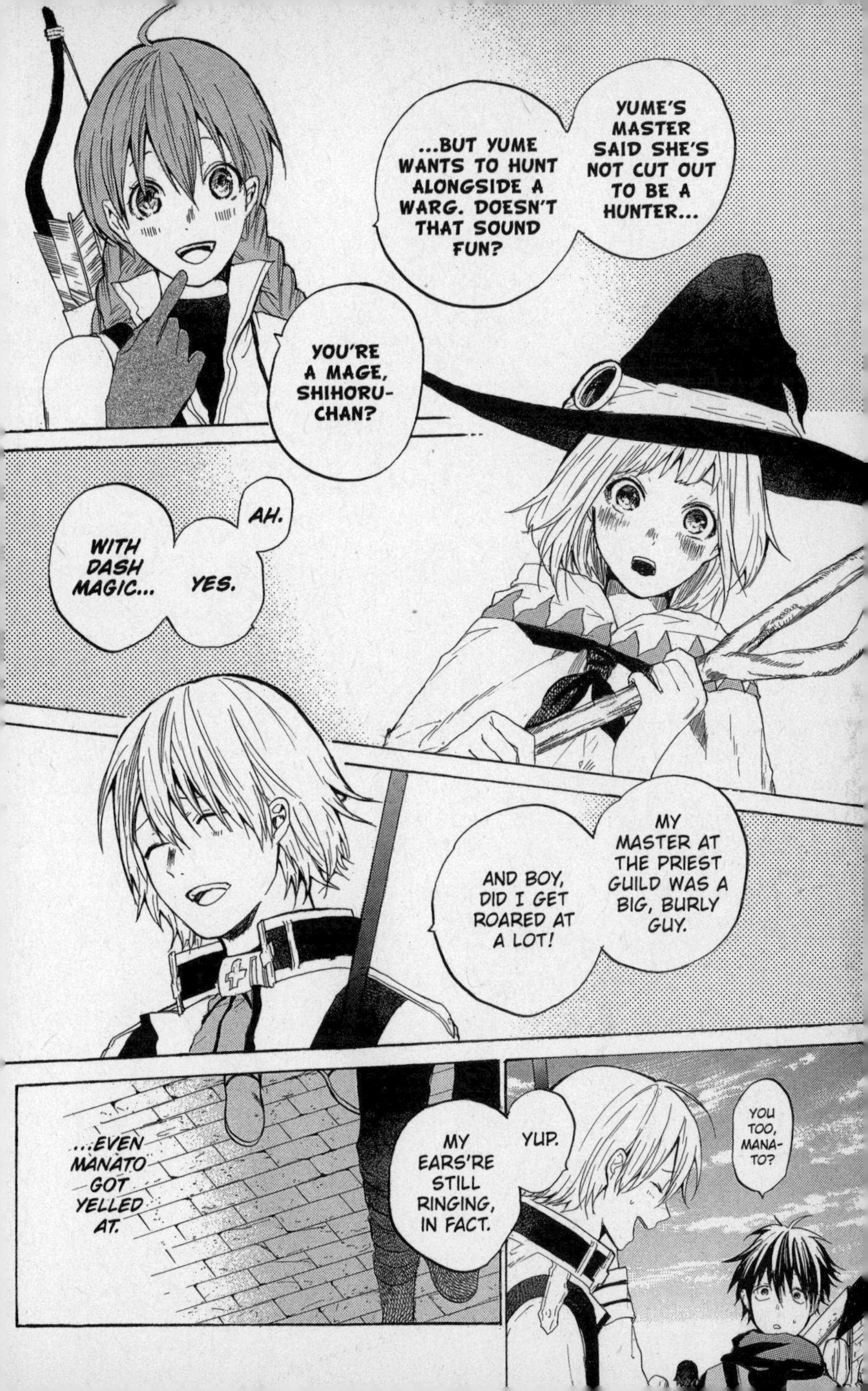
YUME'S MASTER SAID SHE'S NOT CUT OUT TO BE A HUNTER...
...BUT YUME WANTS TO HUNT ALONGSIDE A WARG. DOESN'T THAT SOUND FUN?
YOU'RE A MAGE, SHIHORU-CHAN?
AH.
YES.
WITH DASH MAGIC...
MY MASTER AT THE PRIEST GUILD WAS A BIG, BURLY GUY.
AND BOY, DID I GET ROARED AT A LOT!
YOU TOO, MANATO?
YUP.
MY EARS'RE STILL RINGING, IN FACT.
...EVEN MANATO GOT YELLED AT.

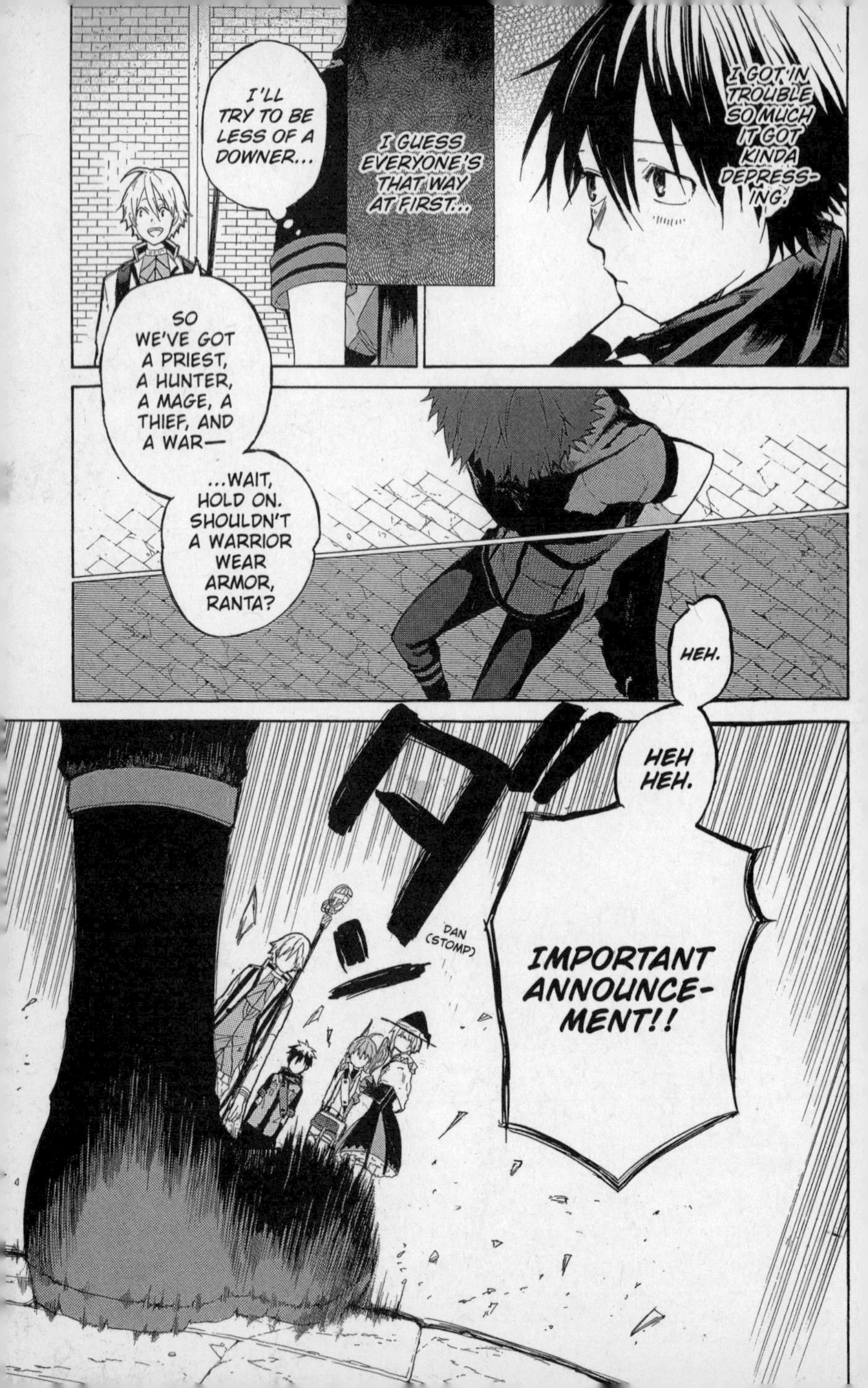
I GOT IN TROUBLE SO MUCH IT GOT KINDA DEPRESS-ING.
I GUESS EVERYONE'S THAT WAY AT FIRST...
I'LL TRY TO BE LESS OF A DOWNER...
SO WE'VE GOT A PRIEST, A HUNTER, A MAGE, A THIEF, AND A WAR—
...WAIT, HOLD ON. SHOULDN'T A WARRIOR WEAR ARMOR, RANTA?
HEH.
HEH HEH.
IMPORTANT ANNOUNCE-MENT!!
DAN (STOMP)

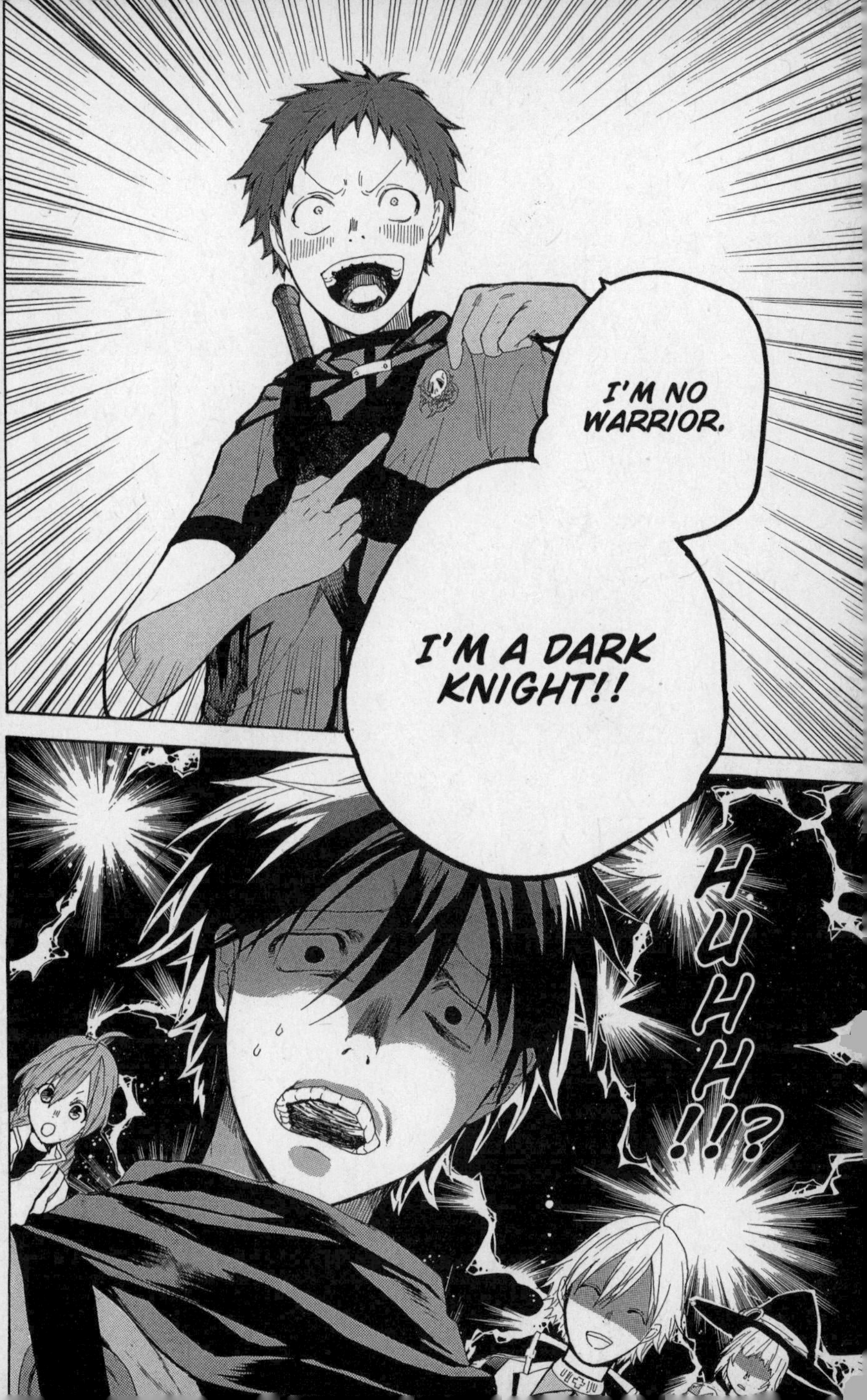
I'M NO WARRIOR.
I'M A DARK KNIGHT!!
HUHHH!!?

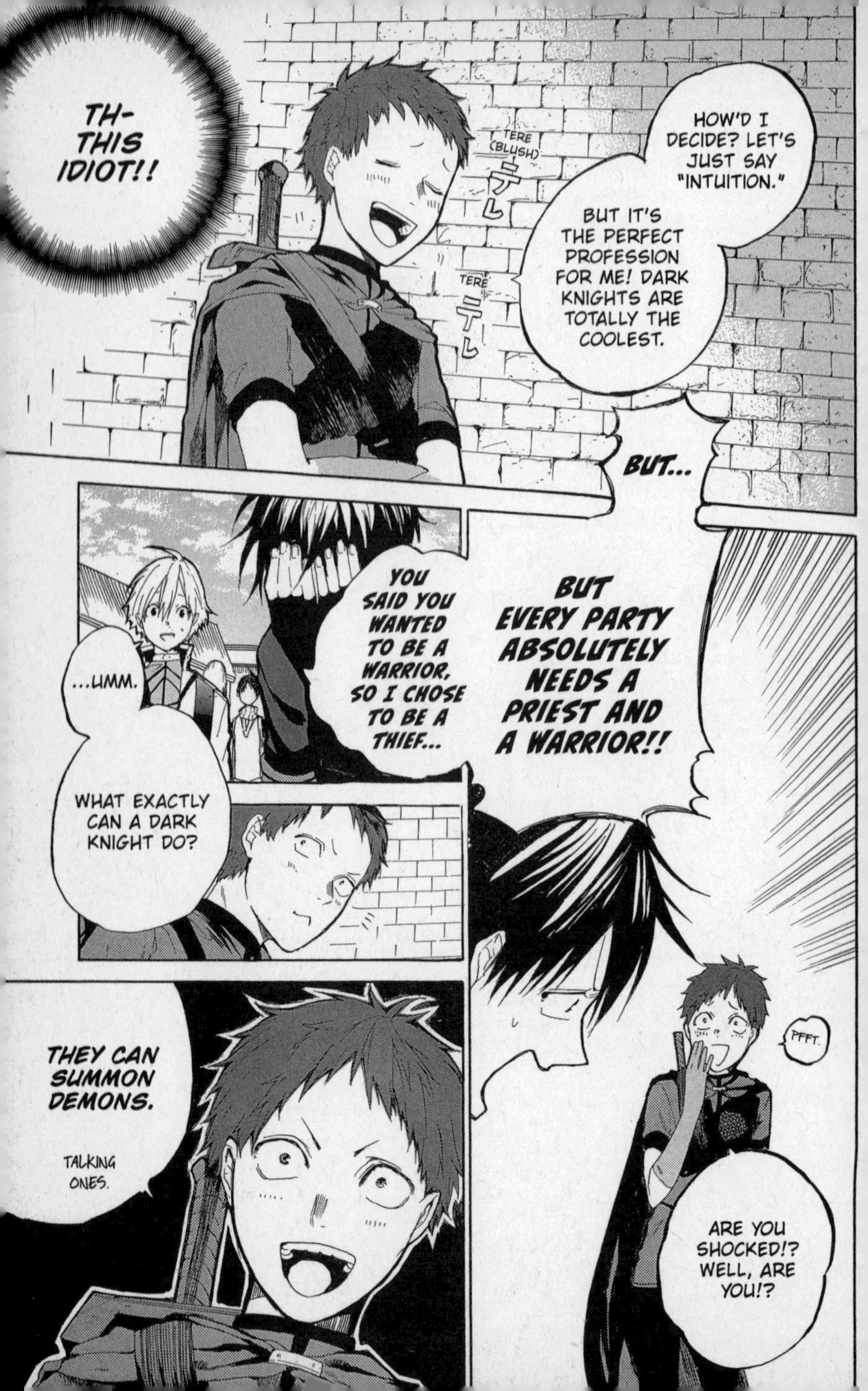
HOW'D I DECIDE? LET'S JUST SAY "INTUITION."
BUT IT'S THE PERFECT PROFESSION FOR ME! DARK KNIGHTS ARE TOTALLY THE COOLEST.
TERE (BLUSH)
テレ
TERE
テレ
TH-THIS IDIOT!!
BUT...
BUT EVERY PARTY ABSOLUTELY NEEDS A PRIEST AND A WARRIOR!!
YOU SAID YOU WANTED TO BE A WARRIOR, SO I CHOSE TO BE A THIEF...
...UMM.
WHAT EXACTLY CAN A DARK KNIGHT DO?
THEY CAN SUMMON DEMONS.
TALKING ONES.
PFFT.
ARE YOU SHOCKED!? WELL, ARE YOU!?

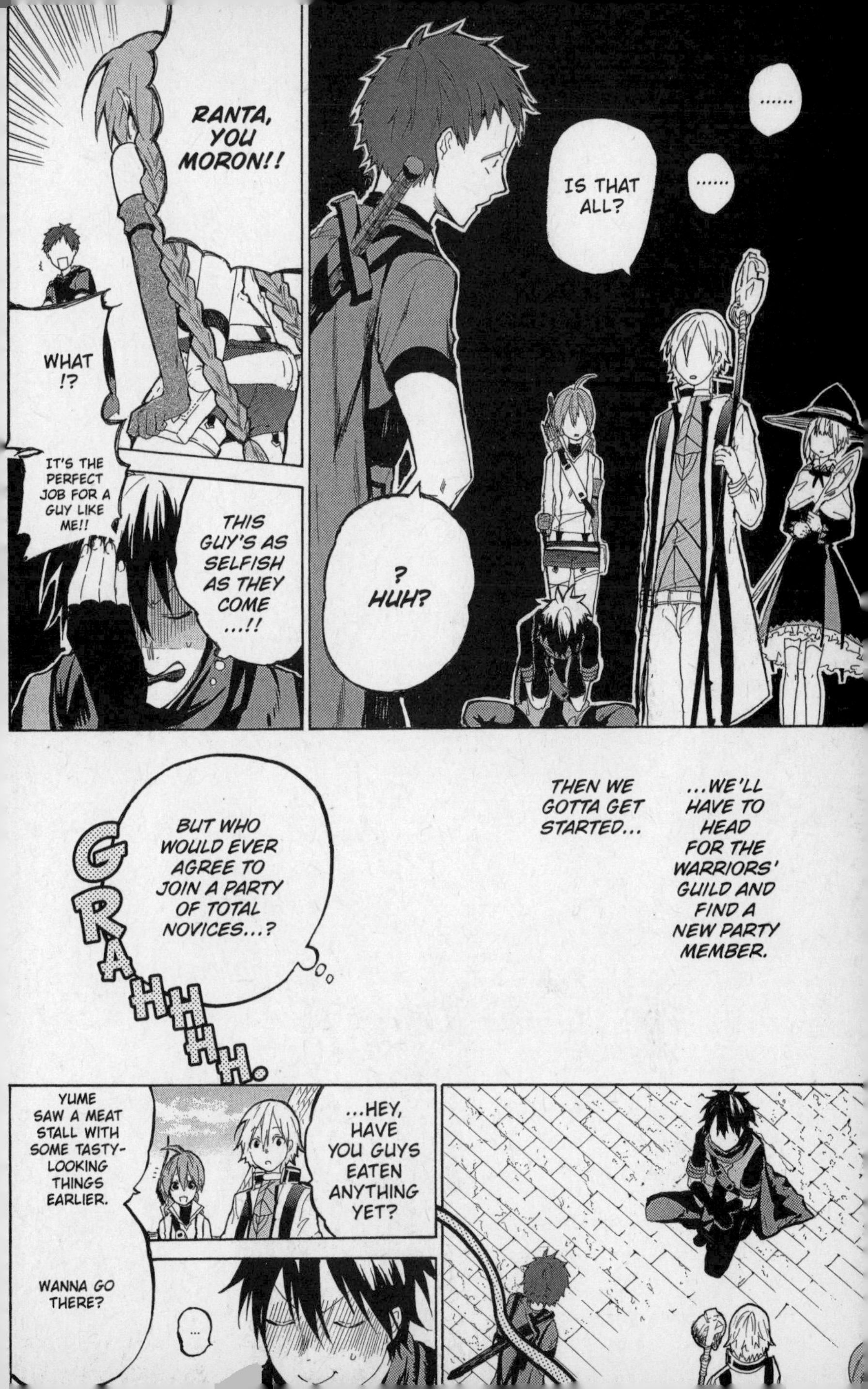
......
......
IS THAT ALL?
? HUH?
RANTA, YOU MORON!!
WHAT !?
IT'S THE PERFECT JOB FOR A GUY LIKE ME!!
THIS GUY'S AS SELFISH AS THEY COME ...!!
...WE'LL HAVE TO HEAD FOR THE WARRIORS' GUILD AND FIND A NEW PARTY MEMBER.
THEN WE GOTTA GET STARTED...
BUT WHO WOULD EVER AGREE TO JOIN A PARTY OF TOTAL NOVICES...?
GRAHHHHH.
...HEY, HAVE YOU GUYS EATEN ANYTHING YET?
YUME SAW A MEAT STALL WITH SOME TASTY-LOOKING THINGS EARLIER.
WANNA GO THERE?
...

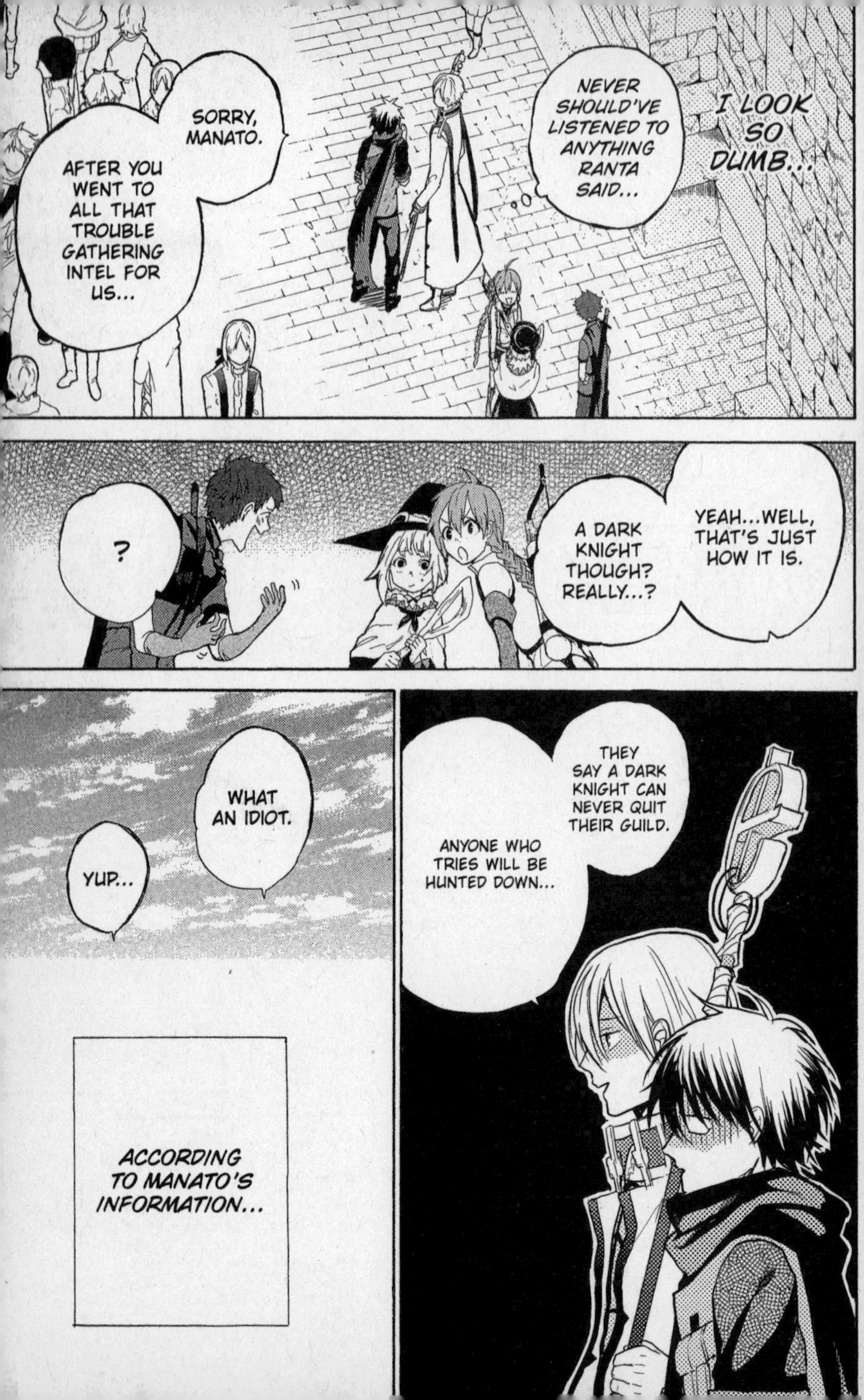

I LOOK SO DUMB...
NEVER SHOULD'VE LISTENED TO ANYTHING RANTA SAID...
SORRY, MANATO.
AFTER YOU WENT TO ALL THAT TROUBLE GATHERING INTEL FOR US...
YEAH...WELL, THAT'S JUST HOW IT IS.
A DARK KNIGHT THOUGH? REALLY...?
?
THEY SAY A DARK KNIGHT CAN NEVER QUIT THEIR GUILD.
ANYONE WHO TRIES WILL BE HUNTED DOWN...
WHAT AN IDIOT.
YUP...
ACCORDING TO MANATO'S INFORMATION...

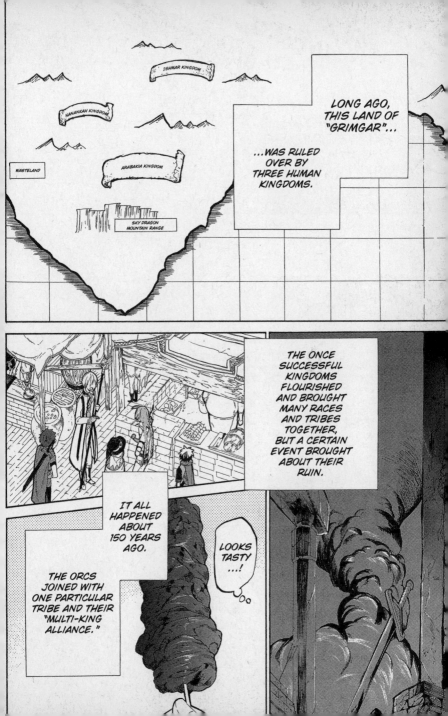

ISHMAR KINGDOM

NANANKAH KINGDOM

ARABAKIA KINGDOM

WASTELAND

SKY DRAGON
MOUNTAIN RANGE

LONG AGO,
THIS LAND OF
"GRIMGAR"...

...WAS RULED
OVER BY
THREE HUMAN
KINGDOMS.

THE ONCE
SUCCESSFUL
KINGDOMS
FLOURISHED
AND BROUGHT
MANY RACES
AND TRIBES
TOGETHER,
BUT A CERTAIN
EVENT BROUGHT
ABOUT THEIR
RUIN.

IT ALL
HAPPENED
ABOUT
150 YEARS
AGO.

LOOKS
TASTY
...!

THE ORCS
JOINED WITH
ONE PARTICULAR
TRIBE AND THEIR
"MULTI-KING
ALLIANCE."

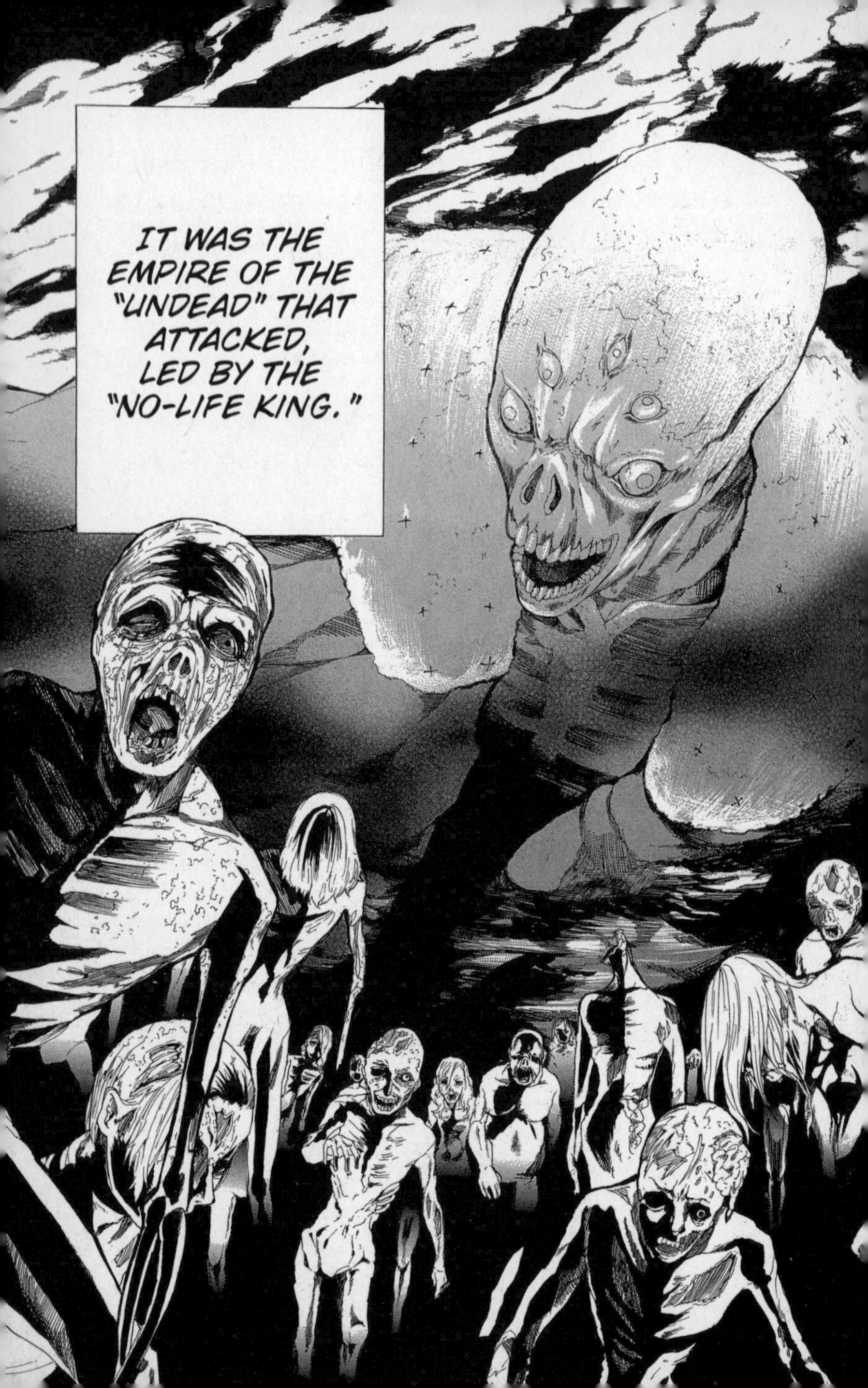
IT WAS THE EMPIRE OF THE "UNDEAD" THAT ATTACKED, LED BY THE "NO-LIFE KING."

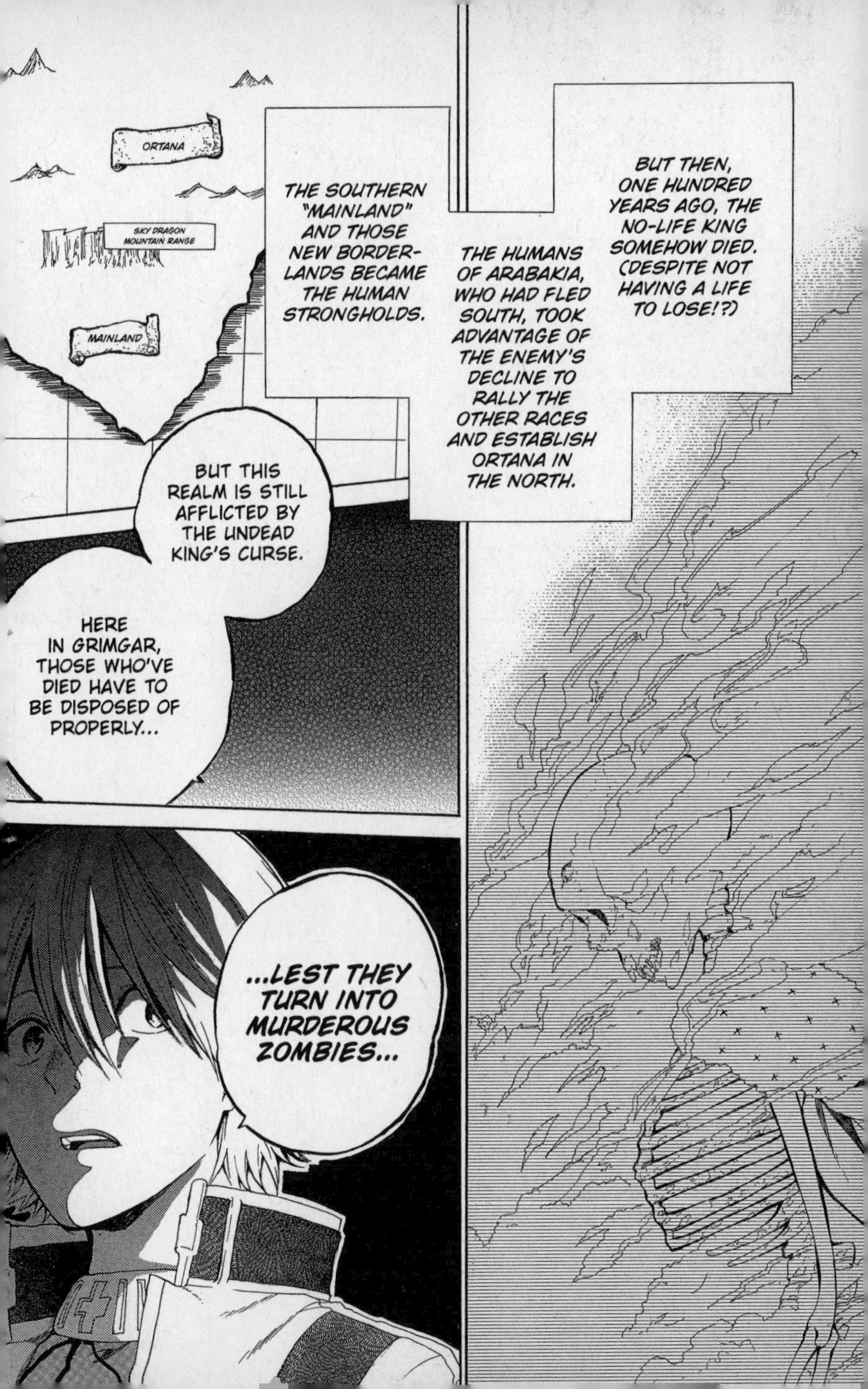
BUT THEN, ONE HUNDRED YEARS AGO, THE NO-LIFE KING SOMEHOW DIED. (DESPITE NOT HAVING A LIFE TO LOSE!?)
THE HUMANS OF ARABAKIA, WHO HAD FLED SOUTH, TOOK ADVANTAGE OF THE ENEMY'S DECLINE TO RALLY THE OTHER RACES AND ESTABLISH ORTANA IN THE NORTH.
THE SOUTHERN "MAINLAND" AND THOSE NEW BORDER-LANDS BECAME THE HUMAN STRONGHOLDS.
ORTANA
SKY DRAGON MOUNTAIN RANGE
MAINLAND
BUT THIS REALM IS STILL AFFLICTED BY THE UNDEAD KING'S CURSE.
HERE IN GRIMGAR, THOSE WHO'VE DIED HAVE TO BE DISPOSED OF PROPERLY...
...LEST THEY TURN INTO MURDEROUS ZOMBIES...

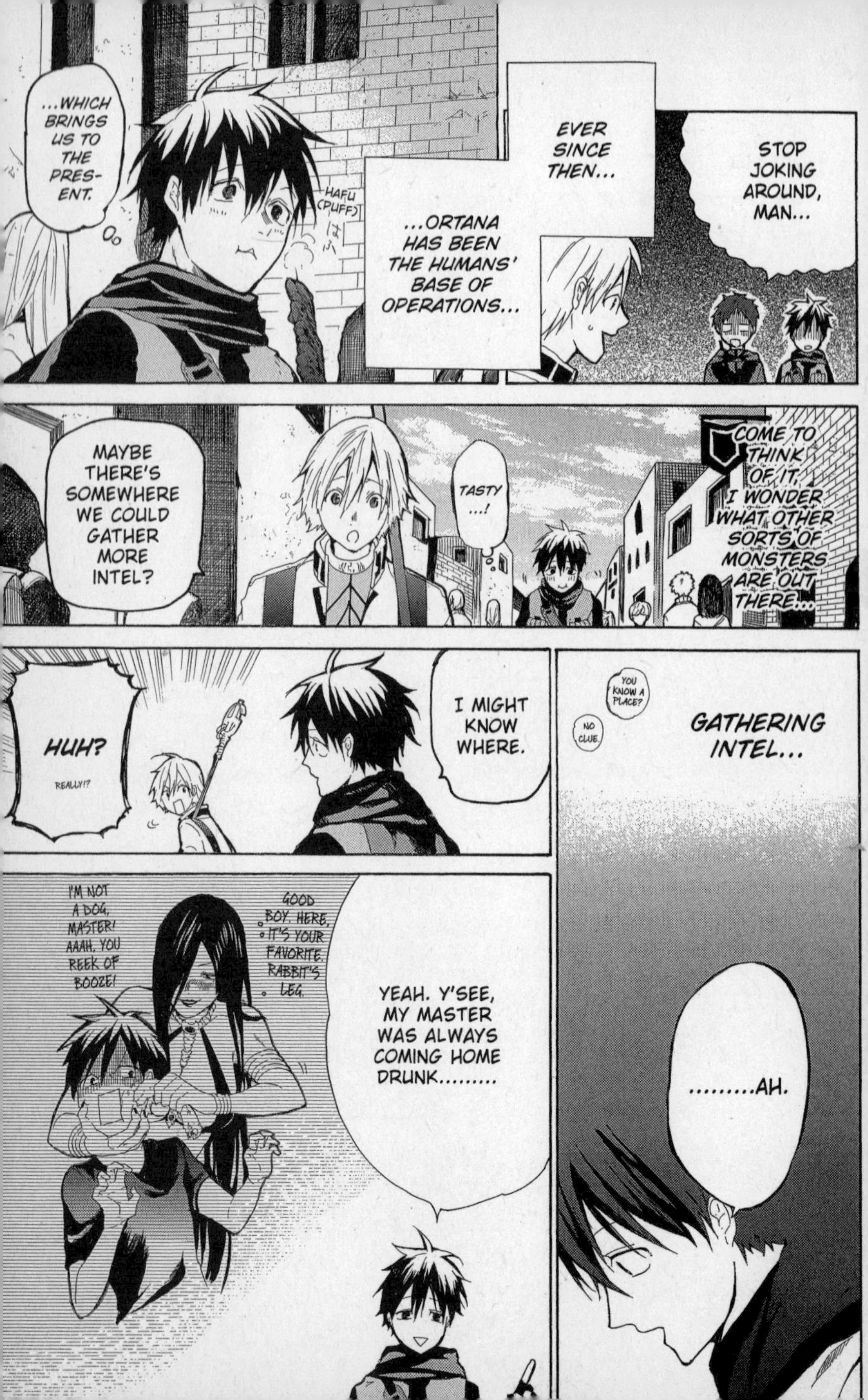
STOP JOKING AROUND, MAN...
EVER SINCE THEN...
...ORTANA HAS BEEN THE HUMANS' BASE OF OPERATIONS...
...WHICH BRINGS US TO THE PRESENT.
HAFU (PUFF)
はふ
COME TO THINK OF IT, I WONDER WHAT OTHER SORTS OF MONSTERS ARE OUT THERE...
TASTY ...!
MAYBE THERE'S SOMEWHERE WE COULD GATHER MORE INTEL?
GATHERING INTEL...
YOU KNOW A PLACE?
NO CLUE.
.........AH.
I MIGHT KNOW WHERE.
HUH?
REALLY!?
YEAH. Y'SEE, MY MASTER WAS ALWAYS COMING HOME DRUNK.........
GOOD BOY. HERE, IT'S YOUR FAVORITE. RABBIT'S LEG.
I'M NOT A DOG, MASTER! AAAH, YOU REEK OF BOOZE!

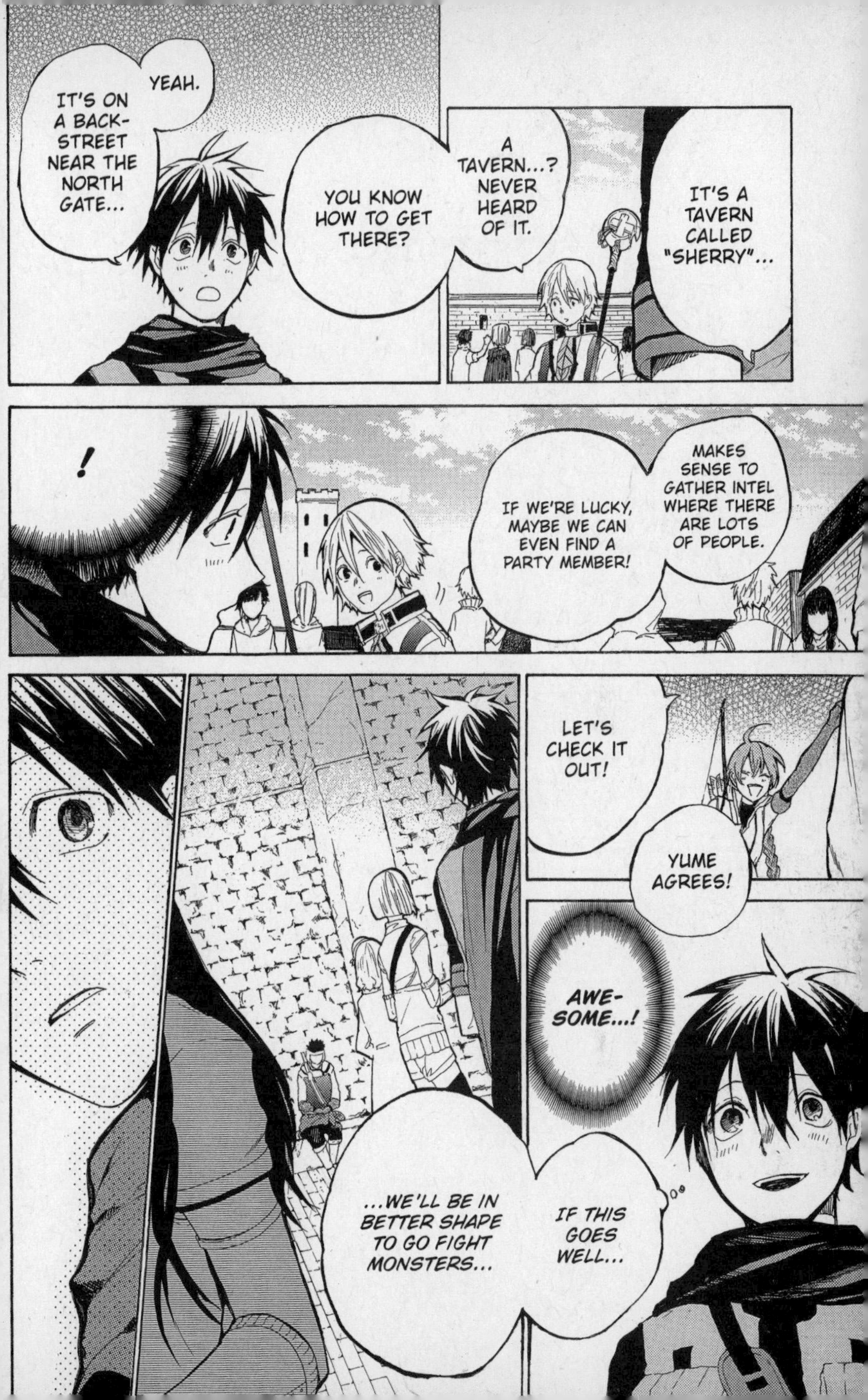
IT'S A TAVERN CALLED "SHERRY"...
A TAVERN...? NEVER HEARD OF IT.
YOU KNOW HOW TO GET THERE?
YEAH.
IT'S ON A BACK-STREET NEAR THE NORTH GATE...
MAKES SENSE TO GATHER INTEL WHERE THERE ARE LOTS OF PEOPLE.
IF WE'RE LUCKY, MAYBE WE CAN EVEN FIND A PARTY MEMBER!
!
LET'S CHECK IT OUT!
YUME AGREES!
AWE-SOME...!
IF THIS GOES WELL...
...WE'LL BE IN BETTER SHAPE TO GO FIGHT MONSTERS...

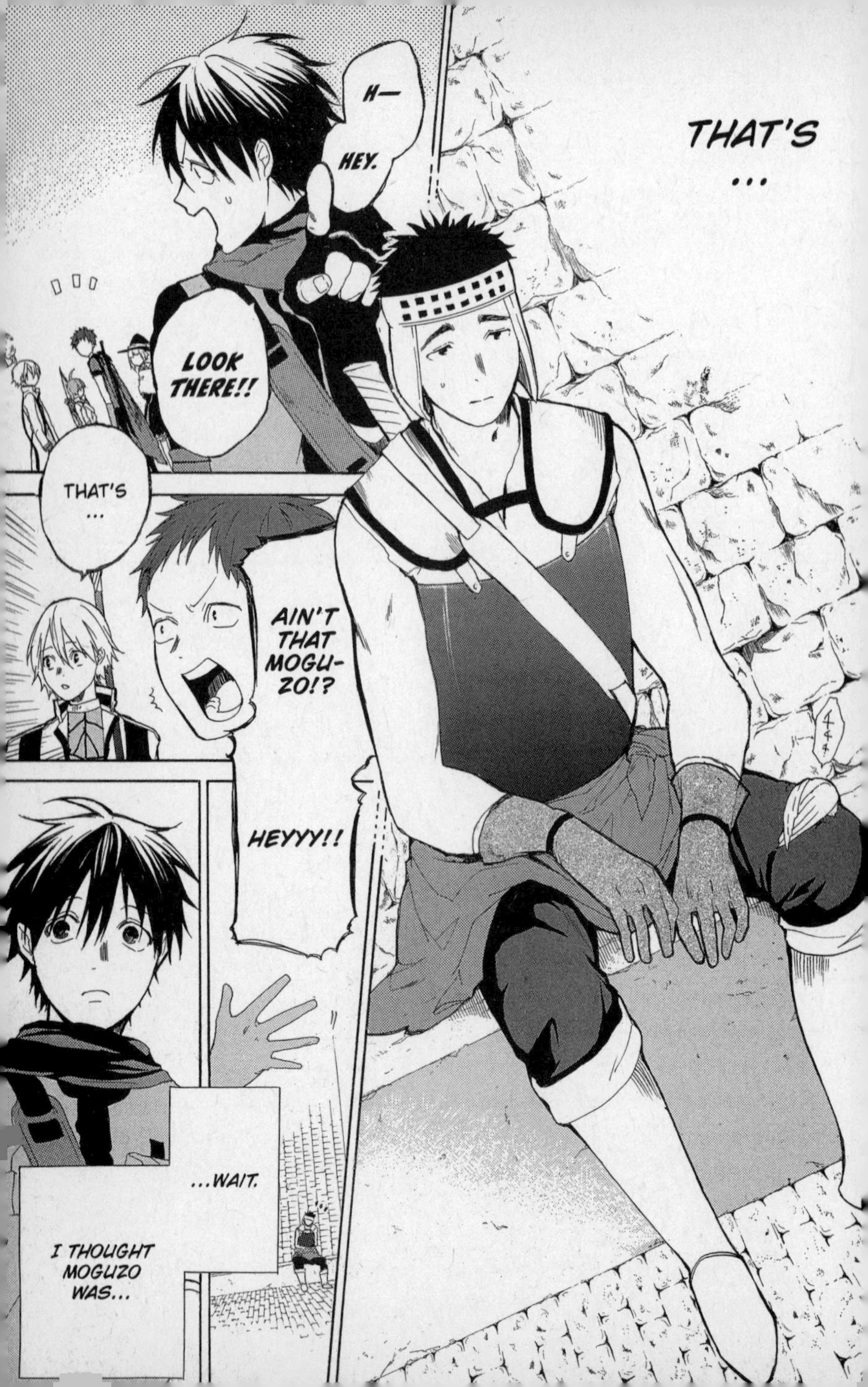
THAT'S ...
H— HEY.
LOOK THERE!!
THAT'S ...
AIN'T THAT MOGU-ZO!?
HEYYY!!
...WAIT.
I THOUGHT MOGUZO WAS...

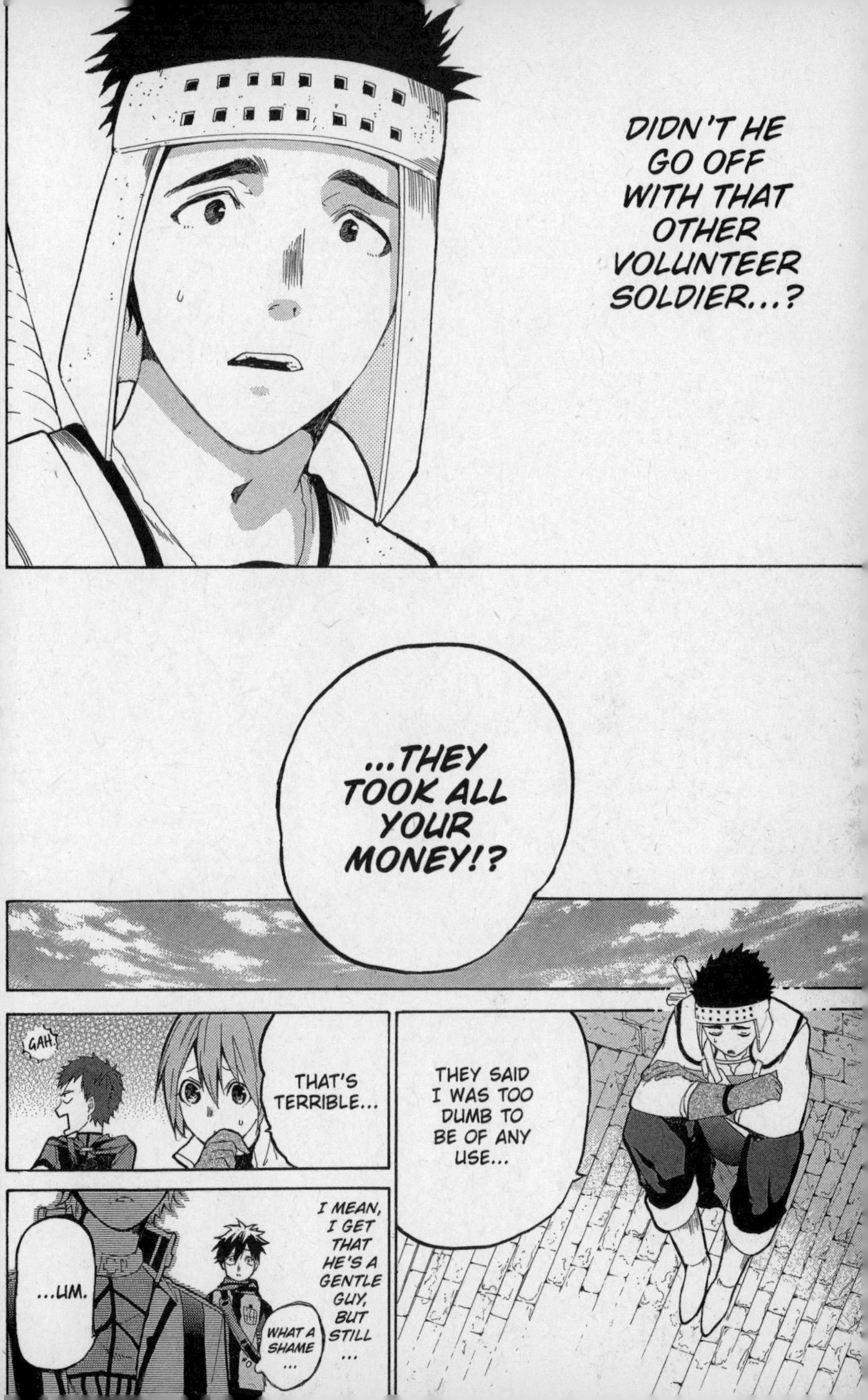
DIDN'T HE GO OFF WITH THAT OTHER VOLUNTEER SOLDIER...?
...THEY TOOK ALL YOUR MONEY!?
THEY SAID I WAS TOO DUMB TO BE OF ANY USE...
THAT'S TERRIBLE...
GAH!
I MEAN, I GET THAT HE'S A GENTLE GUY, BUT STILL...
WHAT A SHAME...
...UM.

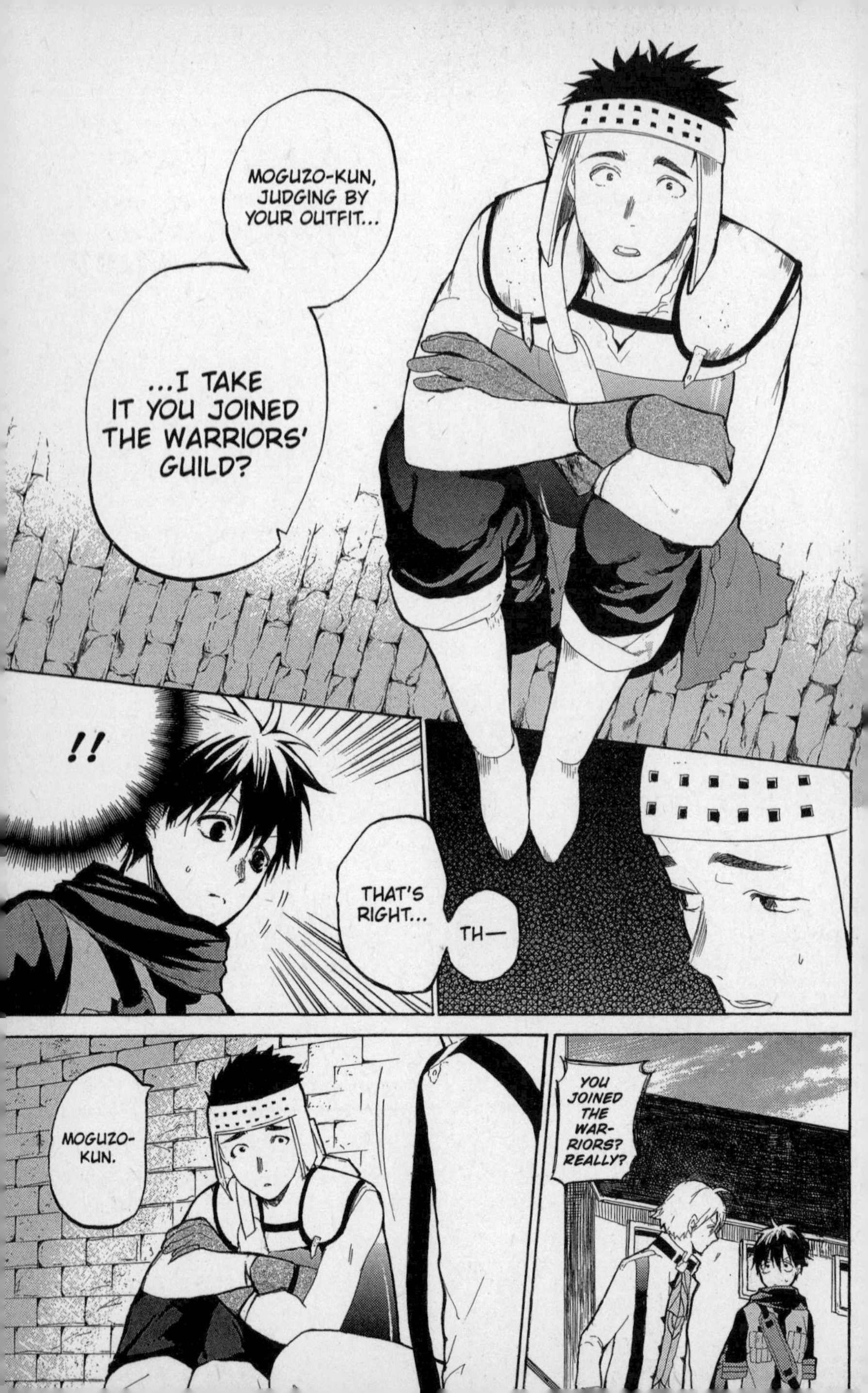
MOGUZO-KUN, JUDGING BY YOUR OUTFIT...
...I TAKE IT YOU JOINED THE WARRIORS' GUILD?
THAT'S RIGHT...
TH—
!!
YOU JOINED THE WAR-RIORS? REALLY?
MOGUZO-KUN.

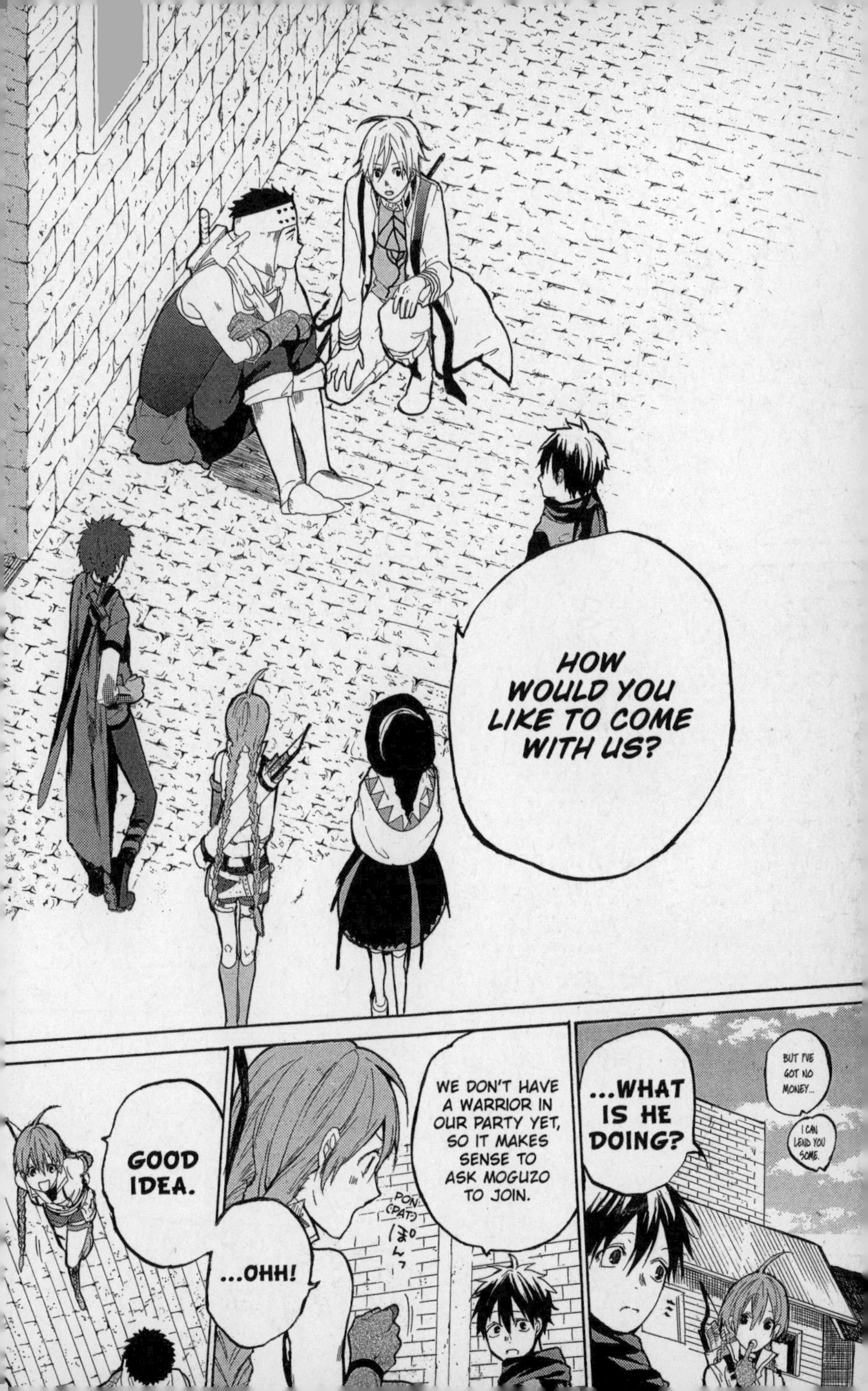
HOW WOULD YOU LIKE TO COME WITH US?
BUT I'VE GOT NO MONEY...
I CAN LEND YOU SOME.
...WHAT IS HE DOING?
WE DON'T HAVE A WARRIOR IN OUR PARTY YET, SO IT MAKES SENSE TO ASK MOGUZO TO JOIN.
PON (PAT)
ぽんっ
...OHH!
GOOD IDEA.

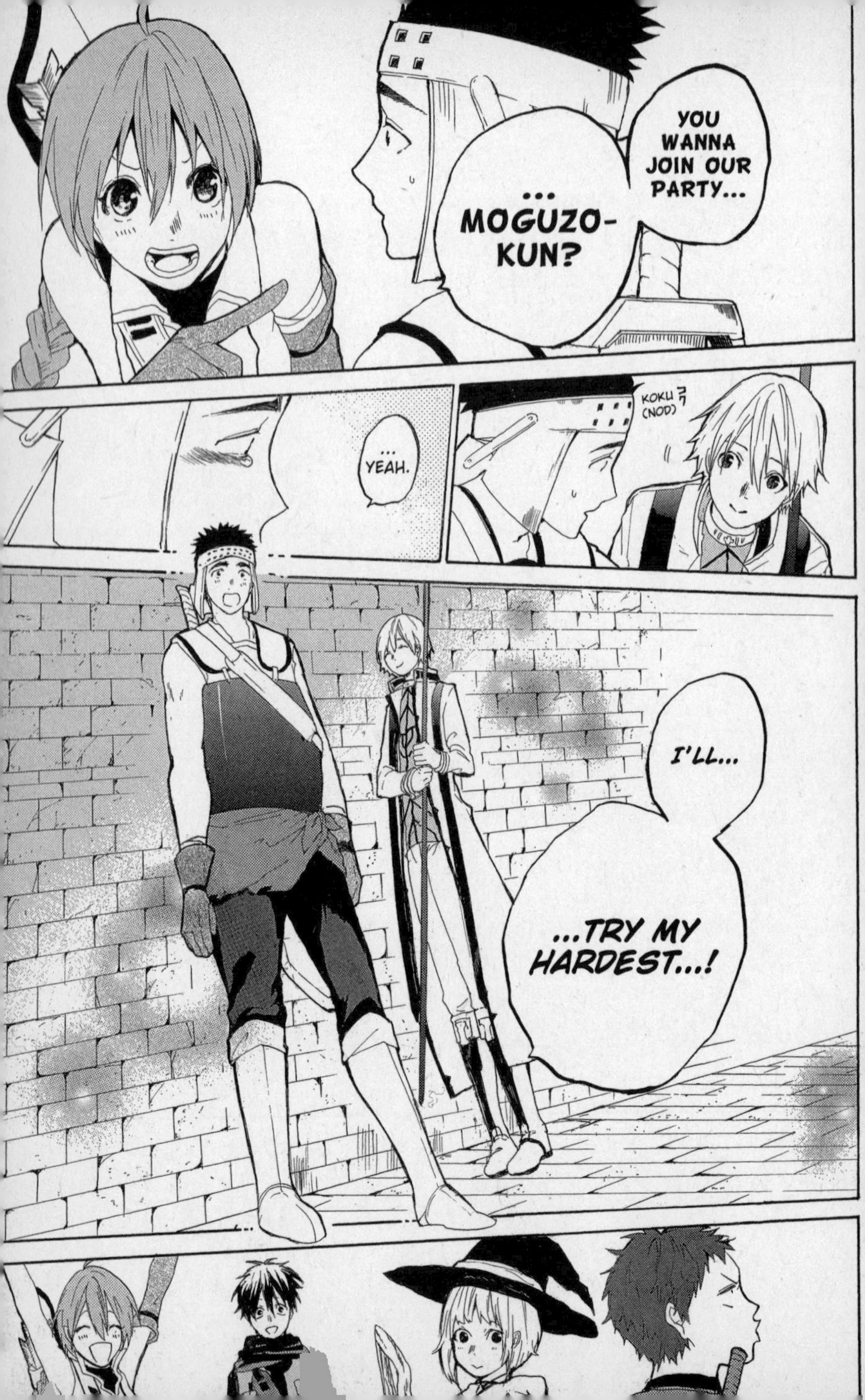
YOU WANNA JOIN OUR PARTY...
...MOGUZO-KUN?
KOKU (NOD)
...YEAH.
I'LL...
...TRY MY HARDEST...!

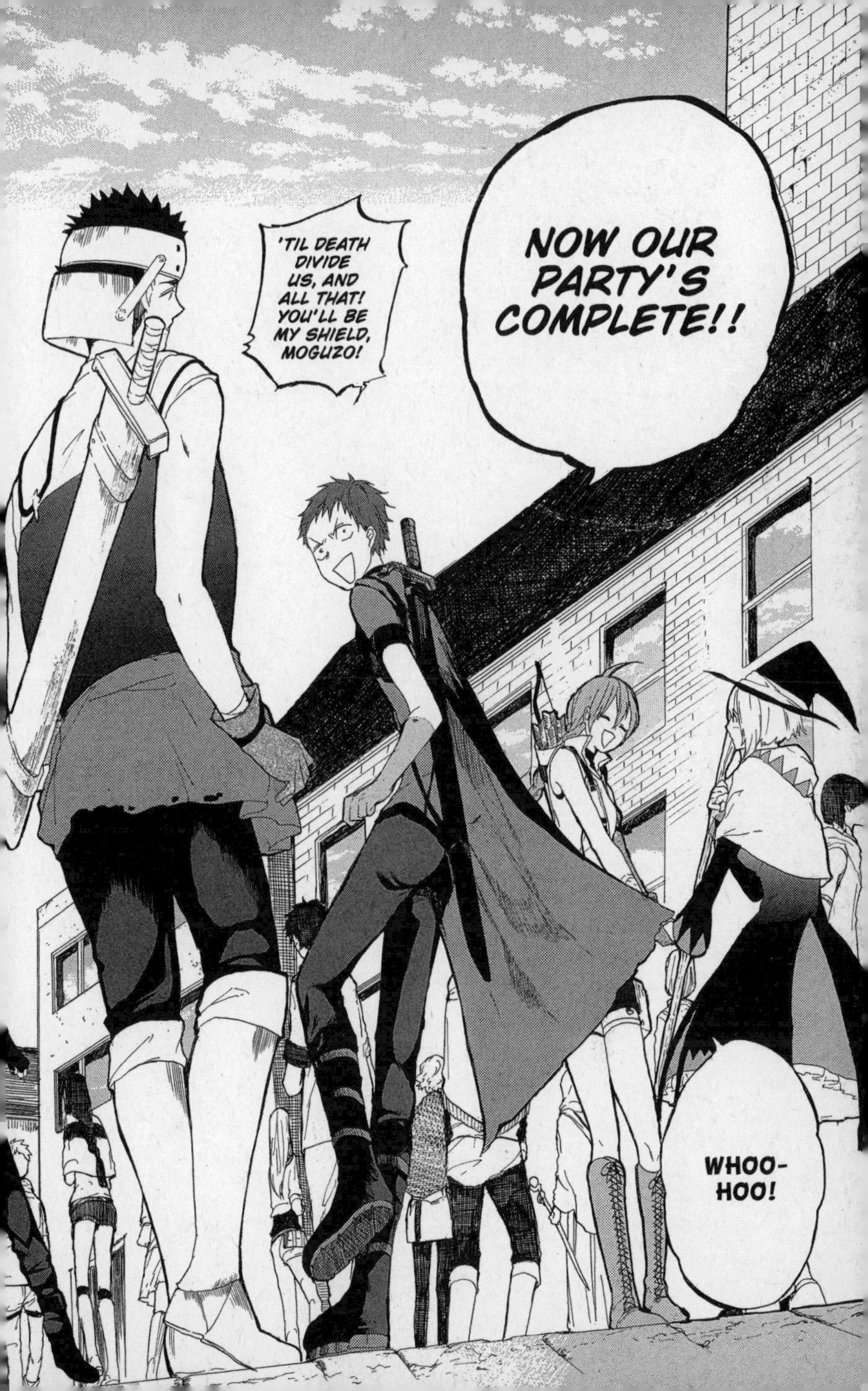
NOW OUR PARTY'S COMPLETE!!
'TIL DEATH DIVIDE US, AND ALL THAT! YOU'LL BE MY SHIELD, MOGUZO!
WHOO-HOO!

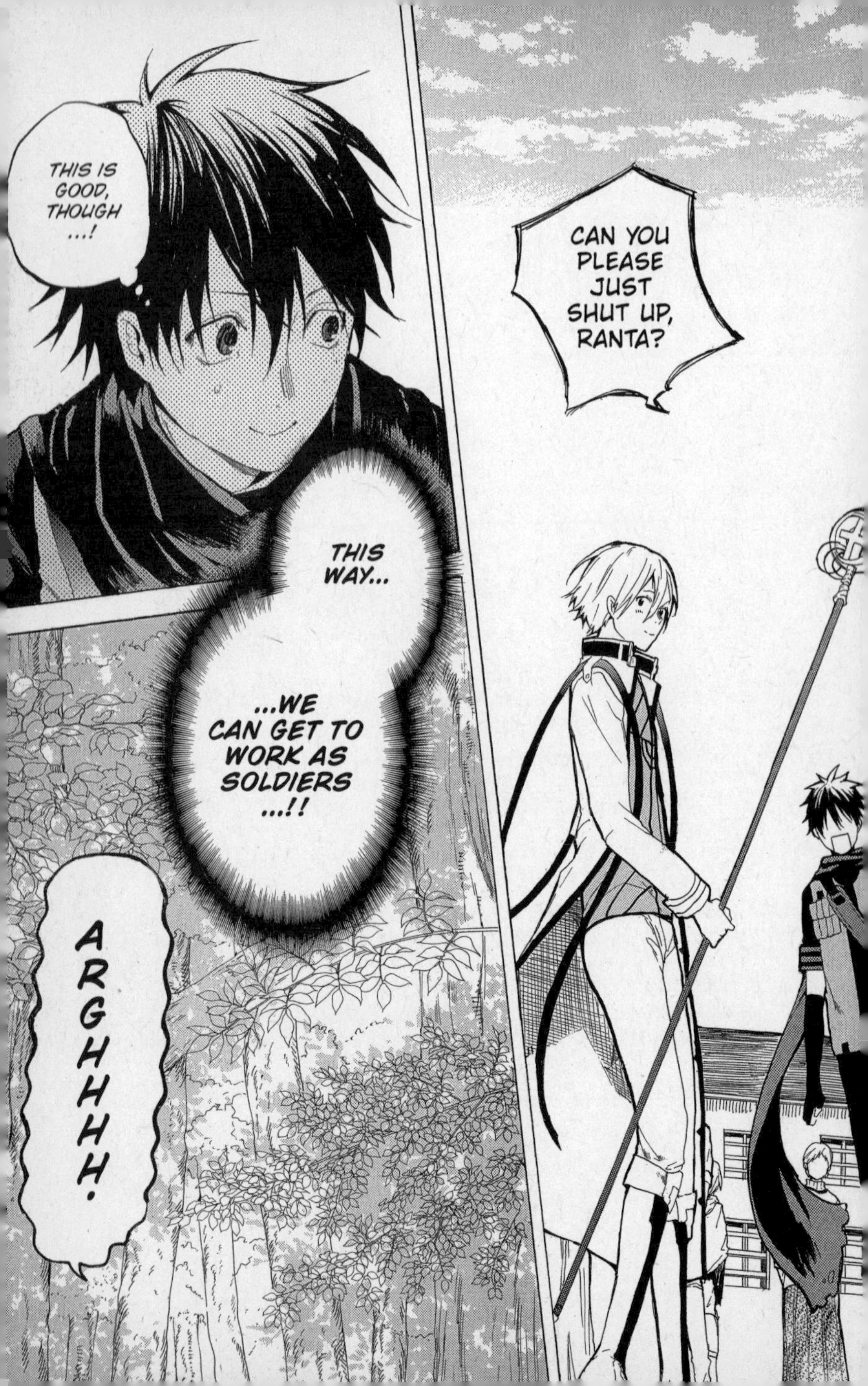
CAN YOU PLEASE JUST SHUT UP, RANTA?
THIS IS GOOD, THOUGH ...!
THIS WAY...
...WE CAN GET TO WORK AS SOLDIERS ...!!
ARGHHHH!

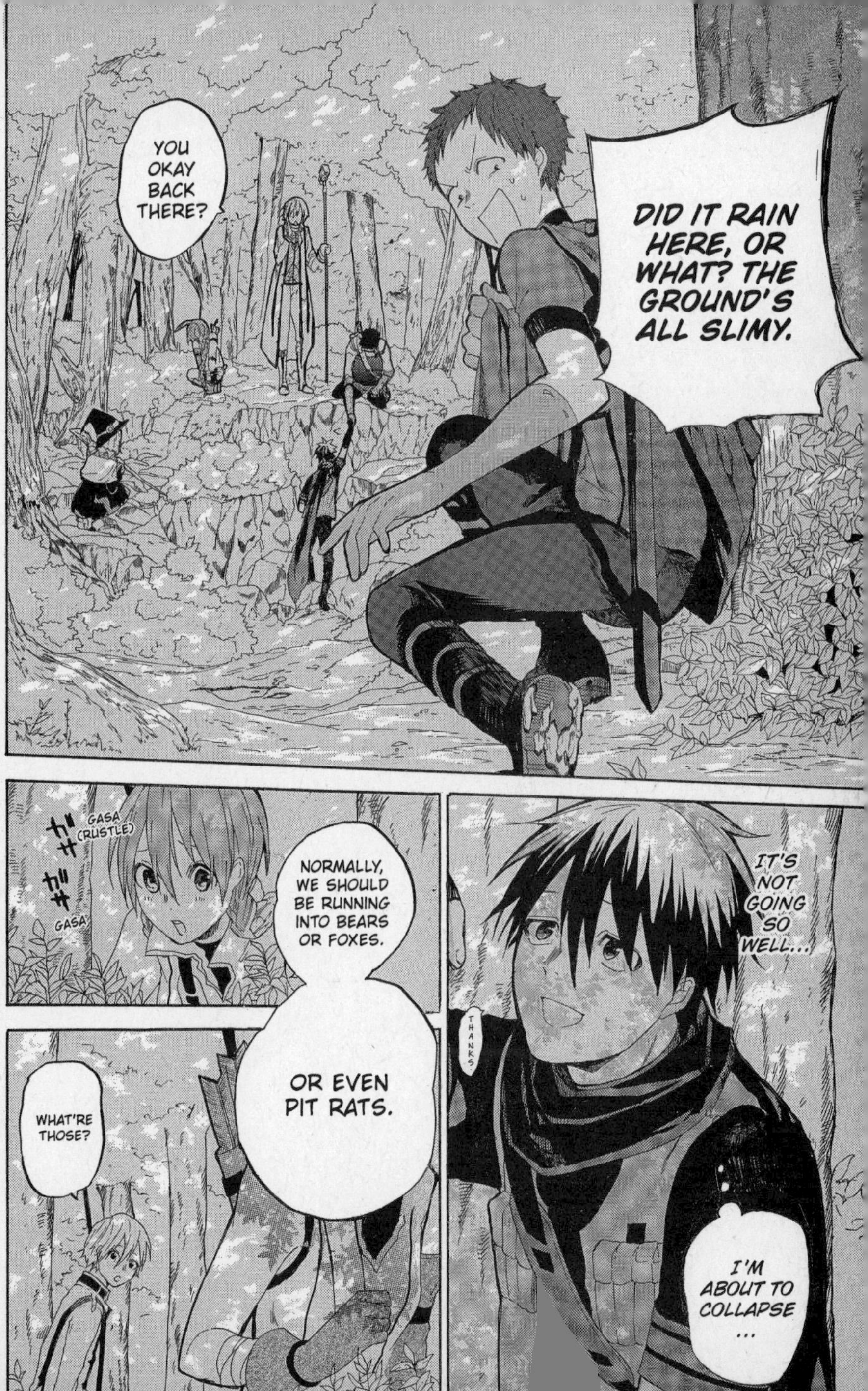
DID IT RAIN HERE, OR WHAT? THE GROUND'S ALL SLIMY.
YOU OKAY BACK THERE?
IT'S NOT GOING SO WELL...
THANKS.
I'M ABOUT TO COLLAPSE...
ガサ
GASA (RUSTLE)
ガサ
GASA
NORMALLY, WE SHOULD BE RUNNING INTO BEARS OR FOXES.
OR EVEN PIT RATS.
WHAT'RE THOSE?

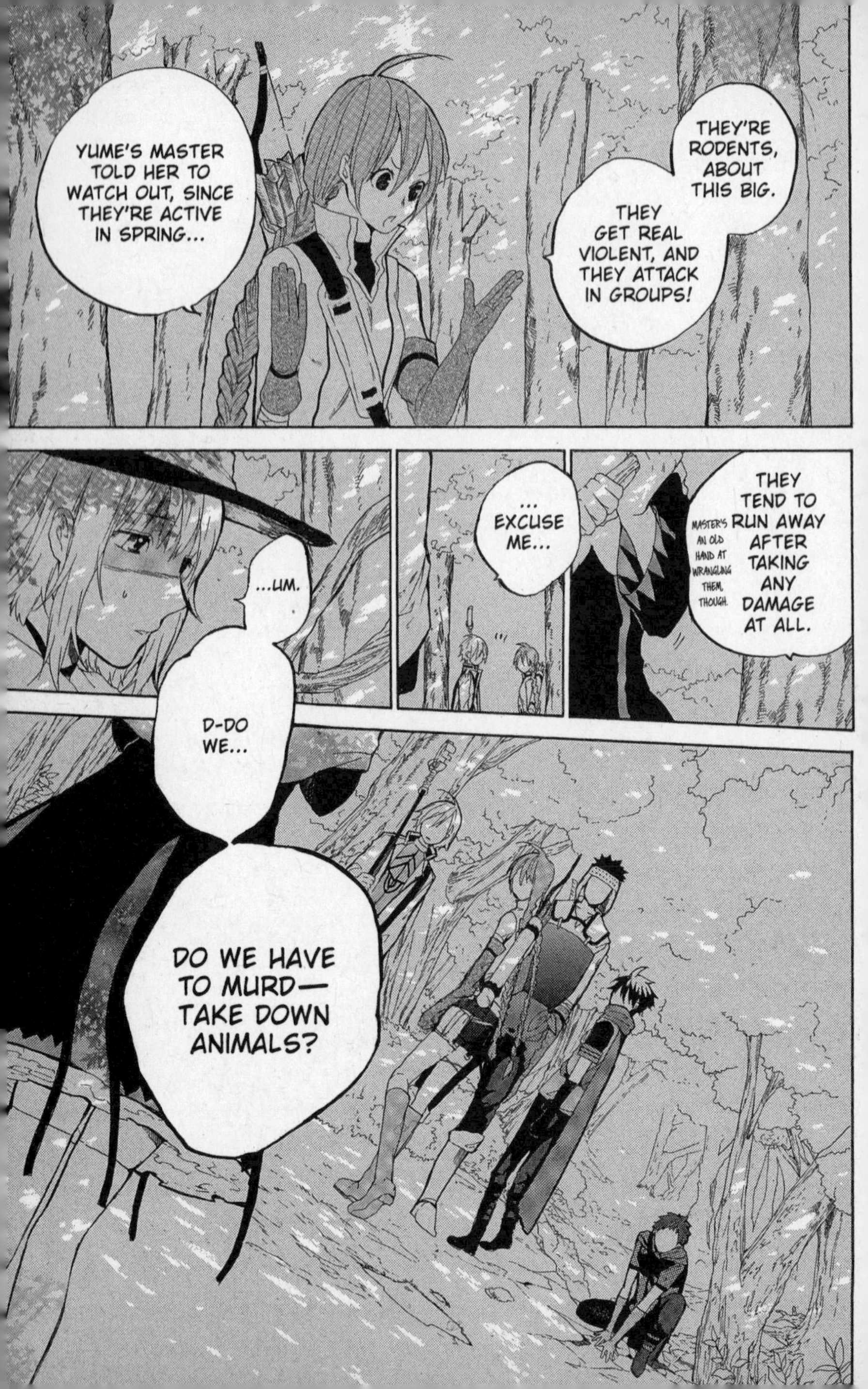
THEY'RE RODENTS, ABOUT THIS BIG.
THEY GET REAL VIOLENT, AND THEY ATTACK IN GROUPS!
YUME'S MASTER TOLD HER TO WATCH OUT, SINCE THEY'RE ACTIVE IN SPRING...
THEY TEND TO RUN AWAY AFTER TAKING ANY DAMAGE AT ALL.
MASTER'S AN OLD HAND AT WRANGLING THEM, THOUGH.
... EXCUSE ME...
...UM.
D-DO WE...
DO WE HAVE TO MURD— TAKE DOWN ANIMALS?

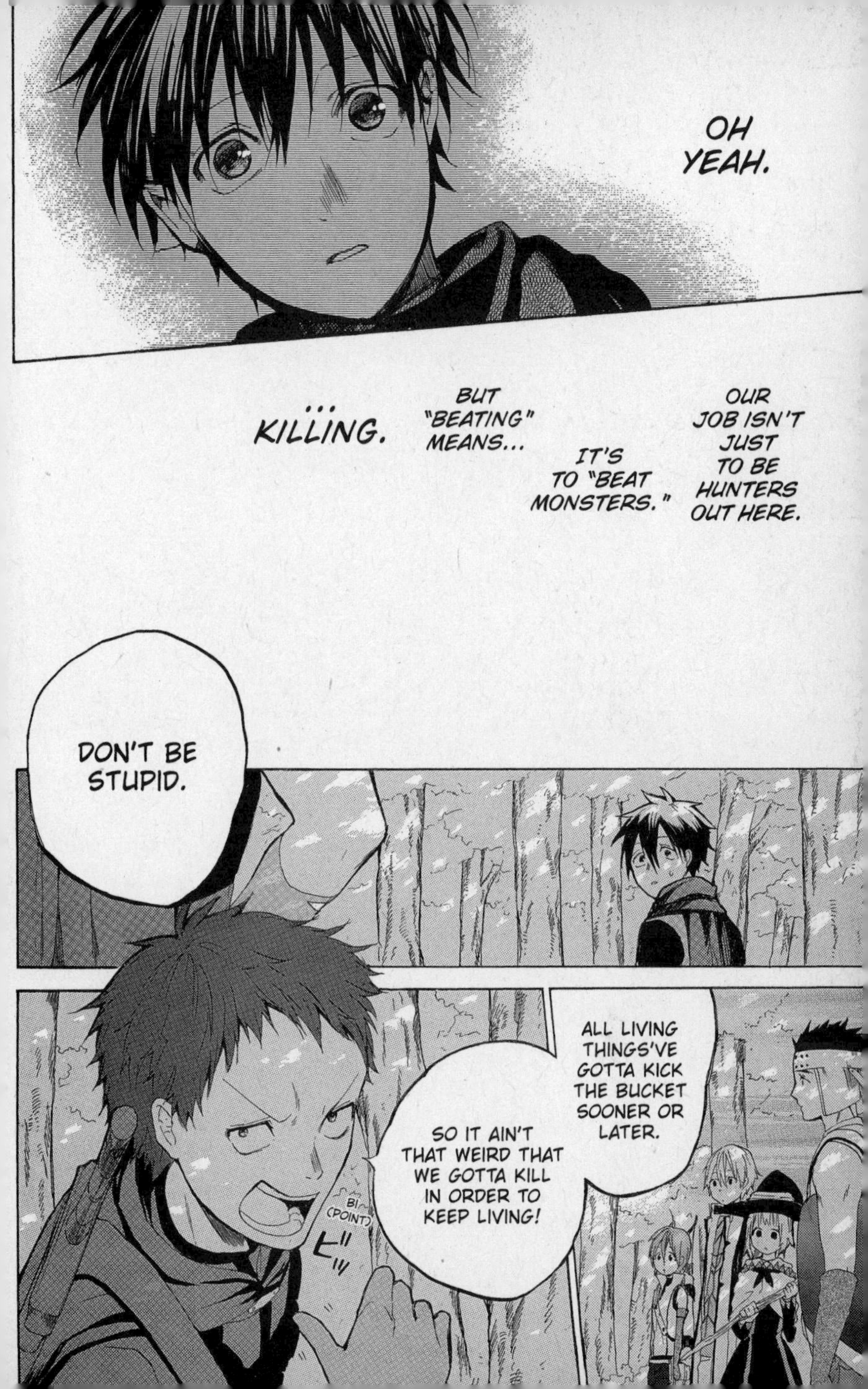
OH YEAH.
OUR JOB ISN'T JUST TO BE HUNTERS OUT HERE.
IT'S TO "BEAT MONSTERS."
BUT "BEATING" MEANS...
...KILLING.
DON'T BE STUPID.
ALL LIVING THINGS'VE GOTTA KICK THE BUCKET SOONER OR LATER.
SO IT AIN'T THAT WEIRD THAT WE GOTTA KILL IN ORDER TO KEEP LIVING!
BI (POINT)

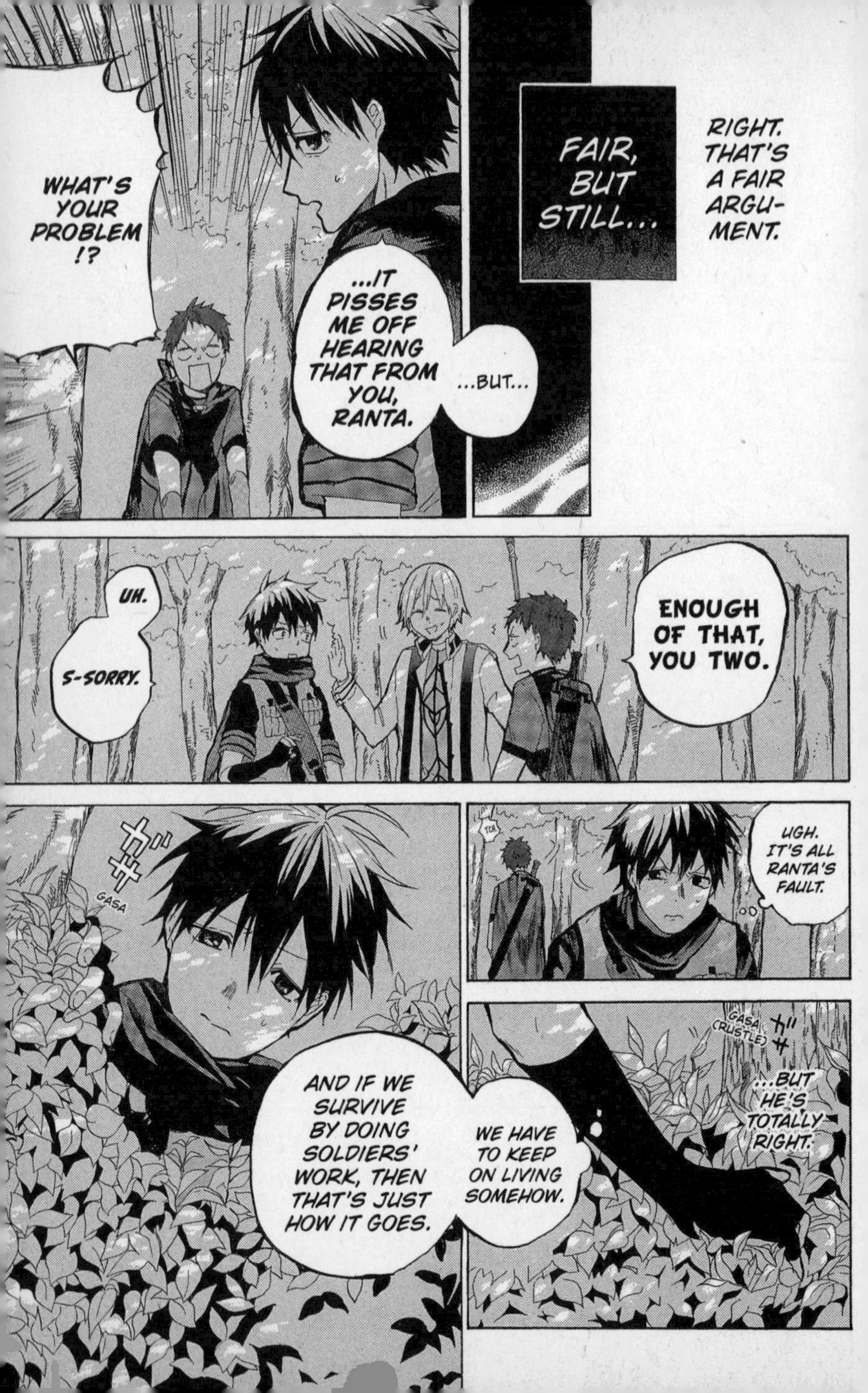
RIGHT. THAT'S A FAIR ARGUMENT.
FAIR, BUT STILL...
...BUT...
...IT PISSES ME OFF HEARING THAT FROM YOU, RANTA.
WHAT'S YOUR PROBLEM!?
ENOUGH OF THAT, YOU TWO.
UH.
S-SORRY.
TCH
UGH. IT'S ALL RANTA'S FAULT.
GASA (RUSTLE)
...BUT HE'S TOTALLY RIGHT.
WE HAVE TO KEEP ON LIVING SOMEHOW.
AND IF WE SURVIVE BY DOING SOLDIERS' WORK, THEN THAT'S JUST HOW IT GOES.
GASA

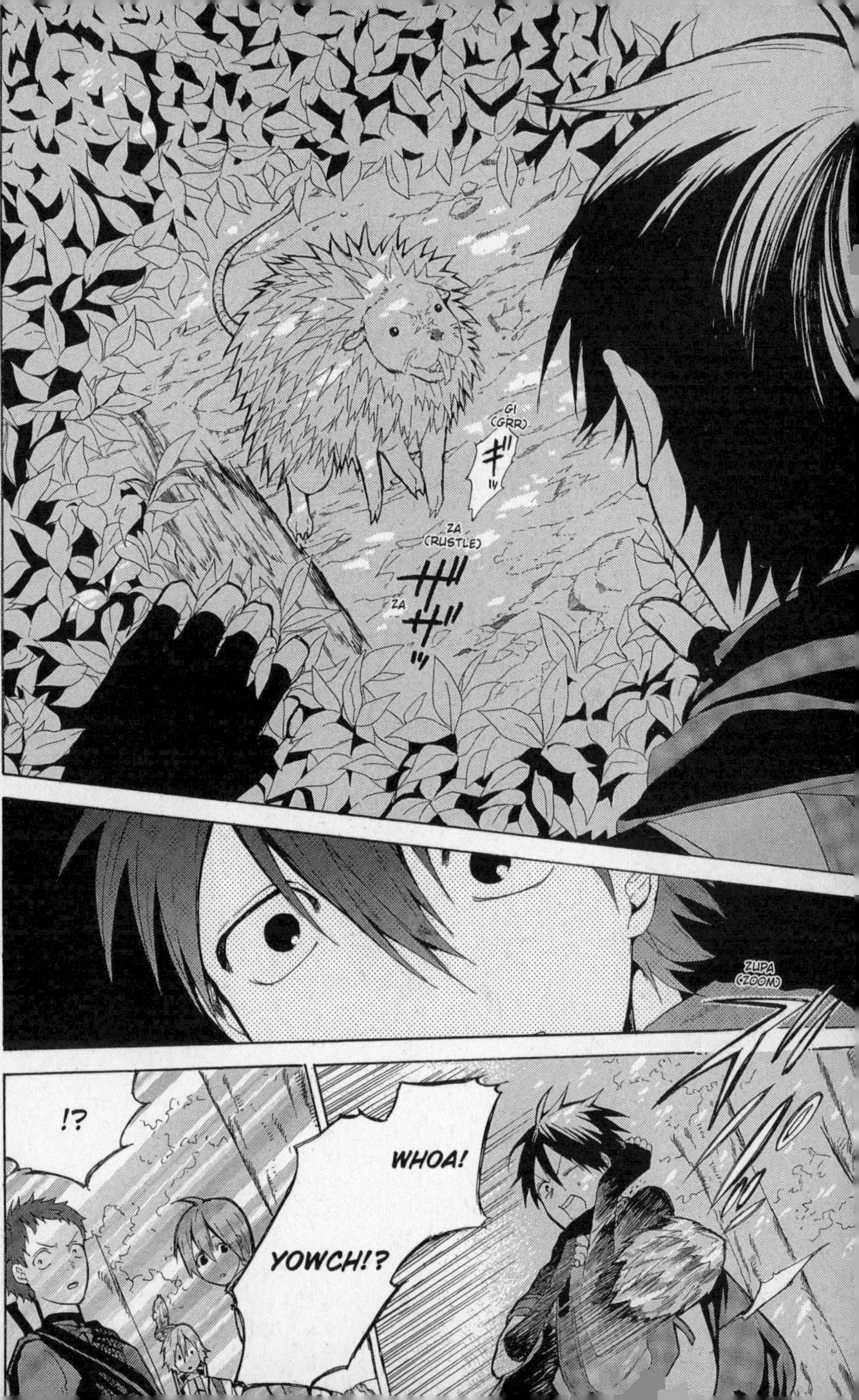
GI
(GRR)
ギッ
ZA
(RUSTLE)
ZA
ザザッ
ZUPA
(ZOOM)
WHOA!
YOWCH!?
!?

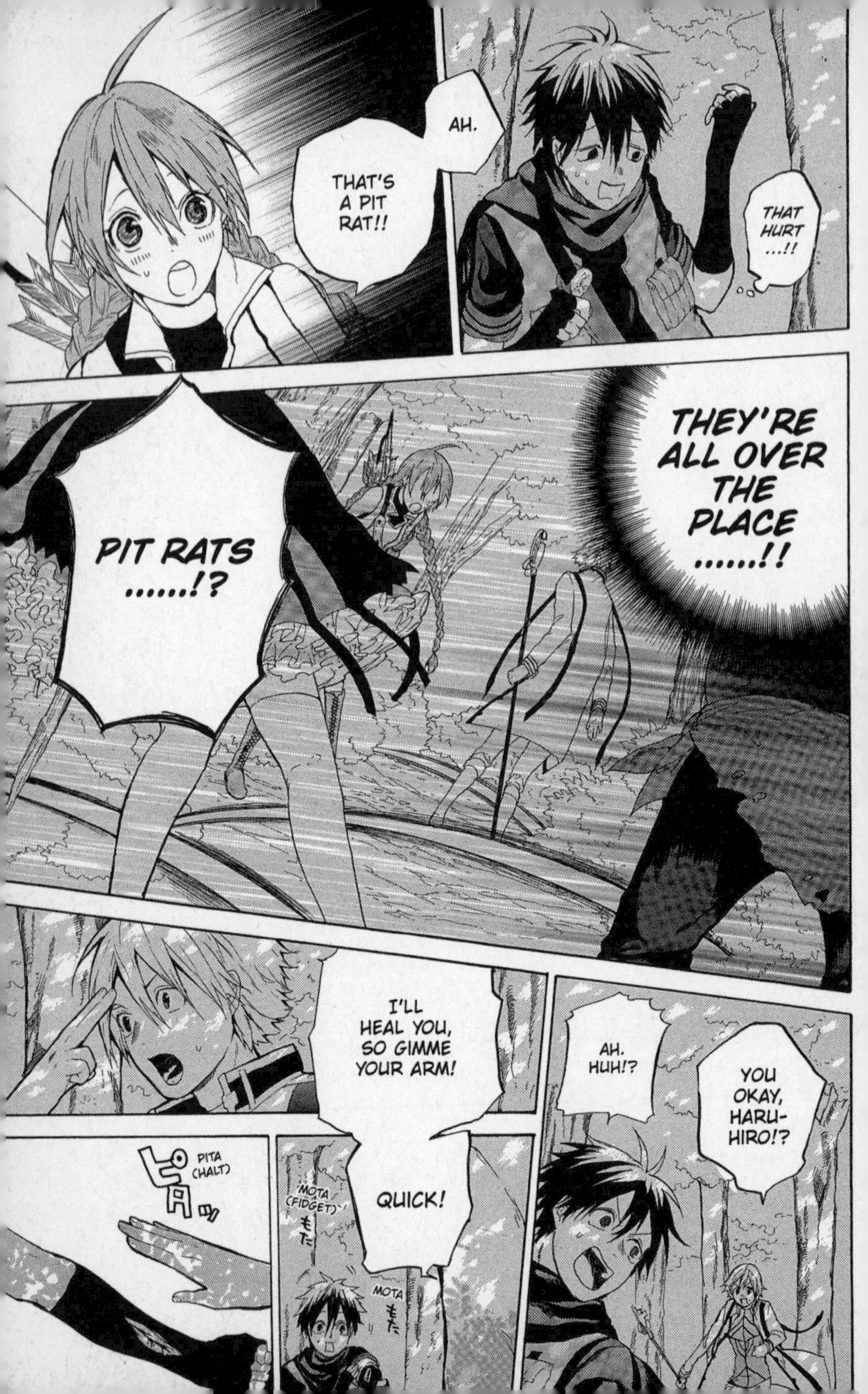
THAT HURT ...!!
AH.
THAT'S A PIT RAT!!
THEY'RE ALL OVER THE PLACE ......!!
PIT RATS ......!?
YOU OKAY, HARU-HIRO!?
AH. HUH!?
I'LL HEAL YOU, SO GIMME YOUR ARM!
QUICK!
MOTA (FIDGET)
MOTA
PITA (HALT)

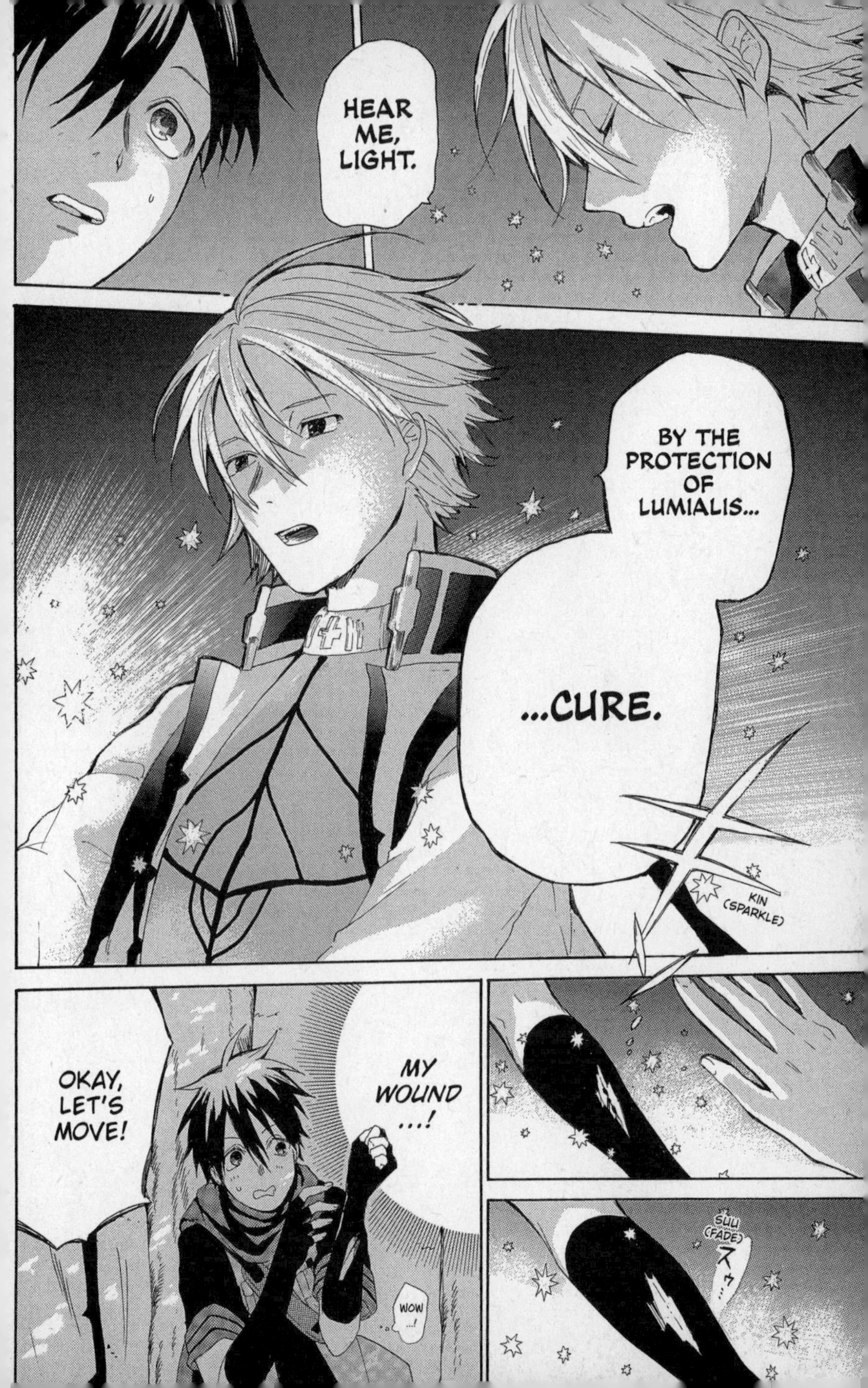
HEAR ME, LIGHT.
BY THE PROTECTION OF LUMIALIS...
...CURE.
KIN (SPARKLE)
SUU (FADE)
スゥ…
MY WOUND ...!
OKAY, LET'S MOVE!
WOW ...!

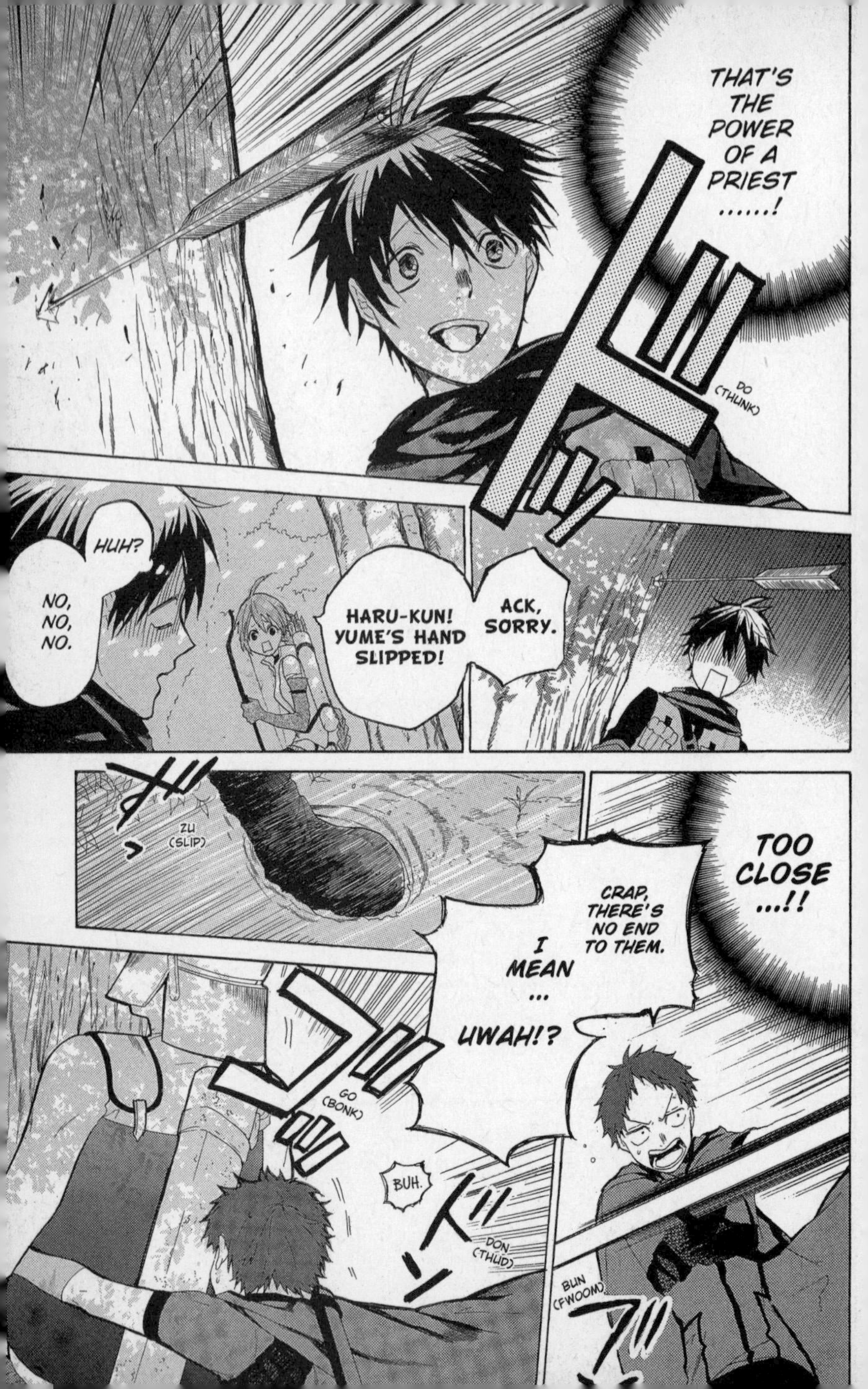
THAT'S THE POWER OF A PRIEST ......!
DO (THUNK)
ACK, SORRY.
HARU-KUN! YUME'S HAND SLIPPED!
HUH?
NO, NO, NO.
TOO CLOSE ...!!
CRAP, THERE'S NO END TO THEM.
ZU (SLIP)
I MEAN ...
UWAH!?
GO (BONK)
BUH.
DON (THUD)
BUN (FWOOM)

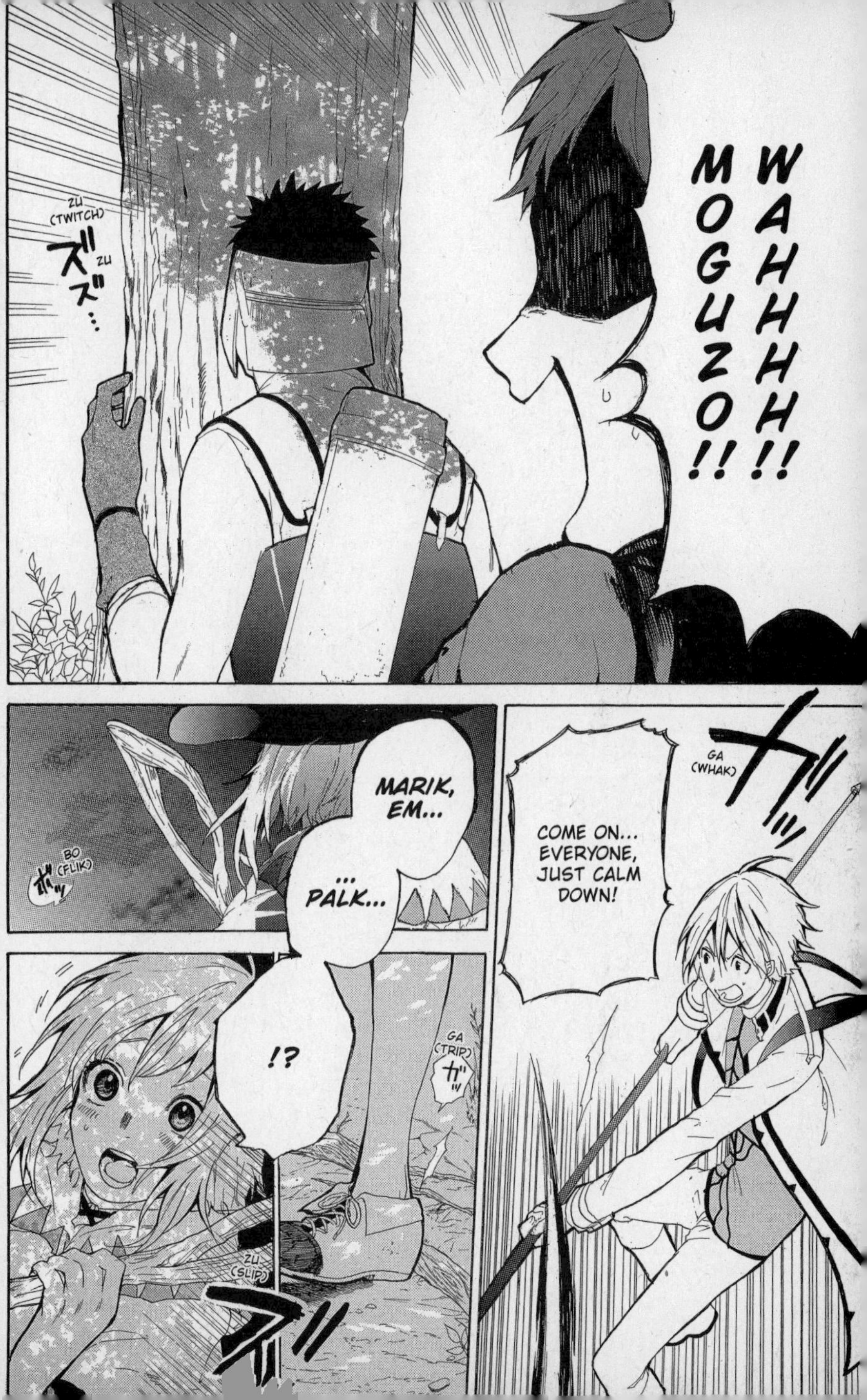
WAHHHHH!!
MOGUZO!!
ZU (TWITCH)
ズズ…
ZU
GA (WHAK)
ガッ
COME ON... EVERYONE, JUST CALM DOWN!
MARIK, EM...
... PALK...
BO (FLIK)
ボッ
!?
GA (TRIP)
ガッ
ZU (SLIP)
ズッ

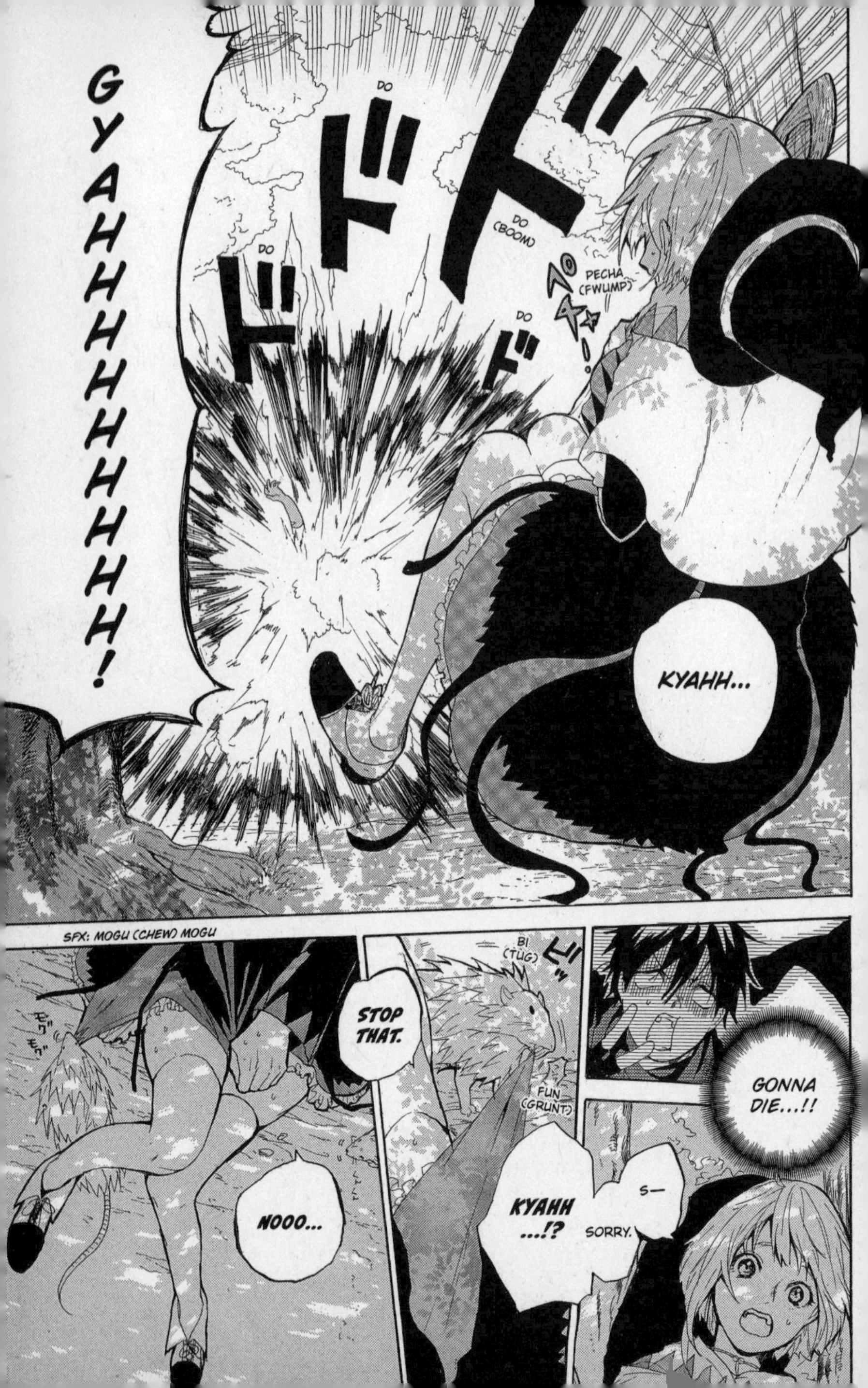
GYAHHHHHHHHH!
DO
DO (BOOM)
DO
DO
PECHA (FWUMP)
KYAHH...
SFX: MOGU (CHEW) MOGU
GONNA DIE...!!
S— SORRY.
BI (TUG)
STOP THAT.
FUN (GRUNT)
KYAHH ...!?
NOOO...

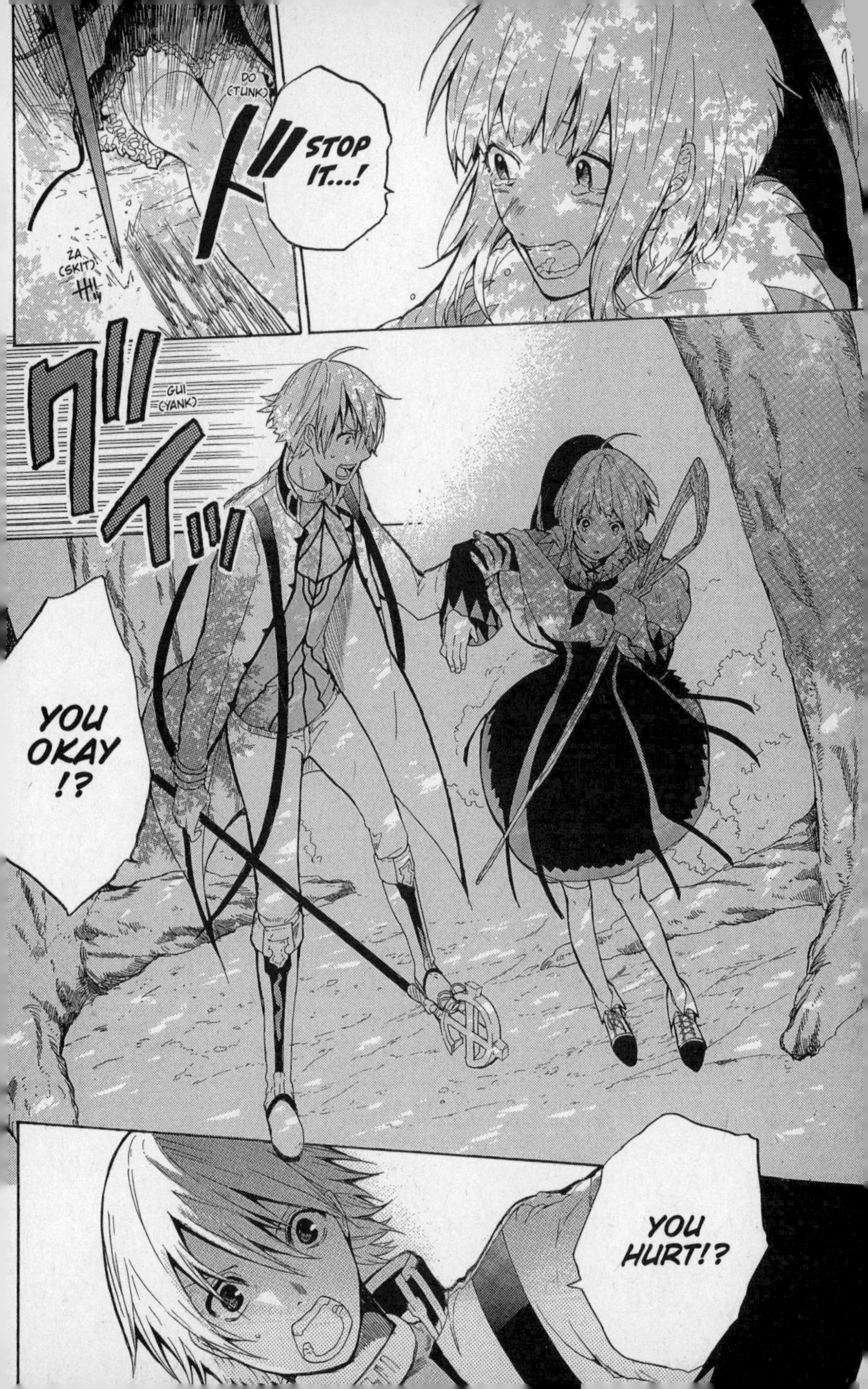
DO (TUNK)
STOP IT...!
ZA (SKIT)
GUI (YANK)
YOU OKAY !?
YOU HURT!?

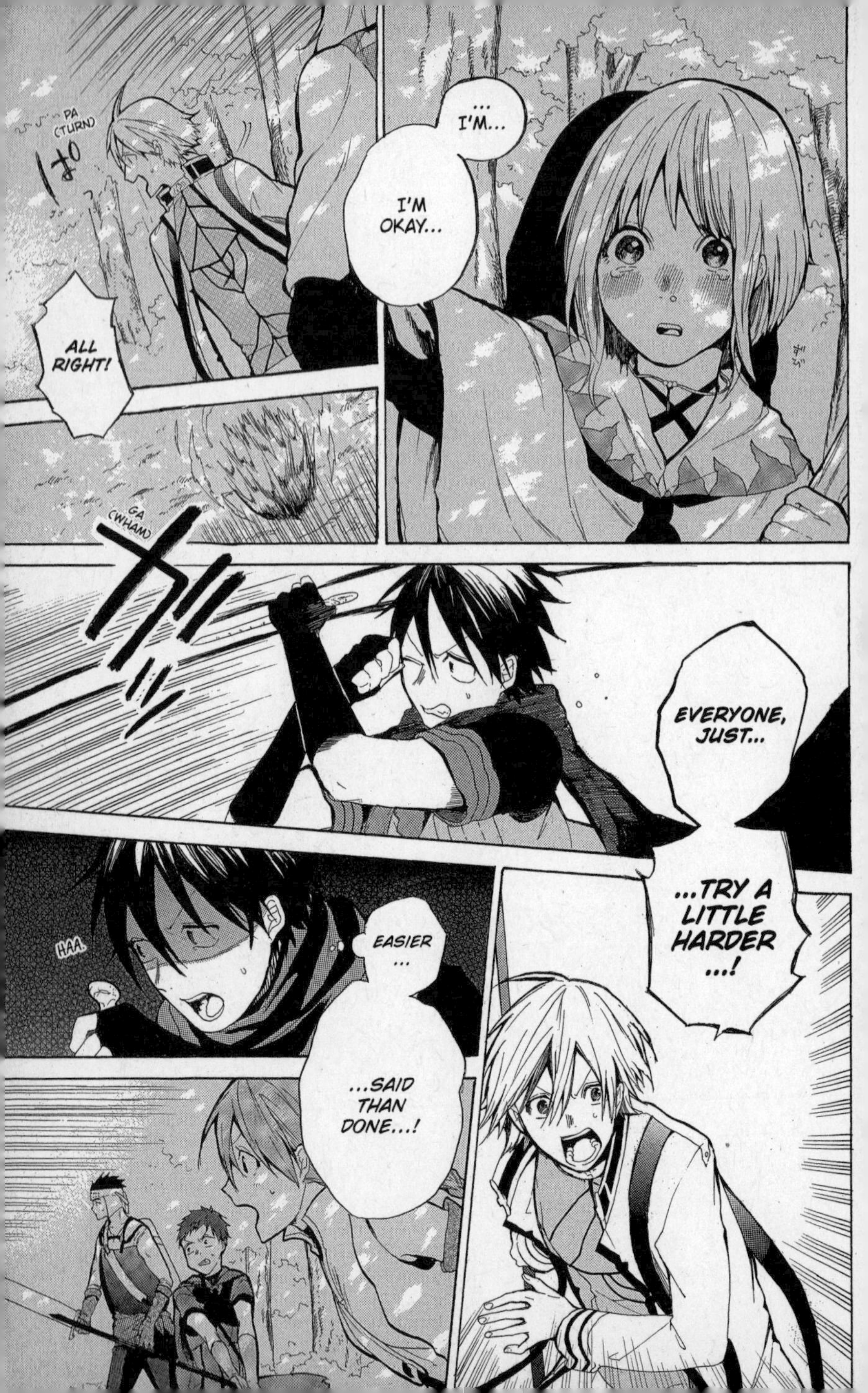
... I'M...
I'M OKAY...
PA (TURN)
ALL RIGHT!
GA (WHAM)
EVERYONE, JUST...
...TRY A LITTLE HARDER ...!
HAA.
EASIER ...
...SAID THAN DONE...!

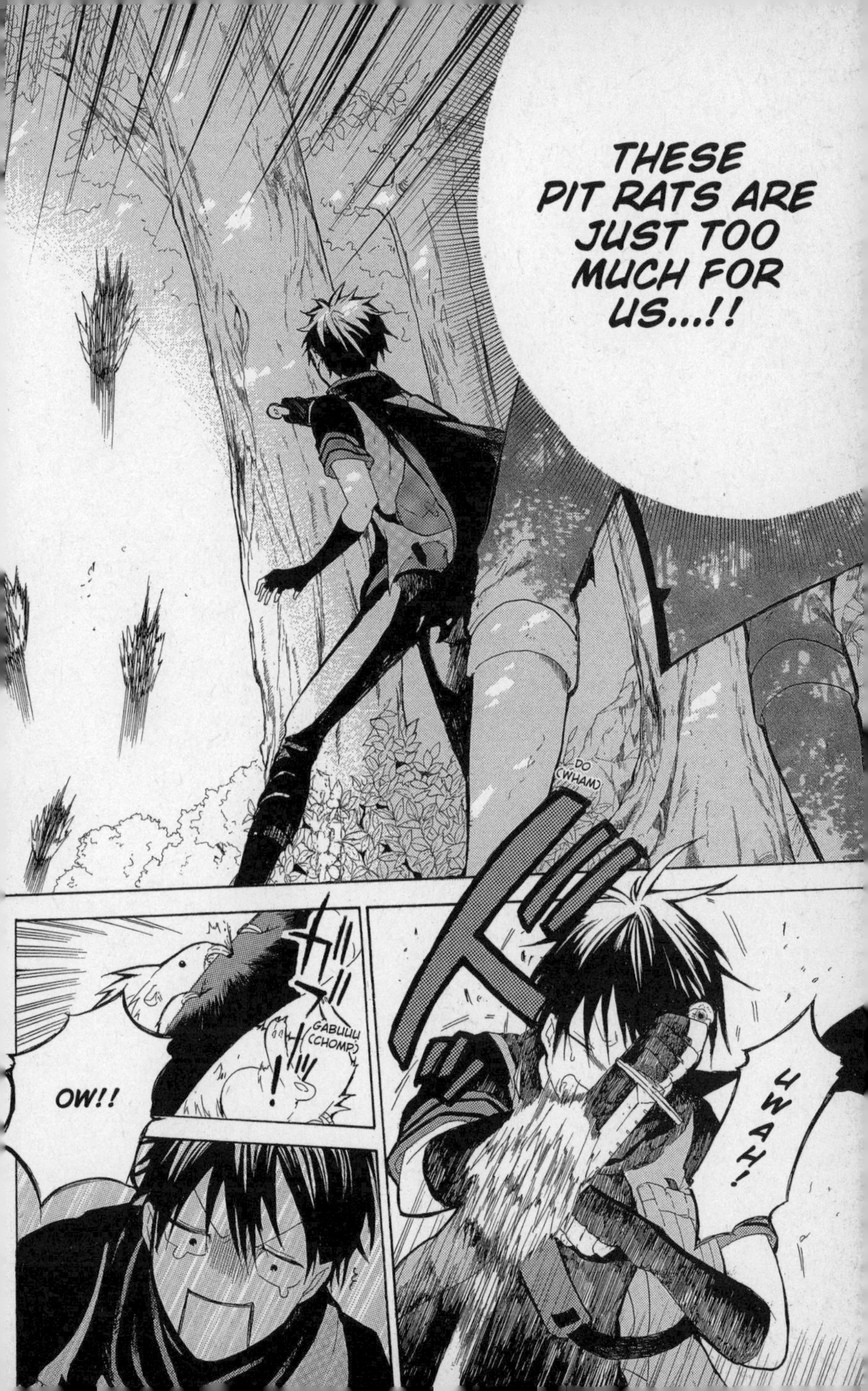
THESE PIT RATS ARE JUST TOO MUCH FOR US...!!
DO (WHAM)
UWAH!
GABUUU (CHOMP)
OW!!

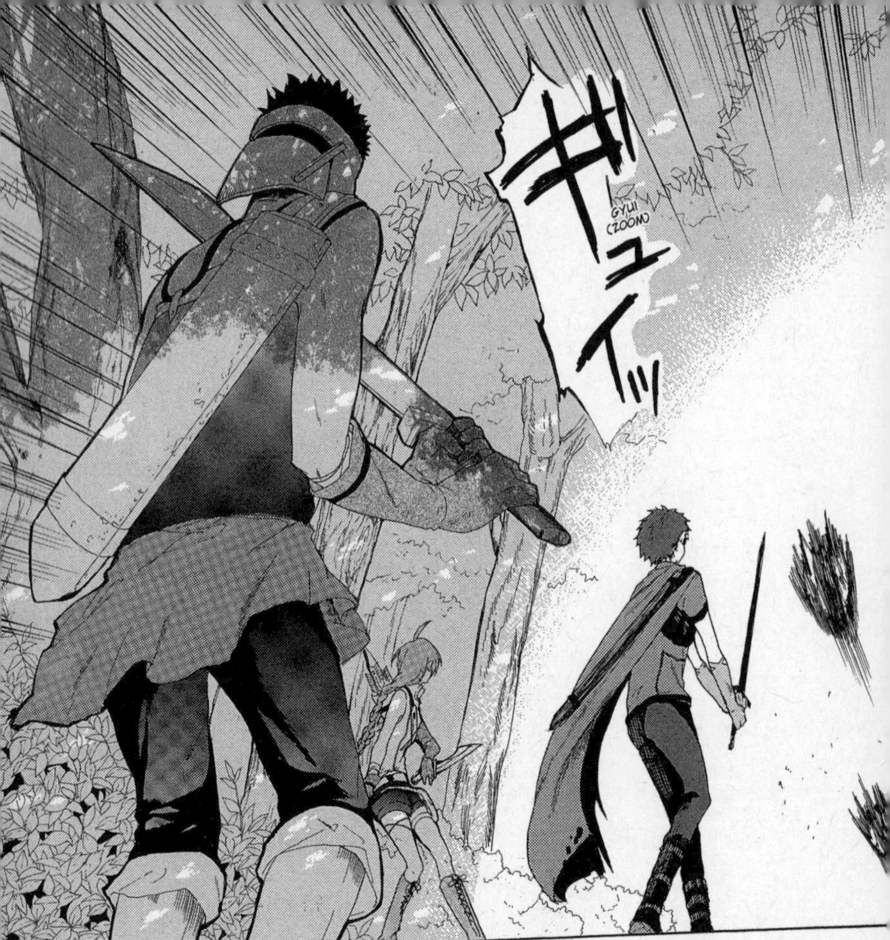
GYUI
(ZOOM)

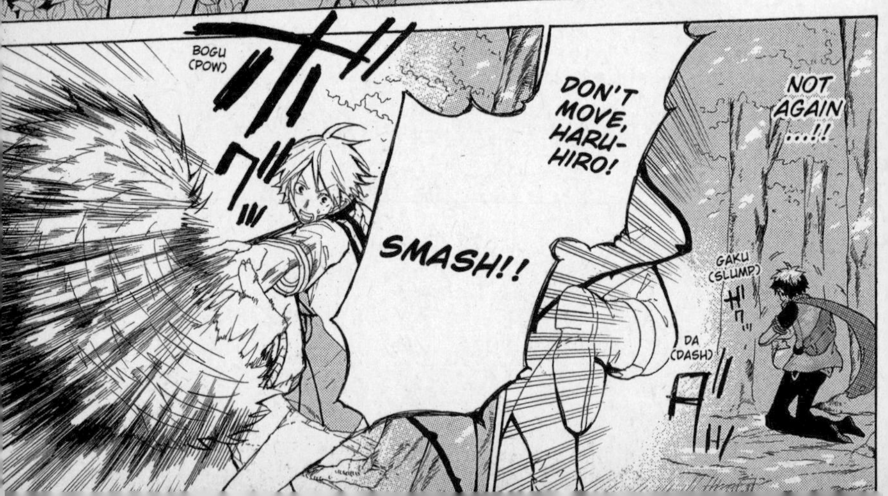
NOT AGAIN ...!!
DON'T MOVE, HARU-HIRO!
BOGU
(POW)
SMASH!!
GAKU
(SLUMP)
DA
(DASH)

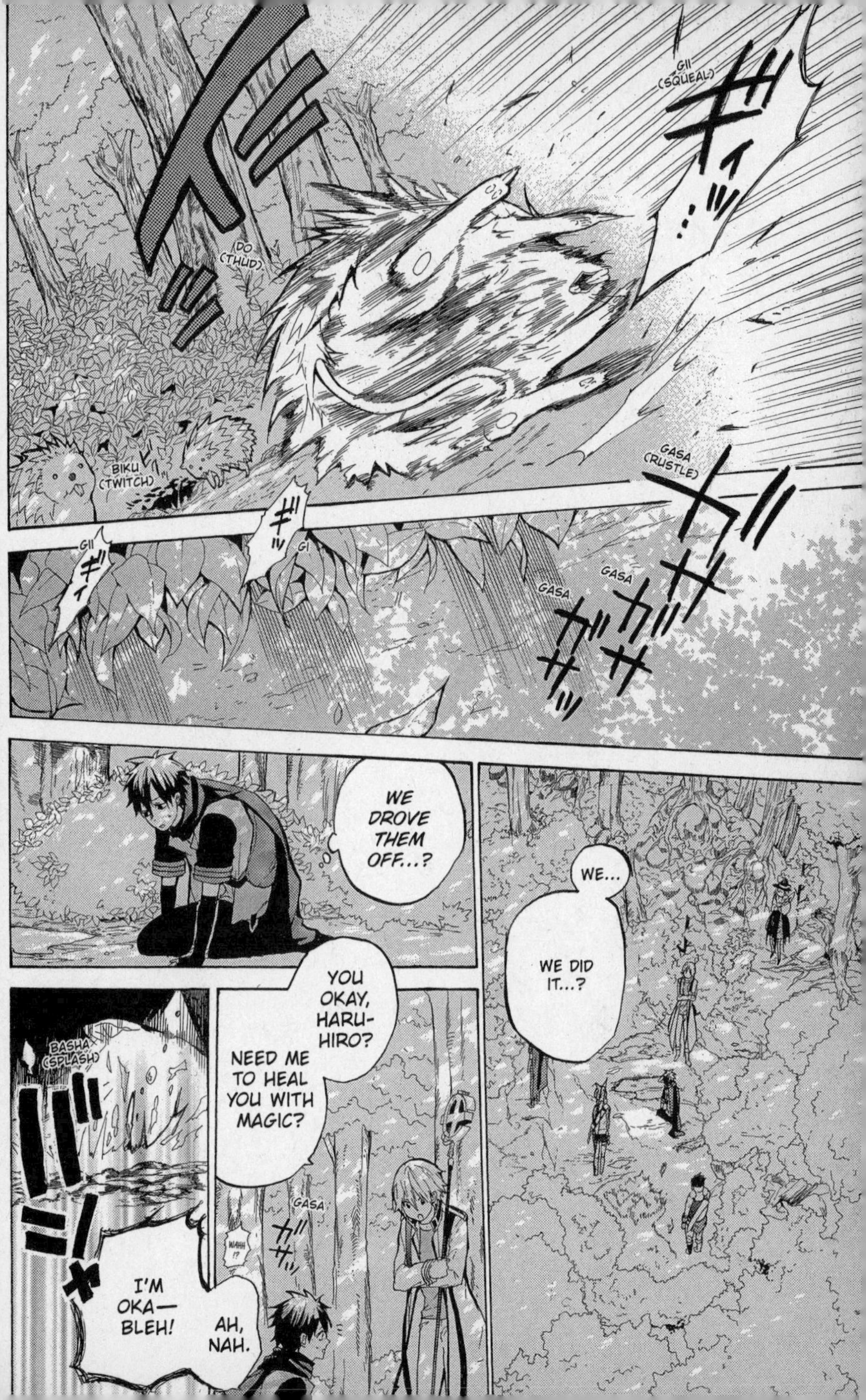

GII (SQUEAL)
DO (THUD)
GASA (RUSTLE)
BIKU (TWITCH)
GASA
GASA
GI
GII
WE...
WE DID IT...?
WE DROVE THEM OFF...?
YOU OKAY, HARUHIRO?
NEED ME TO HEAL YOU WITH MAGIC?
GASA
WAHH!?
AH, NAH.
I'M OKA— BLEH!
BASHA (SPLASH)

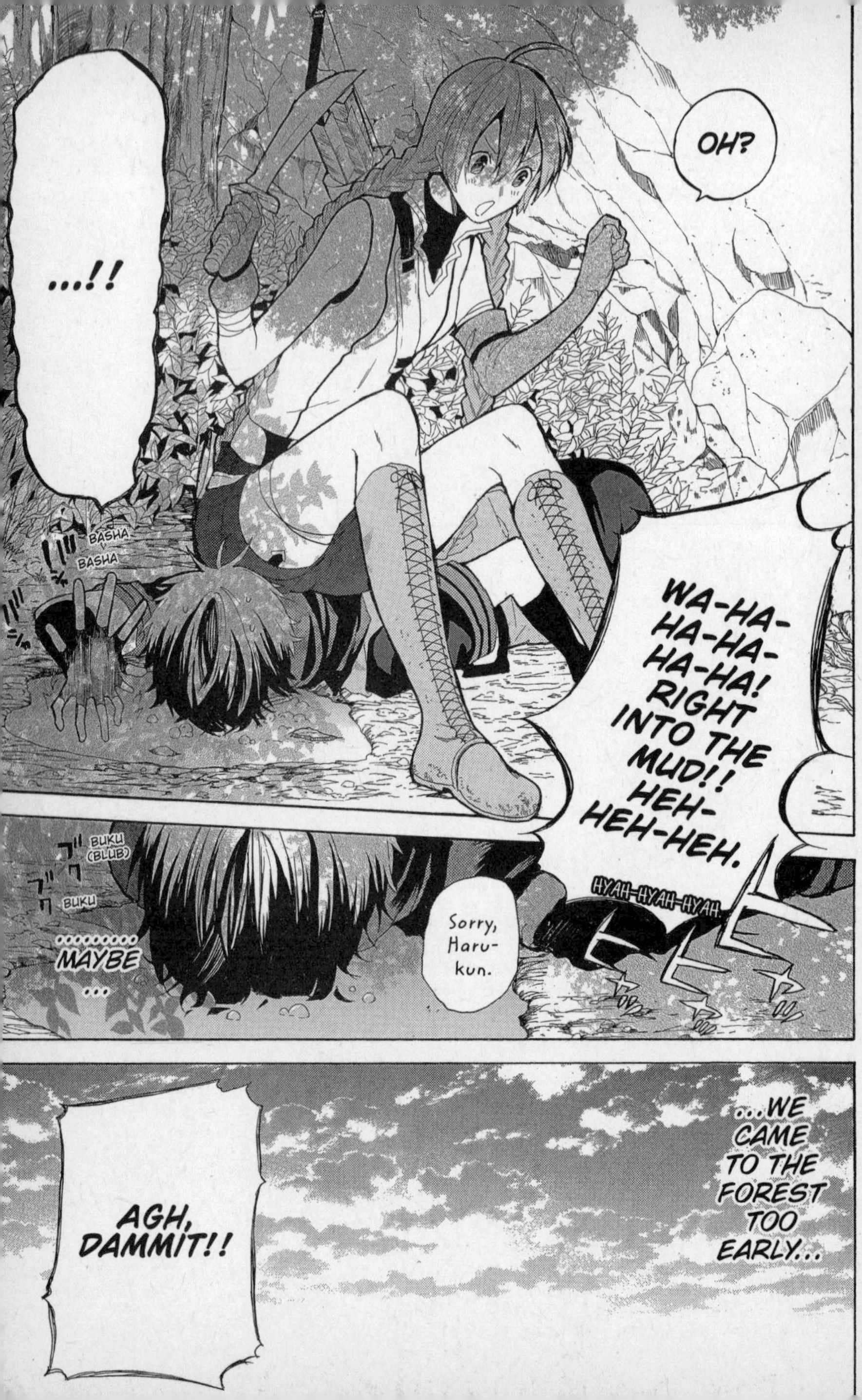
OH?
...!!
WA-HA-HA-HA-HA-HA! RIGHT INTO THE MUD!! HEH-HEH-HEH.
BASHA BASHA
HYAH-HYAH-HYAH.
Sorry, Haru-kun.
BUKU (BLUB) BUKU
.........MAYBE...
...WE CAME TO THE FOREST TOO EARLY...
AGH, DAMMIT!!

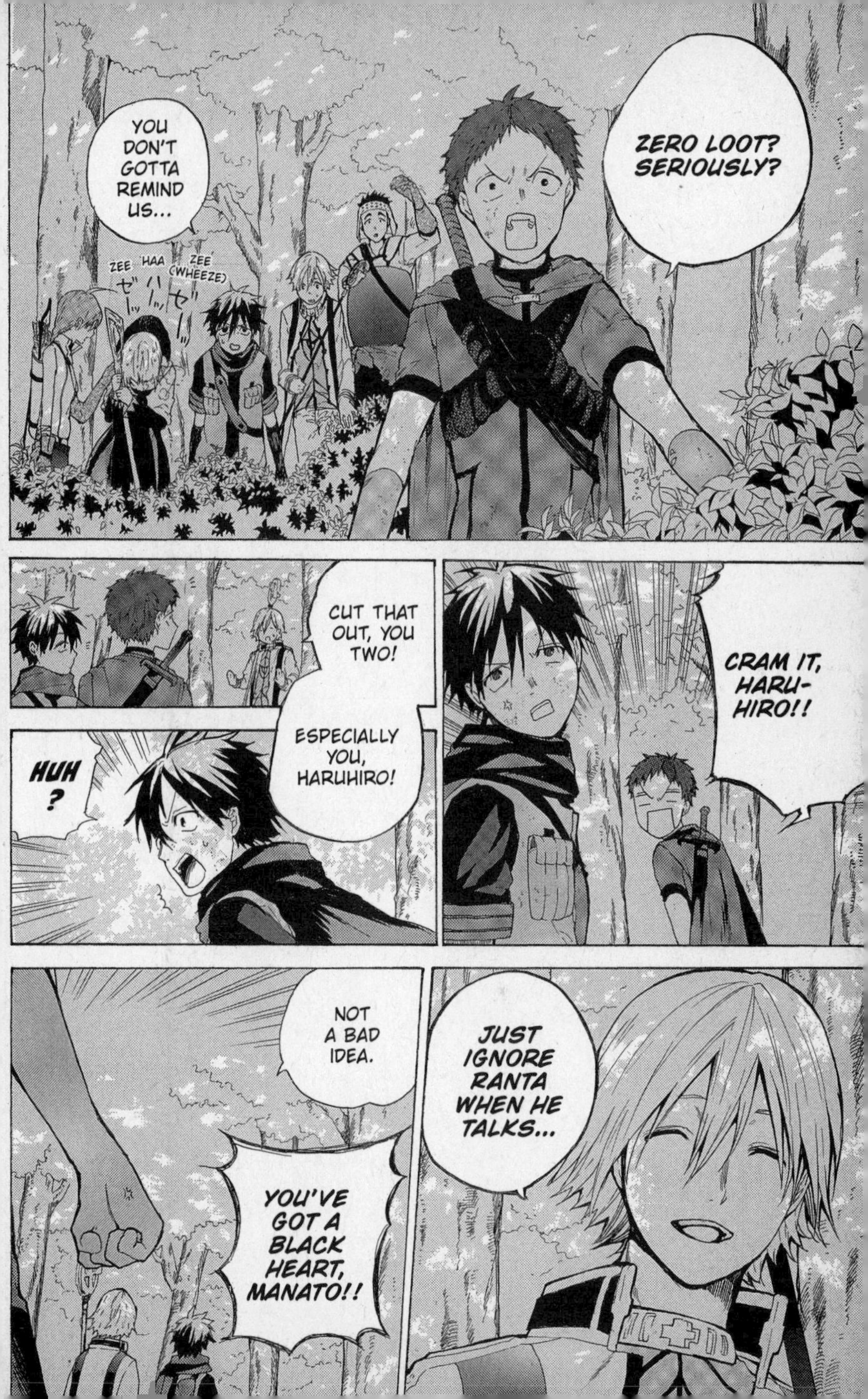
ZERO LOOT? SERIOUSLY?
YOU DON'T GOTTA REMIND US...
ZEE HAA ZEE (WHEEZE)
CRAM IT, HARU-HIRO!!
CUT THAT OUT, YOU TWO!
ESPECIALLY YOU, HARUHIRO!
HUH?
JUST IGNORE RANTA WHEN HE TALKS...
NOT A BAD IDEA.
YOU'VE GOT A BLACK HEART, MANATO!!

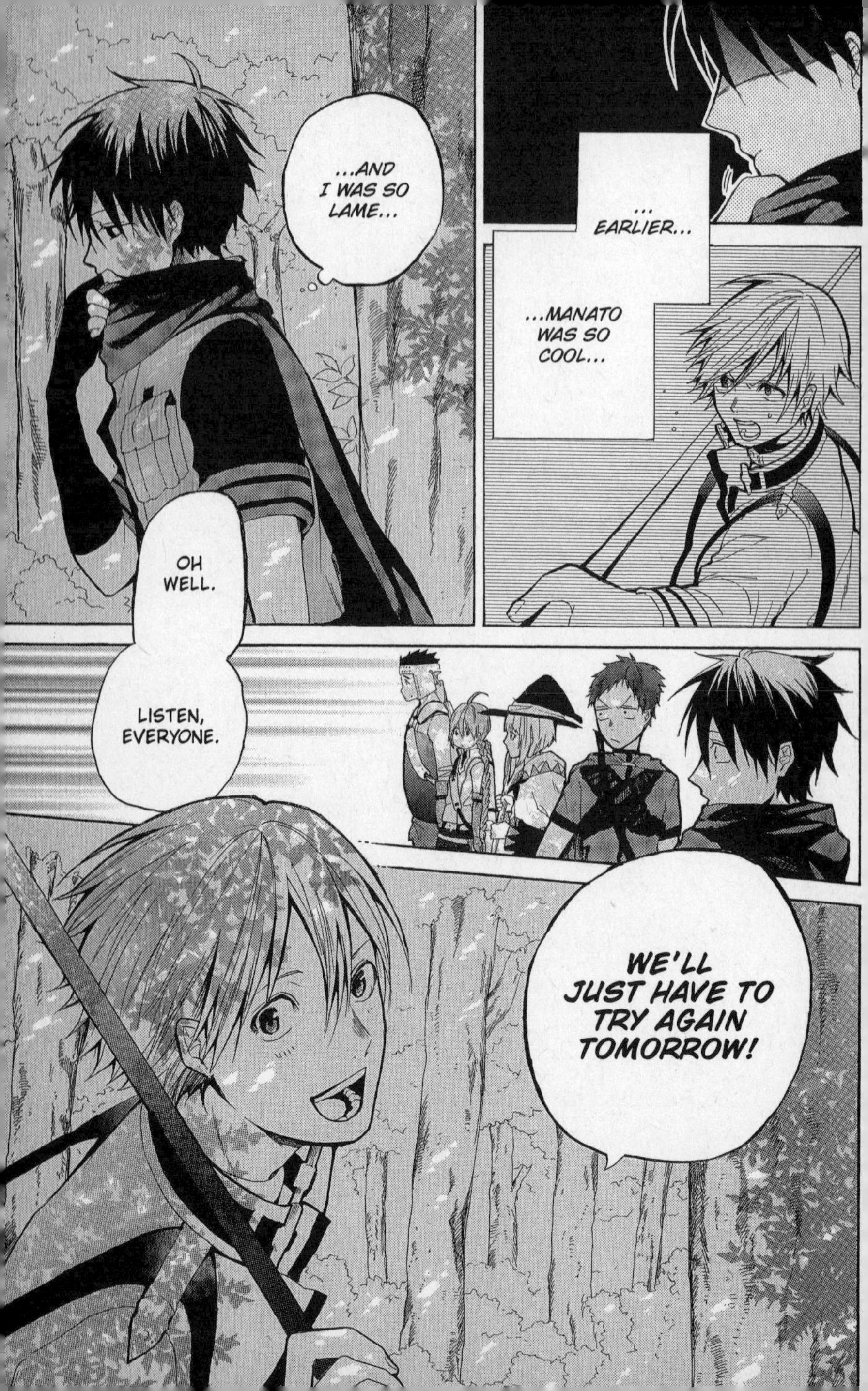
...EARLIER...
...MANATO WAS SO COOL...
...AND I WAS SO LAME...
OH WELL.
LISTEN, EVERYONE.
WE'LL JUST HAVE TO TRY AGAIN TOMORROW!

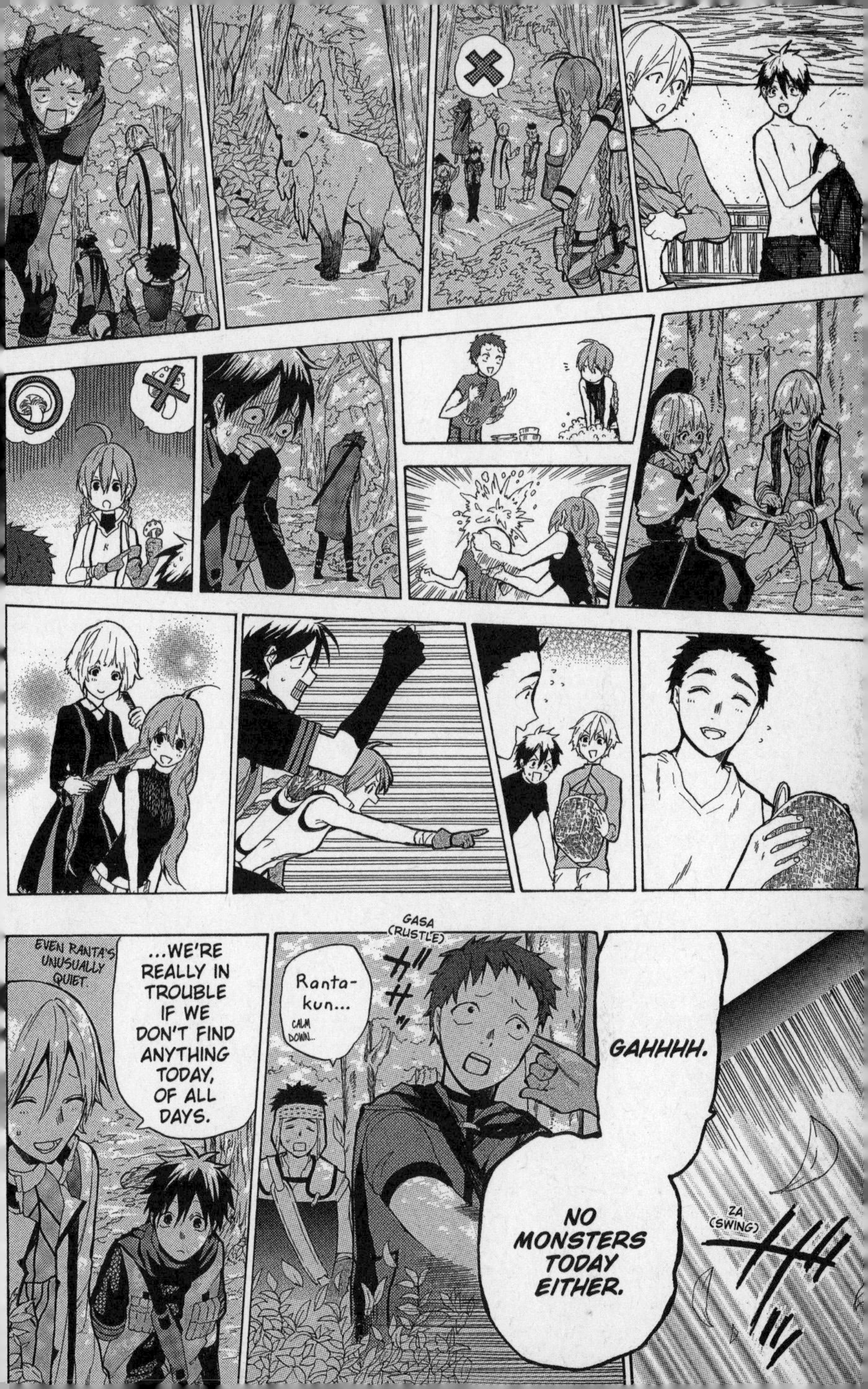
ZA (SWING)
GAHHHH.
NO MONSTERS TODAY EITHER.
GASA (RUSTLE)
Ranta-kun...
CALM DOWN...
...WE'RE REALLY IN TROUBLE IF WE DON'T FIND ANYTHING TODAY, OF ALL DAYS.
EVEN RANTA'S UNUSUALLY QUIET.

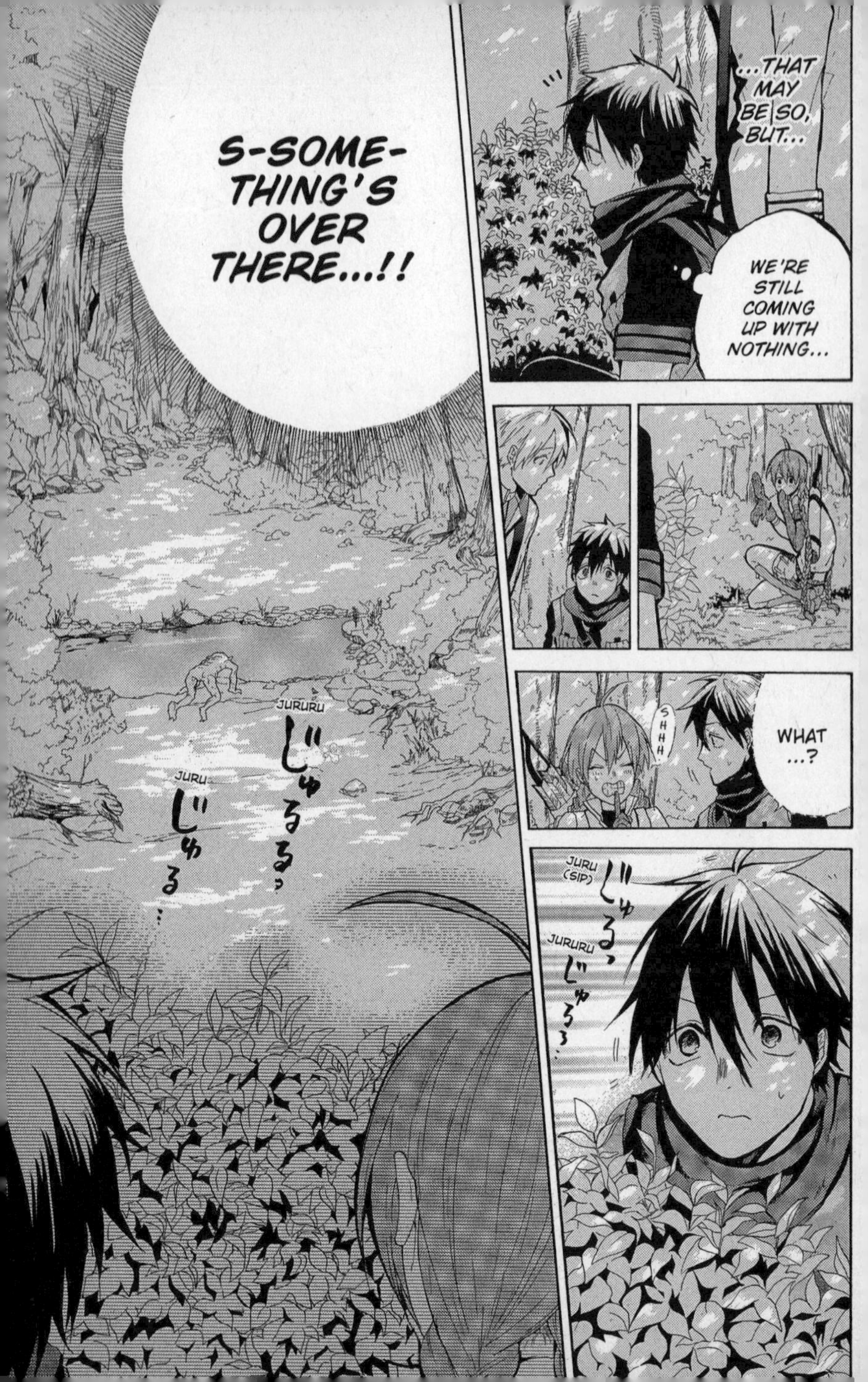
...THAT MAY BE SO, BUT...
WE'RE STILL COMING UP WITH NOTHING...
WHAT ...?
SHHH
JURU (SIP)
じゅるっ
JURURU
じゅるる
S-SOME-THING'S OVER THERE...!!
JURURU
じゅるるっ
JURU
じゅる

NOTE

CONGRATULATIONS ON VOLUME 1!

RANTA IS SO WONDERFULLY OBNOXIOUS!

-SHIRAI

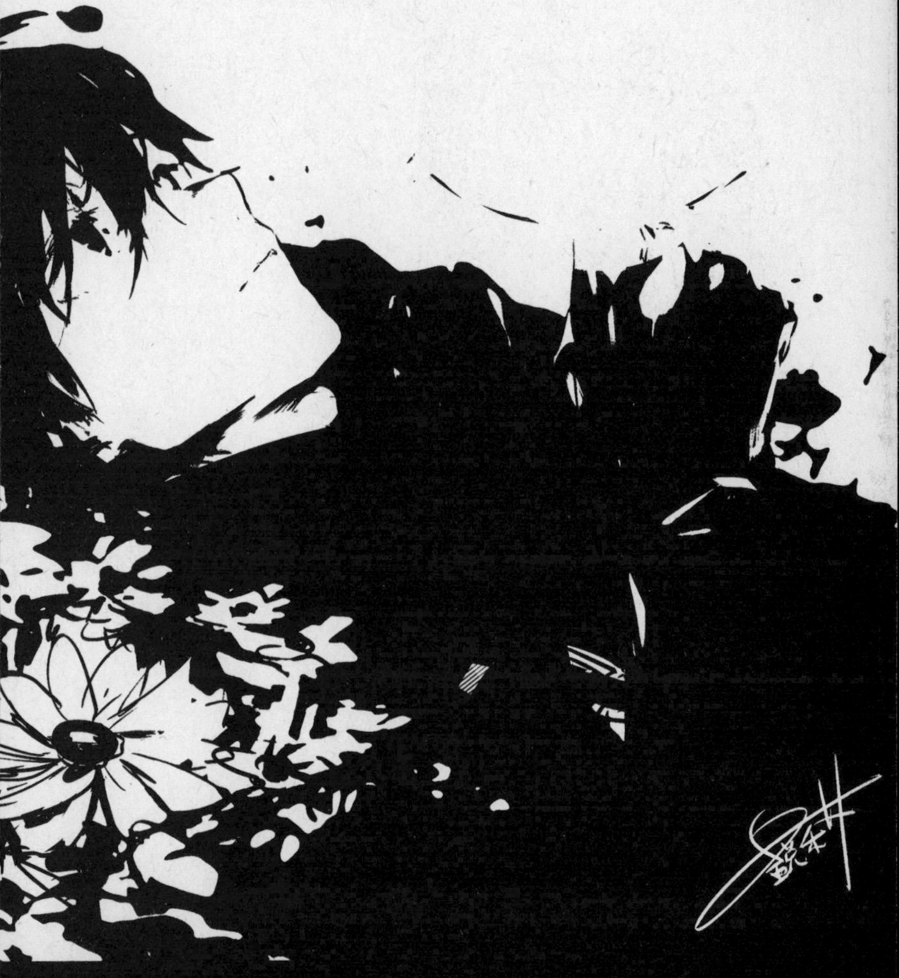

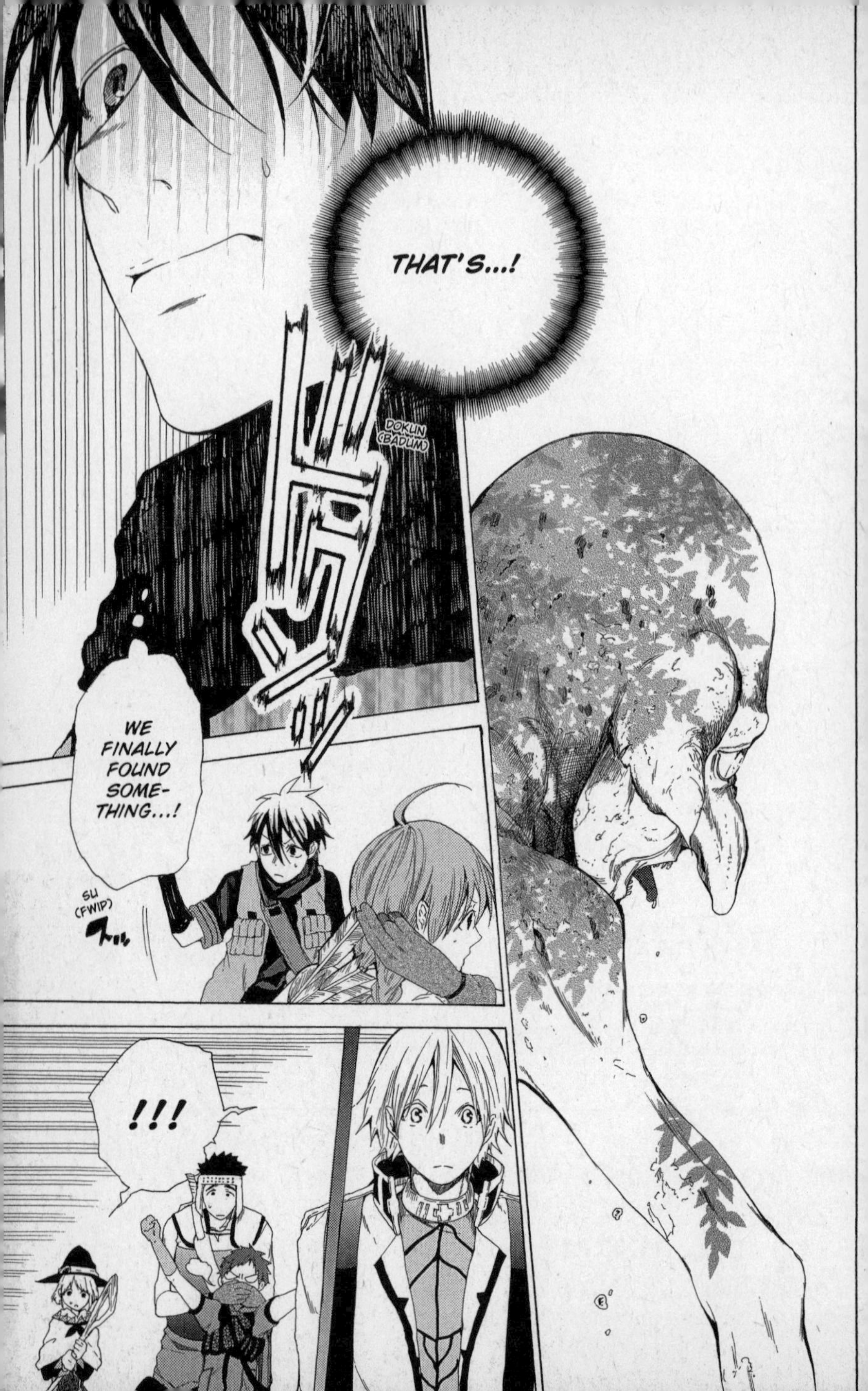
THAT'S...!
DOKUN (BADUM)
WE FINALLY FOUND SOME-THING...!
SU (FWIP)
!!!

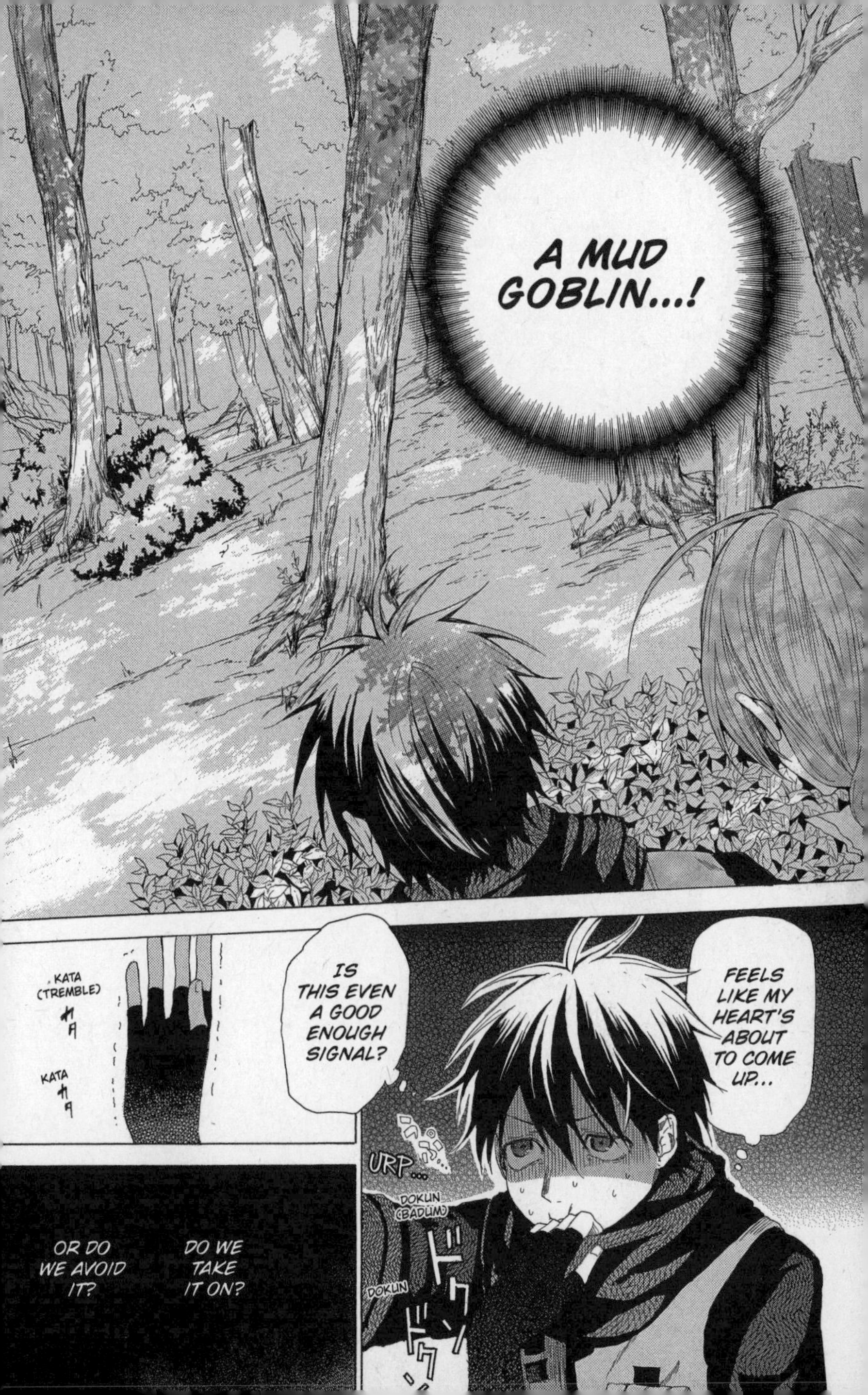
A MUD GOBLIN...!
FEELS LIKE MY HEART'S ABOUT TO COME UP...
IS THIS EVEN A GOOD ENOUGH SIGNAL?
URP...
DOKUN (BADUM)
ドクン
DOKUN
ドクン
KATA (TREMBLE)
カタ
KATA
カタ
DO WE TAKE IT ON?
OR DO WE AVOID IT?

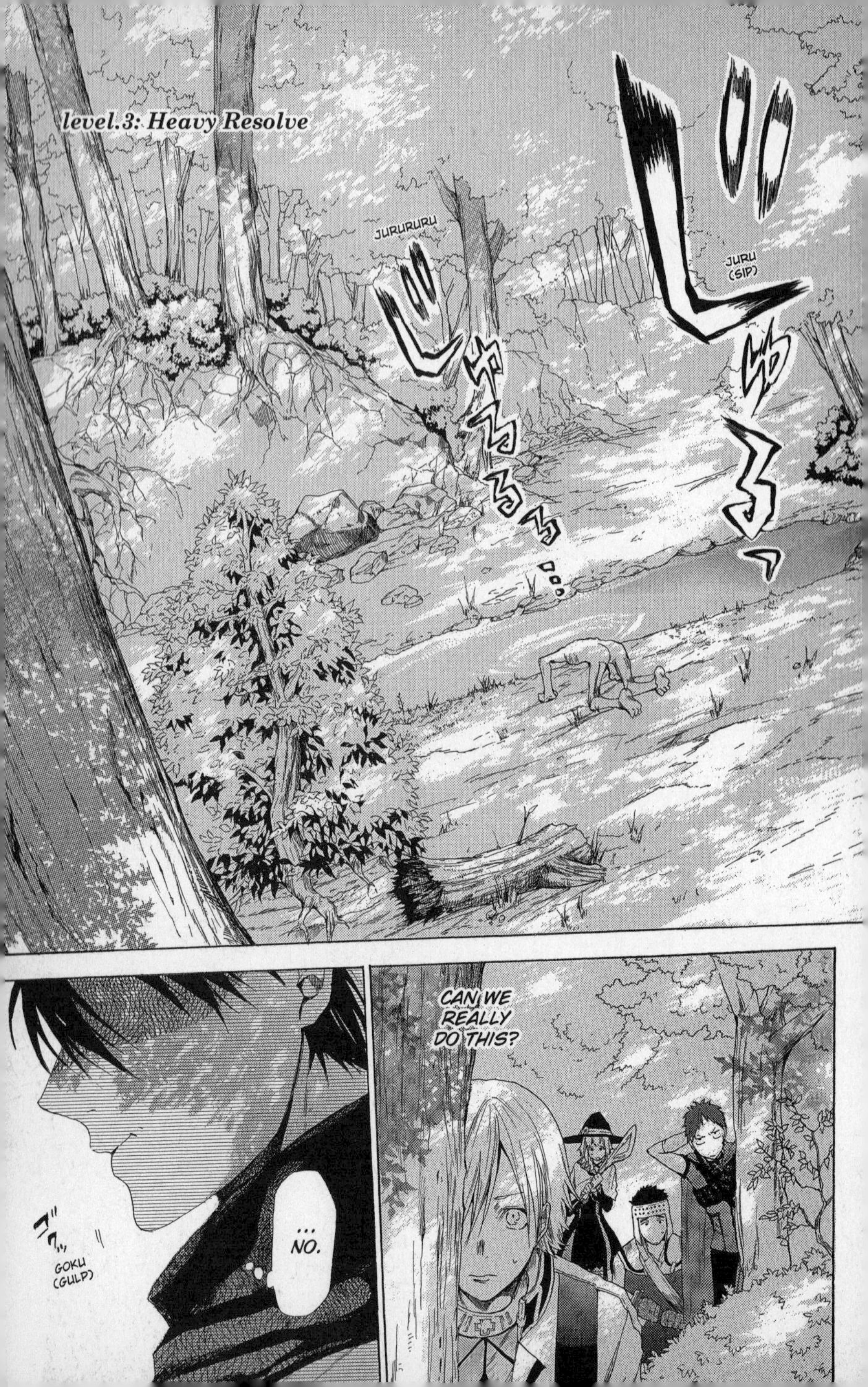
level.3: Heavy Resolve
JURU (SIP)
JURURURU
CAN WE REALLY DO THIS?
... NO.
GOKU (GULP)

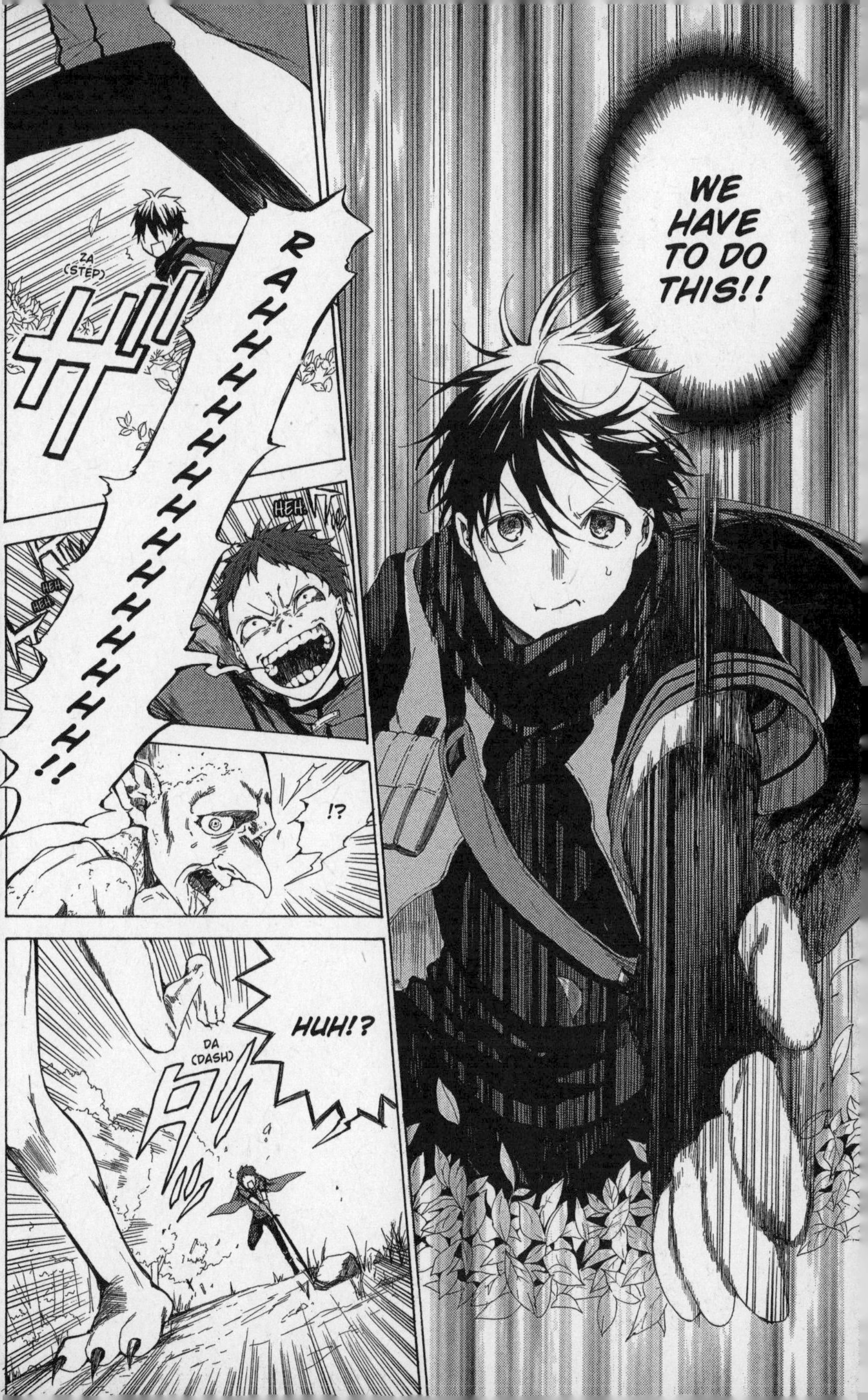
WE HAVE TO DO THIS!!
ZA (STEP)
RAHHHHHHHHHHHHHHH!!
HEH.
HEH. HEH.
!?
HUH!?
DA (DASH)

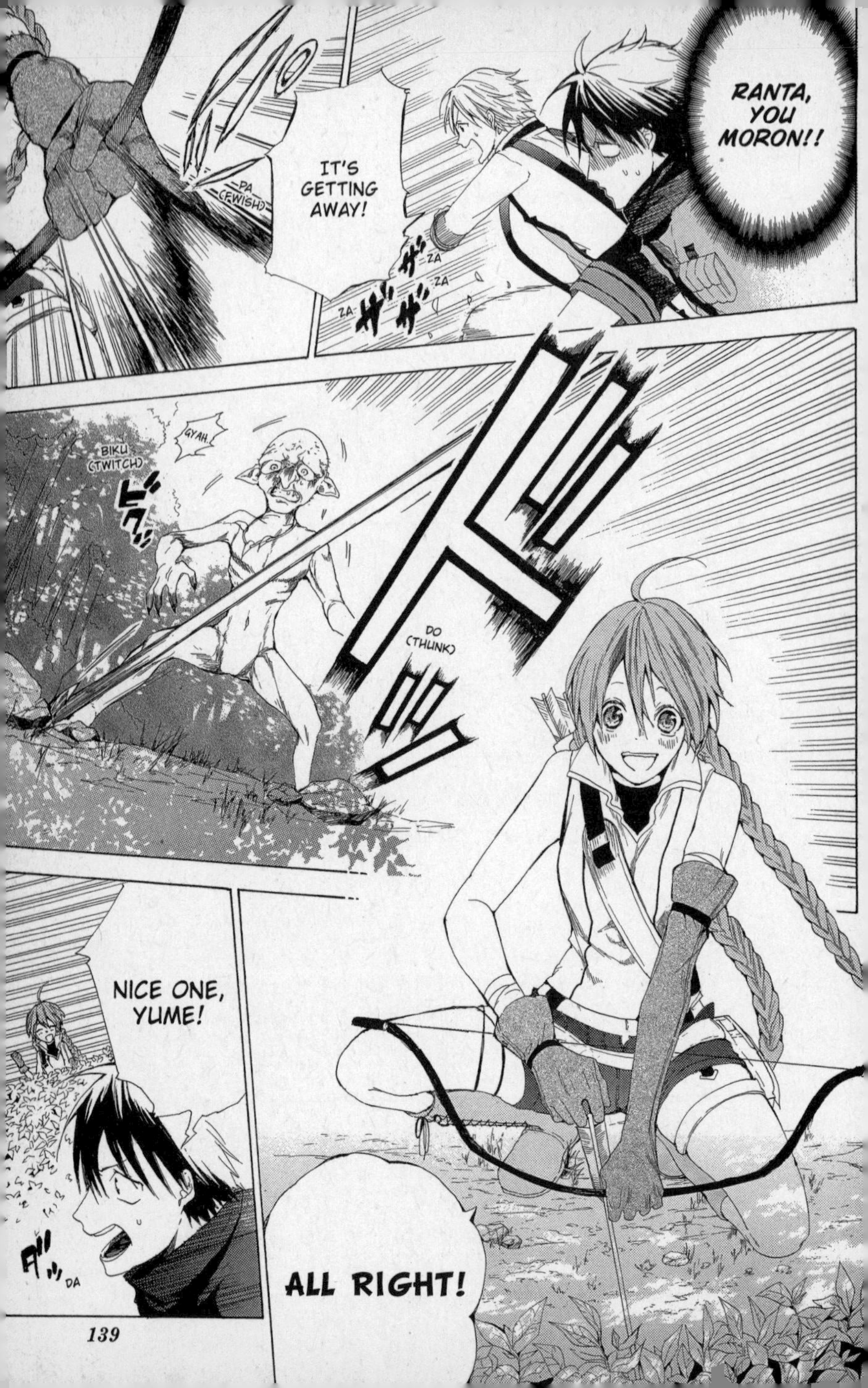
RANTA, YOU MORON!!
IT'S GETTING AWAY!
ZA
ZA
ZA
PA (FWISH)
DO (THUNK)
GYAH!
BIKU (TWITCH)
ALL RIGHT!
NICE ONE, YUME!
DA

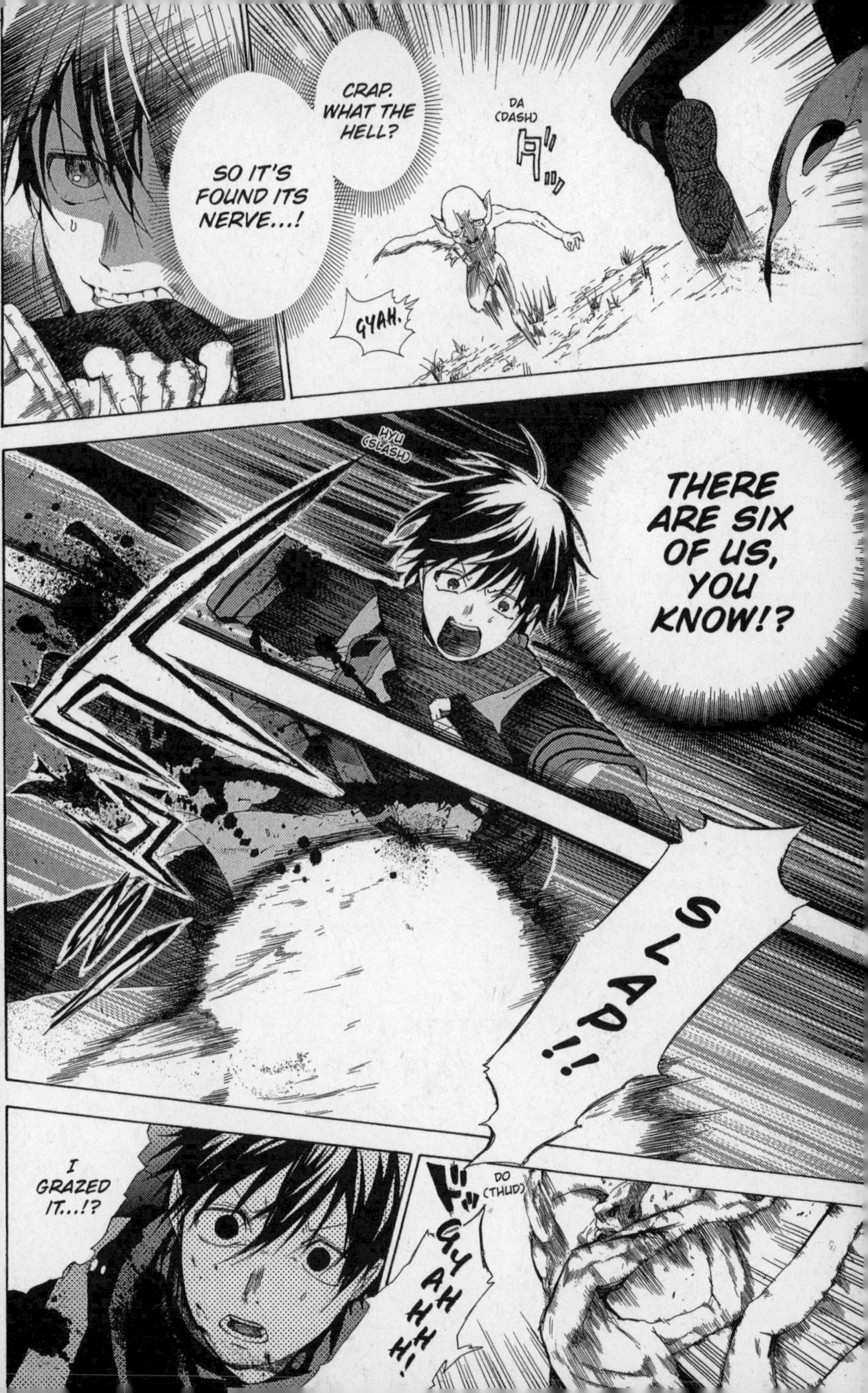
DA (DASH)
GYAH.
CRAP. WHAT THE HELL?
SO IT'S FOUND ITS NERVE...!
THERE ARE SIX OF US, YOU KNOW!?
HYU (SLASH)
SLAP!!
DO (THUD)
GYAHHHH!
I GRAZED IT...!?

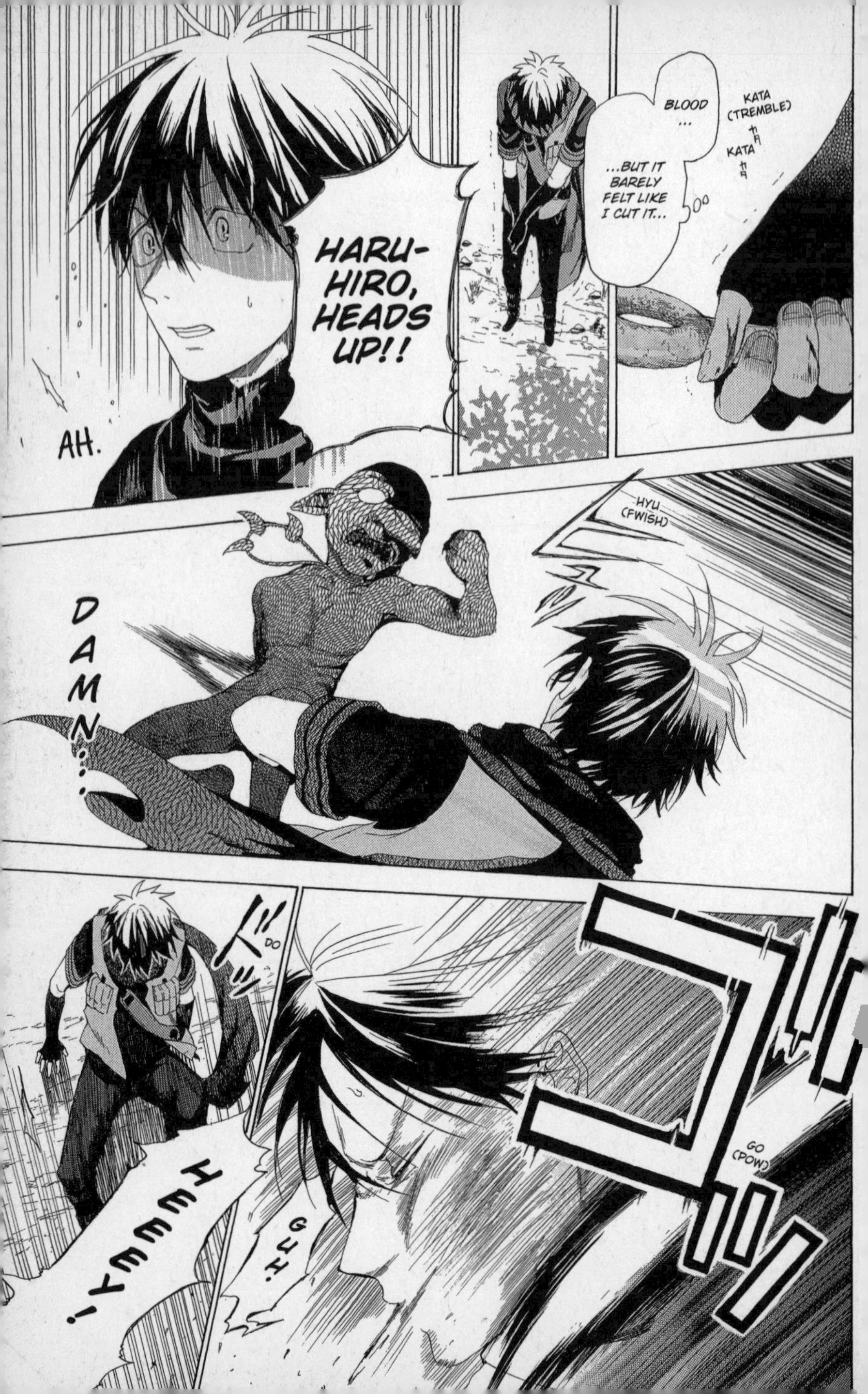
KATA (TREMBLE)
KATA
BLOOD...
...BUT IT BARELY FELT LIKE I CUT IT...
HARU-HIRO, HEADS UP!!
AH.
HYU (FWISH)
DAMN...
GO (POW)
GUH.
DO
HEEEEY!

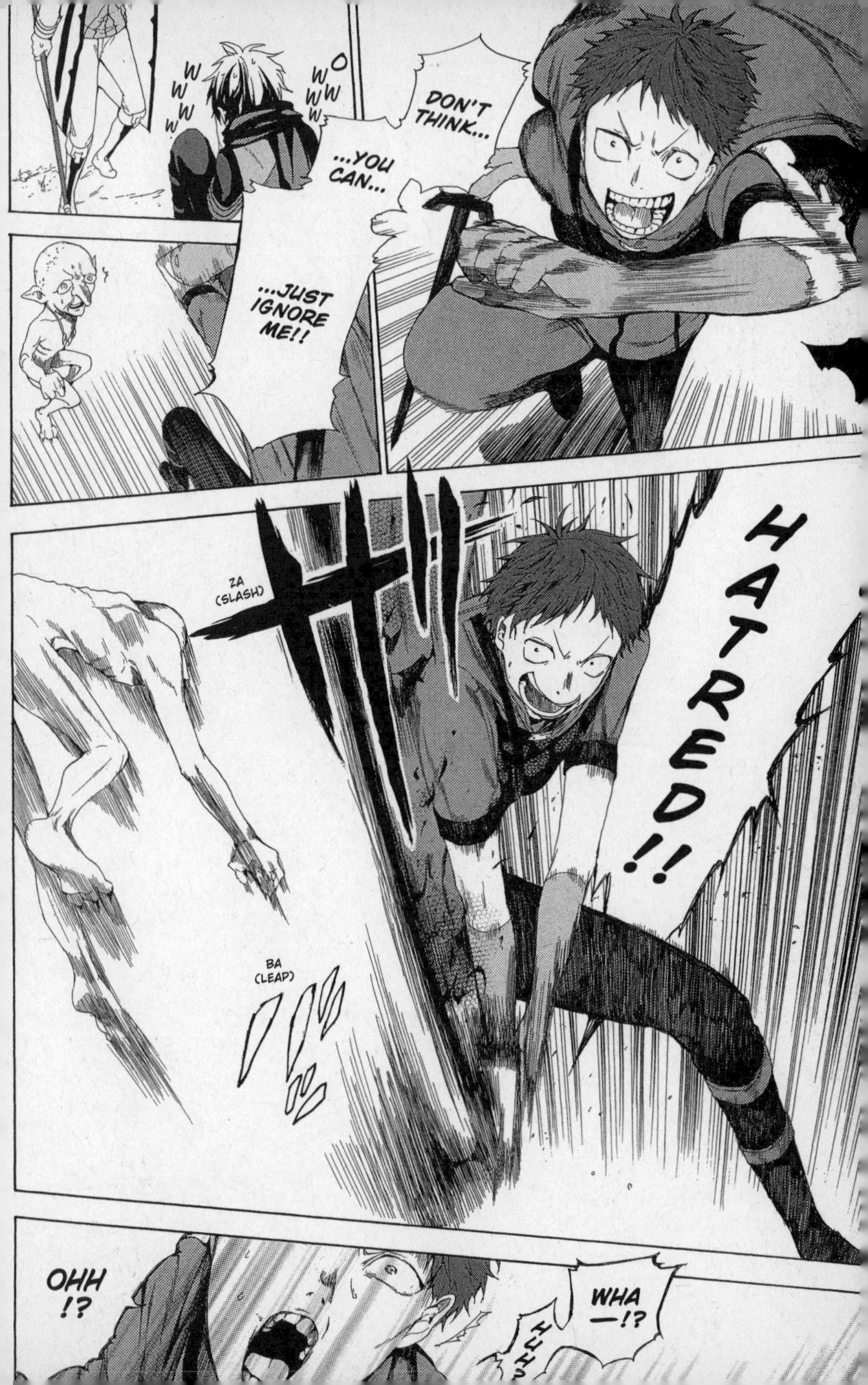
DON'T THINK...
...YOU CAN...
...JUST IGNORE ME!!
WWWWW
OWWWW
HATRED!!
ZA (SLASH)
BA (LEAP)
WHA—!?
HUH
OHH!?

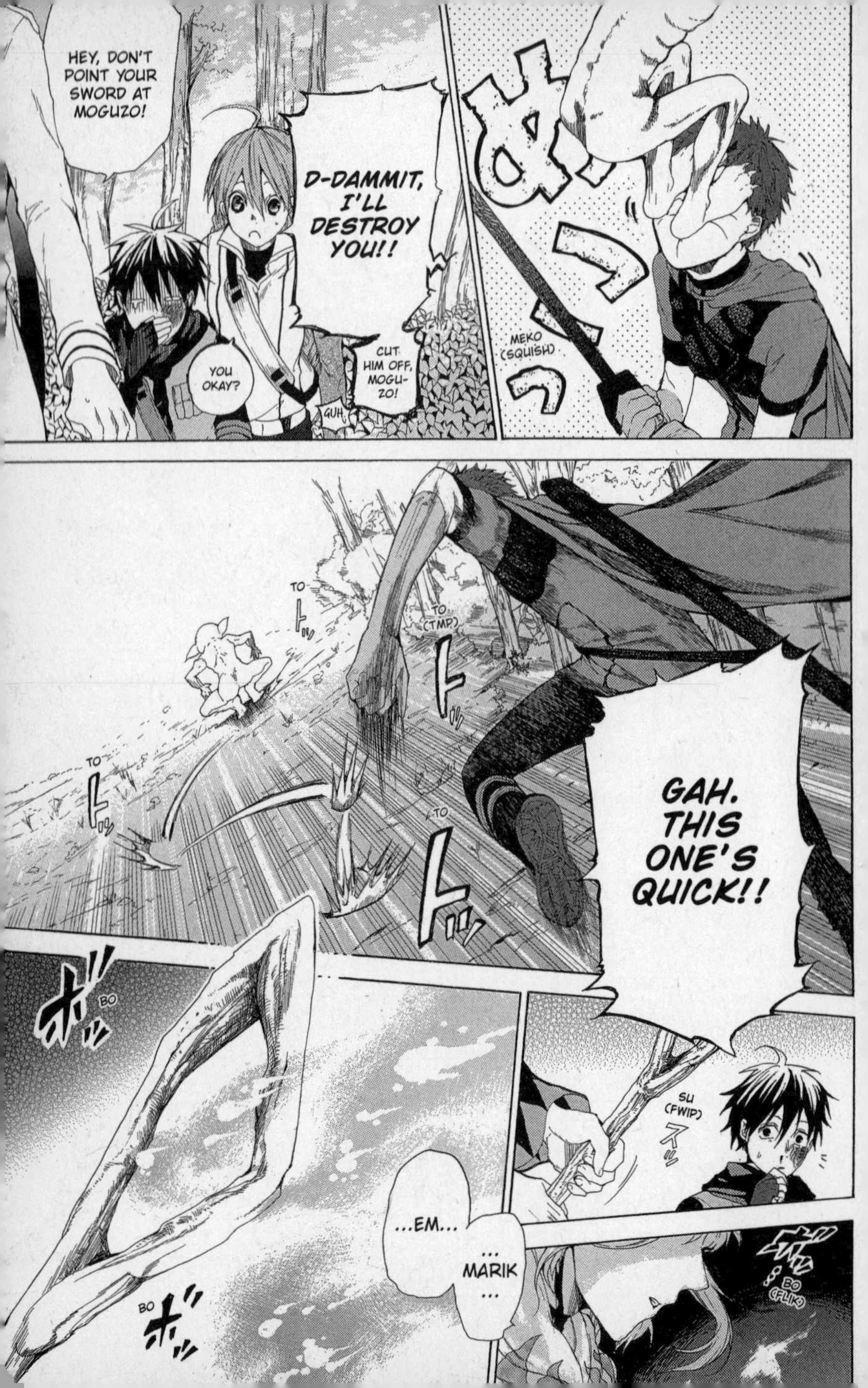
MEKO (SQUISH)
D-DAMMIT, I'LL DESTROY YOU!!
HEY, DON'T POINT YOUR SWORD AT MOGUZO!
CUT HIM OFF, MOGUZO!
GUH
YOU OKAY?
TO (TMP)
TO
GAH. THIS ONE'S QUICK!!
TO
TO
SU (FWIP)
BO (FLIK)
BO
...EM...
... MARIK ...
BO

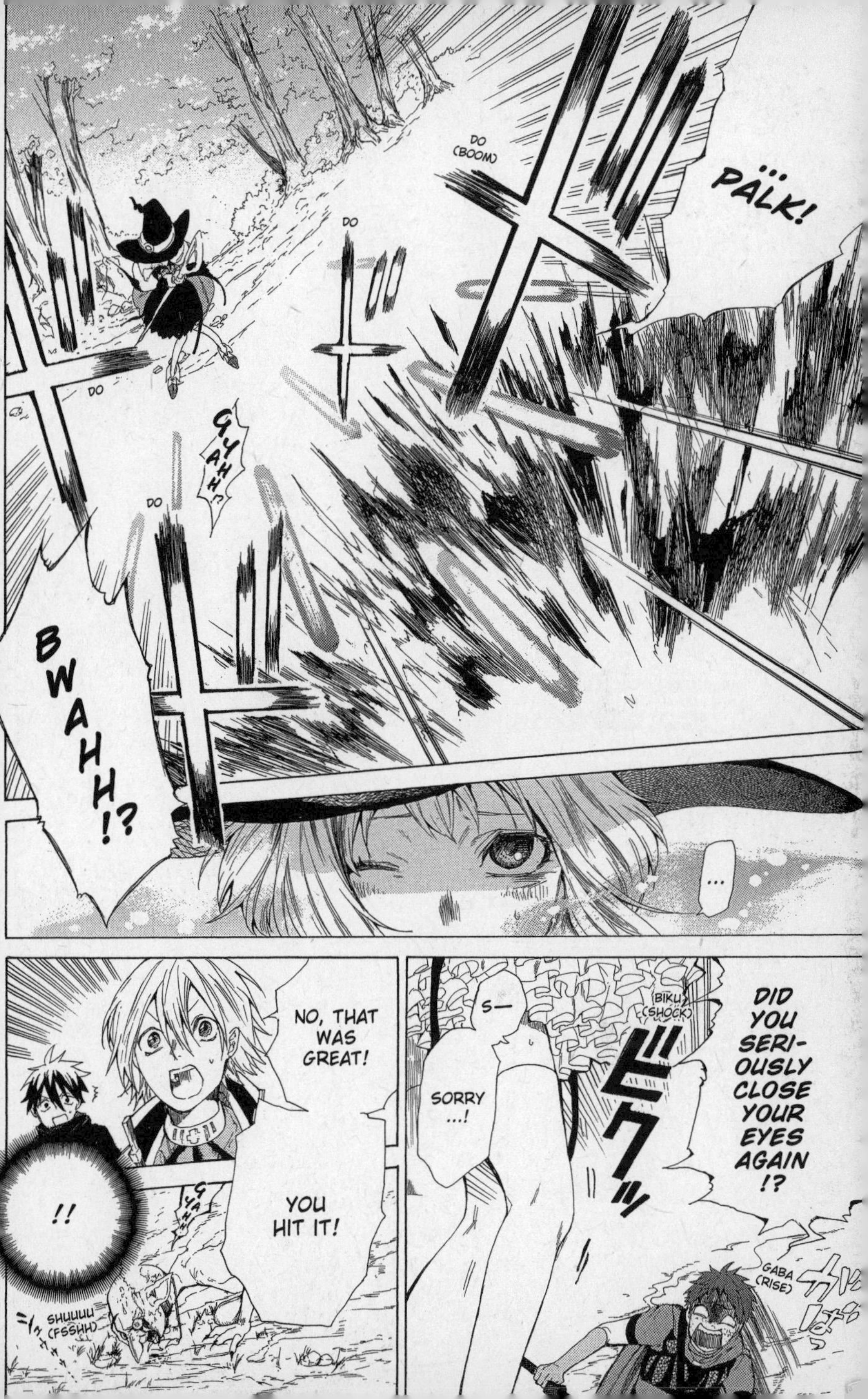
... PÄLK!
DO (BOOM)
DO
GYAHH!?
DO
DO
BWAHH!?
...
DID YOU SERI-OUSLY CLOSE YOUR EYES AGAIN!?
BIKU (SHOCK)
S—
SORRY ...!
GABA (RISE)
NO, THAT WAS GREAT!
YOU HIT IT!
GYAHH
!!
SHUUUU (FSSHH)

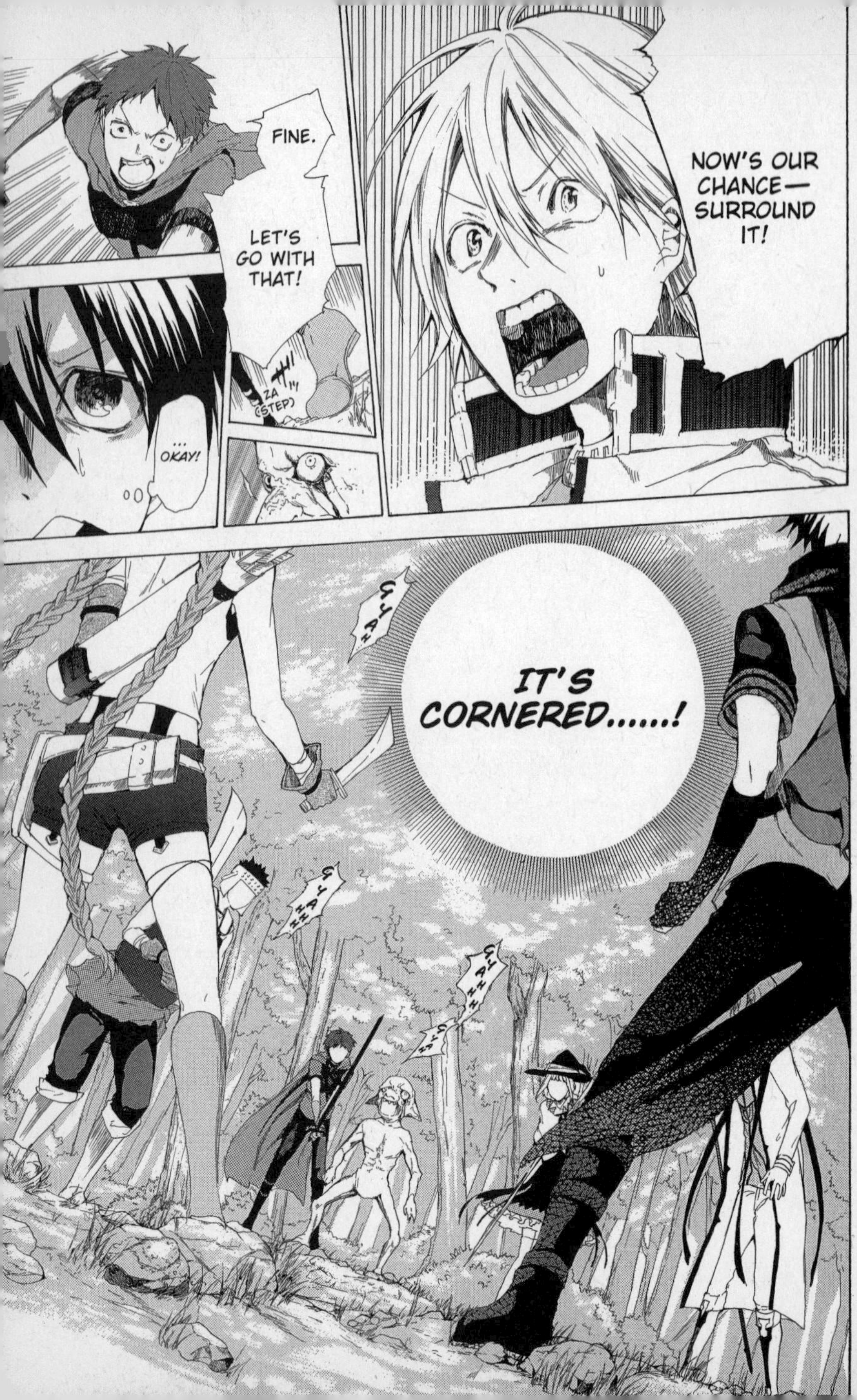
NOW'S OUR CHANCE—SURROUND IT!
FINE.
LET'S GO WITH THAT!
ZA (STEP)
... OKAY!
IT'S CORNERED......!
GYAH
GYAHHH
GYAH

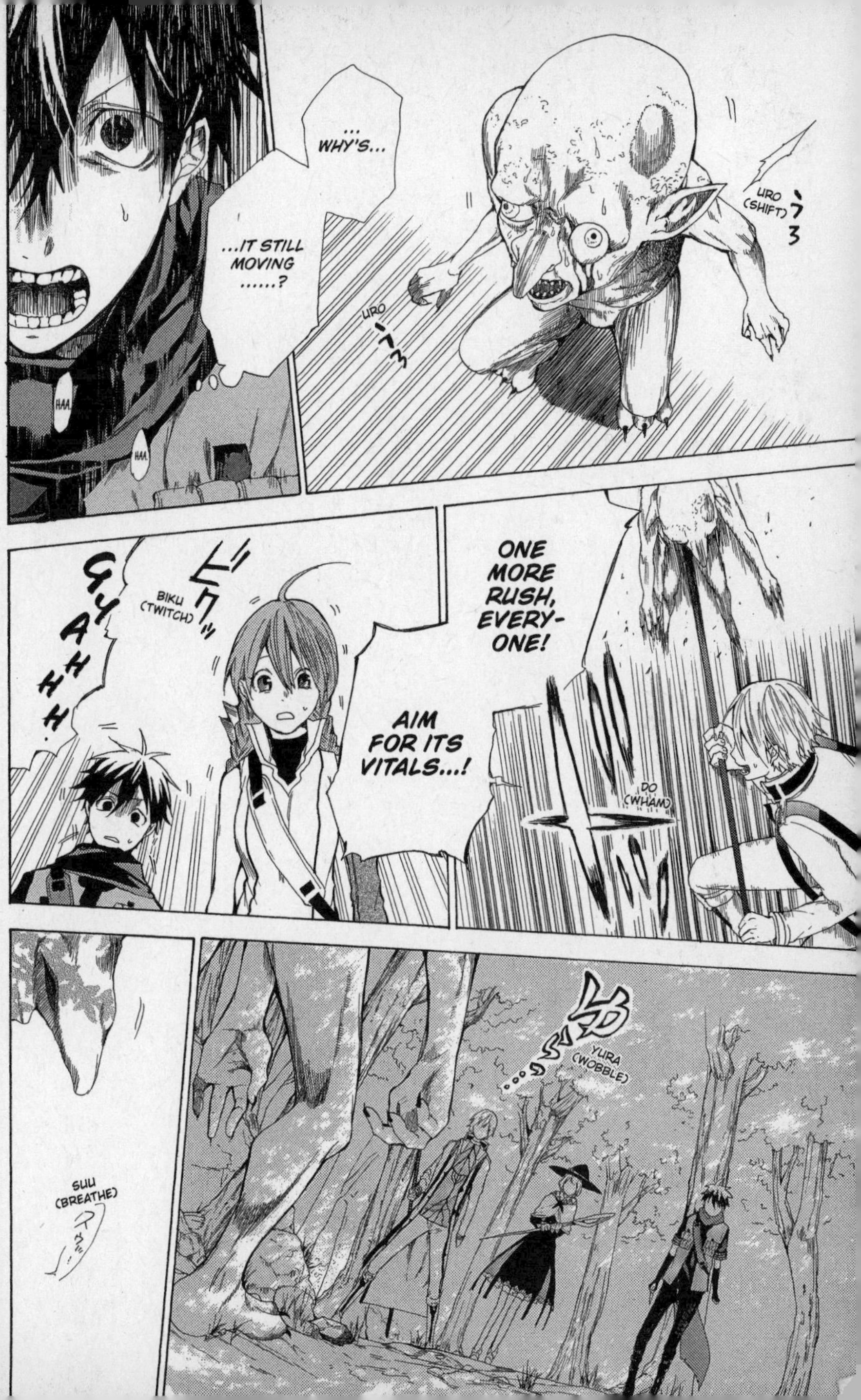
URO (SHIFT)
URO
... WHY'S...
...IT STILL MOVING ......?
HAA
HAA
ONE MORE RUSH, EVERY-ONE!
AIM FOR ITS VITALS...!
DO (WHAM)
BIKU (TWITCH)
GYAHHHH.
YURA (WOBBLE)
SUU (BREATHE)

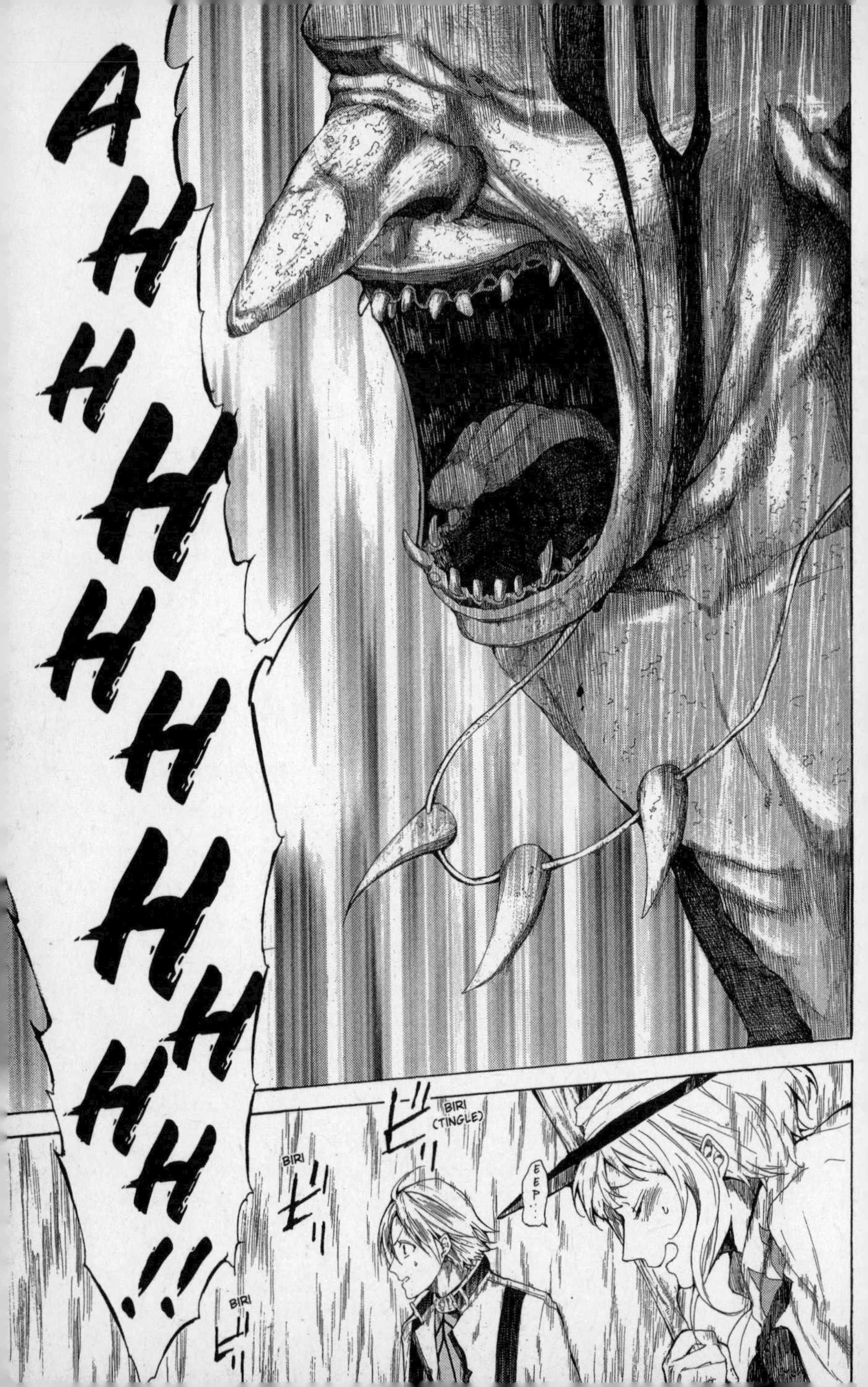
AHHHHHHHHH!!
EEP...
BIRI (TINGLE)
BIRI
BIRI

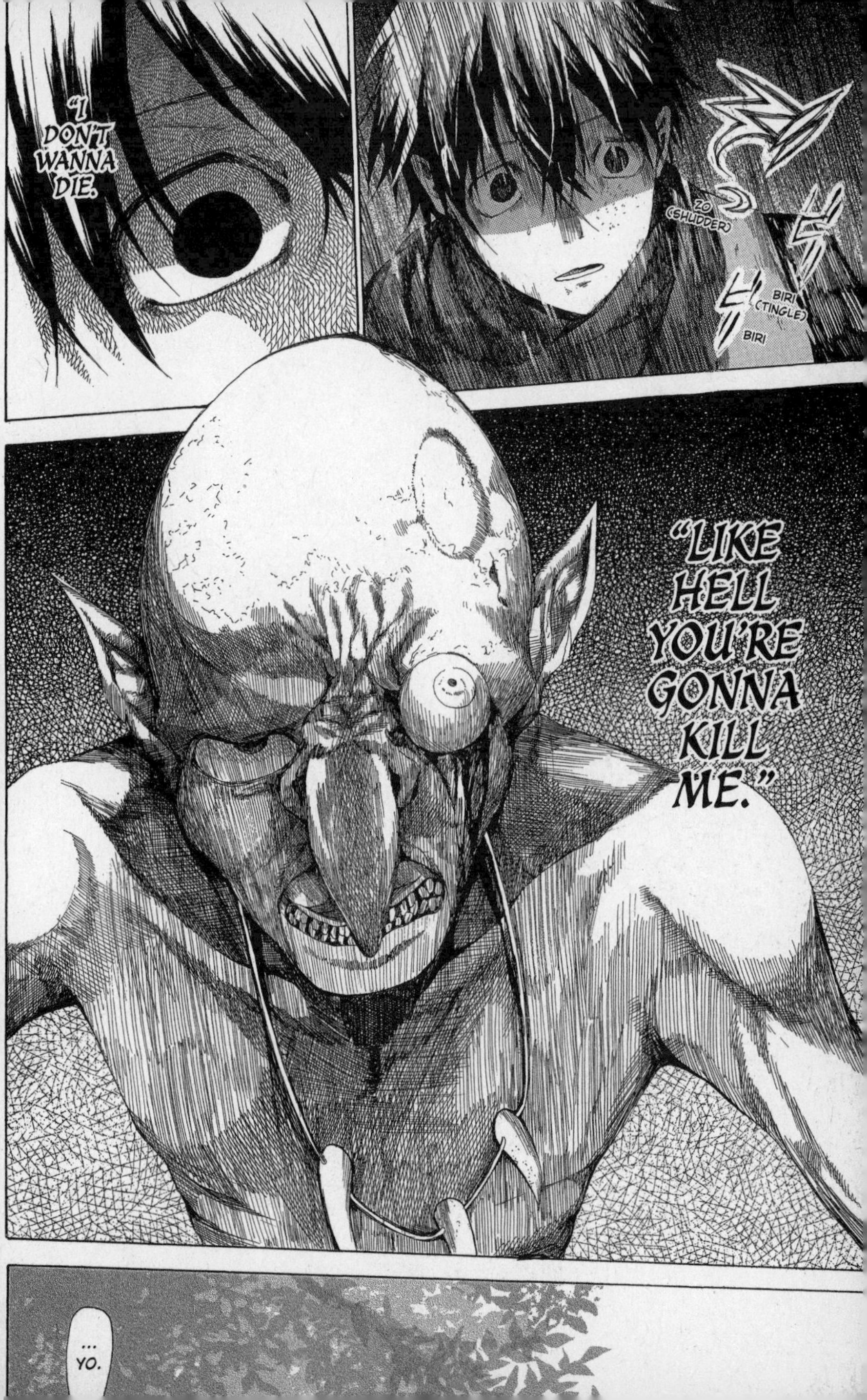
ZO (SHUDDER)
BIRI (TINGLE)
BIRI
"I DON'T WANNA DIE.
"LIKE HELL YOU'RE GONNA KILL ME."
... YO.

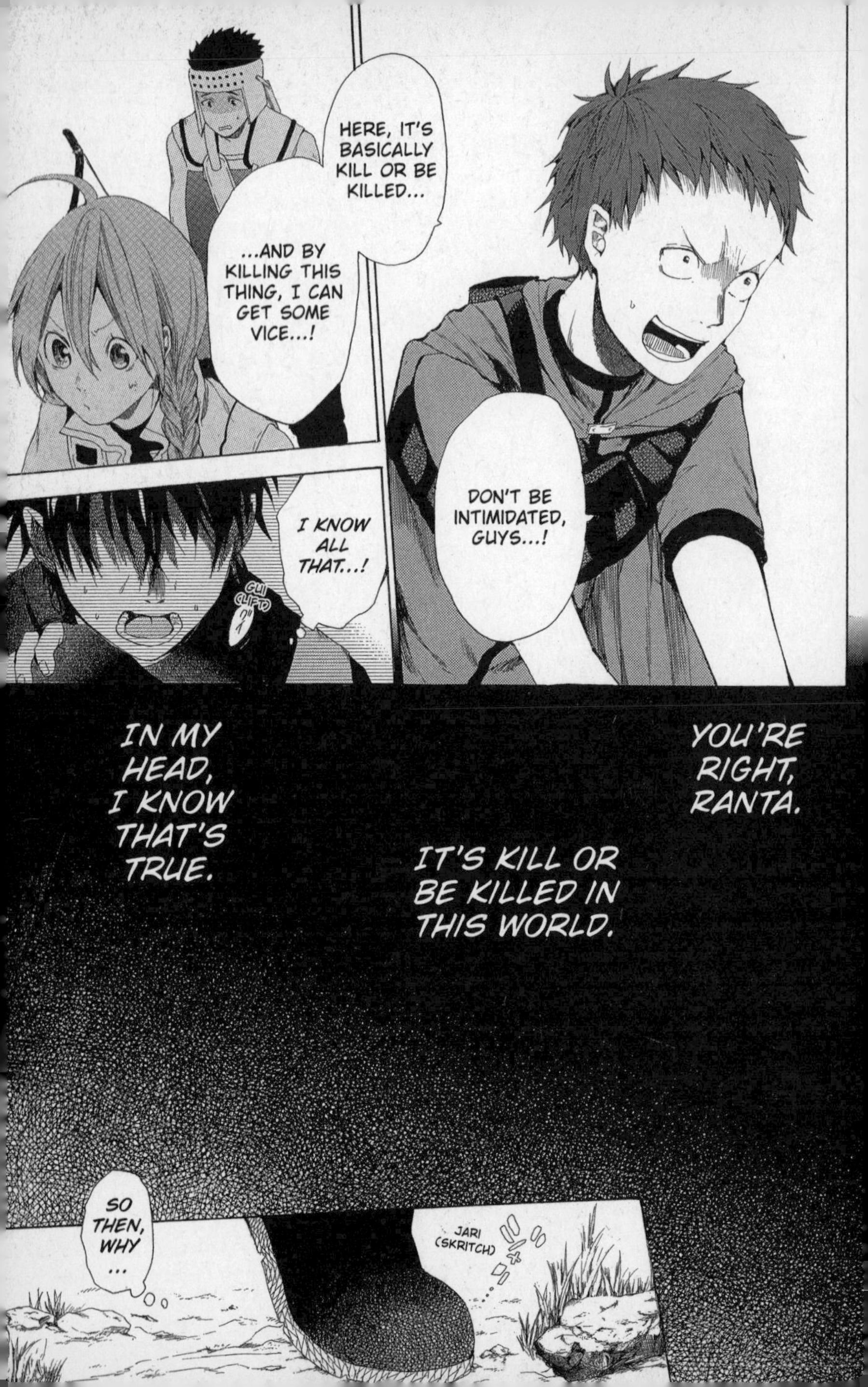
HERE, IT'S BASICALLY KILL OR BE KILLED...
...AND BY KILLING THIS THING, I CAN GET SOME VICE...!
DON'T BE INTIMIDATED, GUYS...!
I KNOW ALL THAT...!
GUI (GRIP)
YOU'RE RIGHT, RANTA.
IT'S KILL OR BE KILLED IN THIS WORLD.
IN MY HEAD, I KNOW THAT'S TRUE.
JARI (SKRITCH)
SO THEN, WHY ...

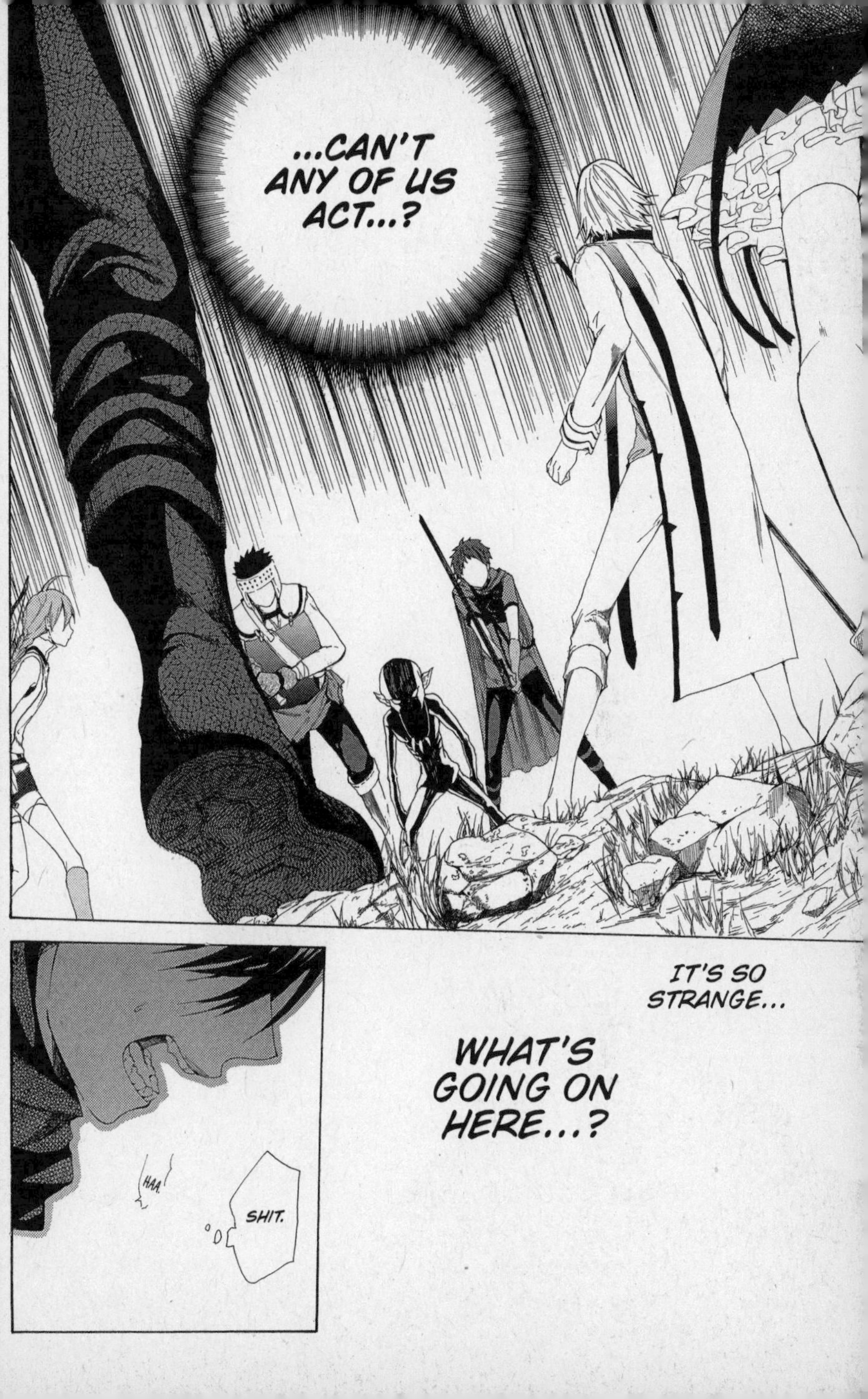
...CAN'T ANY OF US ACT...?
IT'S SO STRANGE...
WHAT'S GOING ON HERE...?
SHIT.
HAA.

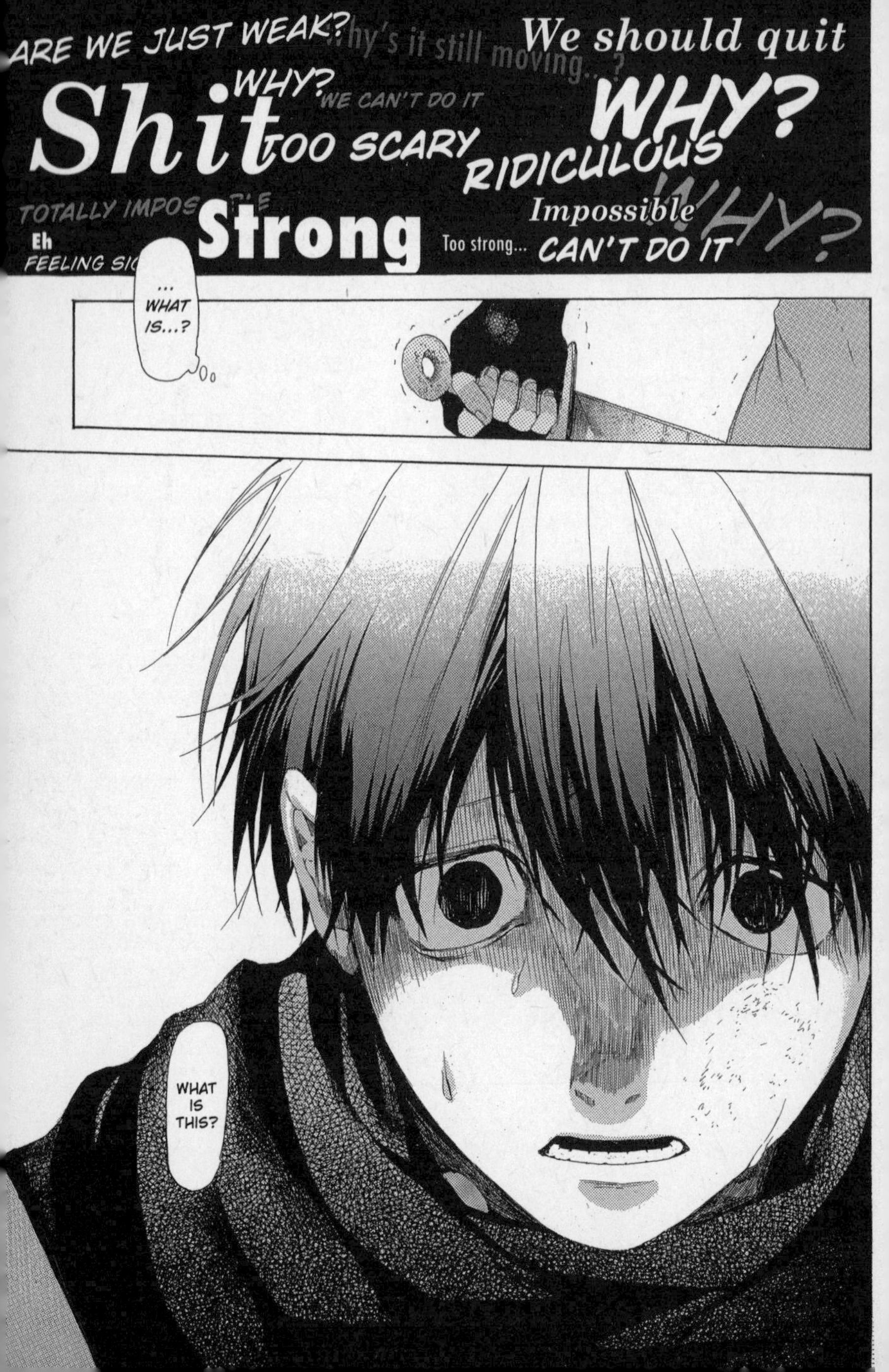
We should quit
WHY?
RIDICULOUS
Impossible
WHY?
CAN'T DO IT
Too strong...
ARE WE JUST WEAK?
WHY?
WE CAN'T DO IT
Shit
TOO SCARY
Strong
Eh
... WHAT IS...?
WHAT IS THIS?

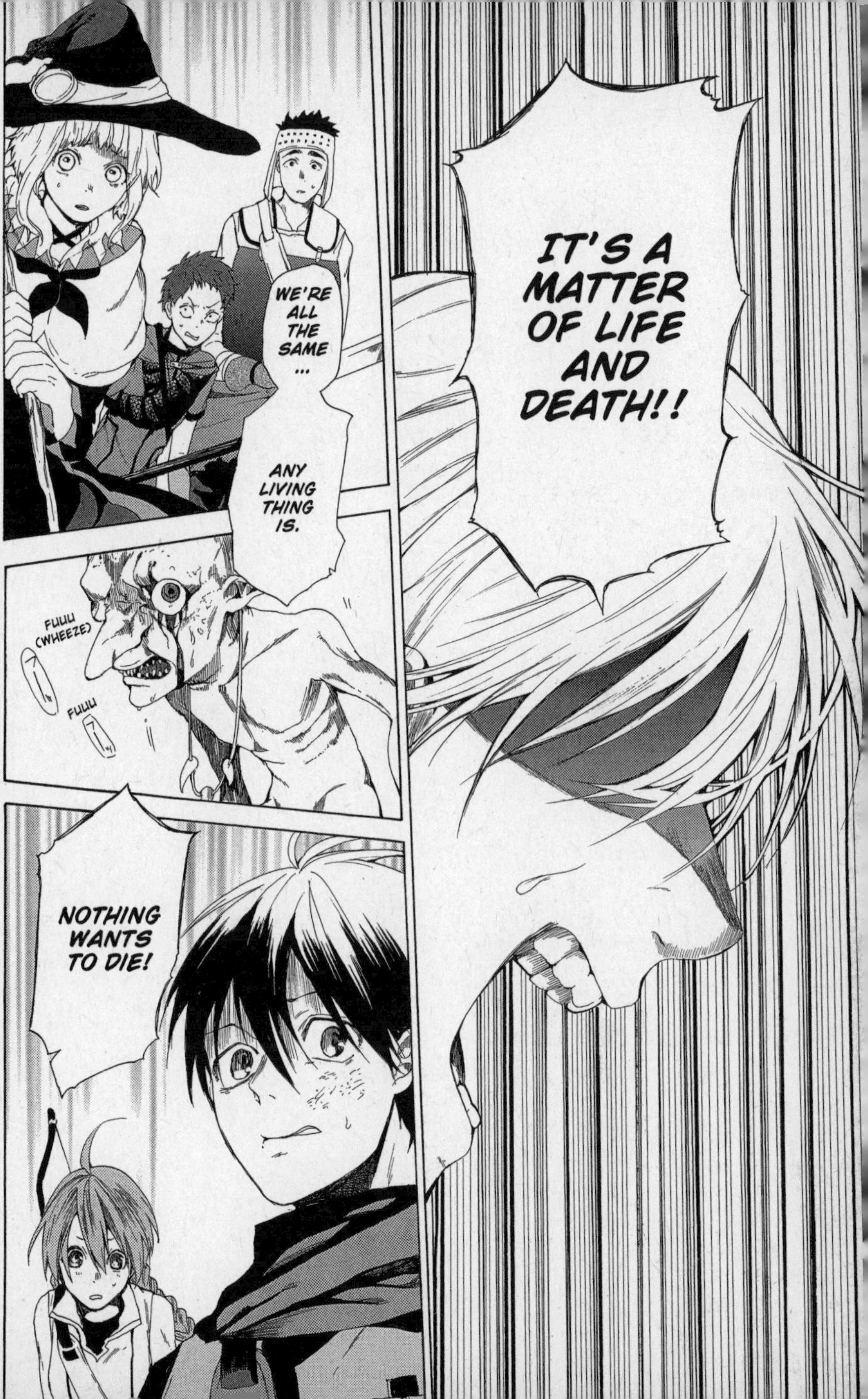
IT'S A MATTER OF LIFE AND DEATH!!
WE'RE ALL THE SAME ...
ANY LIVING THING IS.
FUUU (WHEEZE)
FUUU
NOTHING WANTS TO DIE!

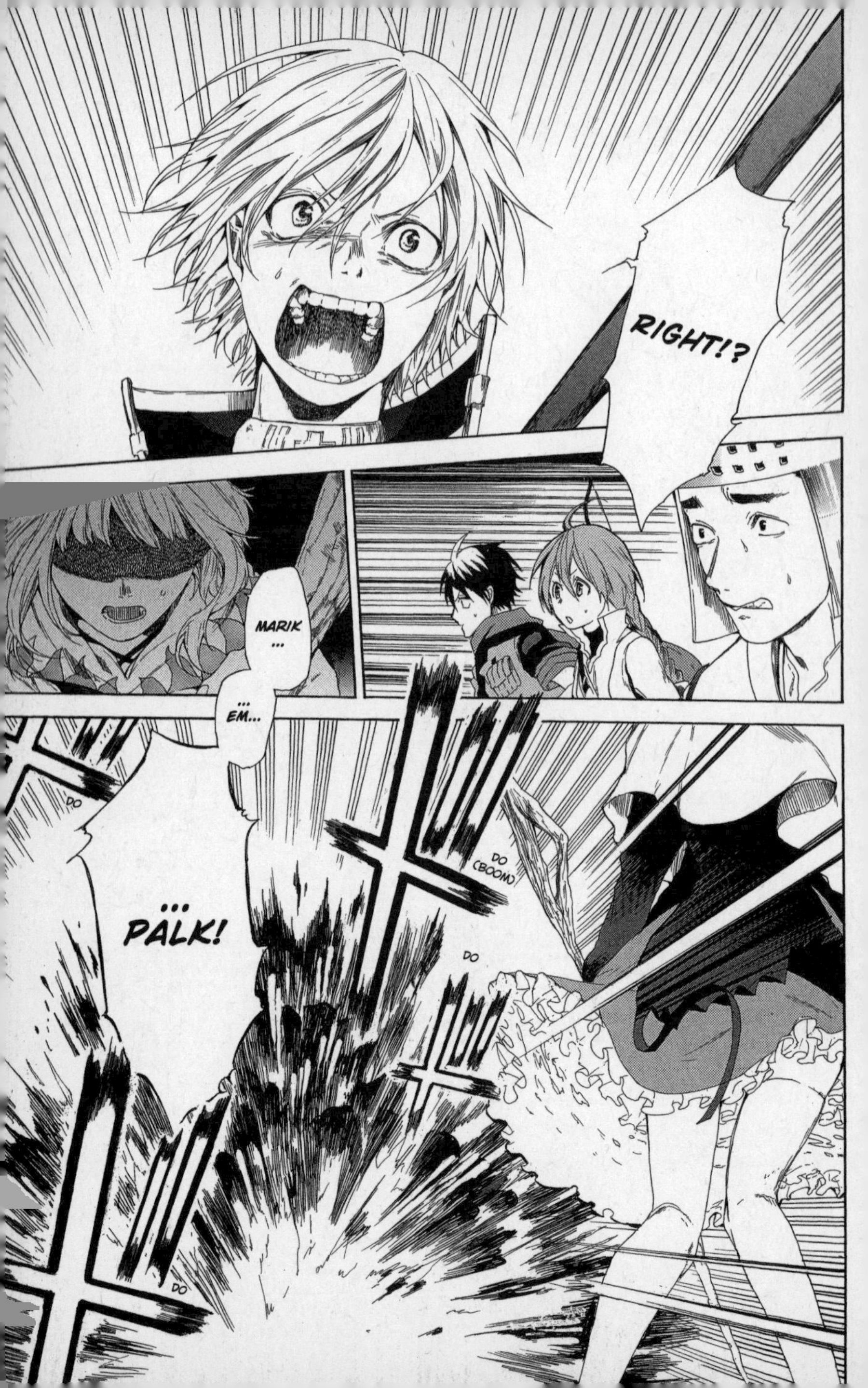
RIGHT!?
MARIK ...
... EM...
DO (BOOM)
DO
DO
... PÄLK!
DO

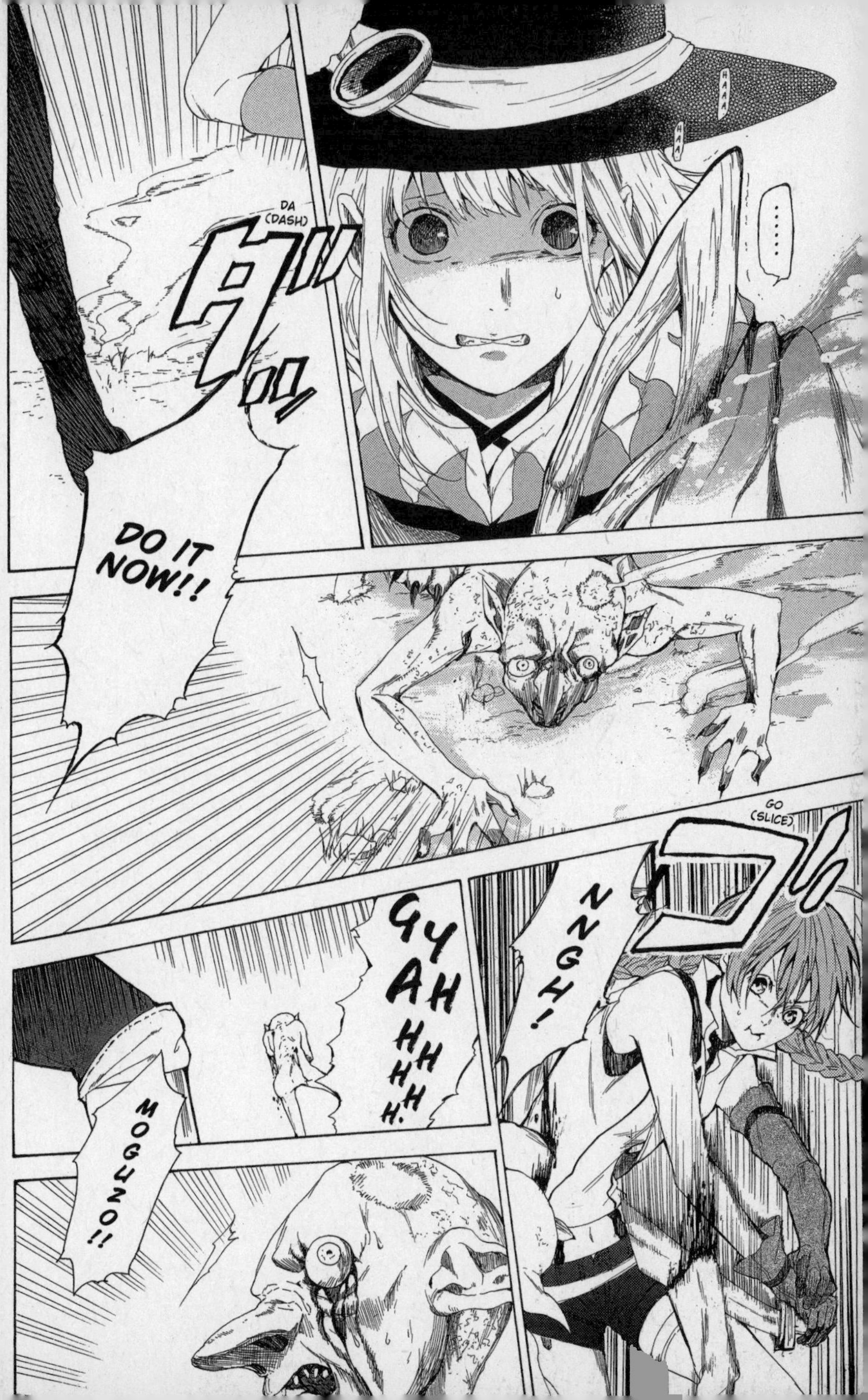
HAAA
HAA
......
DA (DASH)
DO IT NOW!!
GO (SLICE)
NNGH!
GYAHHHHH.
MOGUZO!!

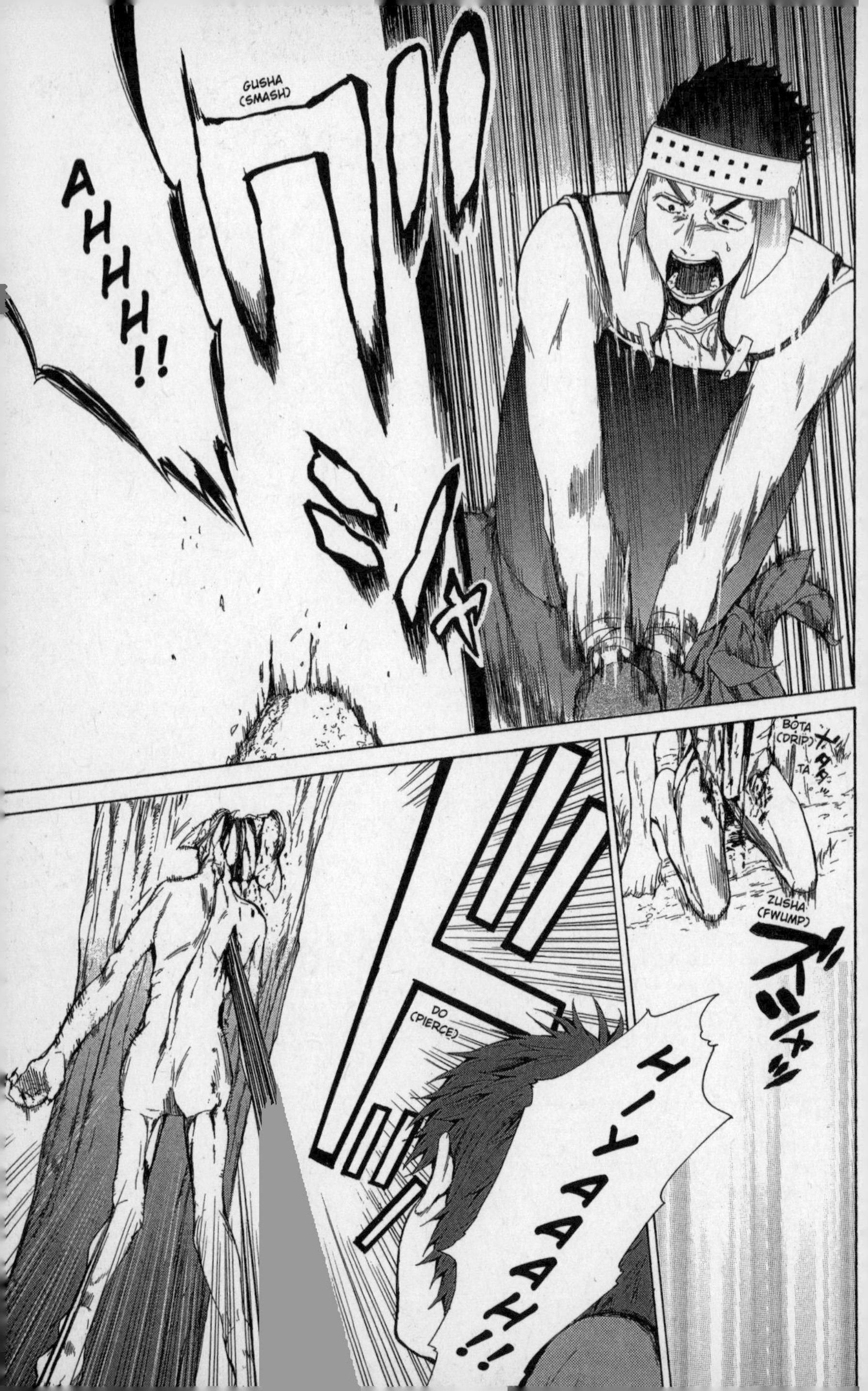
GUSHA (SMASH)
AHHH!!
BOTA (DRIP)
TA
ZUSHA (FWUMP)
HIYAAAAH!!
DO (PIERCE)

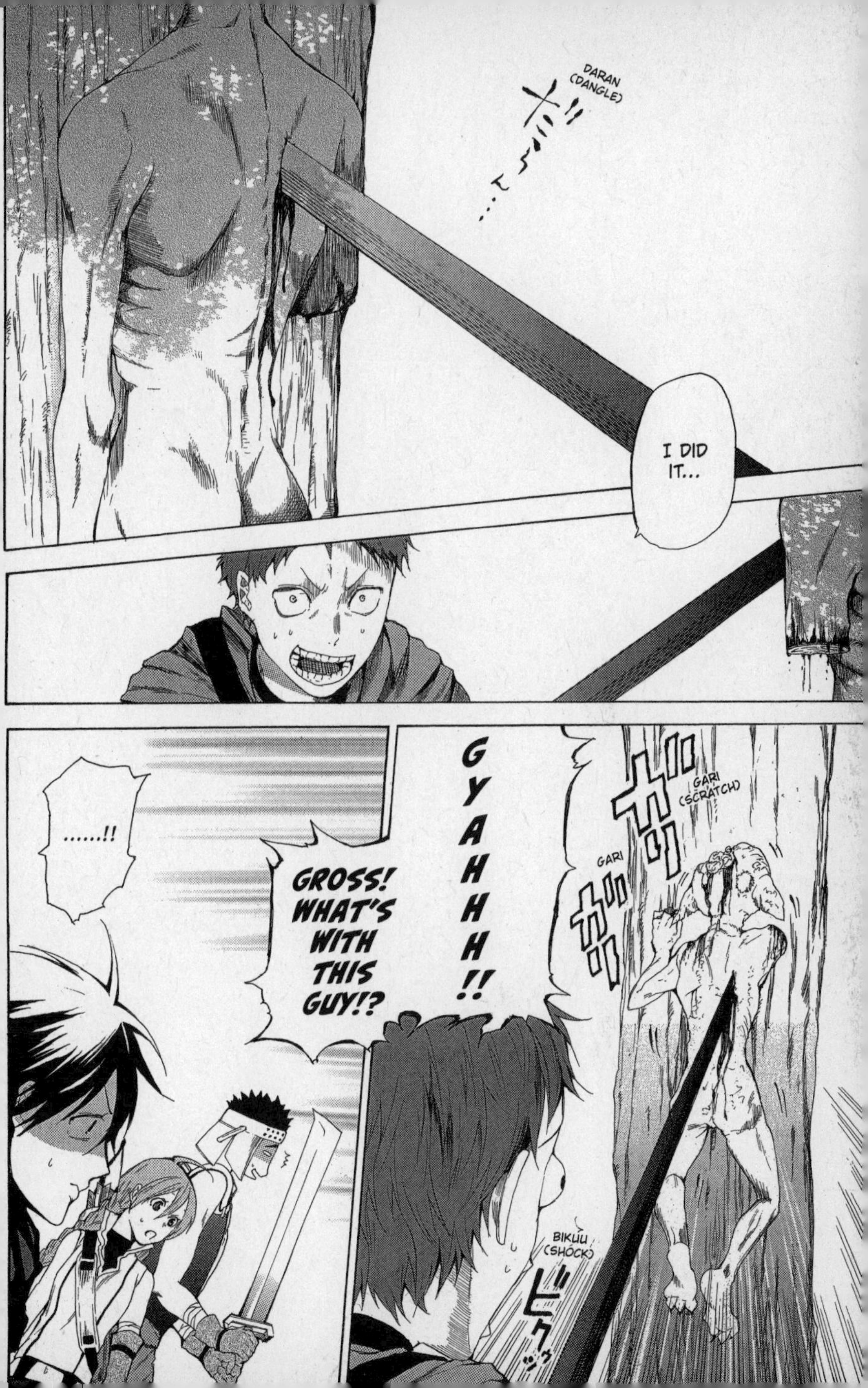
DARAN (DANGLE)
I DID IT...
GARI (SCRATCH)
GARI
GYAHHHH!!
GROSS! WHAT'S WITH THIS GUY!?
......!!
BIKUU (SHOCK)

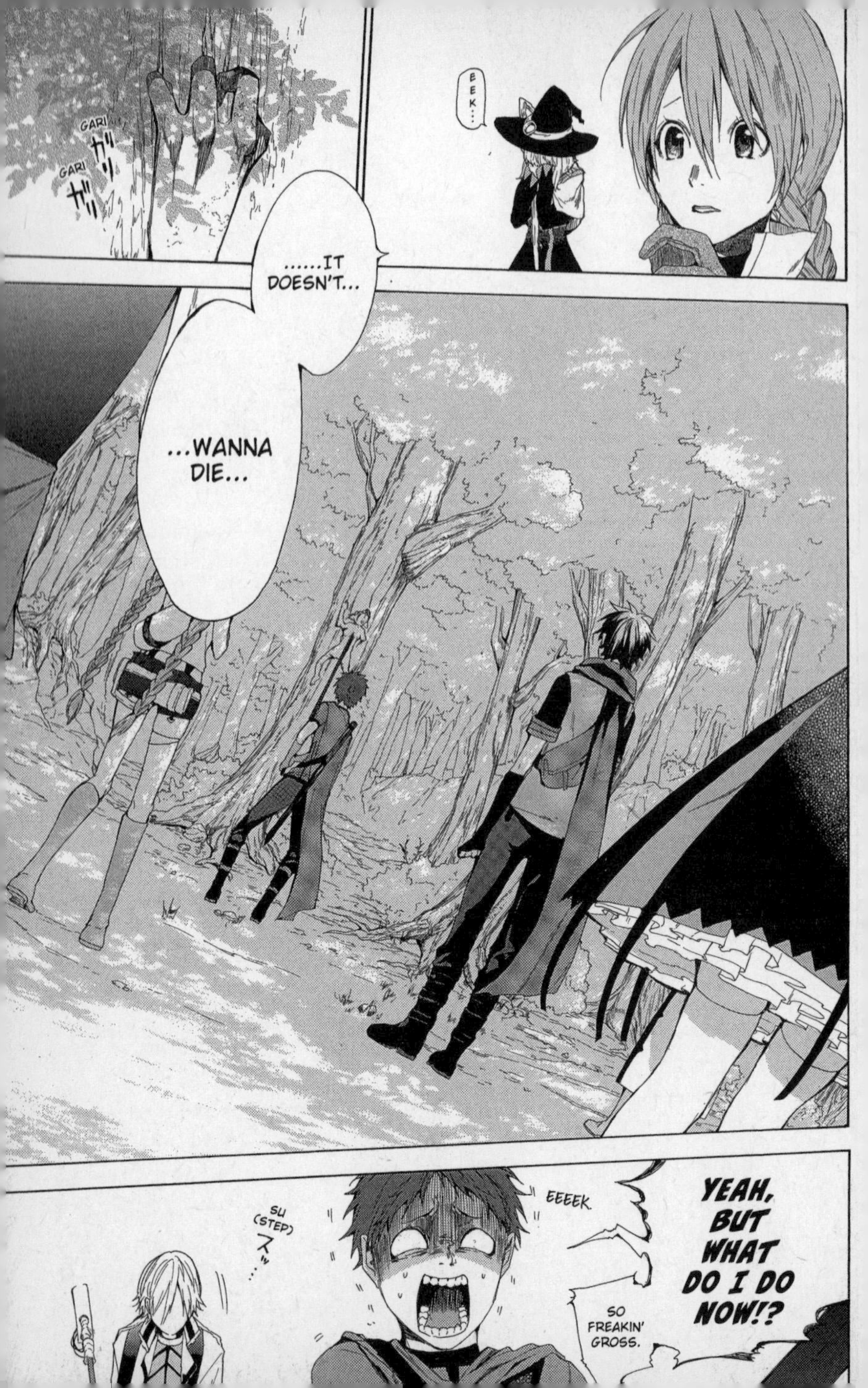
EEK...
GARI ガリ
GARI ガリ
......IT DOESN'T...
...WANNA DIE...
YEAH, BUT WHAT DO I DO NOW!?
EEEEK.
SO FREAKIN' GROSS.
SU (STEP) ス...

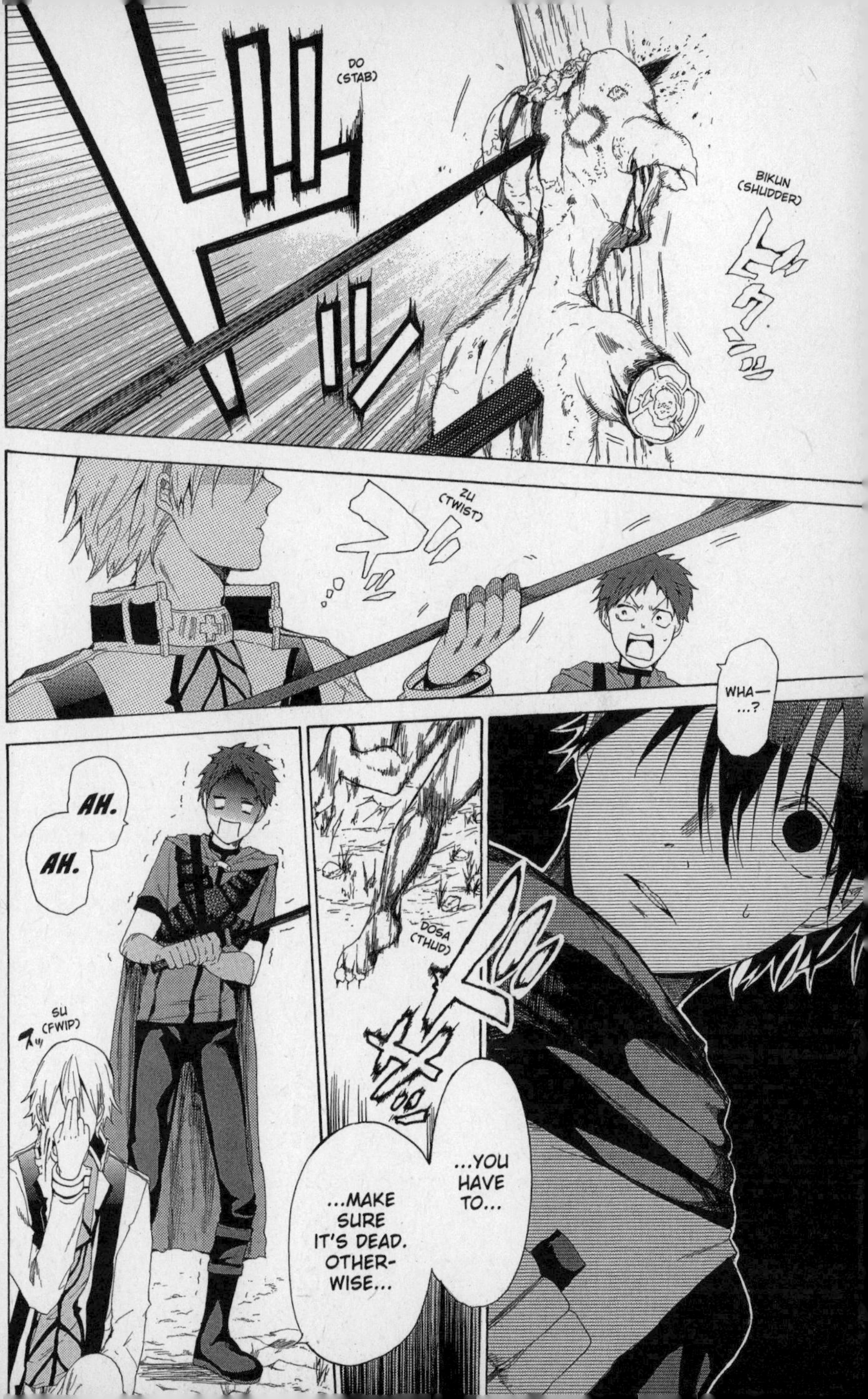
BIKUN (SHUDDER)
DO (STAB)
ZU (TWIST)
WHA— ...?
...YOU HAVE TO...
...MAKE SURE IT'S DEAD. OTHER-WISE...
DOSA (THUD)
AH.
AH.
SU (FWIP)

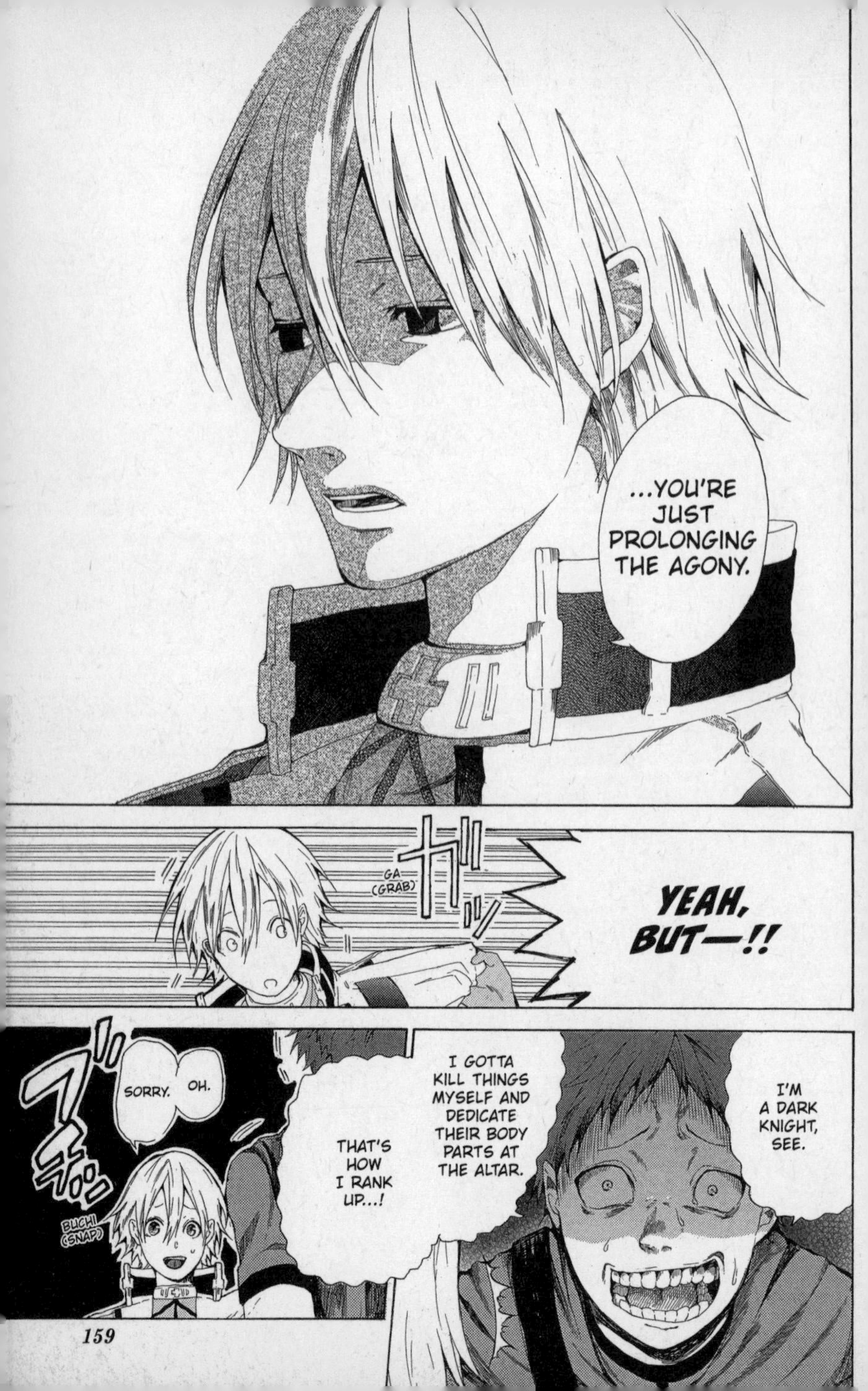
...YOU'RE JUST PROLONGING THE AGONY.
YEAH, BUT—!!
GA (GRAB)
I'M A DARK KNIGHT, SEE.
I GOTTA KILL THINGS MYSELF AND DEDICATE THEIR BODY PARTS AT THE ALTAR.
THAT'S HOW I RANK UP...!
OH.
SORRY.
BUCHI (SNAP)

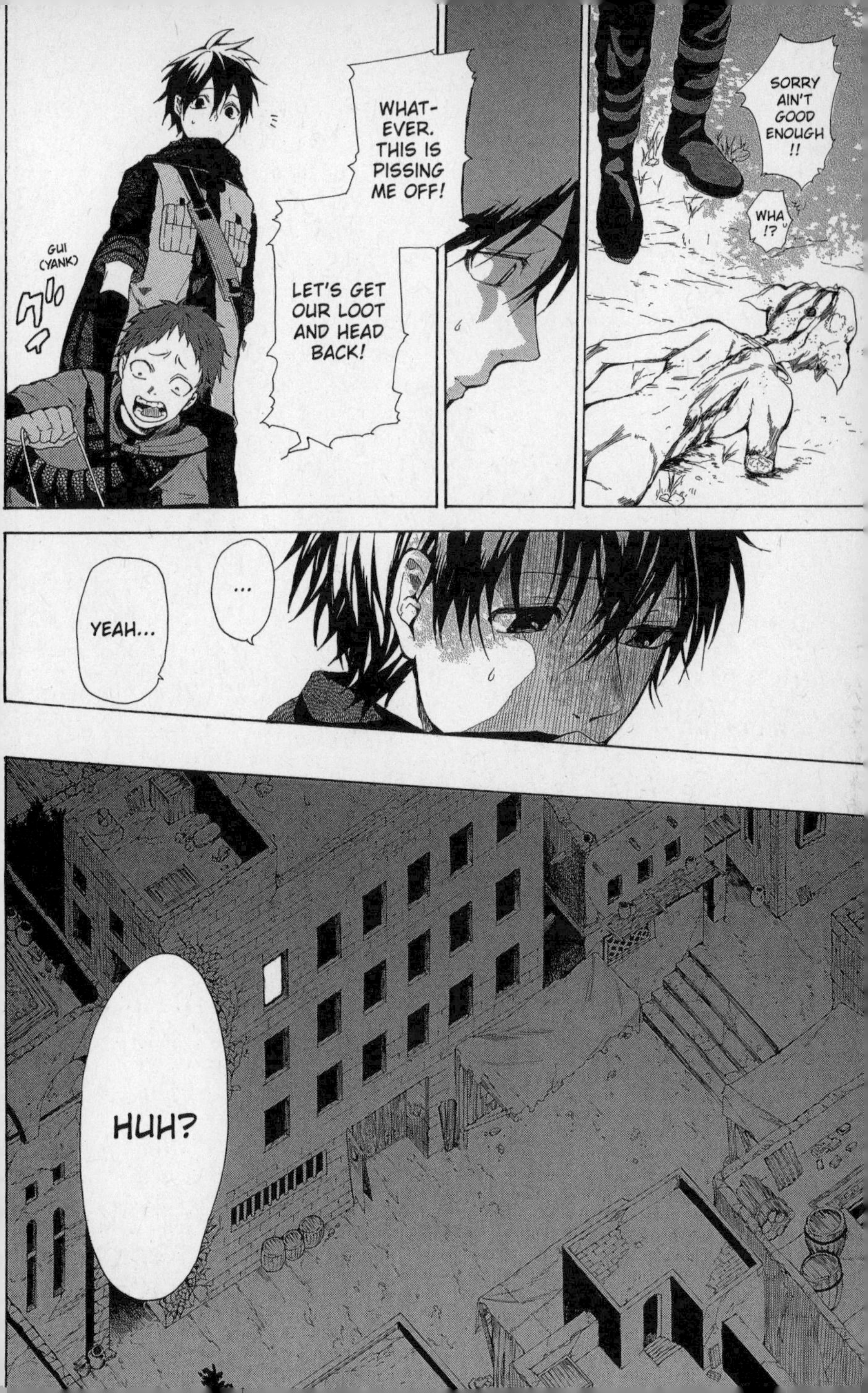
SORRY AIN'T GOOD ENOUGH!!
WHA!?
WHAT-EVER. THIS IS PISSING ME OFF!
LET'S GET OUR LOOT AND HEAD BACK!
GUI (YANK)
...
YEAH...
HUH?

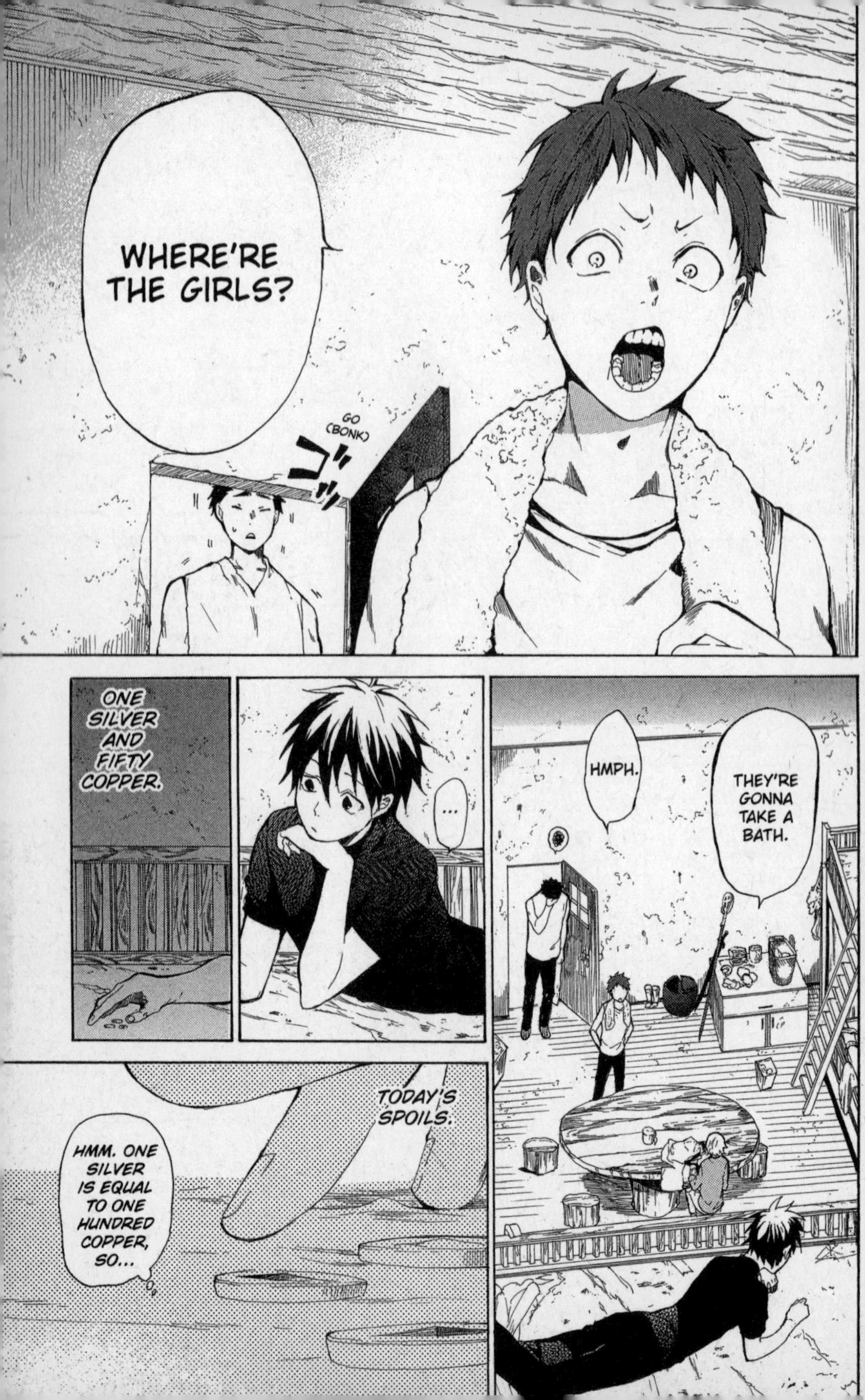
WHERE'RE THE GIRLS?
ゴッ
GO (BONK)
THEY'RE GONNA TAKE A BATH.
HMPH.
...
ONE SILVER AND FIFTY COPPER.
TODAY'S SPOILS.
HMM. ONE SILVER IS EQUAL TO ONE HUNDRED COPPER, SO...

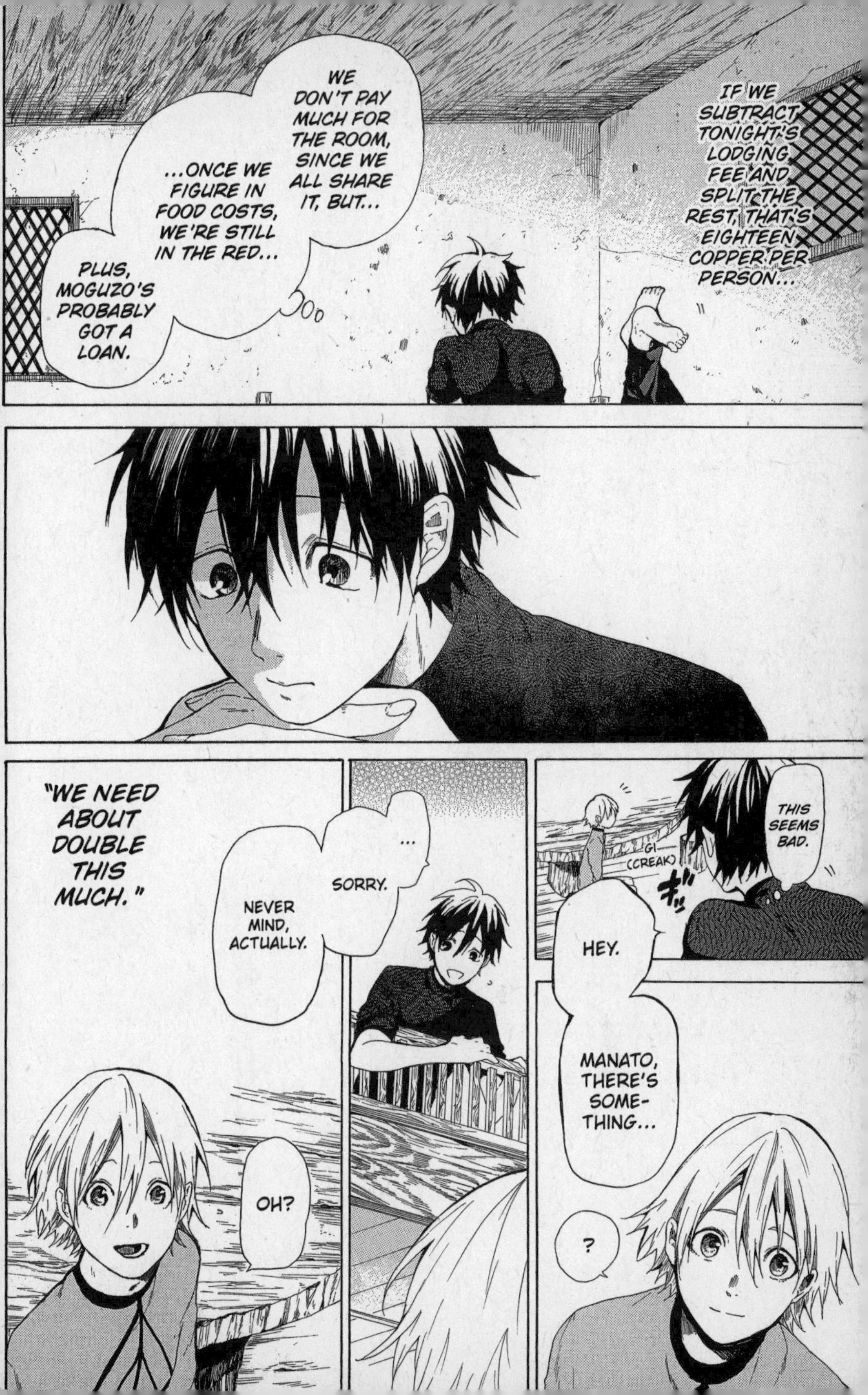
IF WE SUBTRACT TONIGHT'S LODGING FEE AND SPLIT THE REST, THAT'S EIGHTEEN COPPER PER PERSON...
WE DON'T PAY MUCH FOR THE ROOM, SINCE WE ALL SHARE IT, BUT...
...ONCE WE FIGURE IN FOOD COSTS, WE'RE STILL IN THE RED...
PLUS, MOGUZO'S PROBABLY GOT A LOAN.
THIS SEEMS BAD.
GI (CREAK)
HEY.
MANATO, THERE'S SOME-THING...
?
...
SORRY.
NEVER MIND, ACTUALLY.
"WE NEED ABOUT DOUBLE THIS MUCH."
OH?

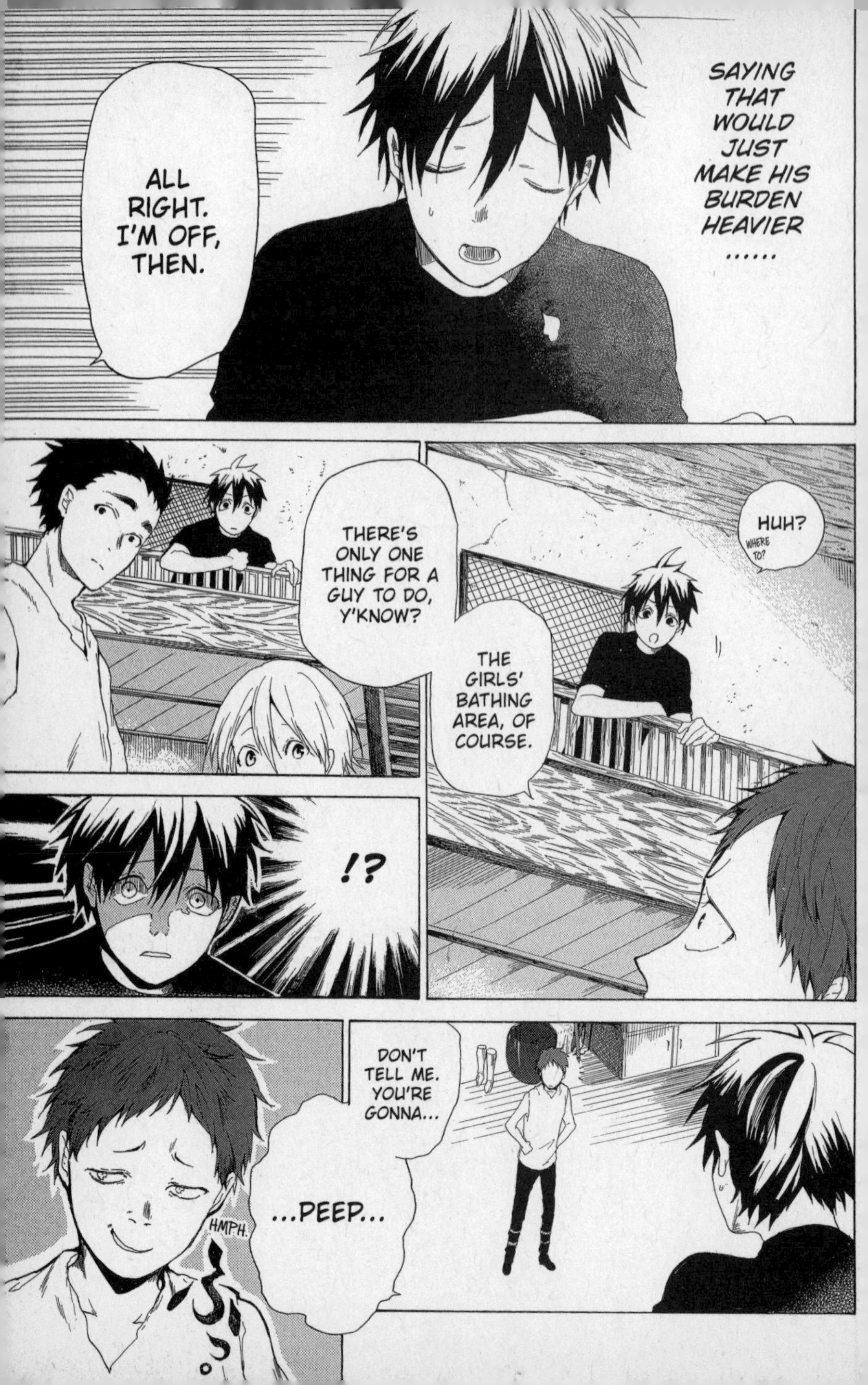
SAYING THAT WOULD JUST MAKE HIS BURDEN HEAVIER......
ALL RIGHT. I'M OFF, THEN.
HUH?
WHERE TO?
THERE'S ONLY ONE THING FOR A GUY TO DO, Y'KNOW?
THE GIRLS' BATHING AREA, OF COURSE.
!?
DON'T TELL ME. YOU'RE GONNA...
...PEEP...
HMPH.

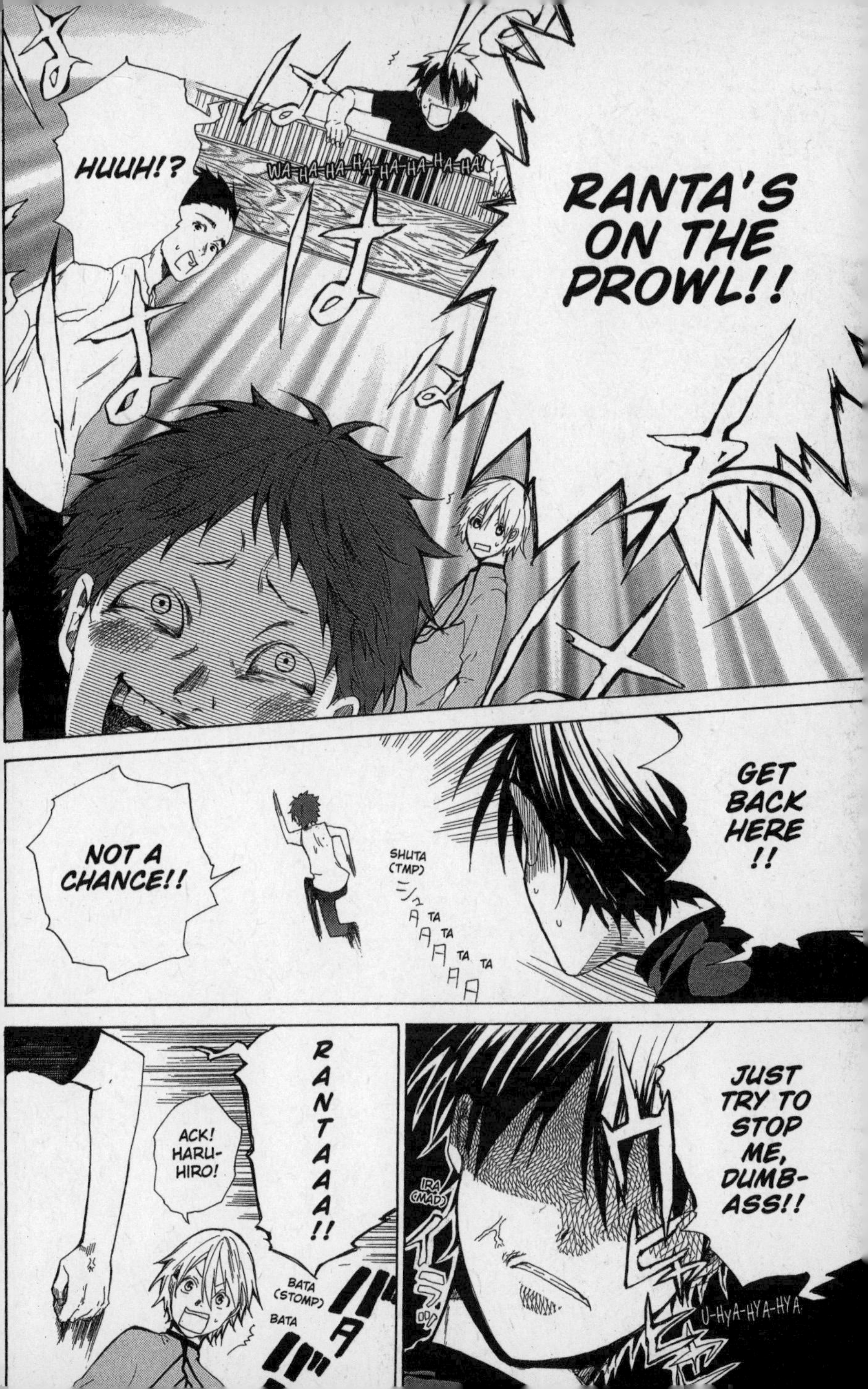
RANTA'S ON THE PROWL!!
WA-HA-HA-HA-HA-HA-HA-HA!
HUUH!?
GET BACK HERE!!
SHUTA (TMP)
TA TA TA TA
NOT A CHANCE!!
JUST TRY TO STOP ME, DUMB-ASS!!
IRA (MAD)
U-HYA-HYA-HYA
RANTAAAA!!
ACK! HARU-HIRO!
BATA (STOMP)
BATA

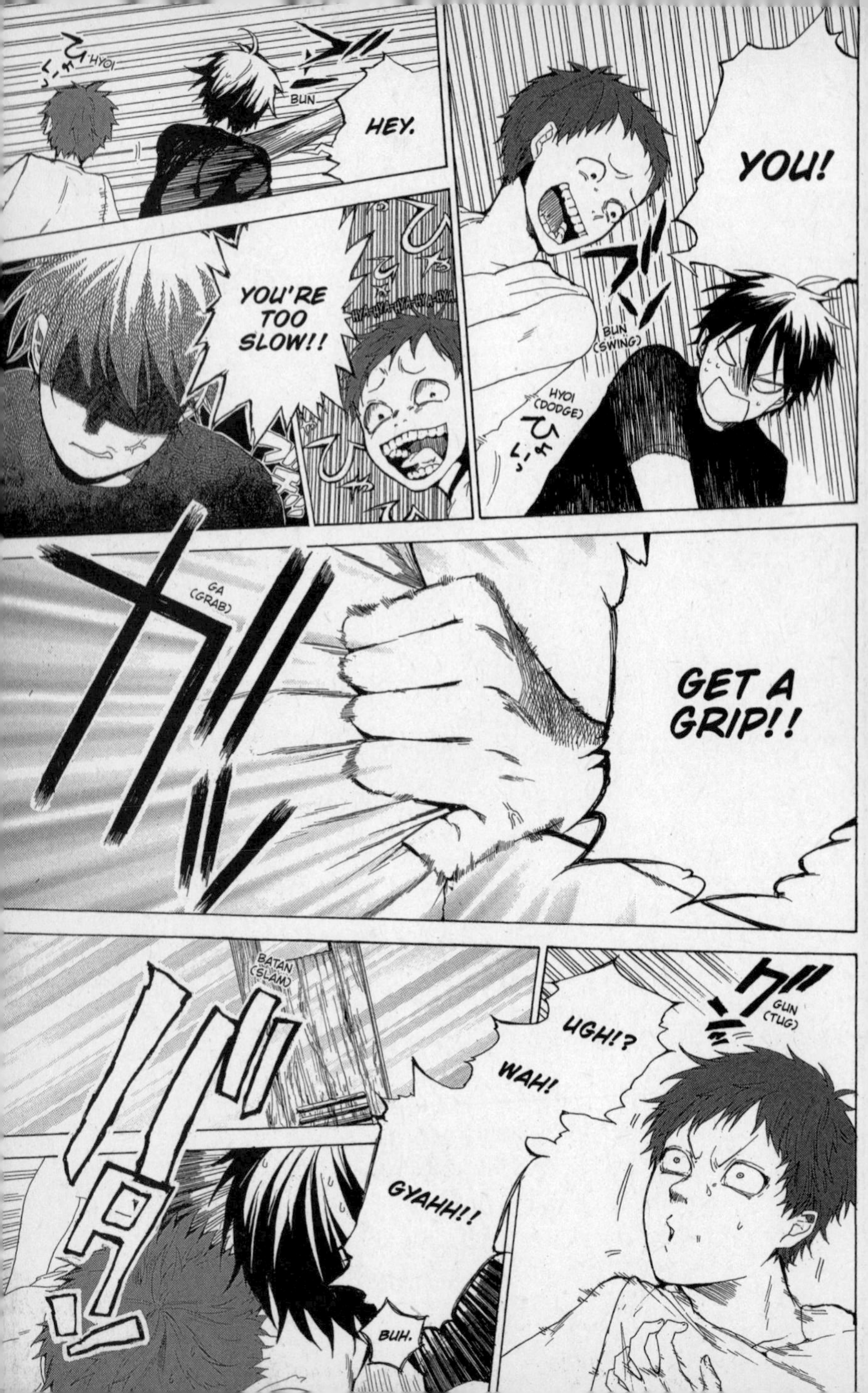
YOU!
BUN (SWING)
HYOI (DODGE)
HYOI
BUN
HEY.
YOU'RE TOO SLOW!!
GA (GRAB)
GET A GRIP!!
GUN (TUG)
UGH!?
WAH!
GYAHH!!
BUH.
BATAN (SLAM)

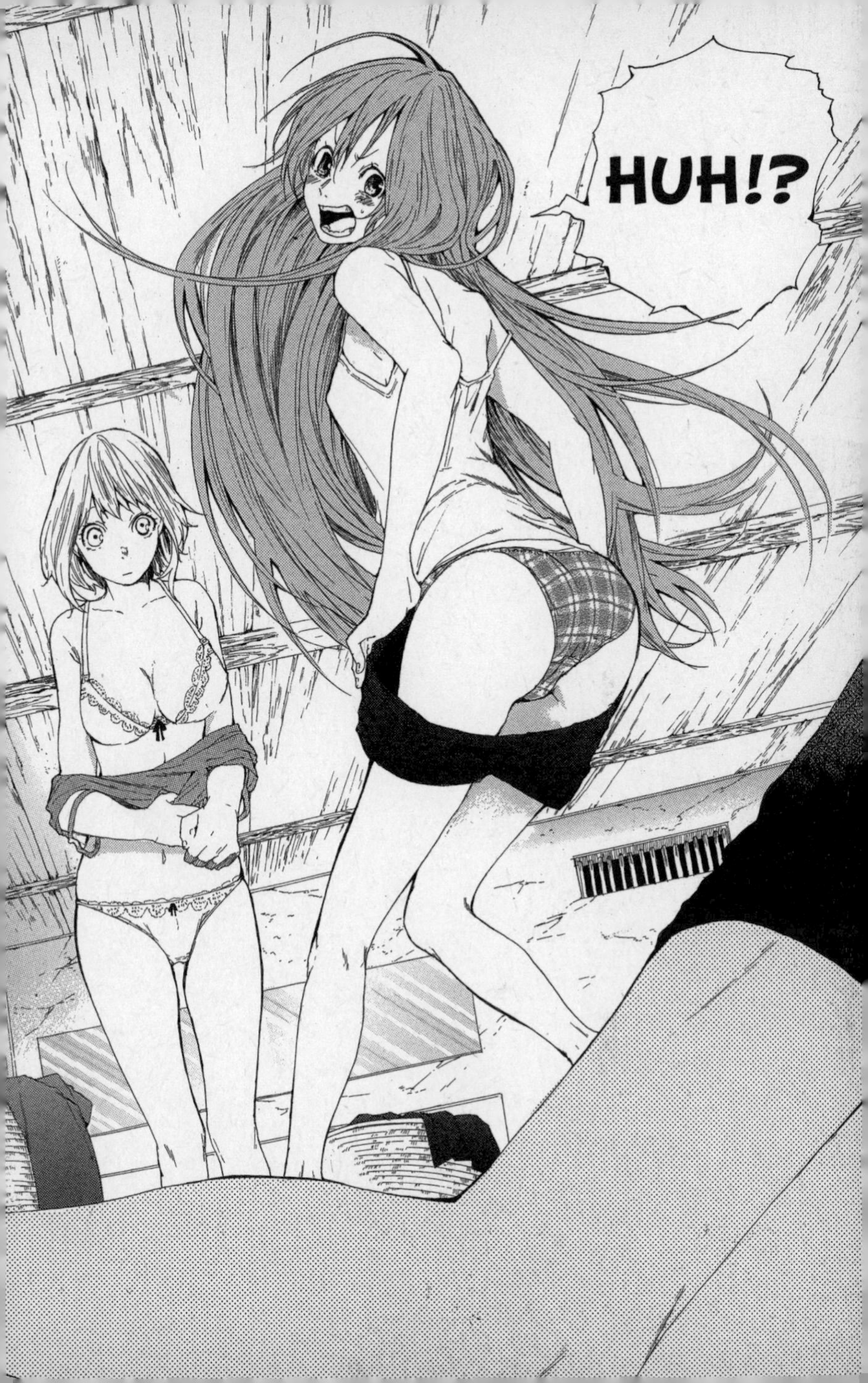
HUH!?

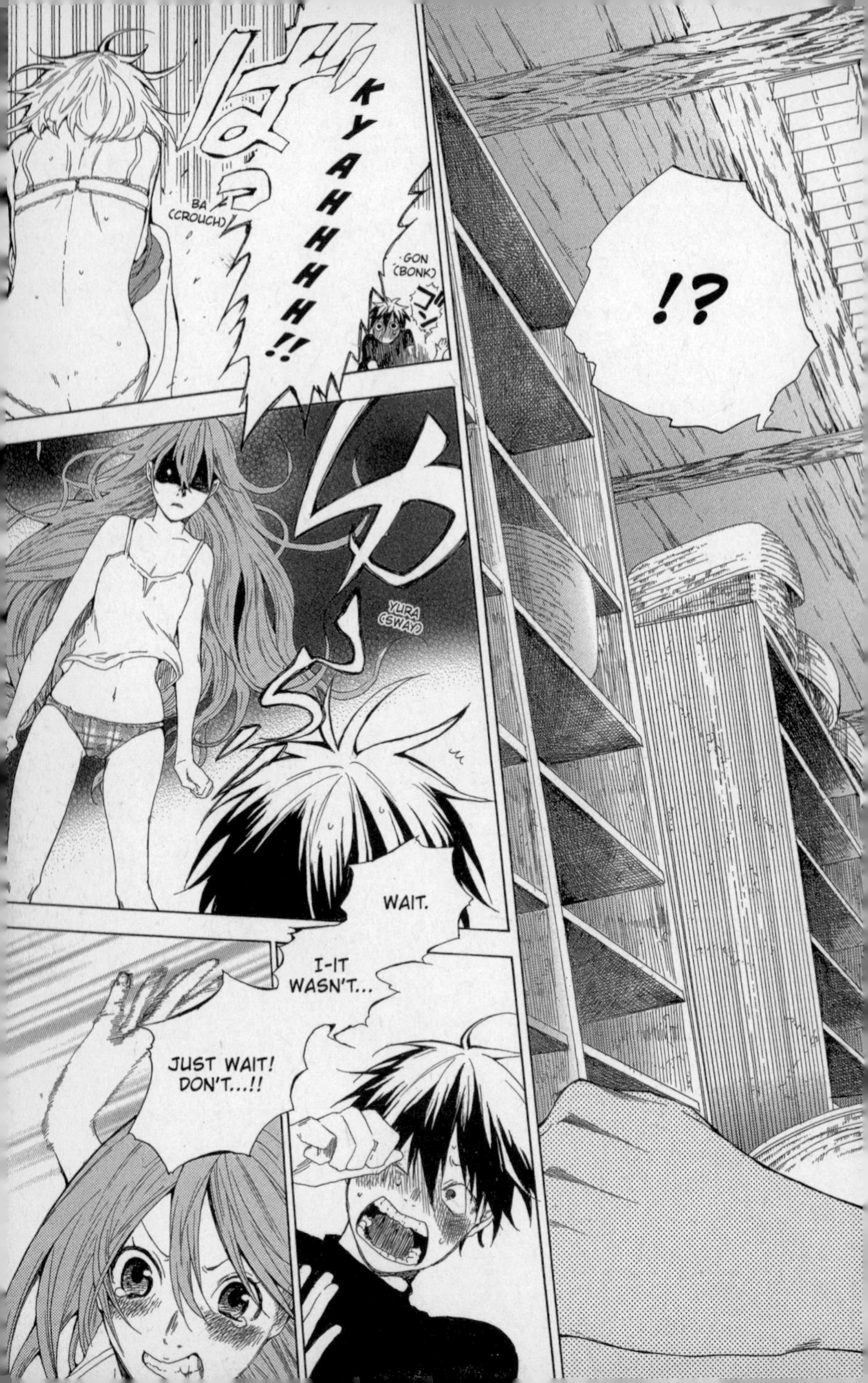
!?
GON
(BONK)
KYAHHHHHH!!
BA
(CROUCH)
YURA
(SWAY)
WAIT.
I-IT
WASN'T...
JUST WAIT!
DON'T...!!

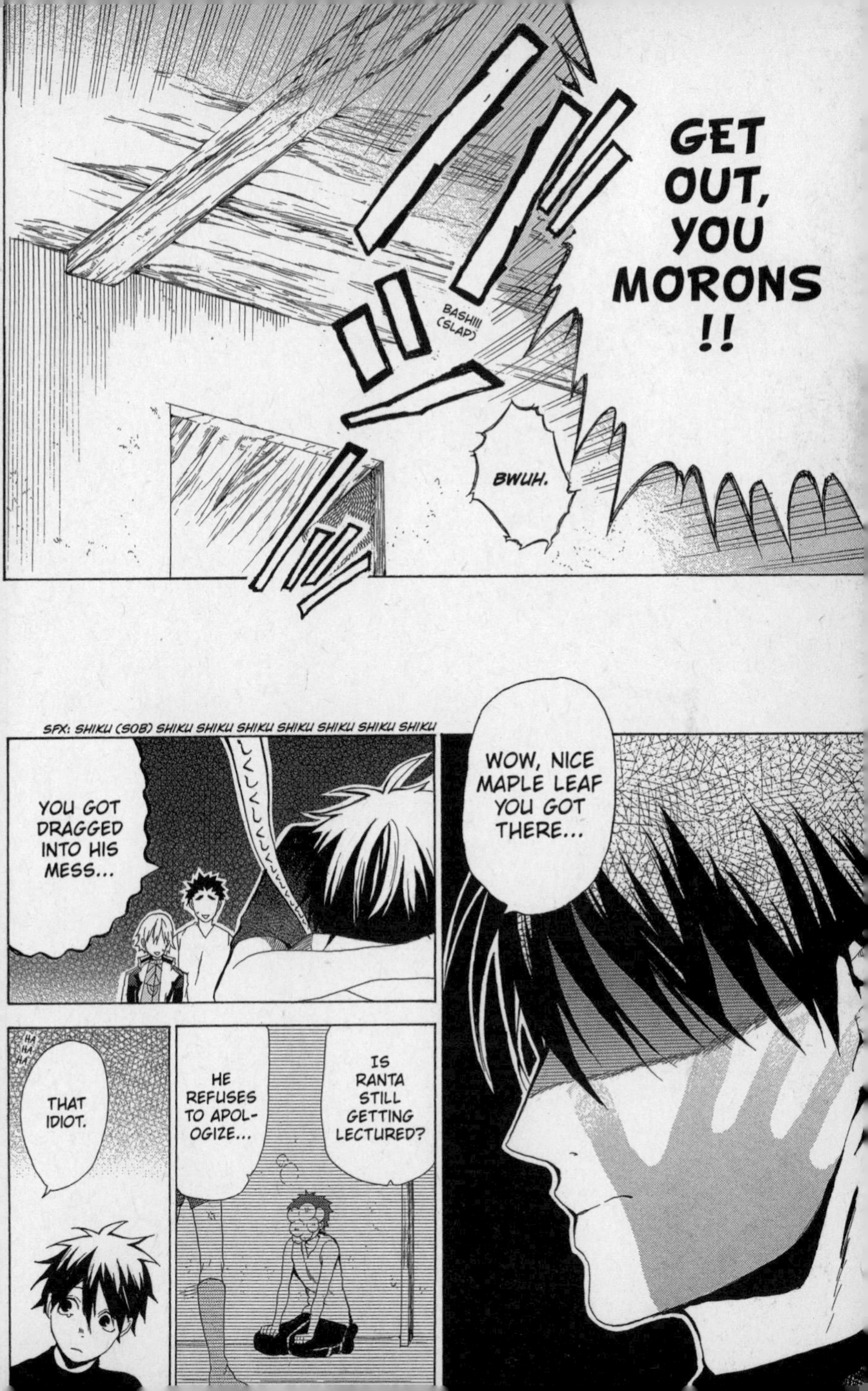
GET OUT, YOU MORONS!!
BASH!!! (SLAP)
BWUH.
WOW, NICE MAPLE LEAF YOU GOT THERE...
SFX: SHIKU (SOB) SHIKU SHIKU SHIKU SHIKU SHIKU SHIKU SHIKU
YOU GOT DRAGGED INTO HIS MESS...
IS RANTA STILL GETTING LECTURED?
HE REFUSES TO APOL-OGIZE...
HA HA HA
THAT IDIOT.

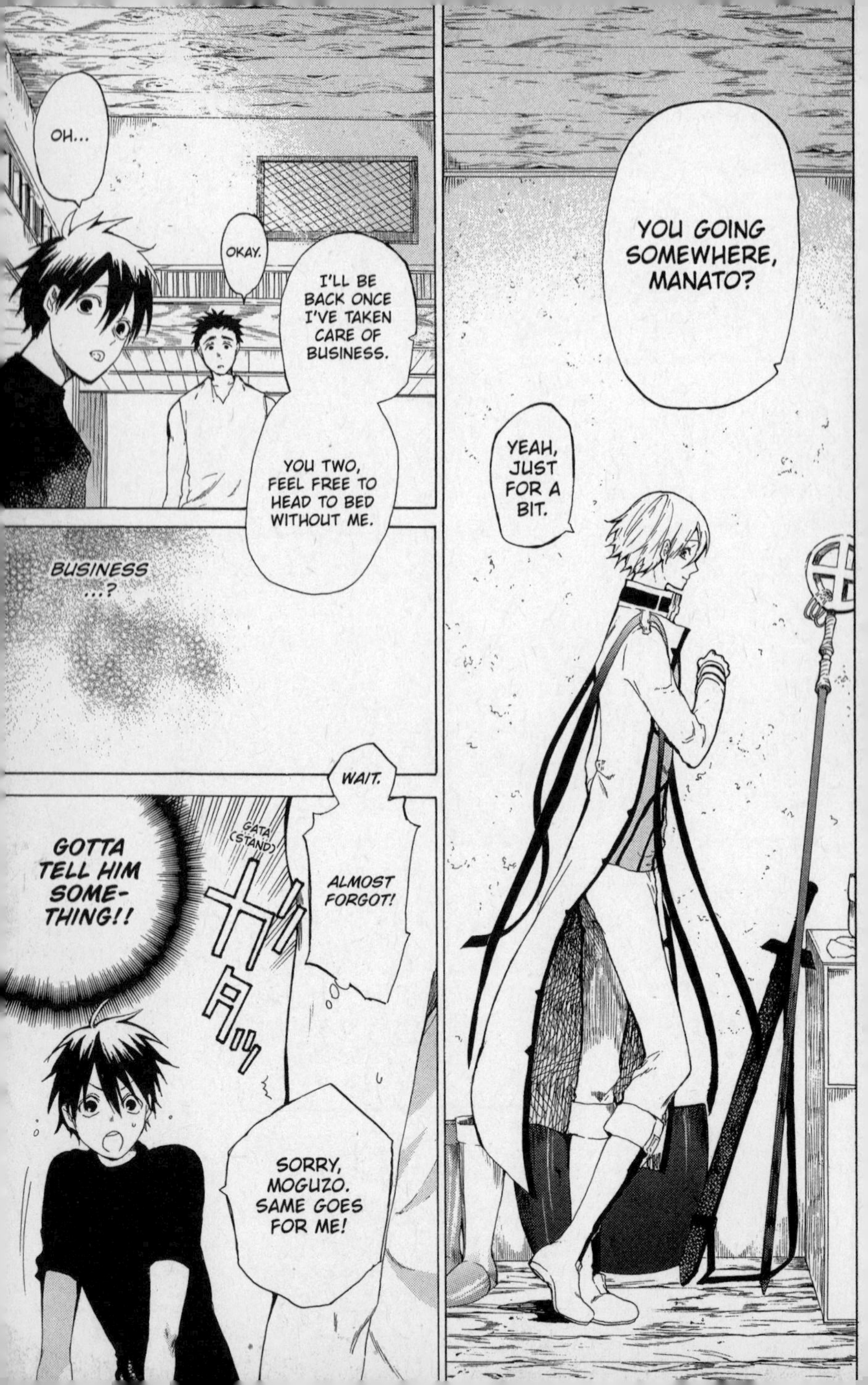
YOU GOING SOMEWHERE, MANATO?
YEAH, JUST FOR A BIT.
I'LL BE BACK ONCE I'VE TAKEN CARE OF BUSINESS.
YOU TWO, FEEL FREE TO HEAD TO BED WITHOUT ME.
OKAY.
OH...
BUSINESS ...?
WAIT.
ALMOST FORGOT!
ガタッ
GATA (STAND)
GOTTA TELL HIM SOME-THING!!
SORRY, MOGUZO. SAME GOES FOR ME!

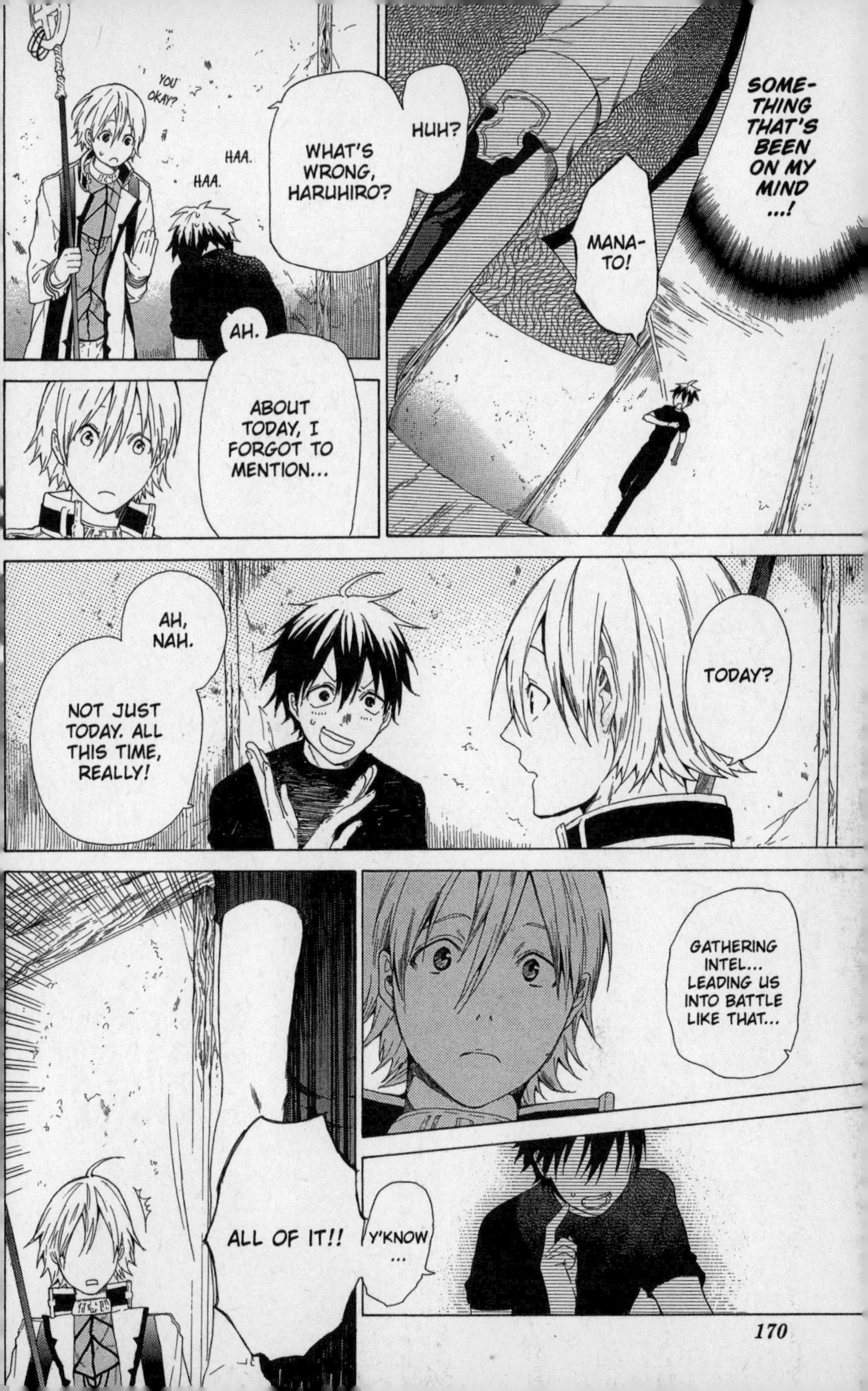
SOME-THING THAT'S BEEN ON MY MIND...!
MANA-TO!
HUH?
WHAT'S WRONG, HARUHIRO?
HAA.
HAA.
YOU OKAY?
AH.
ABOUT TODAY, I FORGOT TO MENTION...
TODAY?
AH, NAH.
NOT JUST TODAY. ALL THIS TIME, REALLY!
GATHERING INTEL... LEADING US INTO BATTLE LIKE THAT...
Y'KNOW...
ALL OF IT!!

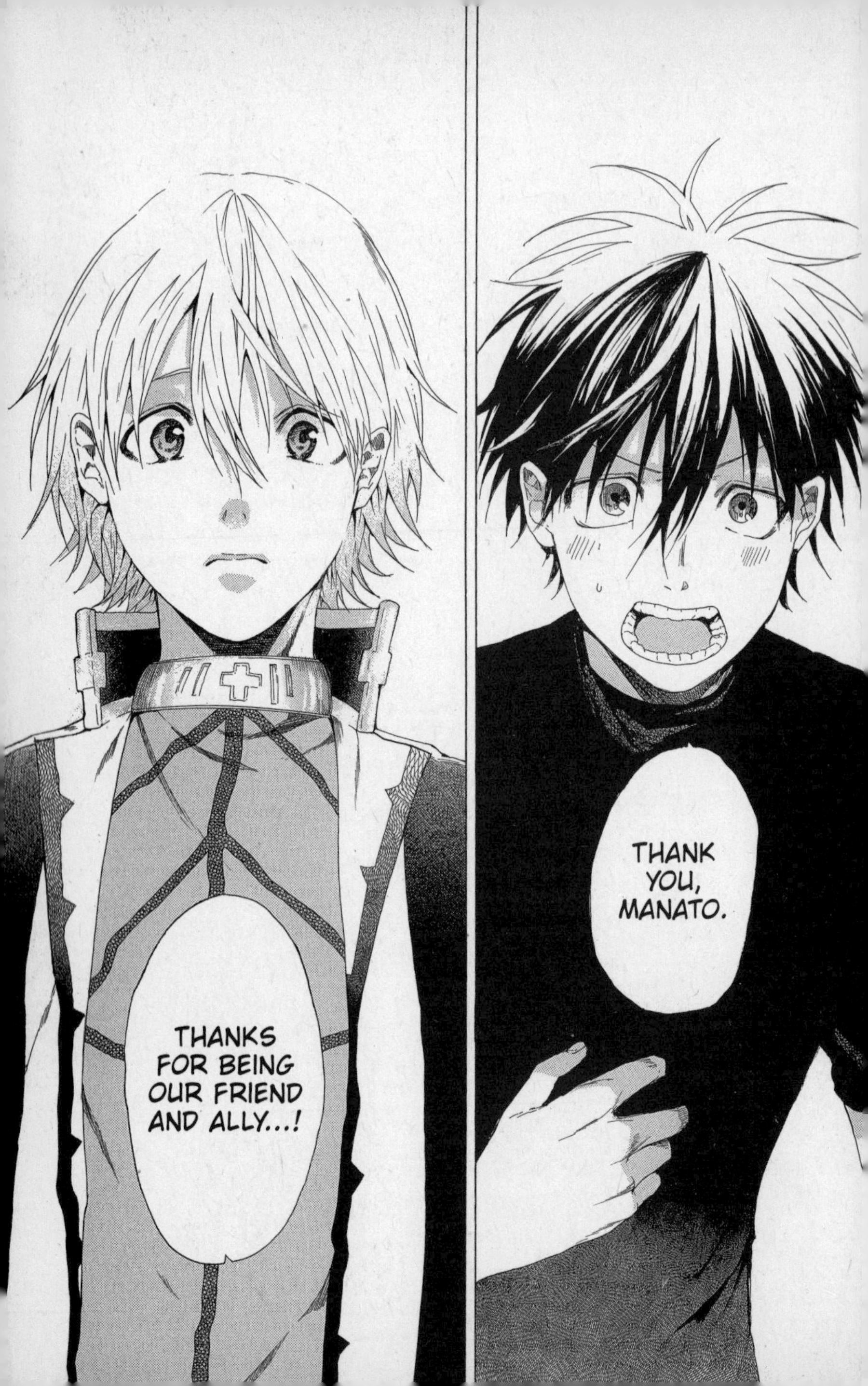
THANK YOU, MANATO.
THANKS FOR BEING OUR FRIEND AND ALLY...!

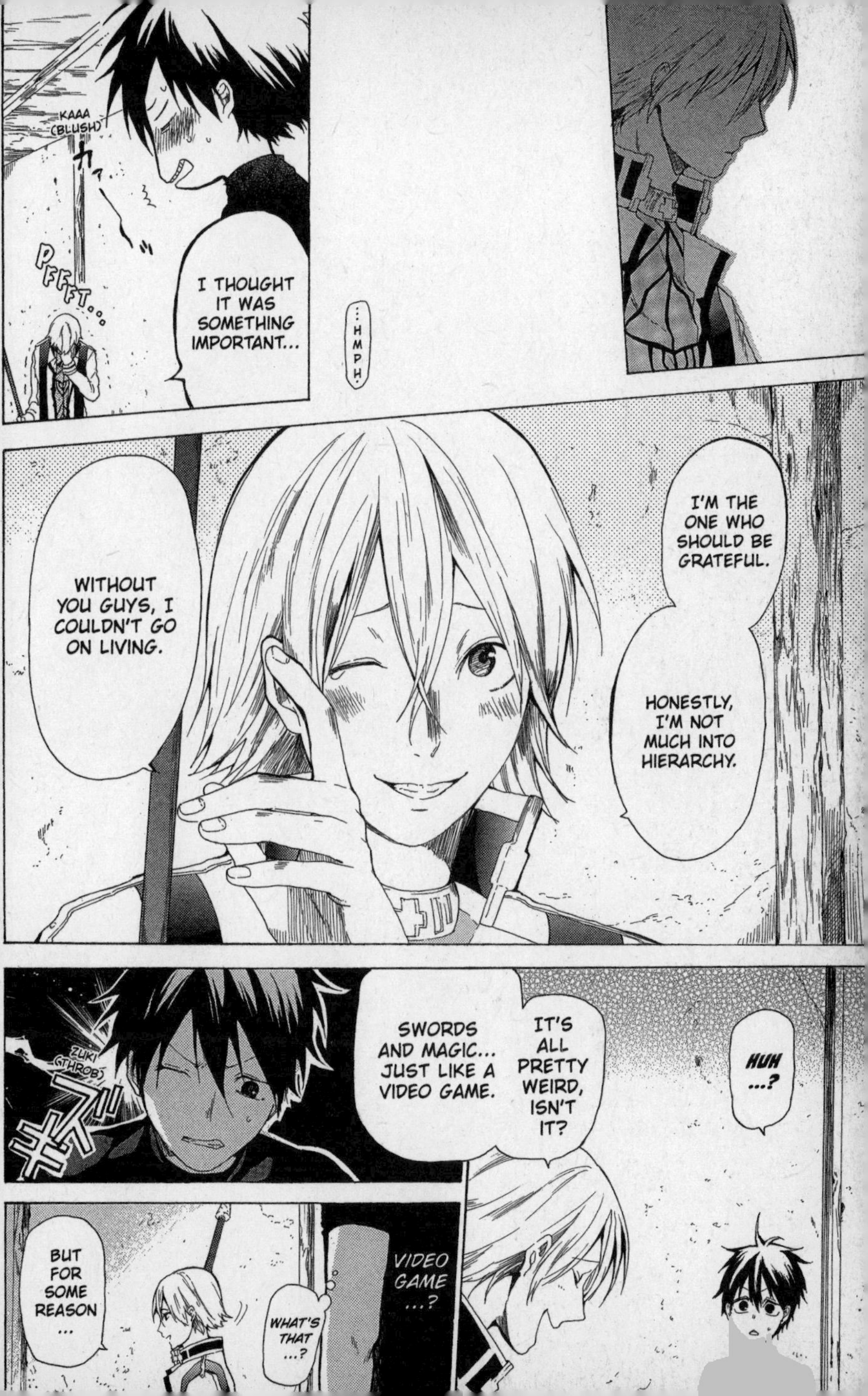
...HMPH.
KAAA (BLUSH)
I THOUGHT IT WAS SOMETHING IMPORTANT...
PFFFT...
I'M THE ONE WHO SHOULD BE GRATEFUL.
HONESTLY, I'M NOT MUCH INTO HIERARCHY.
WITHOUT YOU GUYS, I COULDN'T GO ON LIVING.
HUH ...?
IT'S ALL PRETTY WEIRD, ISN'T IT?
SWORDS AND MAGIC... JUST LIKE A VIDEO GAME.
ZUKI (THROB)
VIDEO GAME ...?
WHAT'S THAT ...?
BUT FOR SOME REASON ...

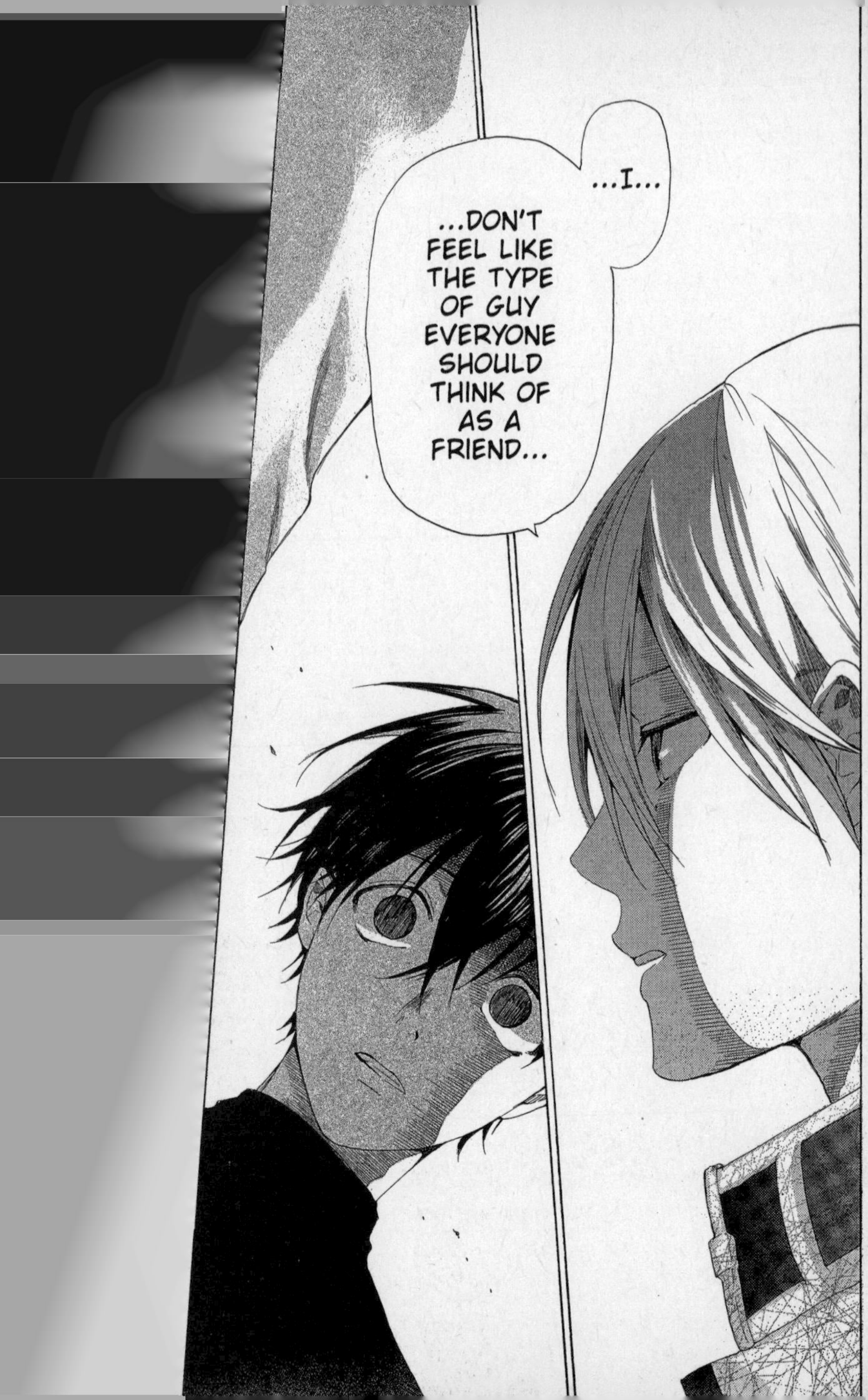
...I...
...DON'T FEEL LIKE THE TYPE OF GUY EVERYONE SHOULD THINK OF AS A FRIEND...

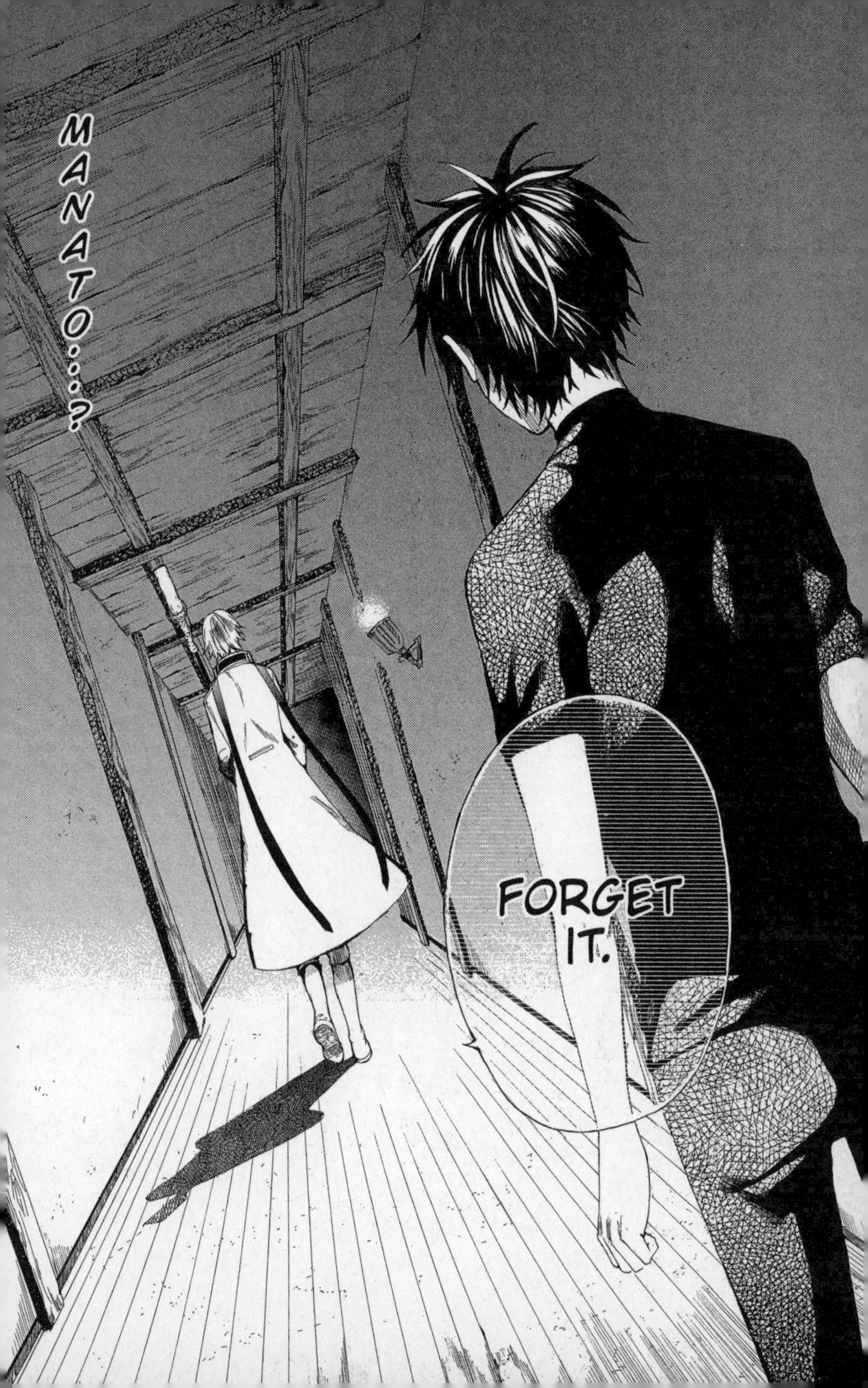
MANATO...?
FORGET IT.

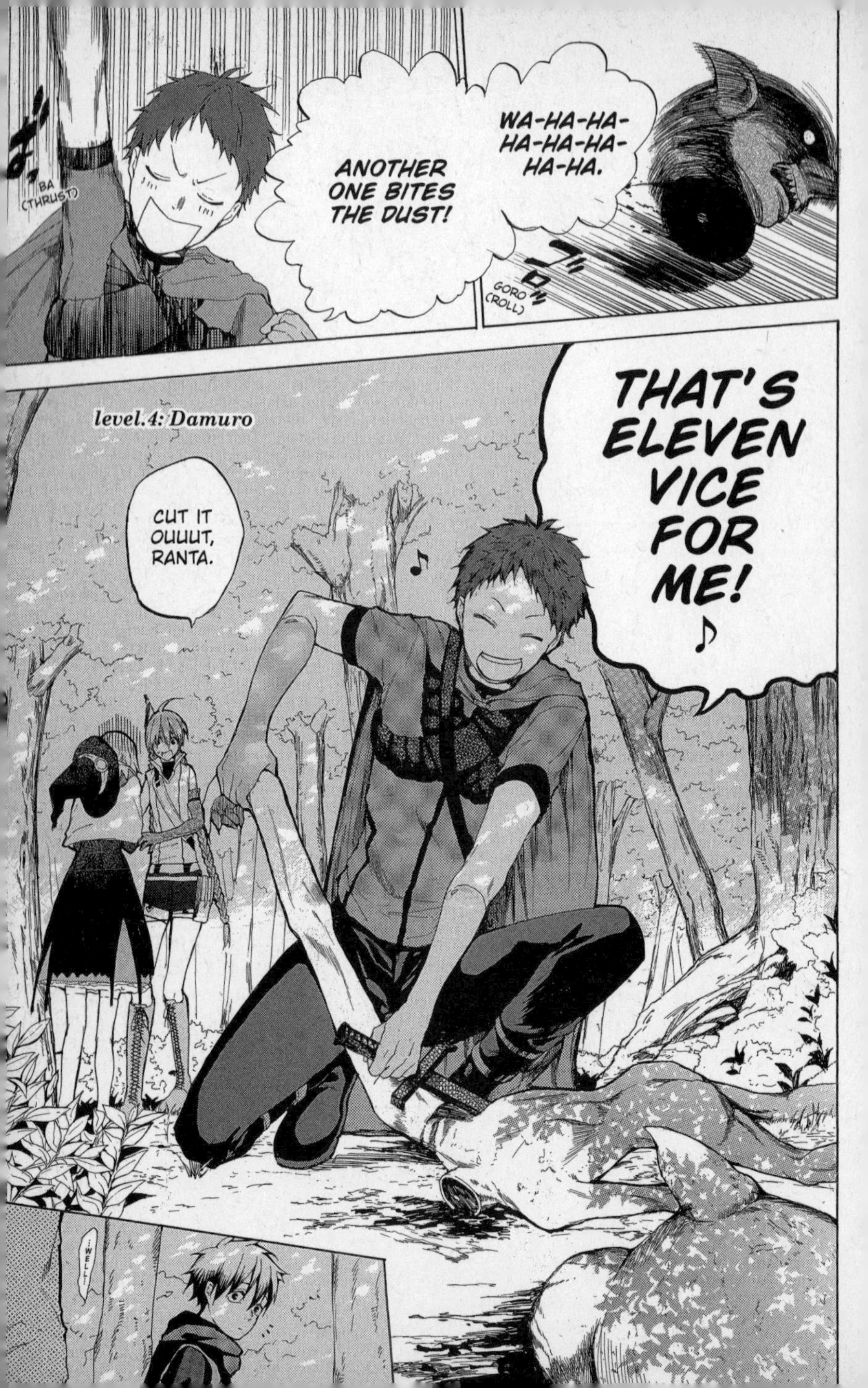
WA-HA-HA-HA-HA-HA-HA-HA.
GORO (ROLL)
ANOTHER ONE BITES THE DUST!
BA (THRUST)
THAT'S ELEVEN VICE FOR ME! ♪
level.4: Damuro
CUT IT OUUUT, RANTA.
...WELL...

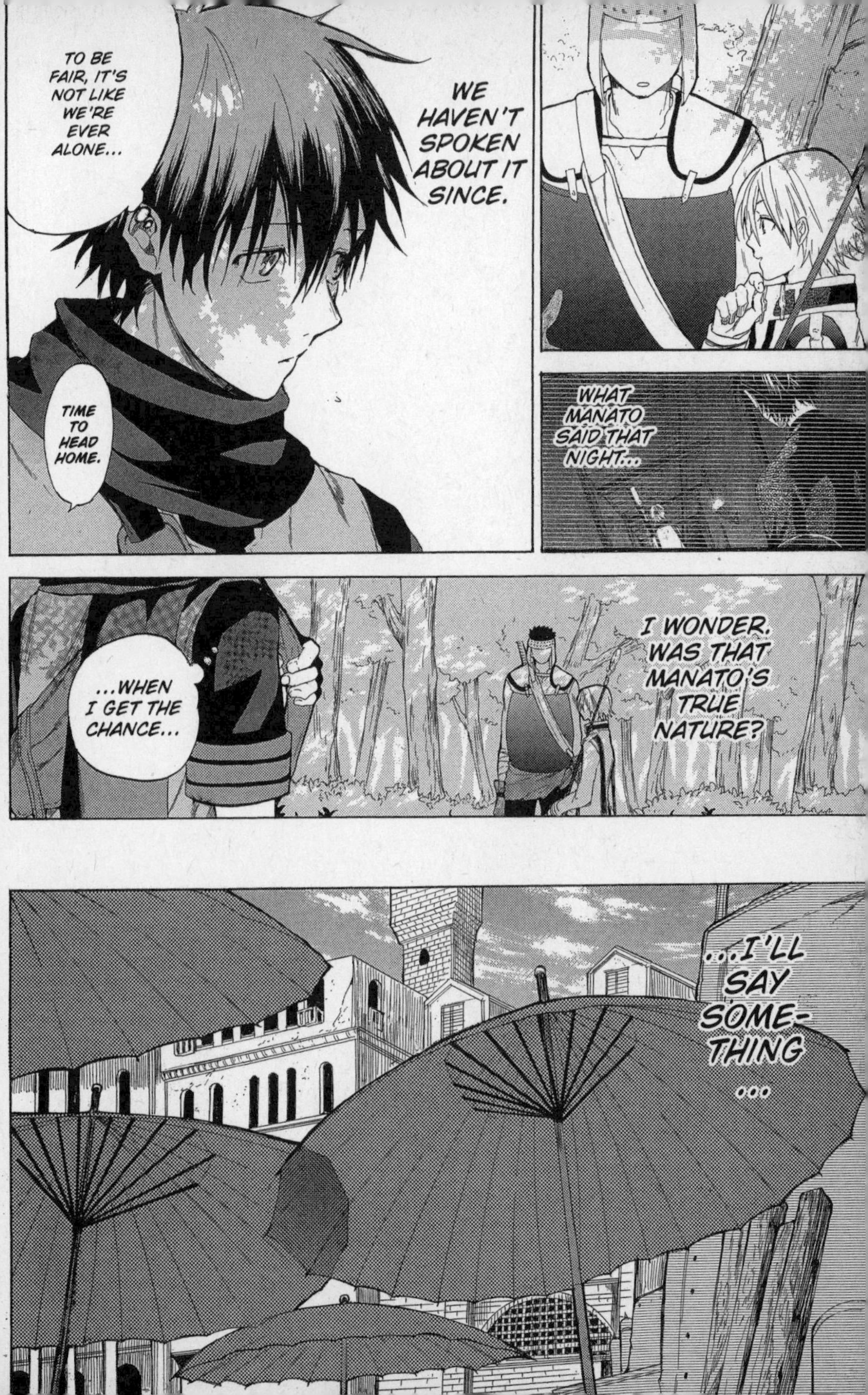
WHAT MANATO SAID THAT NIGHT...
WE HAVEN'T SPOKEN ABOUT IT SINCE.
TO BE FAIR, IT'S NOT LIKE WE'RE EVER ALONE...
TIME TO HEAD HOME.
I WONDER. WAS THAT MANATO'S TRUE NATURE?
...WHEN I GET THE CHANCE...
...I'LL SAY SOME-THING...

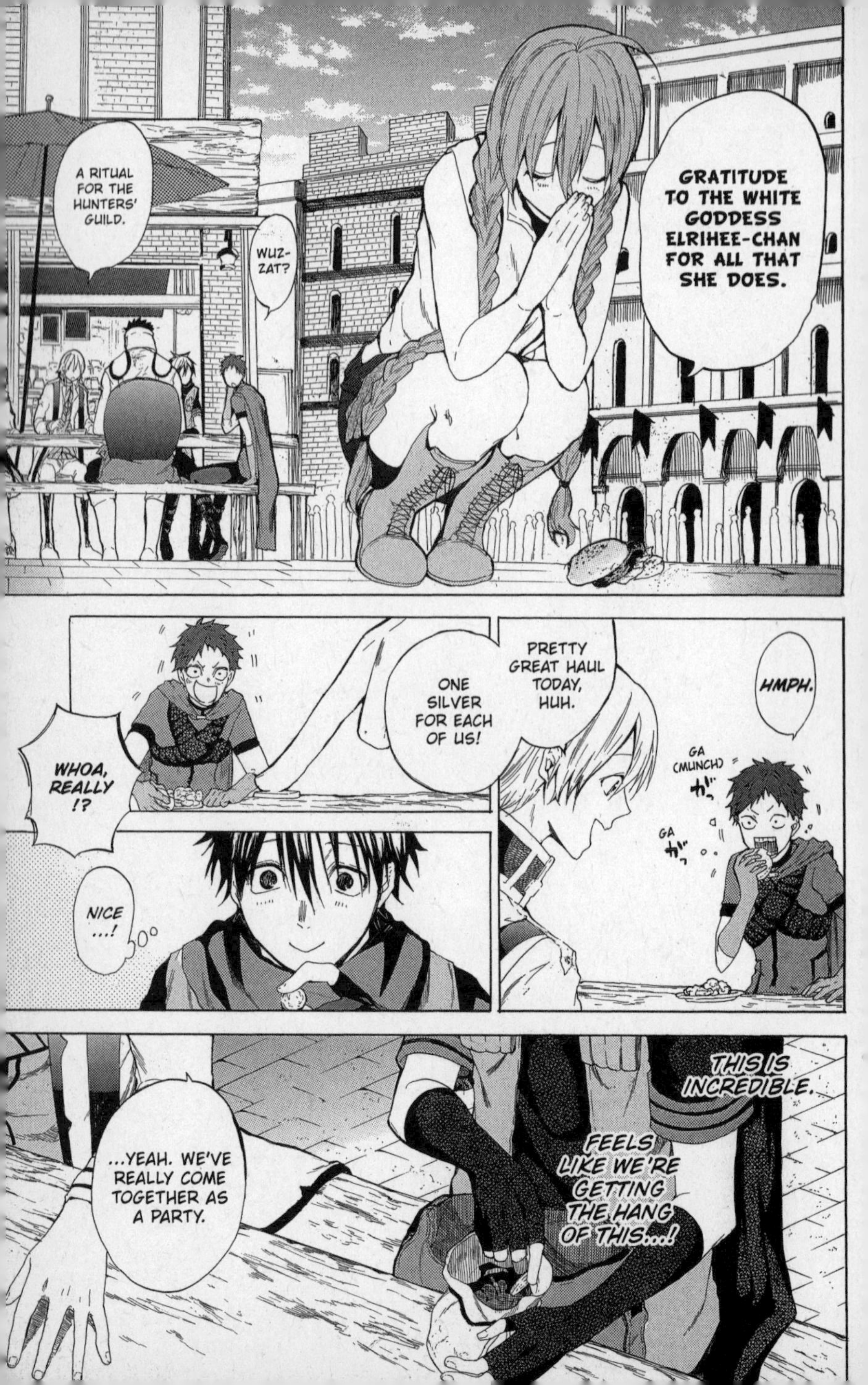
GRATITUDE TO THE WHITE GODDESS ELRIHEE-CHAN FOR ALL THAT SHE DOES.
WUZ-ZAT?
A RITUAL FOR THE HUNTERS' GUILD.
HMPH.
PRETTY GREAT HAUL TODAY, HUH.
GA (MUNCH)
GA
ONE SILVER FOR EACH OF US!
WHOA, REALLY!?
NICE...!
THIS IS INCREDIBLE.
FEELS LIKE WE'RE GETTING THE HANG OF THIS...!
...YEAH. WE'VE REALLY COME TOGETHER AS A PARTY.

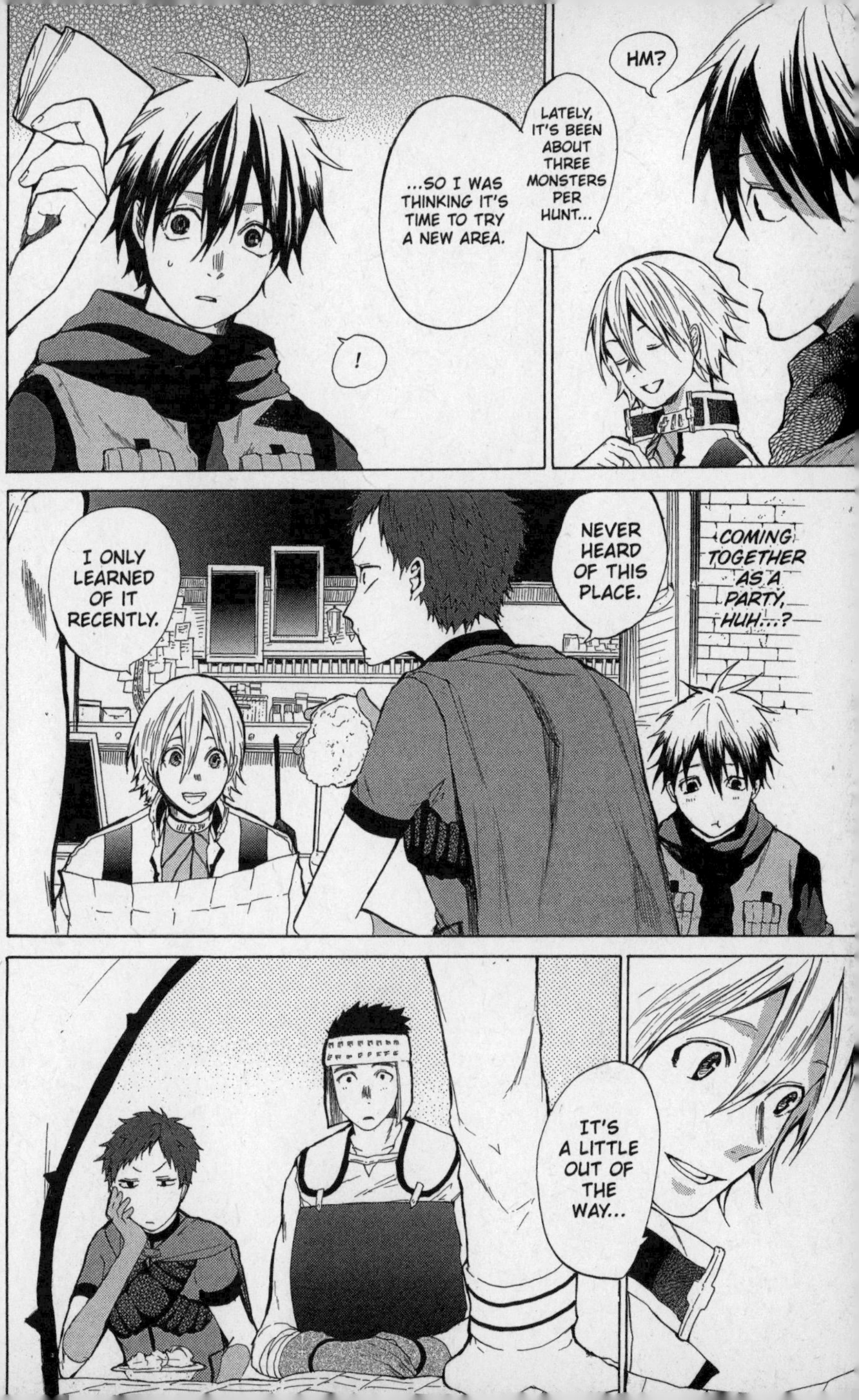
HM?
LATELY, IT'S BEEN ABOUT THREE MONSTERS PER HUNT...
...SO I WAS THINKING IT'S TIME TO TRY A NEW AREA.
!
COMING TOGETHER AS A PARTY, HUH...?
NEVER HEARD OF THIS PLACE.
I ONLY LEARNED OF IT RECENTLY.
IT'S A LITTLE OUT OF THE WAY...

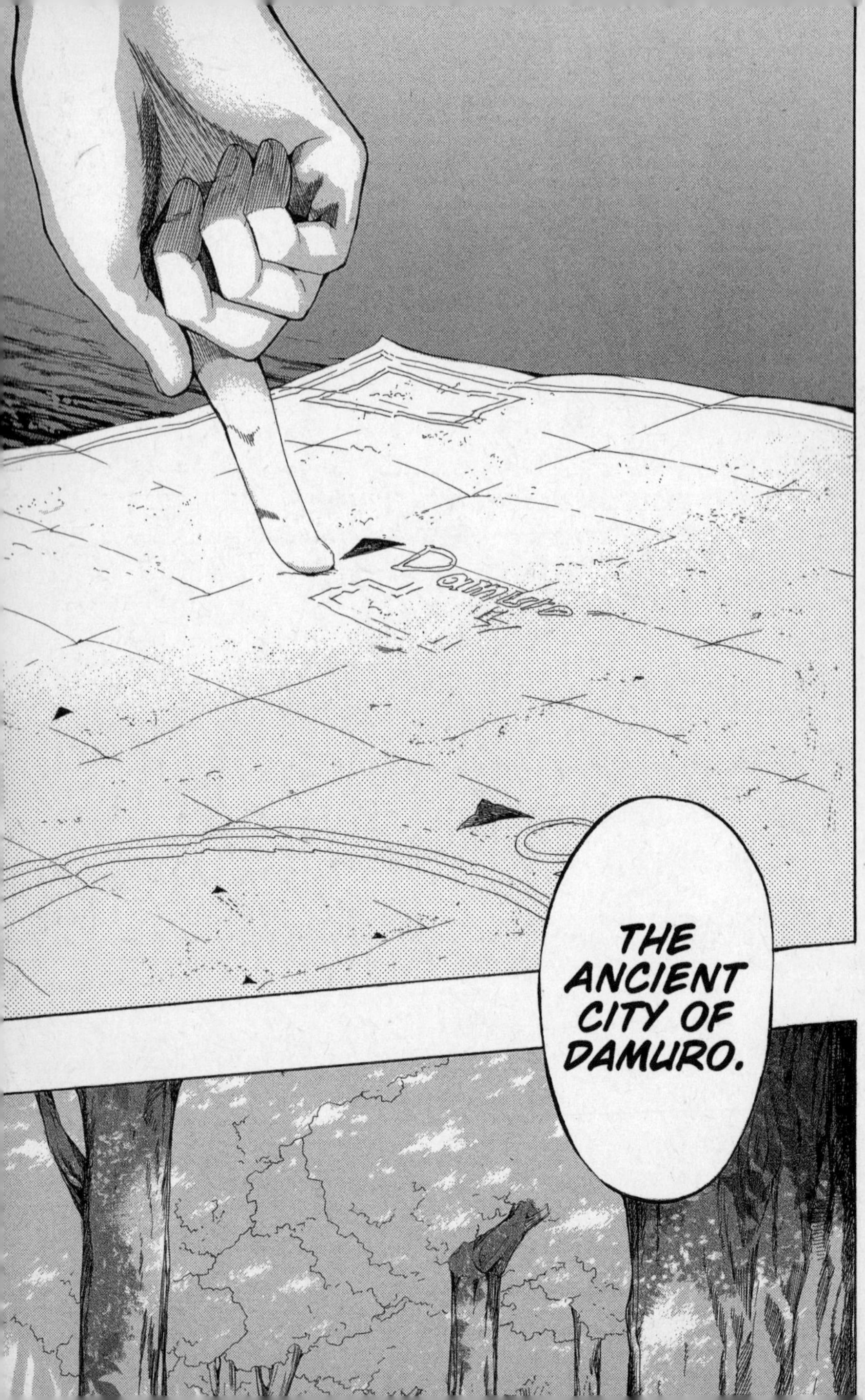
THE ANCIENT CITY OF DAMURO.

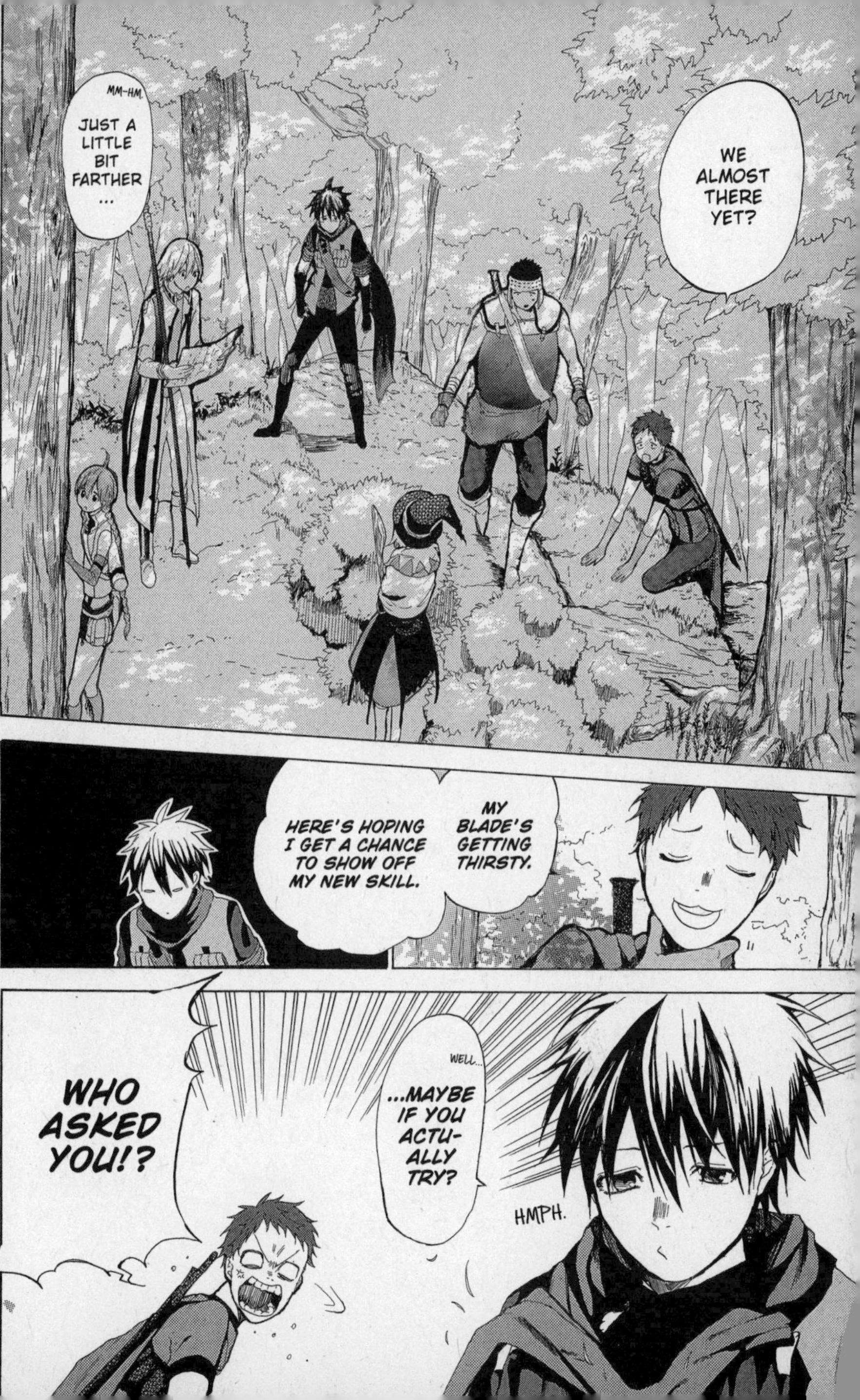
WE ALMOST THERE YET?
MM-HM. JUST A LITTLE BIT FARTHER...
MY BLADE'S GETTING THIRSTY.
HERE'S HOPING I GET A CHANCE TO SHOW OFF MY NEW SKILL.
WELL... ...MAYBE IF YOU ACTU-ALLY TRY?
HMPH.
WHO ASKED YOU!?

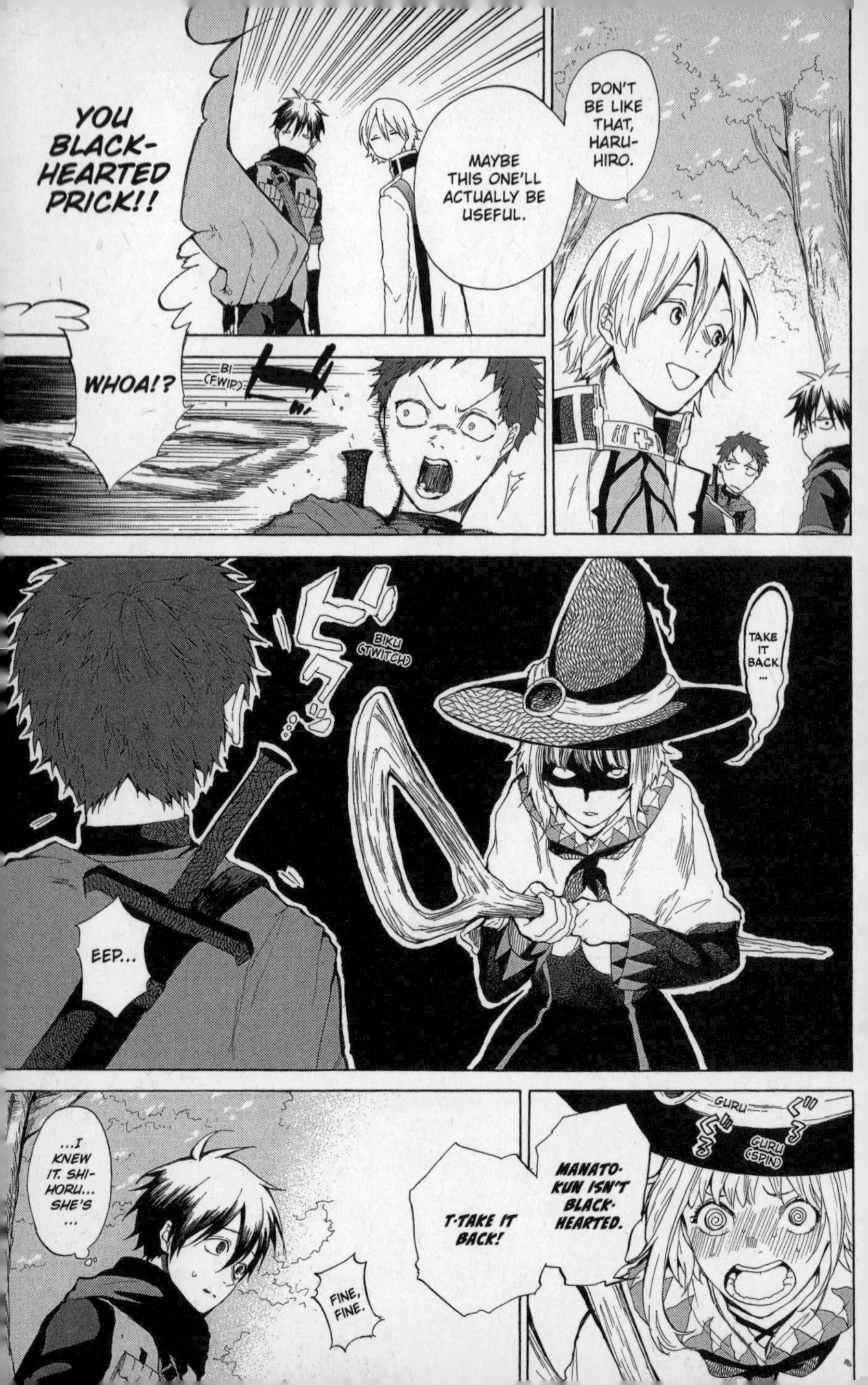
DON'T BE LIKE THAT, HARUHIRO.
MAYBE THIS ONE'LL ACTUALLY BE USEFUL.
YOU BLACK-HEARTED PRICK!!
WHOA!?
BI (FWIP)
TAKE IT BACK...
BIKU (TWITCH)
EEP...
GURU
GURU (SPIN)
MANATO-KUN ISN'T BLACK-HEARTED.
T-TAKE IT BACK!
FINE, FINE.
...I KNEW IT. SHIHORU... SHE'S...

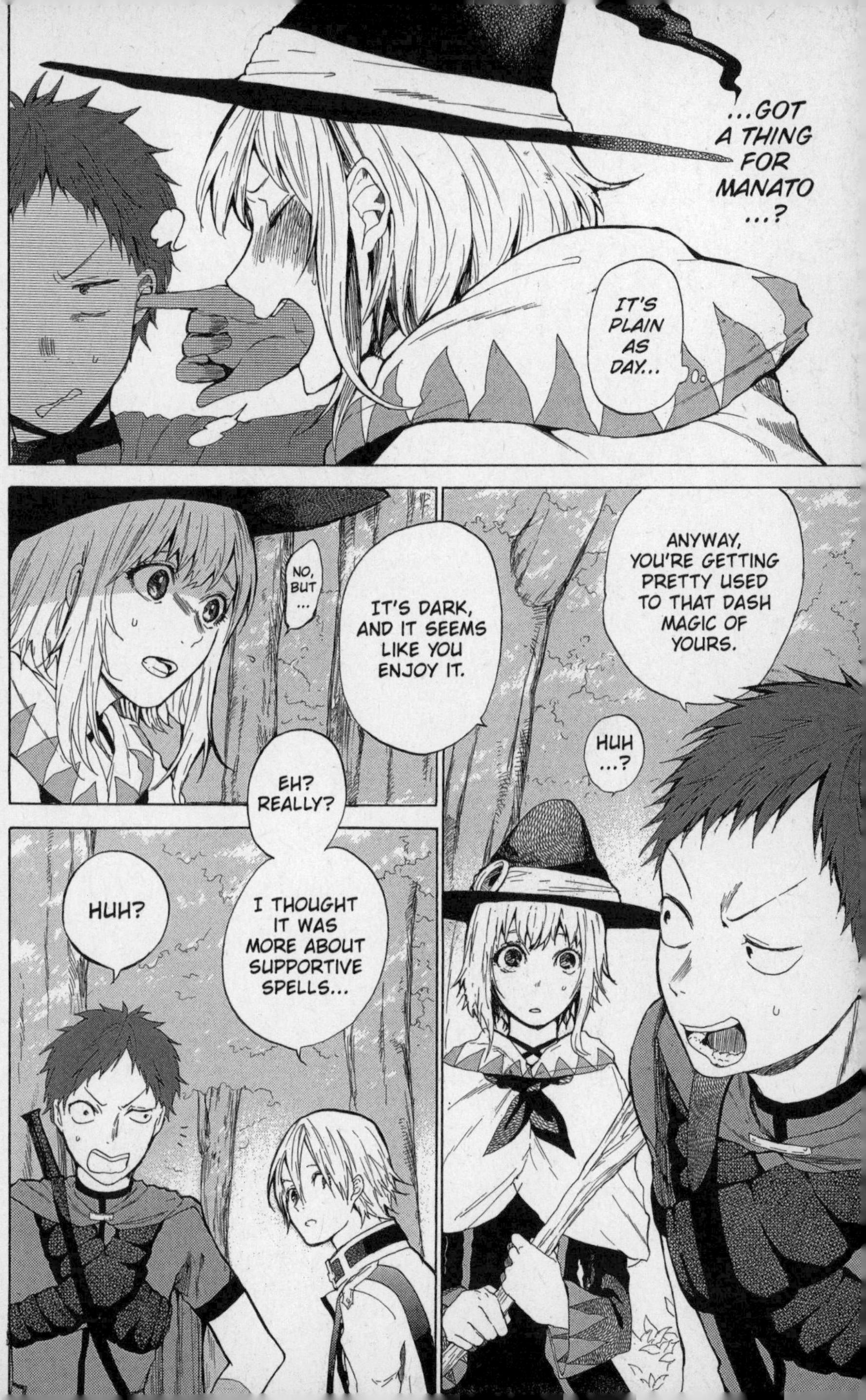
...GOT A THING FOR MANATO ...?
IT'S PLAIN AS DAY...
ANYWAY, YOU'RE GETTING PRETTY USED TO THAT DASH MAGIC OF YOURS.
HUH ...?
IT'S DARK, AND IT SEEMS LIKE YOU ENJOY IT.
NO, BUT ...
EH? REALLY?
I THOUGHT IT WAS MORE ABOUT SUPPORTIVE SPELLS...
HUH?

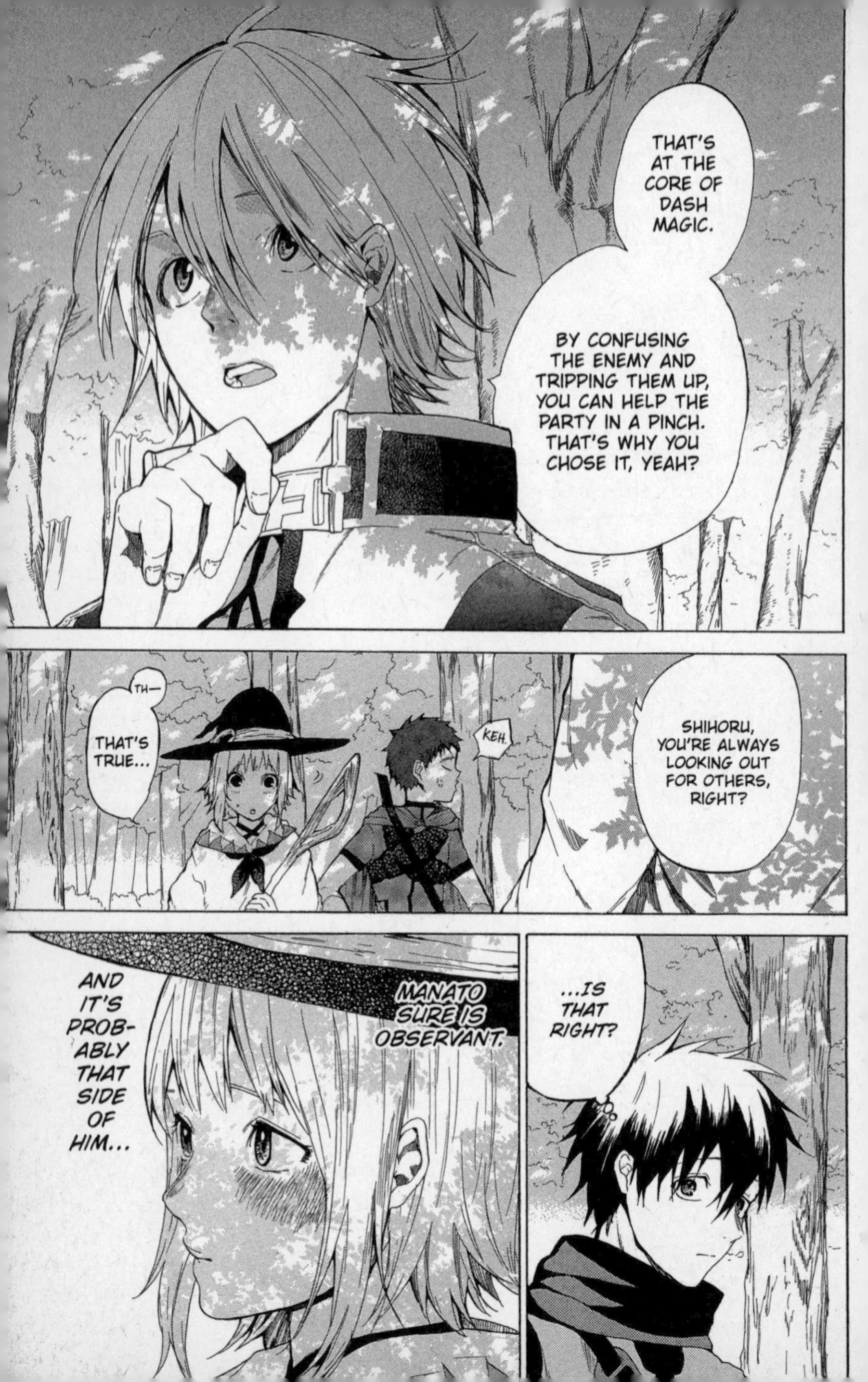
THAT'S AT THE CORE OF DASH MAGIC.
BY CONFUSING THE ENEMY AND TRIPPING THEM UP, YOU CAN HELP THE PARTY IN A PINCH. THAT'S WHY YOU CHOSE IT, YEAH?
SHIHORU, YOU'RE ALWAYS LOOKING OUT FOR OTHERS, RIGHT?
KEH.
TH—
THAT'S TRUE...
...IS THAT RIGHT?
MANATO SURE IS OBSERVANT.
AND IT'S PROBABLY THAT SIDE OF HIM...

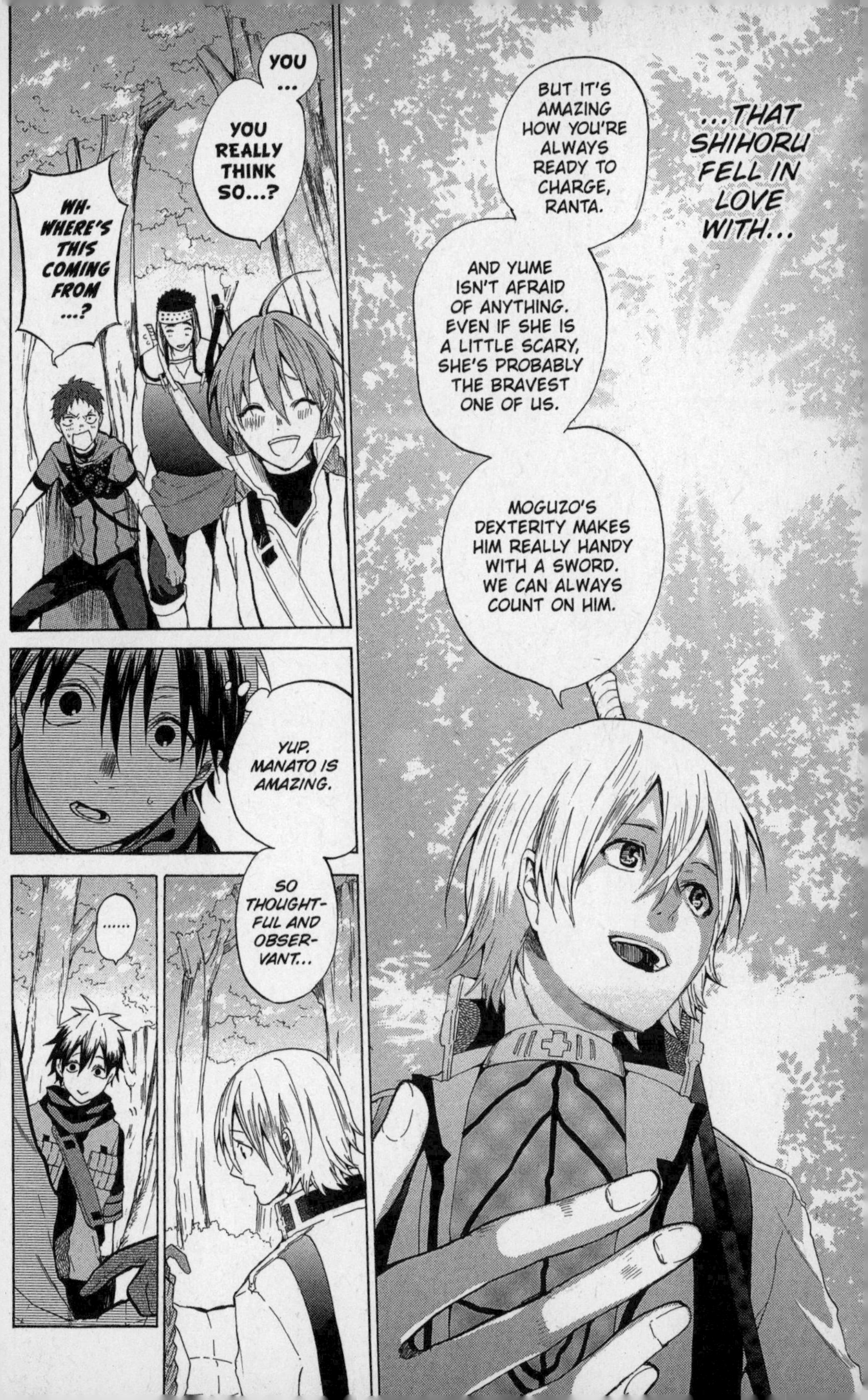
...THAT SHIHORU FELL IN LOVE WITH...
BUT IT'S AMAZING HOW YOU'RE ALWAYS READY TO CHARGE, RANTA.
AND YUME ISN'T AFRAID OF ANYTHING. EVEN IF SHE IS A LITTLE SCARY, SHE'S PROBABLY THE BRAVEST ONE OF US.
MOGUZO'S DEXTERITY MAKES HIM REALLY HANDY WITH A SWORD. WE CAN ALWAYS COUNT ON HIM.
YOU...
YOU REALLY THINK SO...?
WH-WHERE'S THIS COMING FROM...?
YUP. MANATO IS AMAZING.
SO THOUGHTFUL AND OBSERVANT...
......

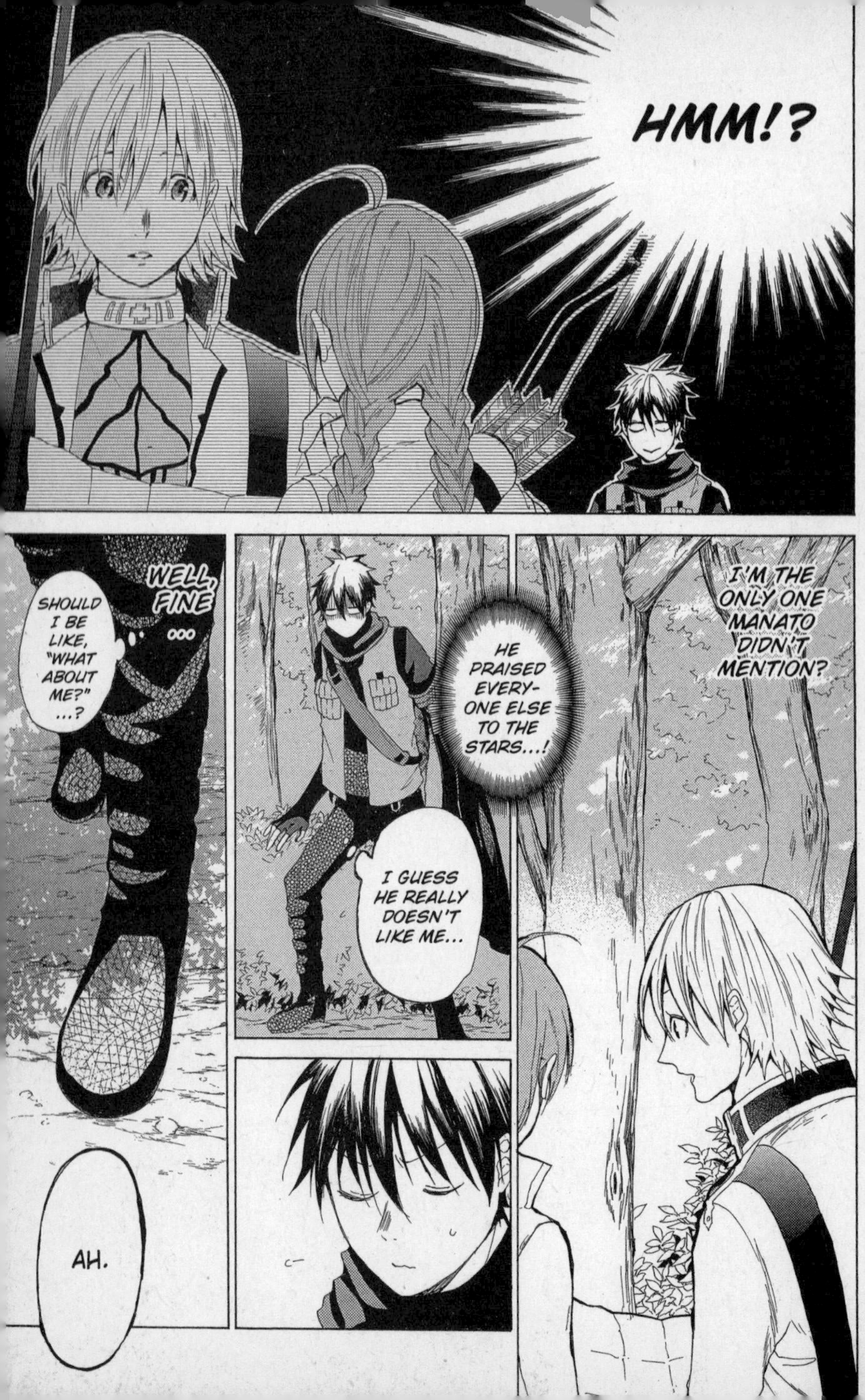
HMM!?
I'M THE ONLY ONE MANATO DIDN'T MENTION?
HE PRAISED EVERY-ONE ELSE TO THE STARS...!
I GUESS HE REALLY DOESN'T LIKE ME...
WELL, FINE ...
SHOULD I BE LIKE, "WHAT ABOUT ME?" ...?
AH.

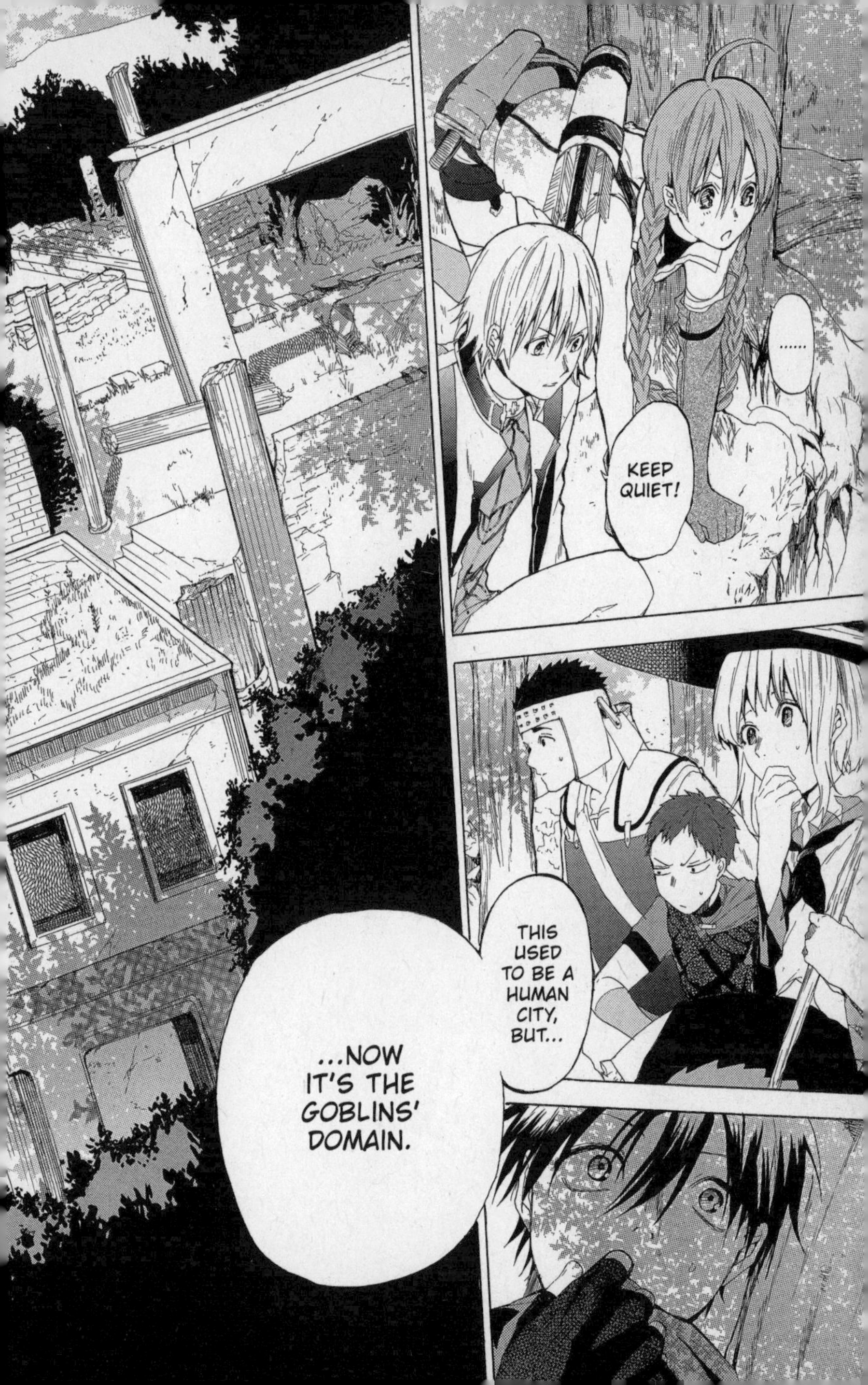
......
KEEP QUIET!
THIS USED TO BE A HUMAN CITY, BUT...
...NOW IT'S THE GOBLINS' DOMAIN.

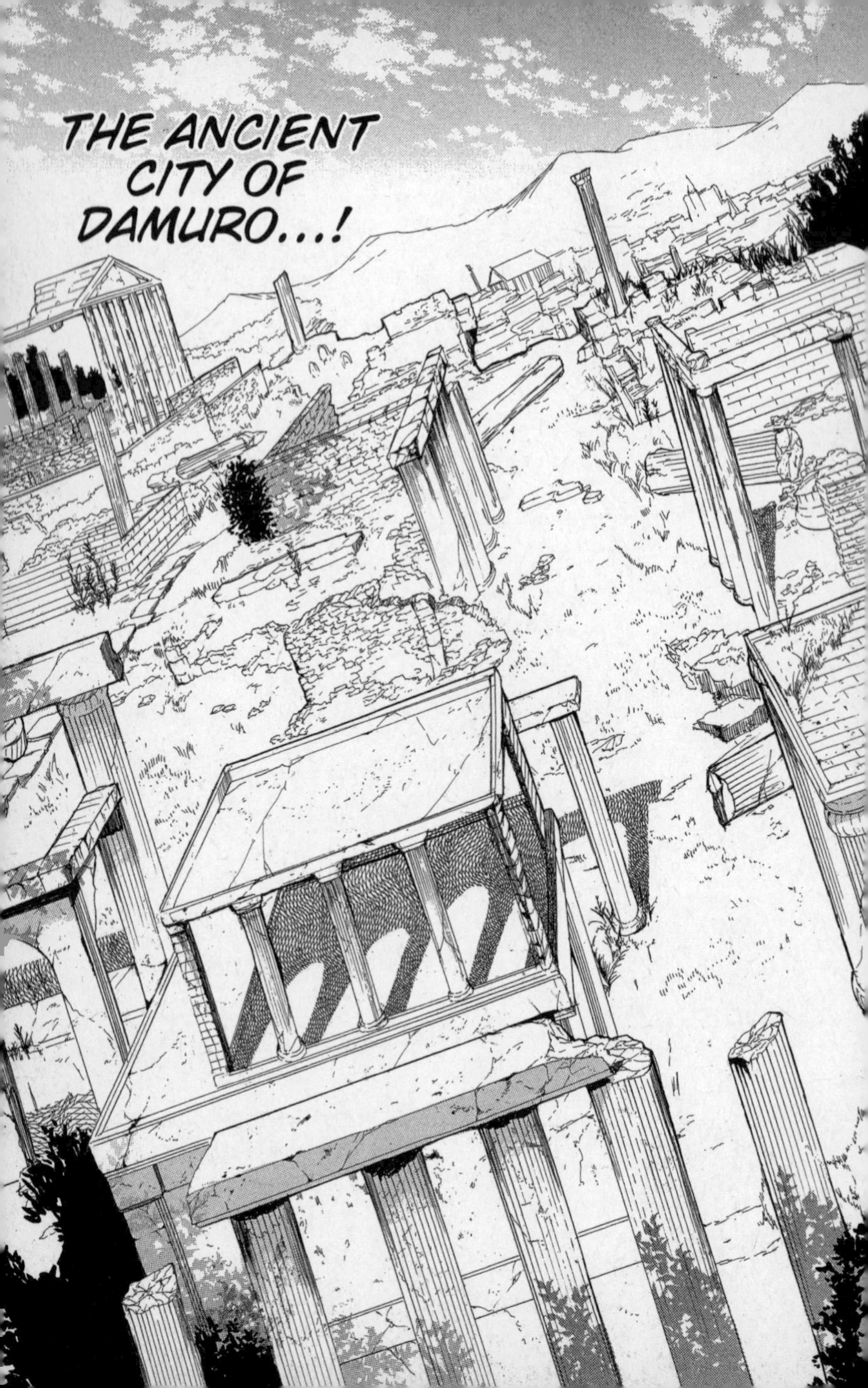
THE ANCIENT CITY OF DAMURO...!

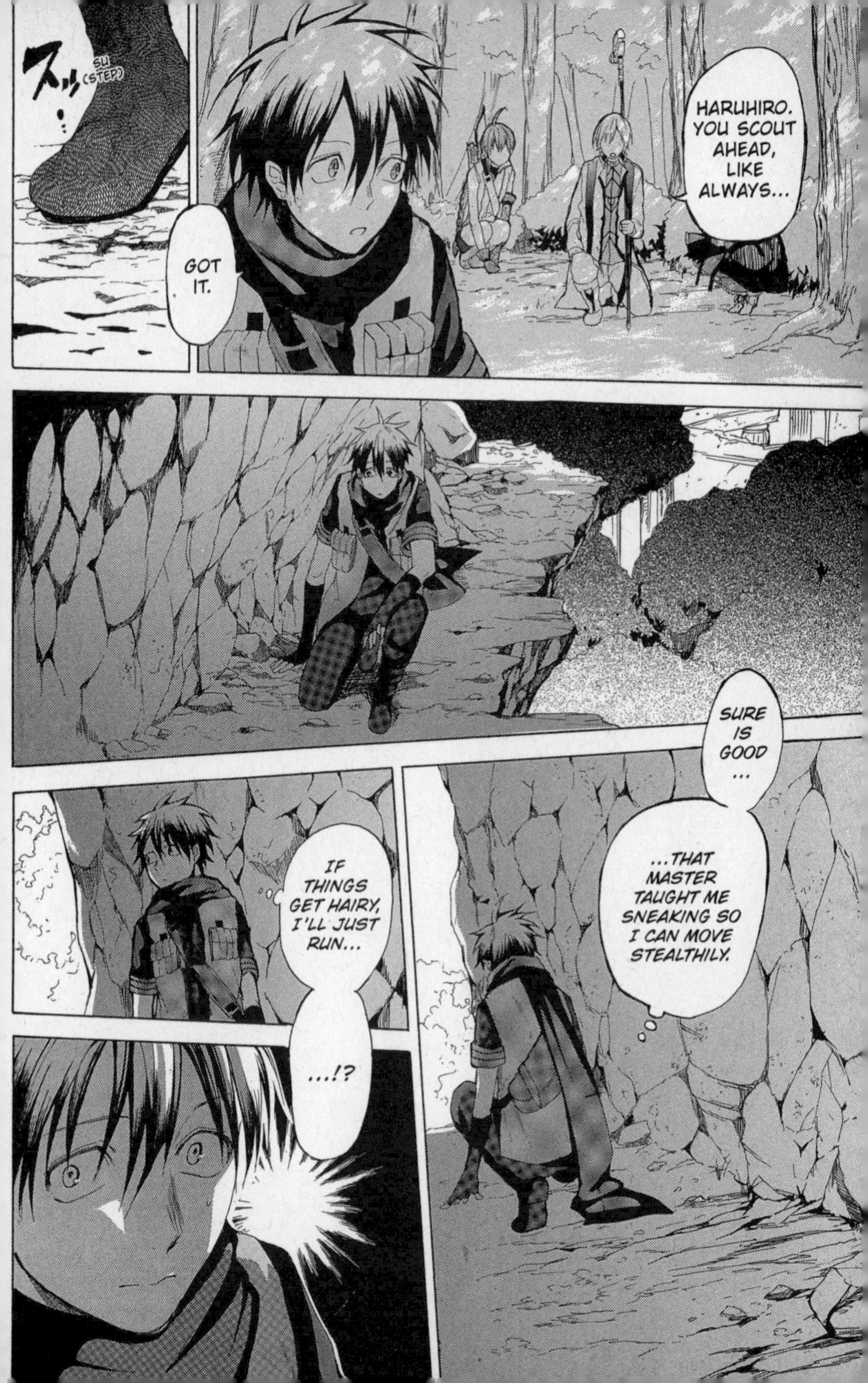
HARUHIRO. YOU SCOUT AHEAD, LIKE ALWAYS...
GOT IT.
スッ
SU (STEP)
SURE IS GOOD...
...THAT MASTER TAUGHT ME SNEAKING SO I CAN MOVE STEALTHILY.
IF THINGS GET HAIRY, I'LL JUST RUN...
...!?

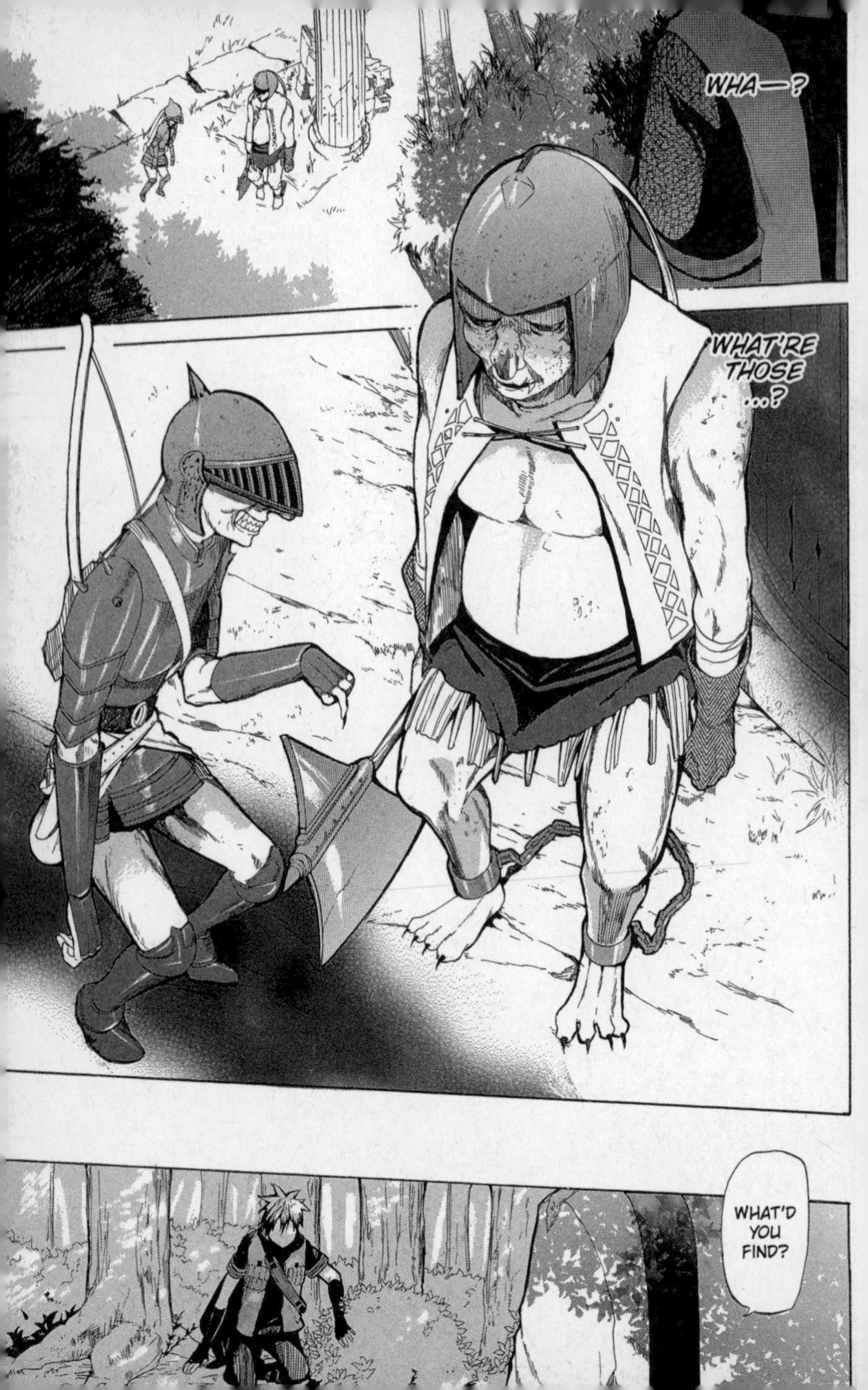
WHA—?
WHAT'RE THOSE ...?
WHAT'D YOU FIND?

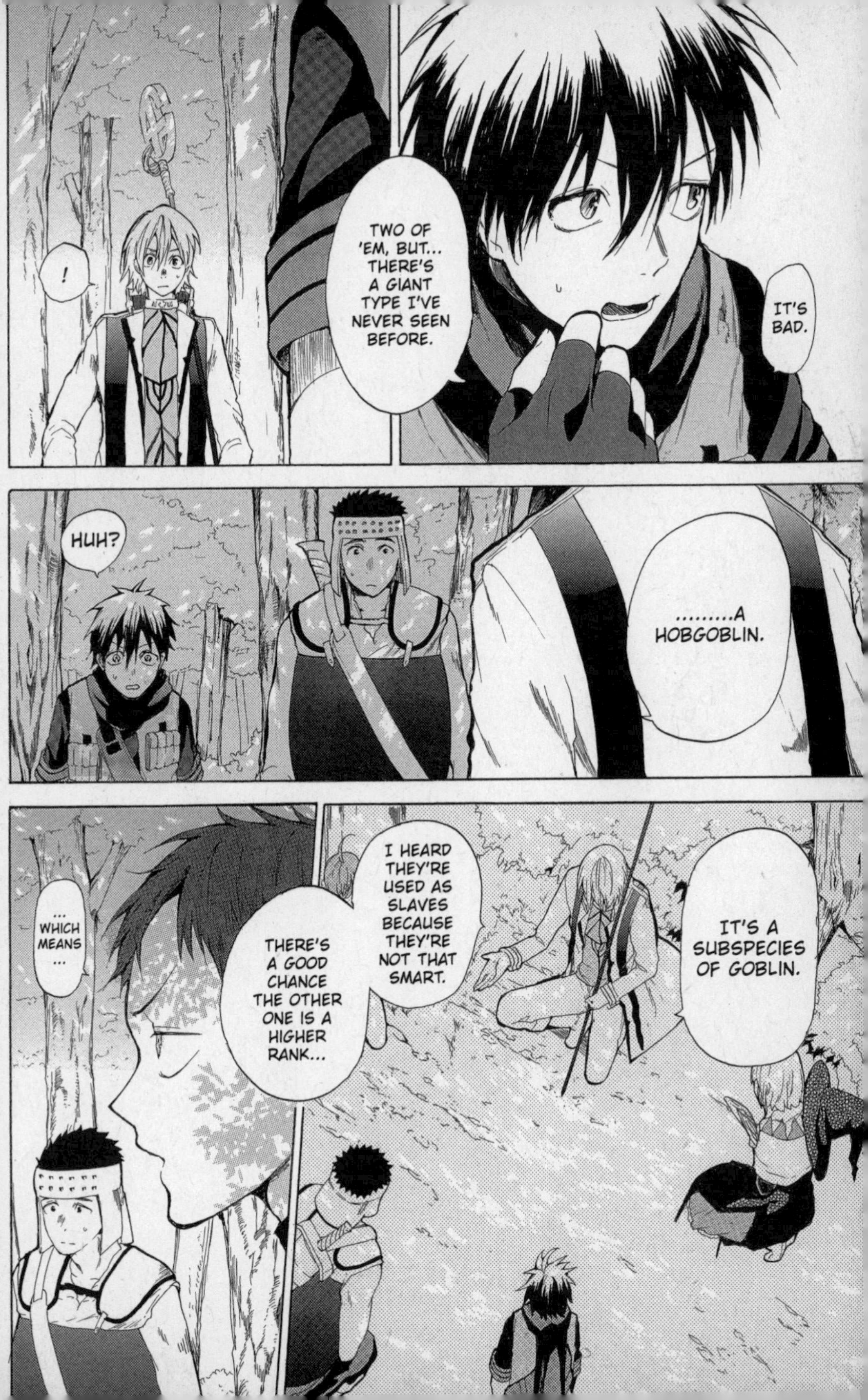
IT'S BAD.
TWO OF 'EM, BUT... THERE'S A GIANT TYPE I'VE NEVER SEEN BEFORE.
!
.........A HOBGOBLIN.
HUH?
IT'S A SUBSPECIES OF GOBLIN.
I HEARD THEY'RE USED AS SLAVES BECAUSE THEY'RE NOT THAT SMART.
THERE'S A GOOD CHANCE THE OTHER ONE IS A HIGHER RANK...
...WHICH MEANS...

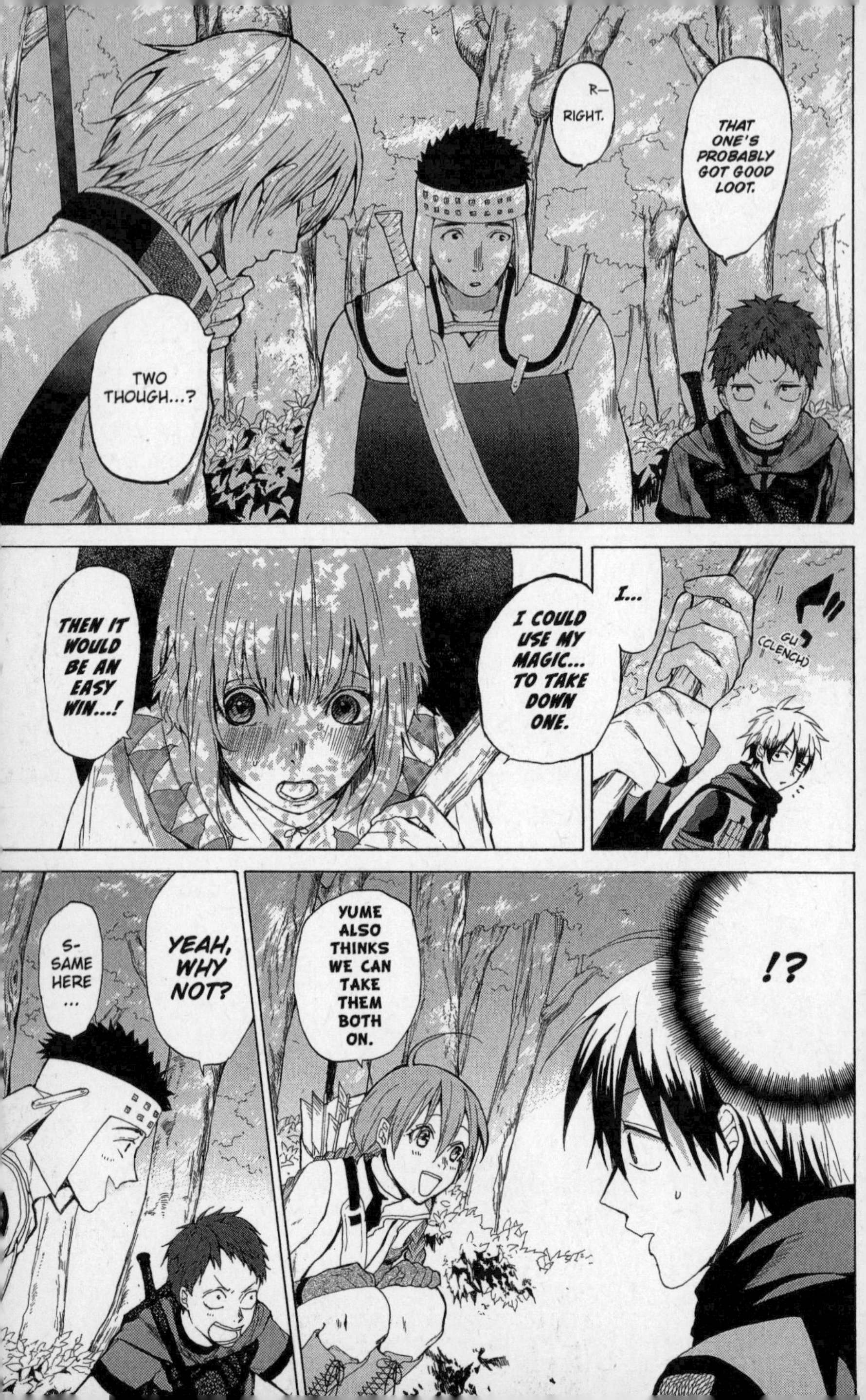
THAT ONE'S PROBABLY GOT GOOD LOOT.
R— RIGHT.
TWO THOUGH...?
I...
I COULD USE MY MAGIC... TO TAKE DOWN ONE.
GU (CLENCH)
THEN IT WOULD BE AN EASY WIN...!
!?
YUME ALSO THINKS WE CAN TAKE THEM BOTH ON.
YEAH, WHY NOT?
S-SAME HERE...

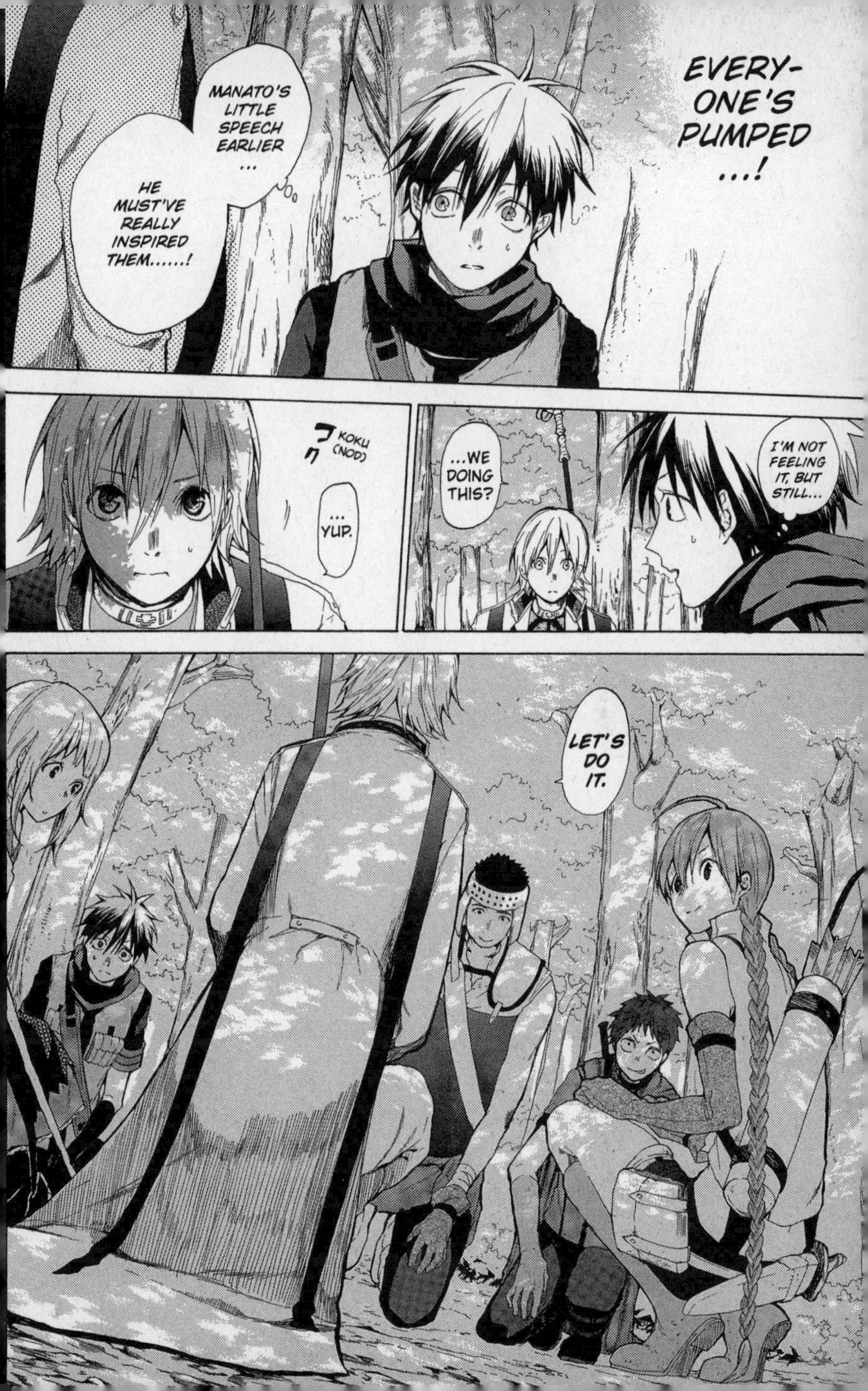
EVERY-ONE'S PUMPED ...!
MANATO'S LITTLE SPEECH EARLIER ...
HE MUST'VE REALLY INSPIRED THEM......!
I'M NOT FEELING IT, BUT STILL...
...WE DOING THIS?
KOKU (NOD)
... YUP.
LET'S DO IT.

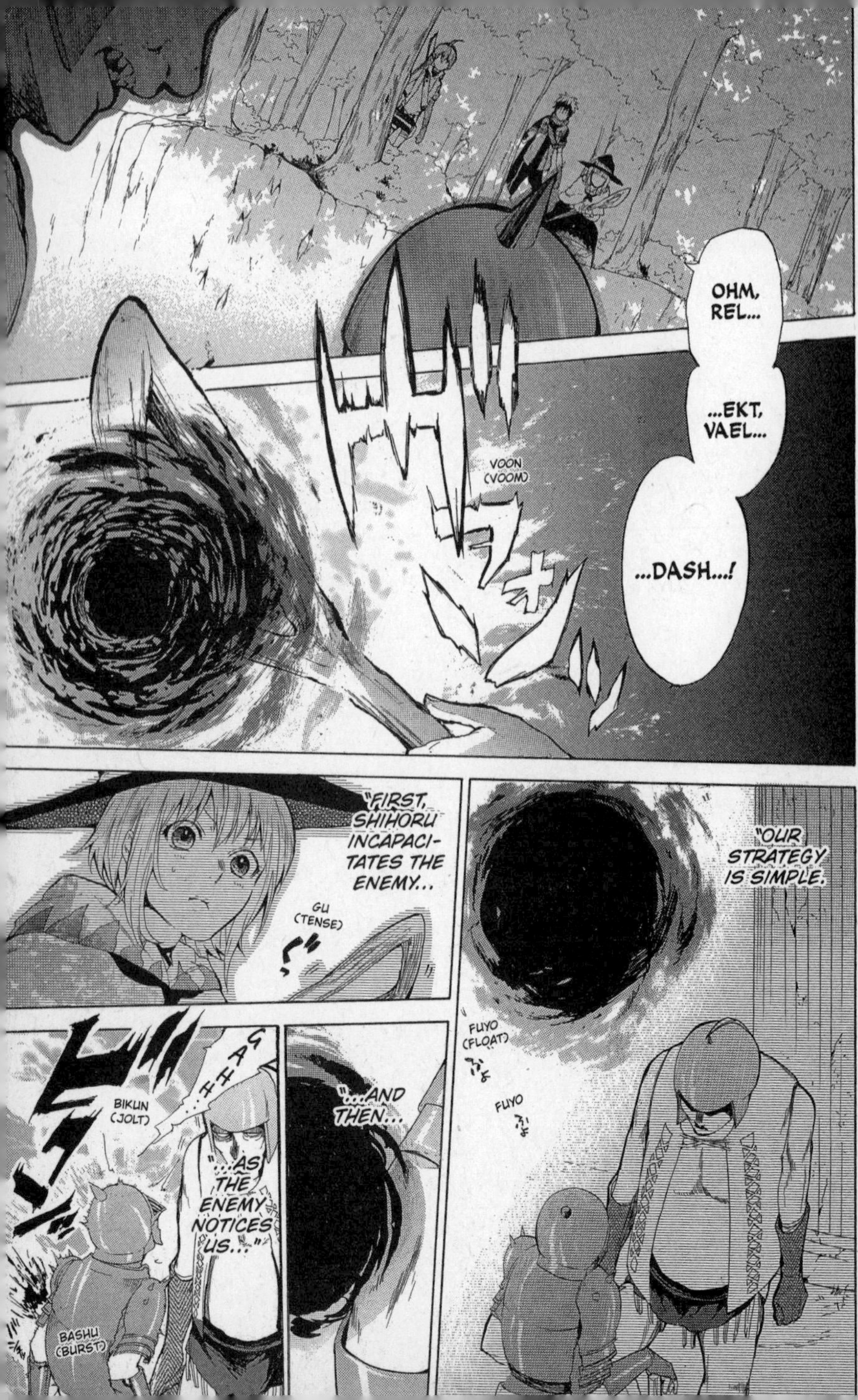
OHM, REL...
...EKT, VAEL...
...DASH...!
VOON (VOOM)
"OUR STRATEGY IS SIMPLE.
FUYO (FLOAT)
FUYO
"FIRST, SHIHORU INCAPACITATES THE ENEMY...
GU (TENSE)
"...AND THEN...
GAHH
BIKUN (JOLT)
"...AS THE ENEMY NOTICES US..."
BASHU (BURST)

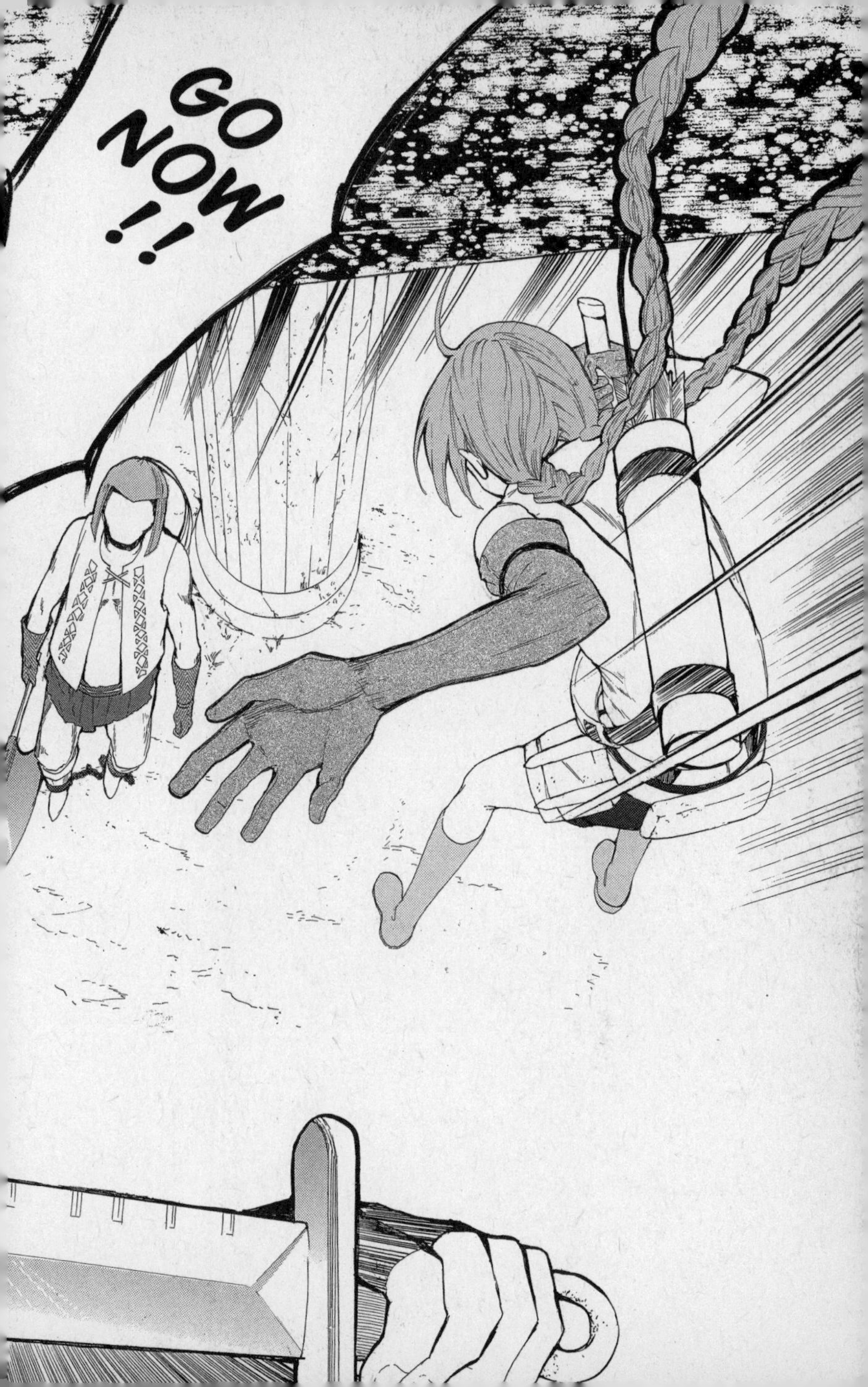
GO NOW!!

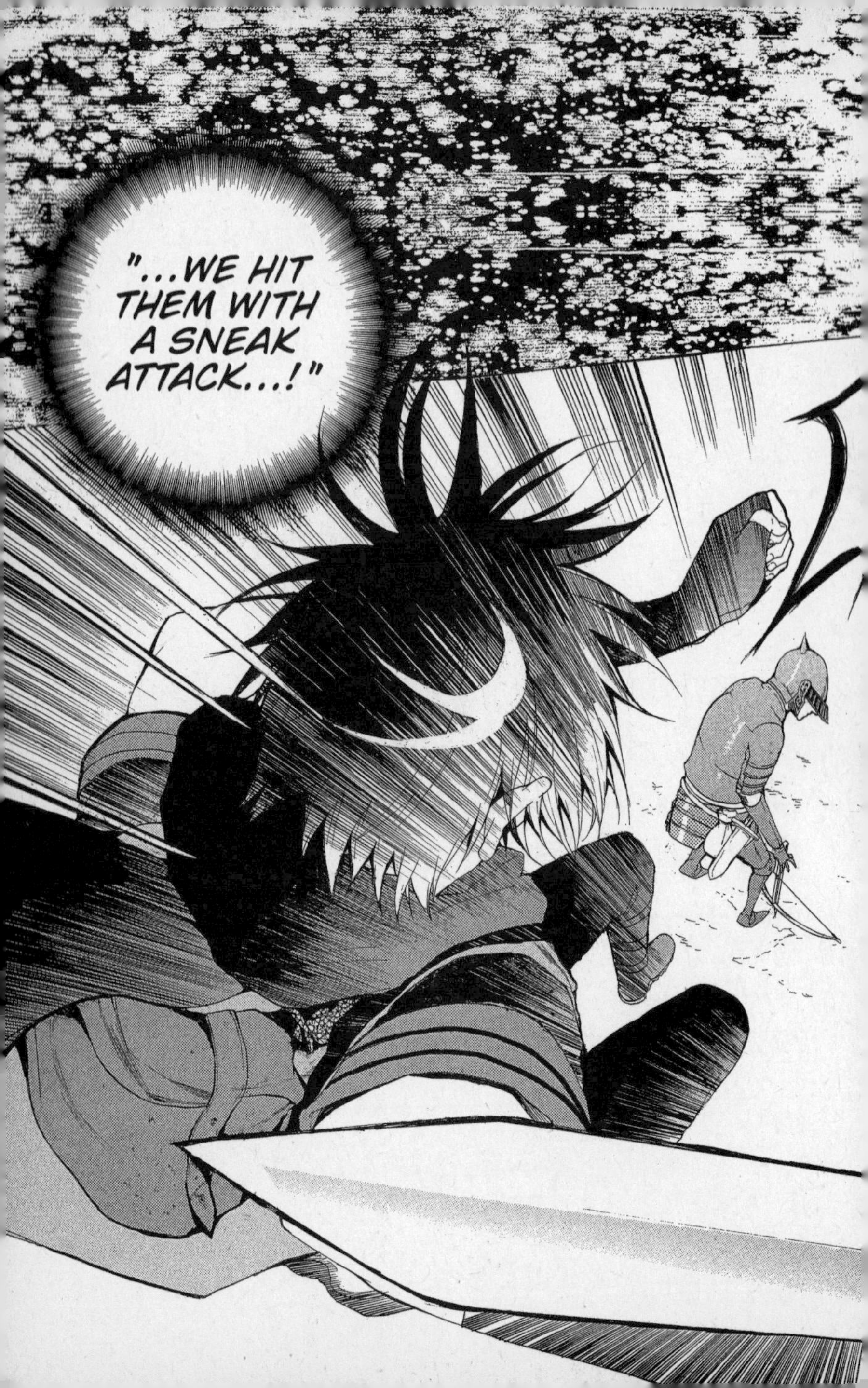
"...WE HIT THEM WITH A SNEAK ATTACK...!"

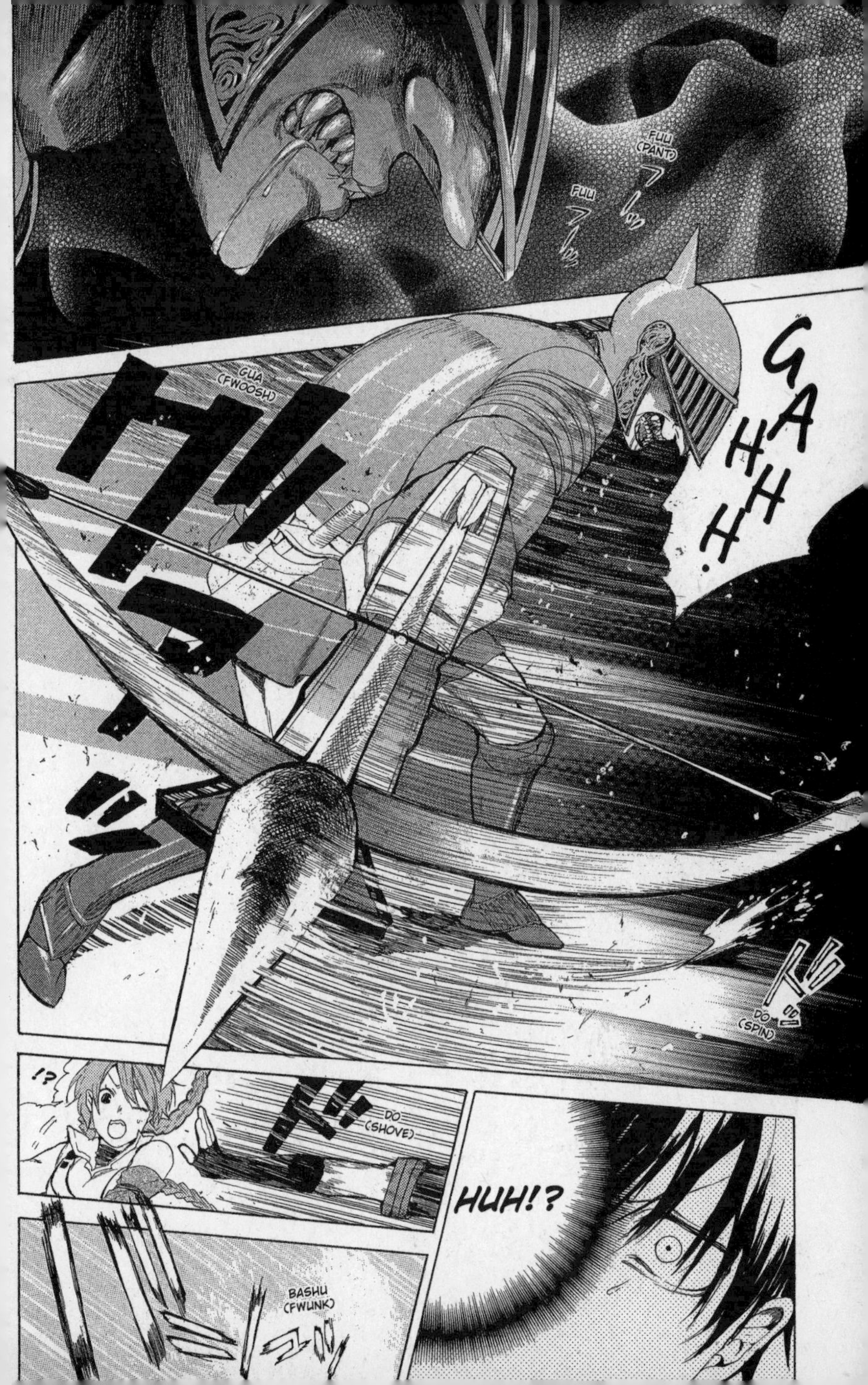
FUU (PANT)
FUU
GAHHH!
GUA (FWOOSH)
DO (SPIN)
HUH!?
DO (SHOVE)
!?
BASHU (FWUNK)

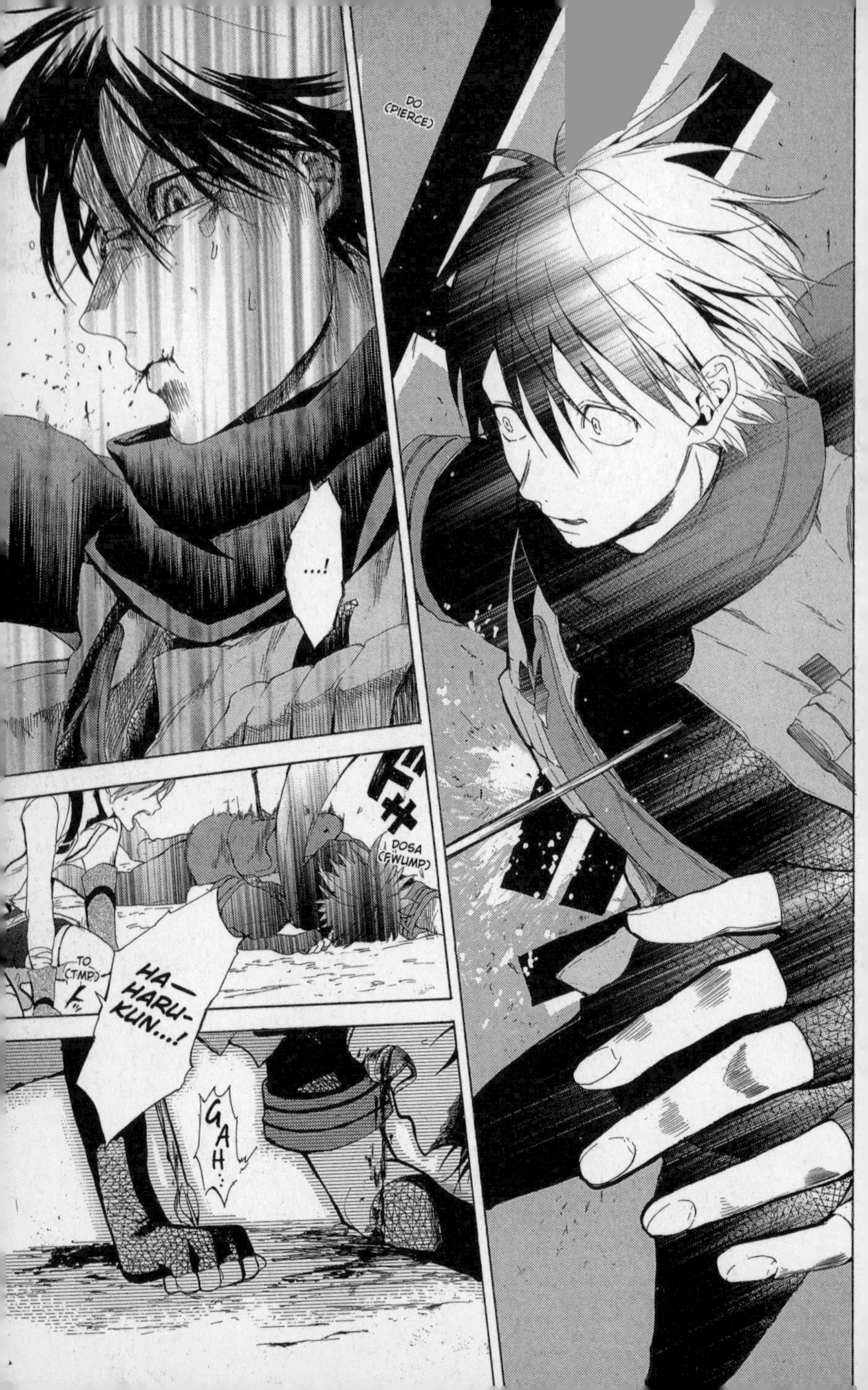
DO
(PIERCE)
...!
DOSA
(FWUMP)
HA-
HARU-
KUN...!
TO
(TMP)
GAH...

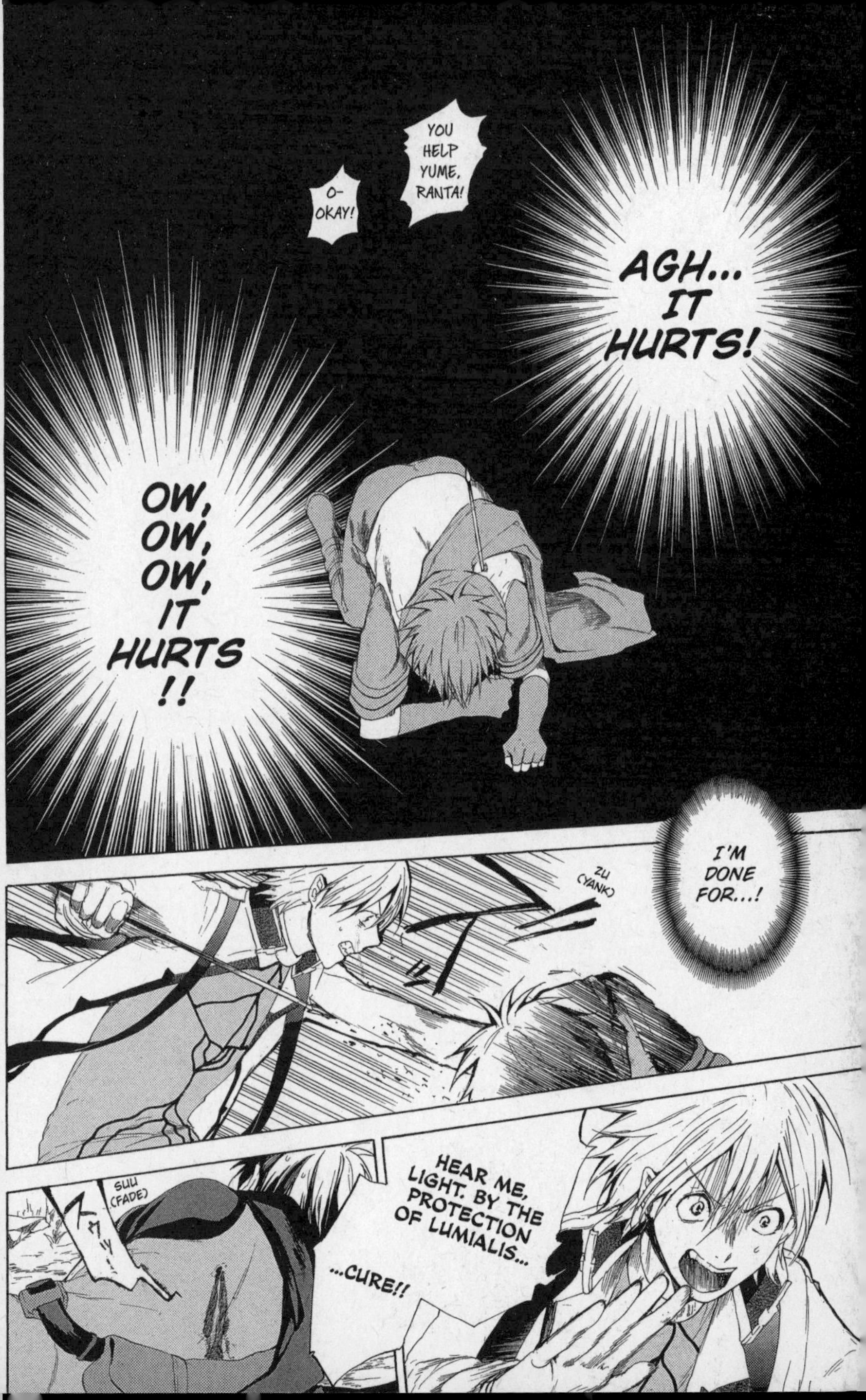
YOU HELP YUME, RANTA!
O-OKAY!
AGH... IT HURTS!
OW, OW, OW, IT HURTS!!
I'M DONE FOR...!
ZU (YANK)
HEAR ME, LIGHT. BY THE PROTECTION OF LUMIALIS...
...CURE!!
SUU (FADE)

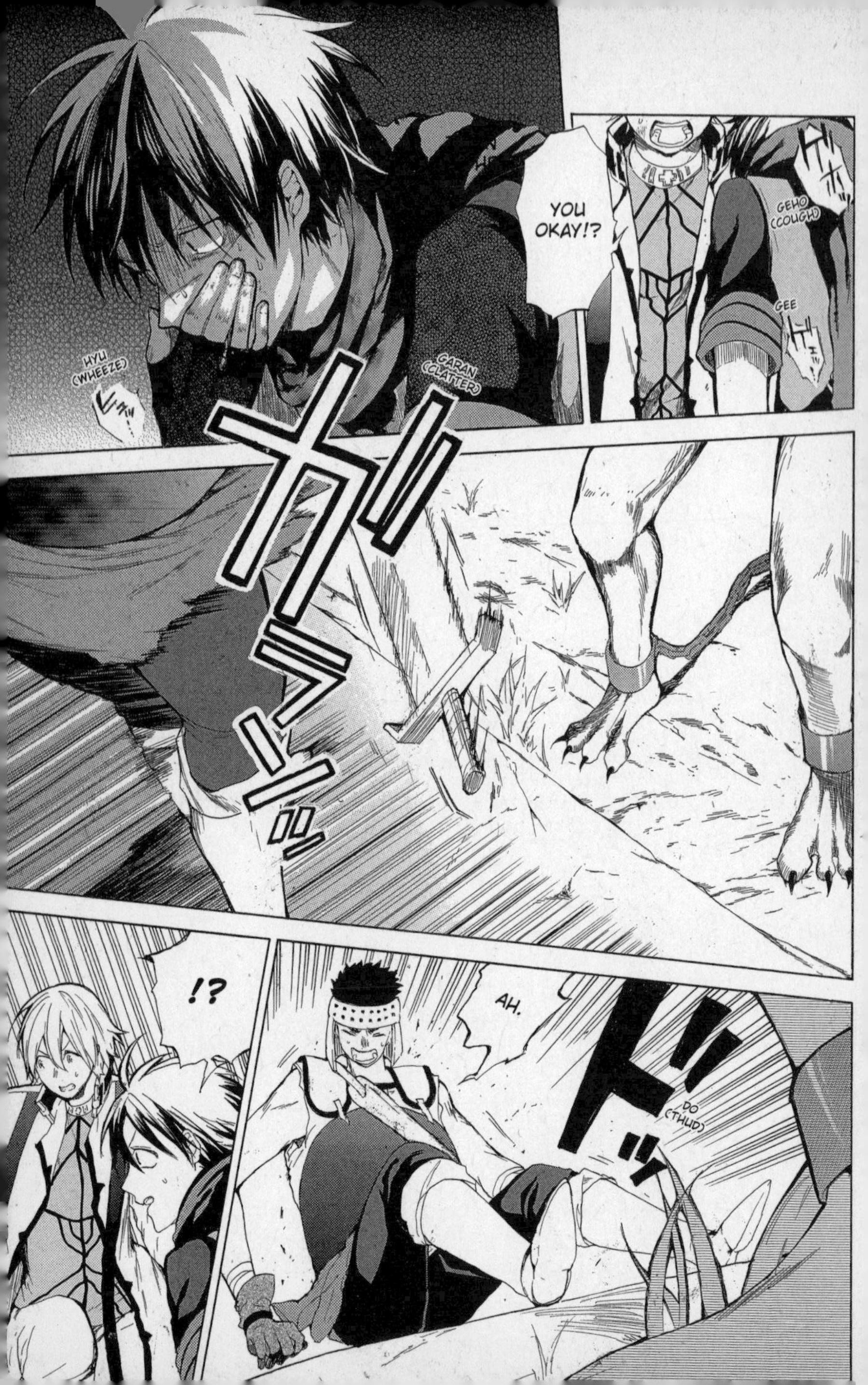
YOU OKAY!?
GEHO (COUGH)
GEE
GARAN (CLATTER)
HYU (WHEEZE)
AH.
DO (THUD)
!?

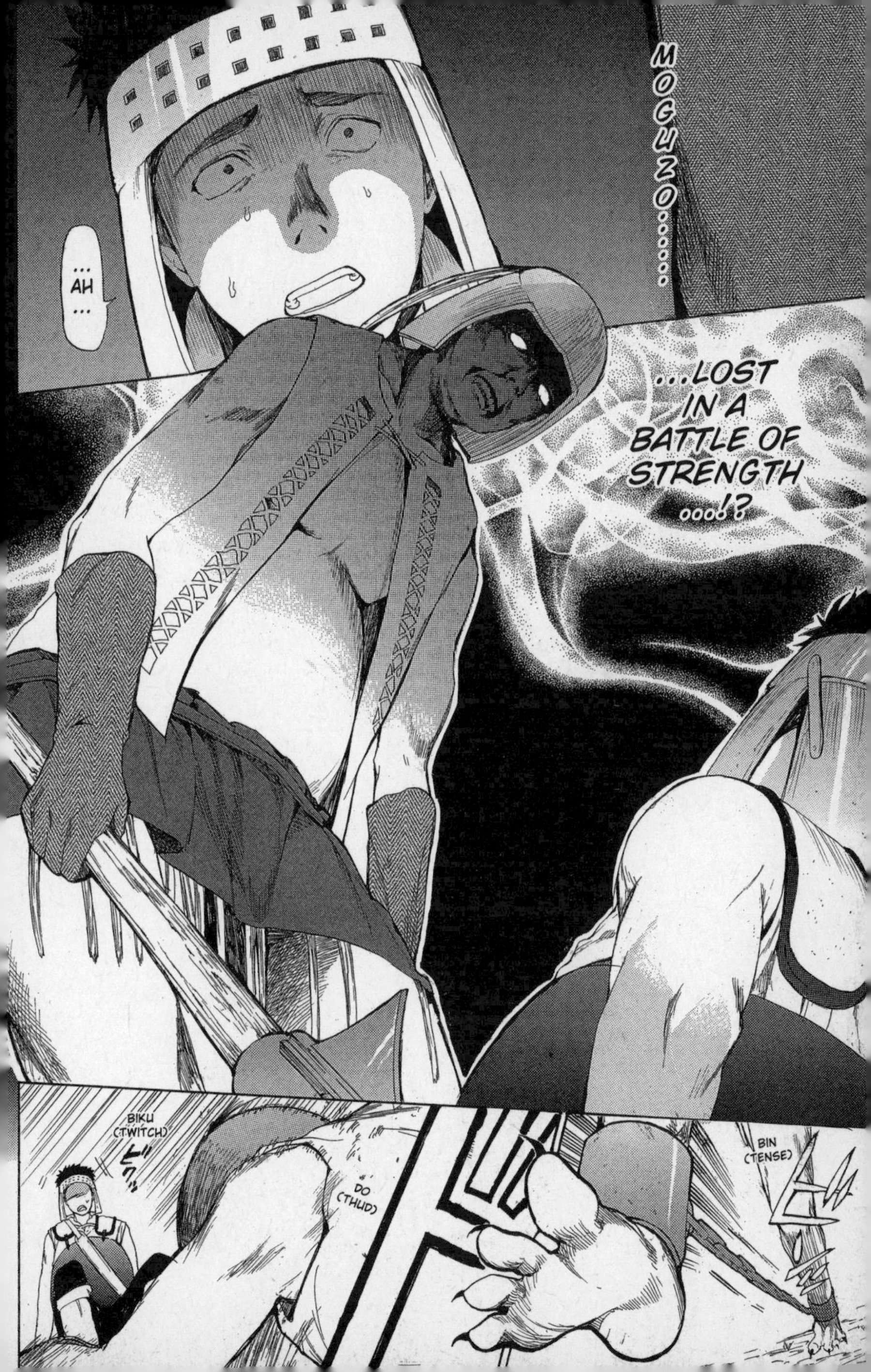
MOGUZO......
...LOST IN A BATTLE OF STRENGTH ...!?
...AH...
BIN (TENSE)
DO (THUD)
BIKU (TWITCH)

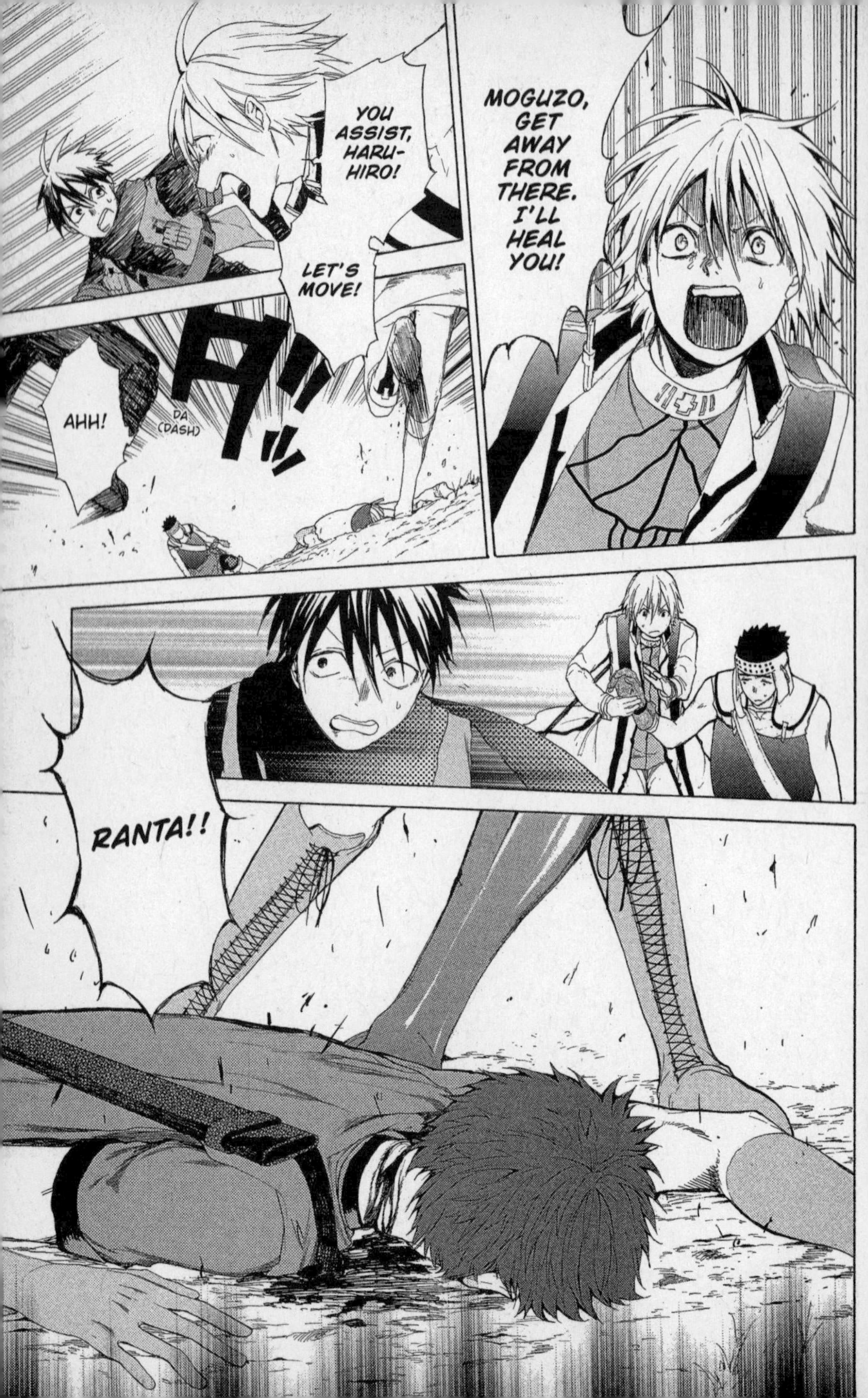
MOGUZO, GET AWAY FROM THERE. I'LL HEAL YOU!
YOU ASSIST, HARU-HIRO!
LET'S MOVE!
DA (DASH)
AHH!
RANTA!!

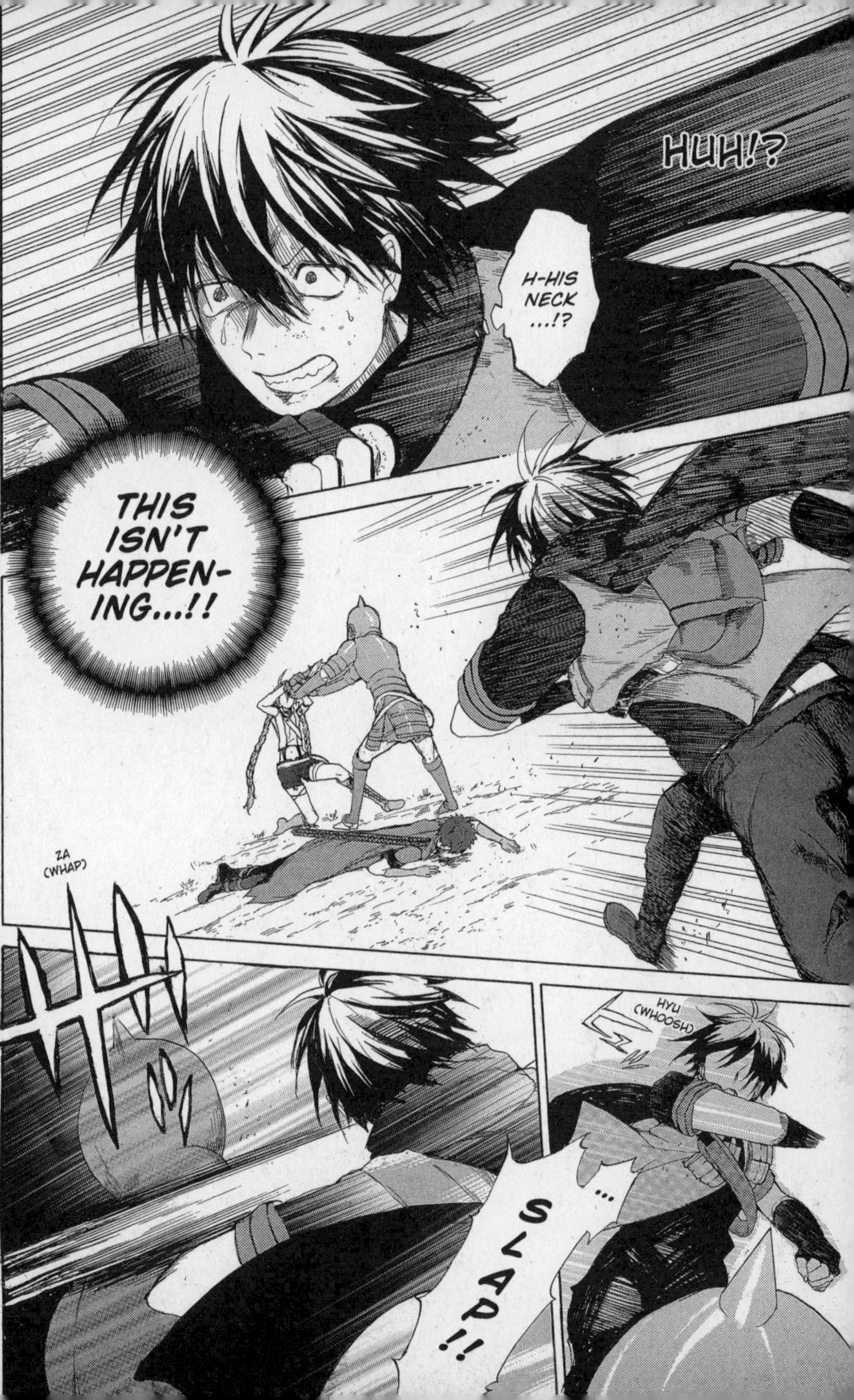

HUH!?
H-HIS NECK ...!?
THIS ISN'T HAPPEN-ING...!!
ZA (WHAP)
HYU (WHOOSH)
...
SLAP!!

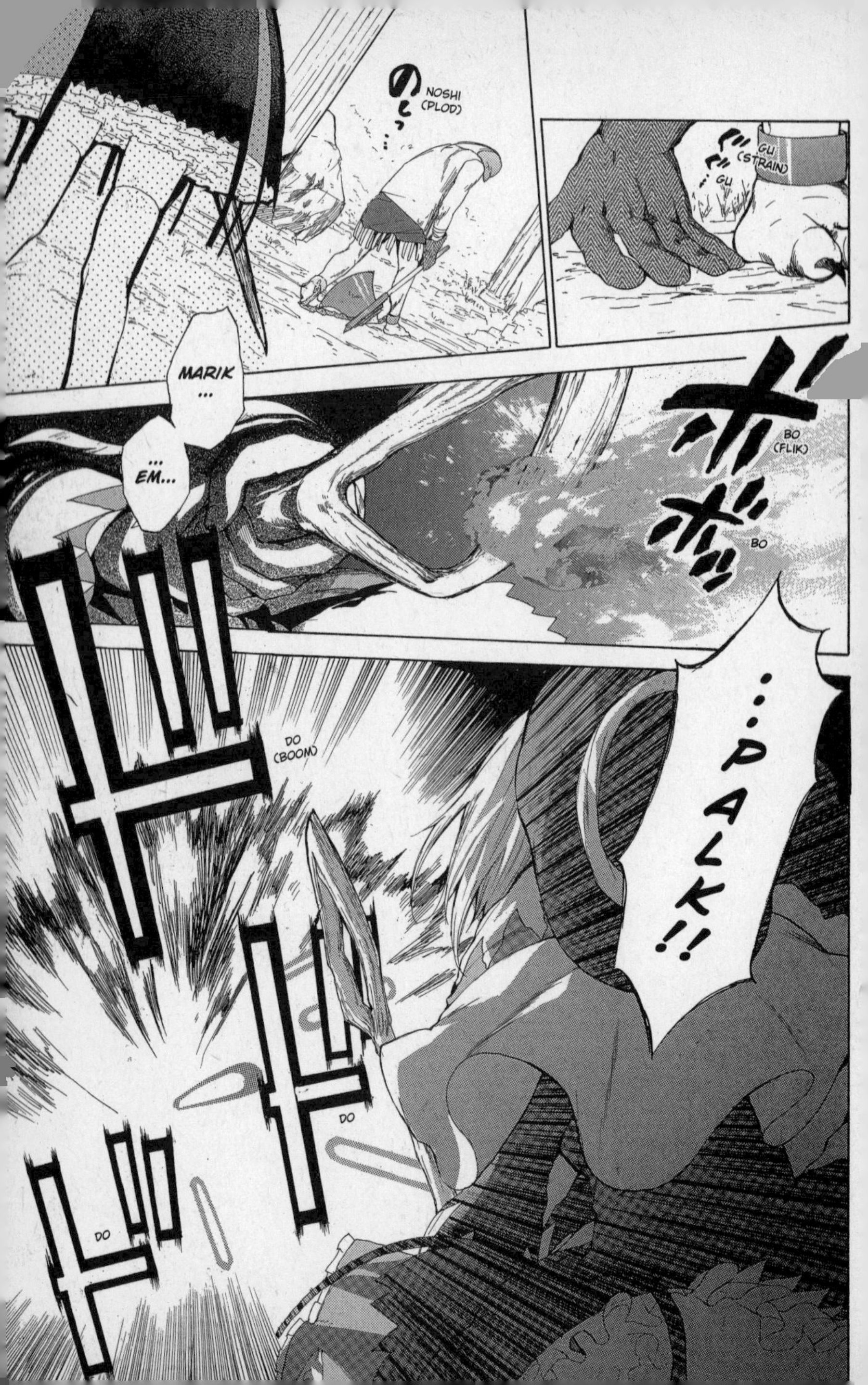

GU (STRAIN)
GU
NOSHI (PLOD)
BO (FLIK)
BO
MARIK …
… EM…
…PALK!!
DO (BOOM)
DO
DO

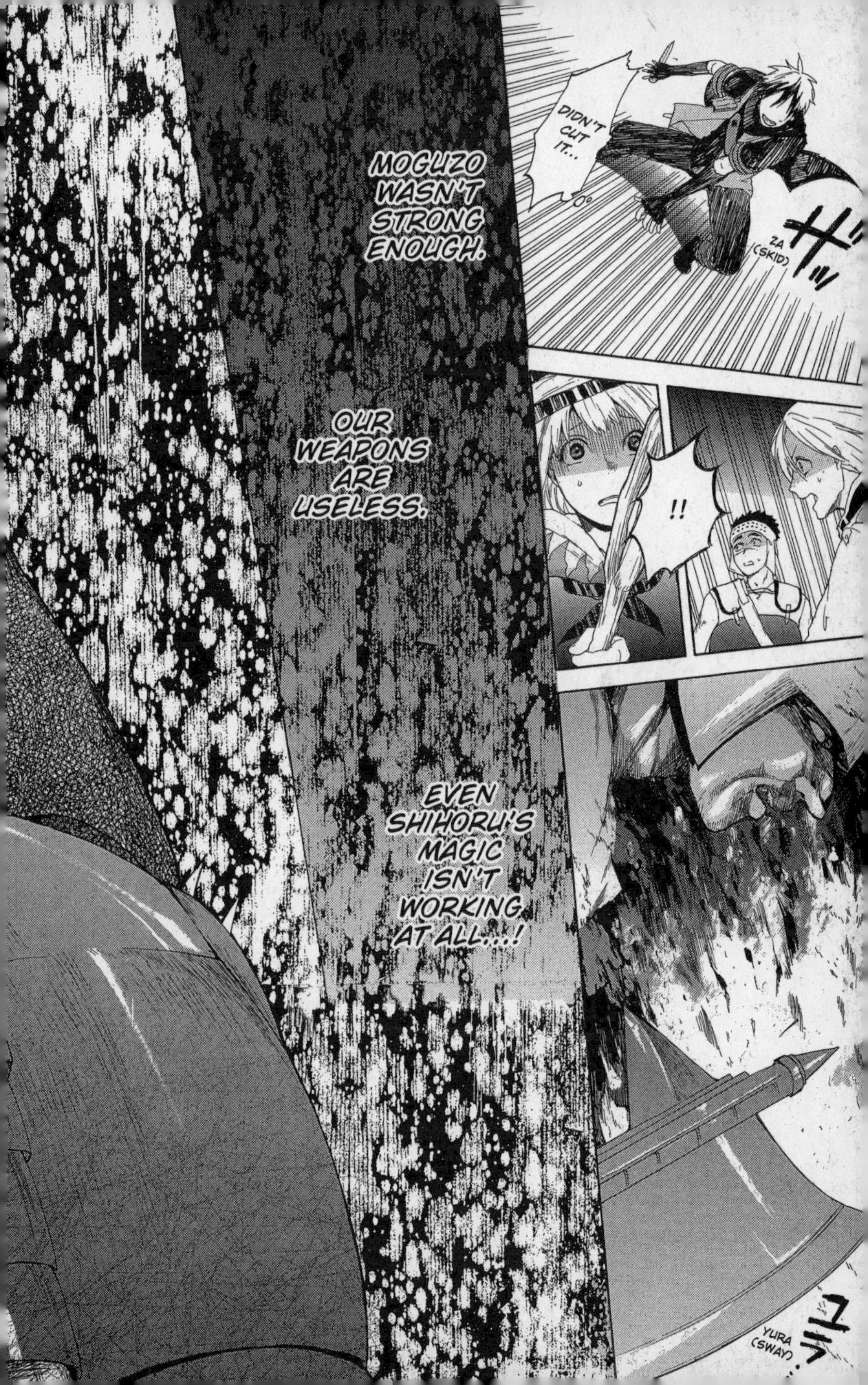

DIDN'T CUT IT...
ZA (SKID)
!!
YURA (SWAY)
MOGUZO WASN'T STRONG ENOUGH.
OUR WEAPONS ARE USELESS.
EVEN SHIHORU'S MAGIC ISN'T WORKING AT ALL...!

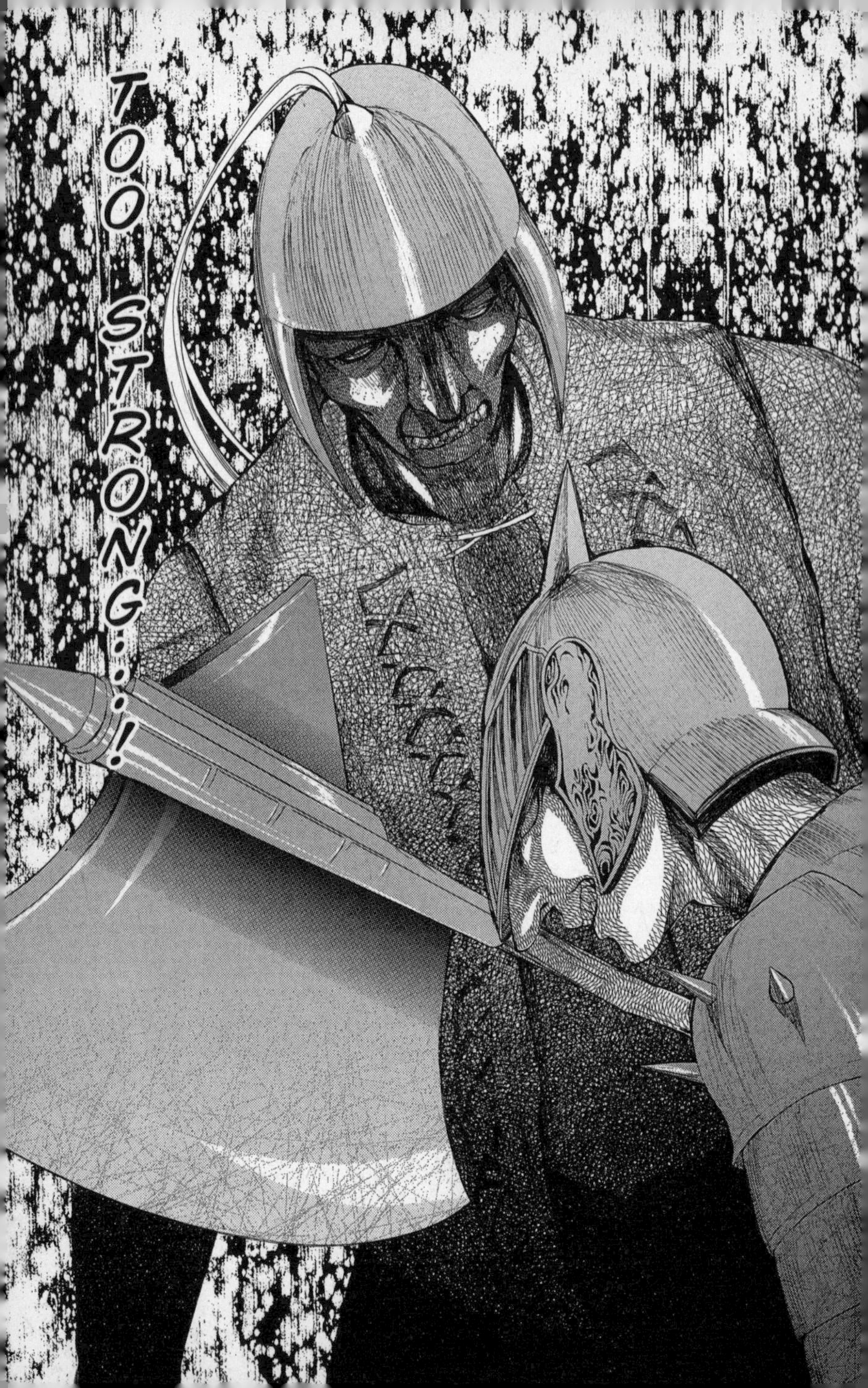
TOO STRONG...!

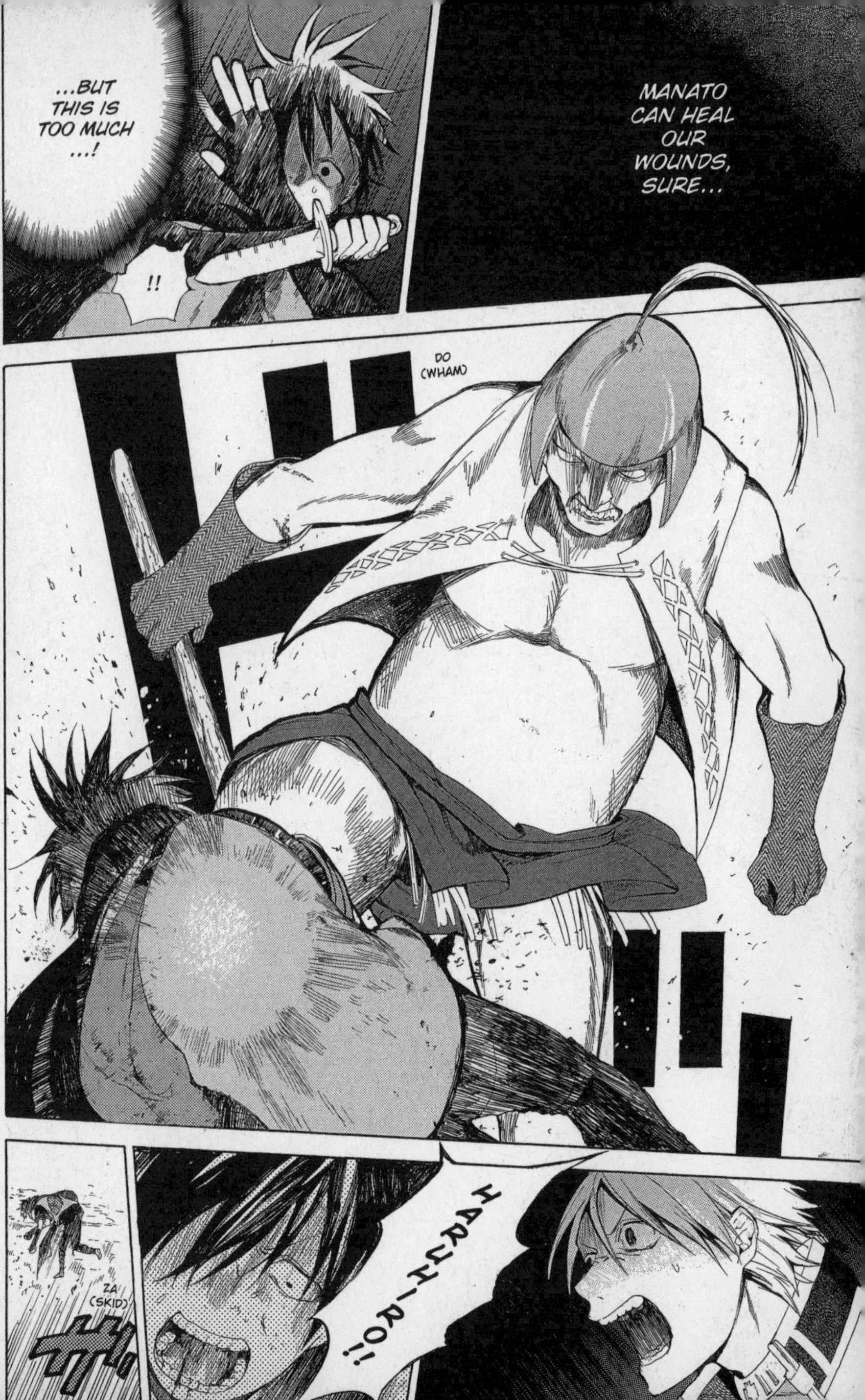
MANATO CAN HEAL OUR WOUNDS, SURE...
...BUT THIS IS TOO MUCH...!
!!
DO (WHAM)
HARUHI-RO!!
ZA (SKID)

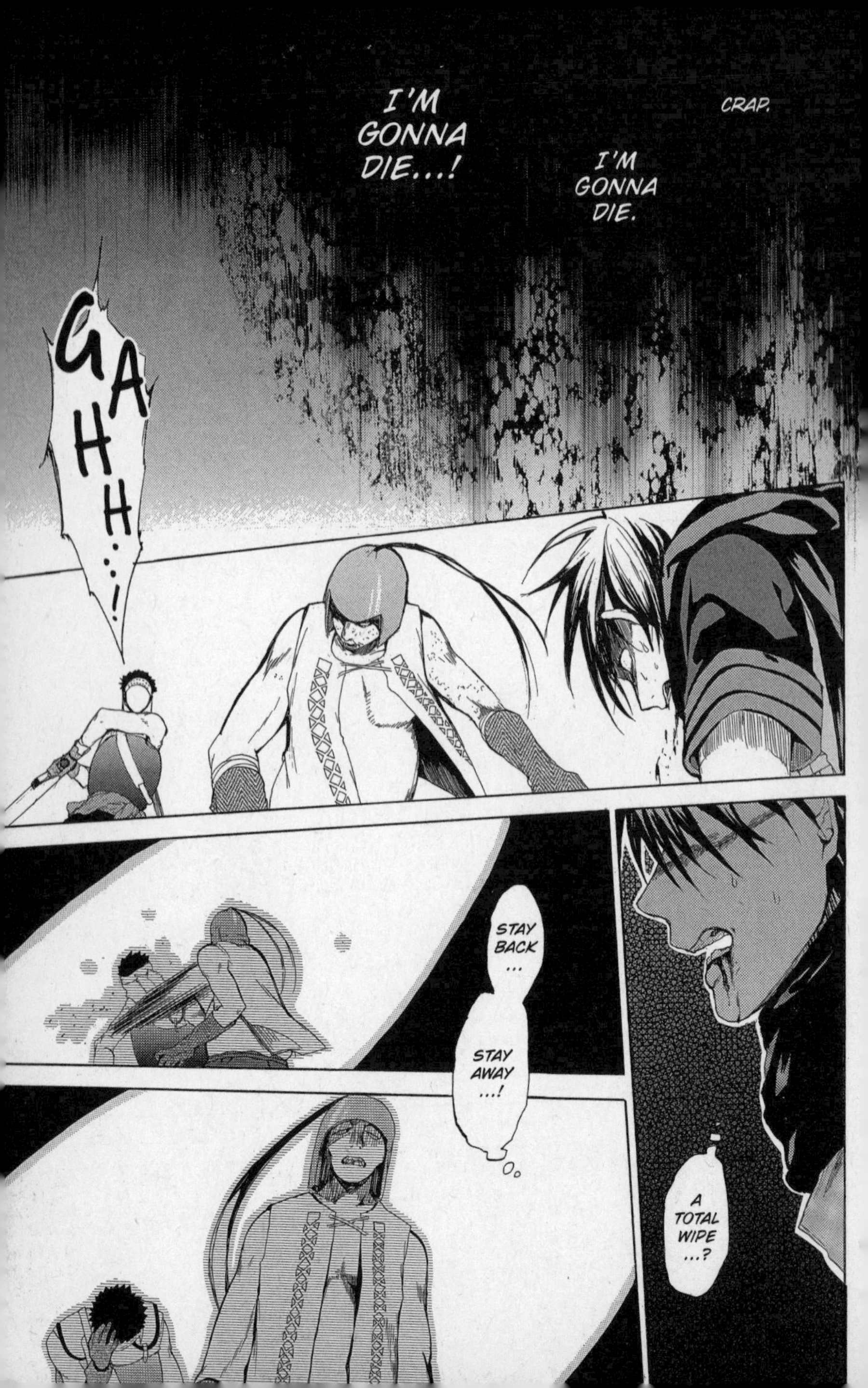
CRAP.
I'M GONNA DIE.
I'M GONNA DIE...!
GAHH...!
A TOTAL WIPE...?
STAY BACK...
STAY AWAY...!

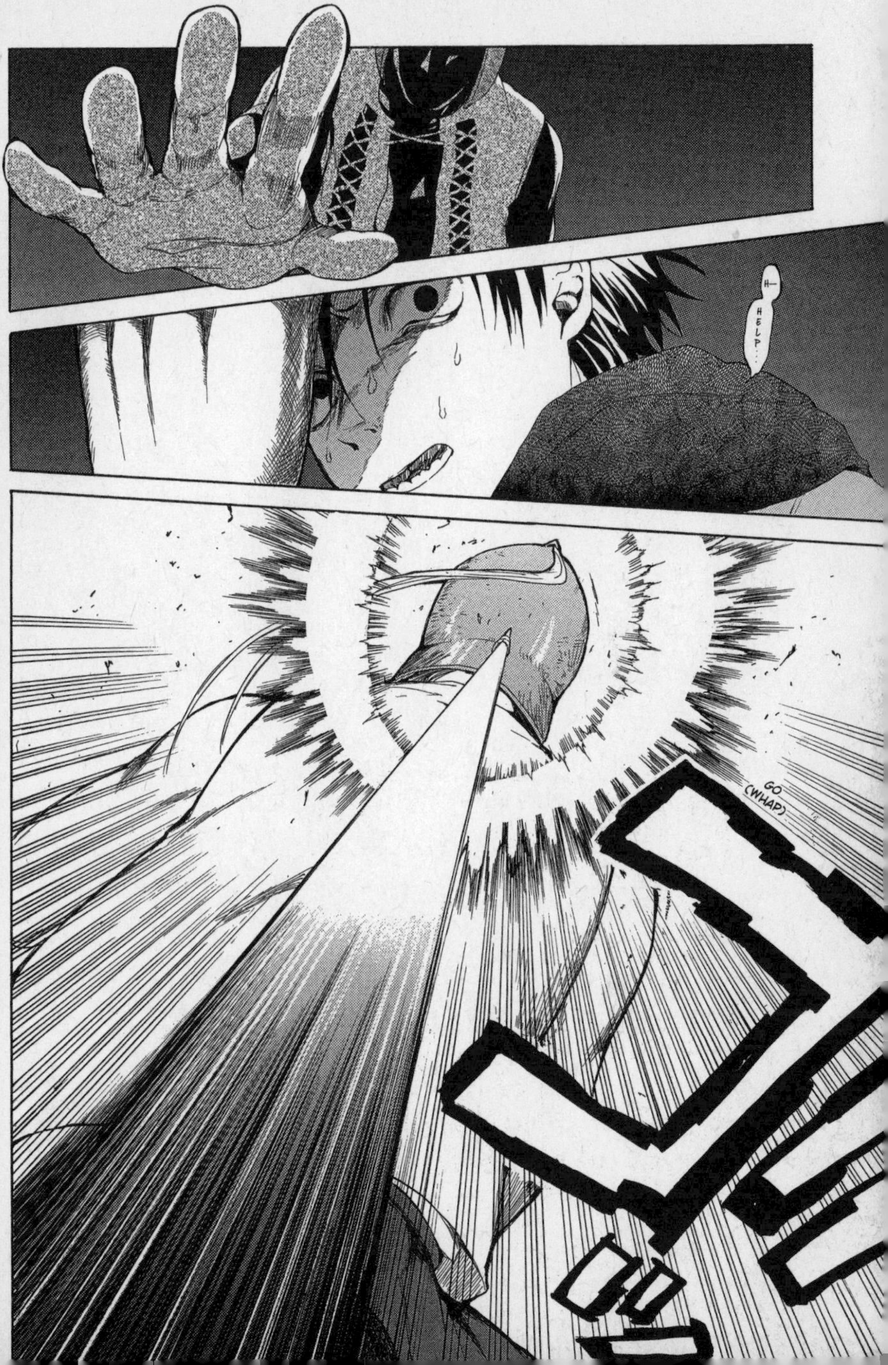
H—
HELP...
GO
(WHAP)

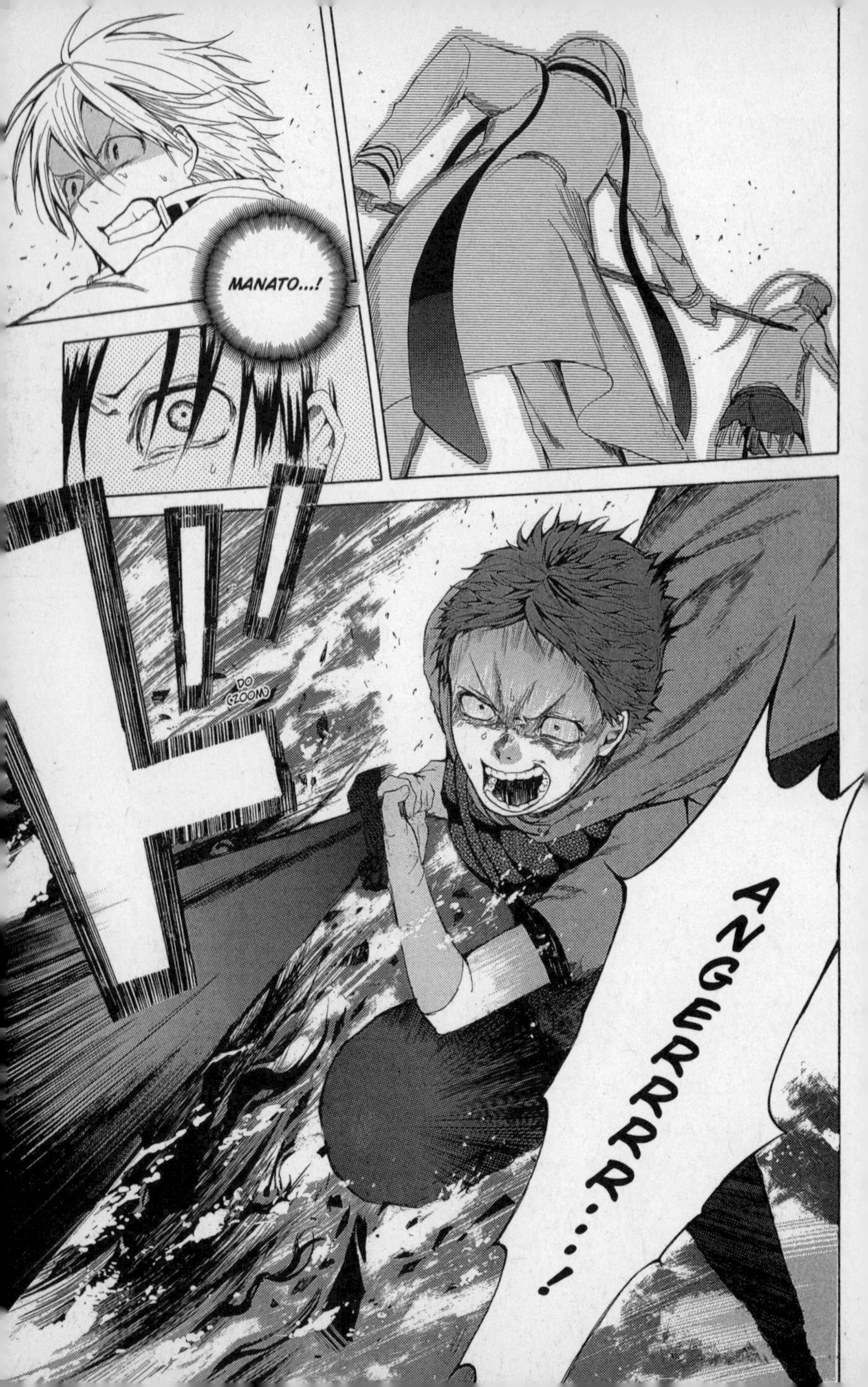
MANATO...!
DO (ZOOM)
ANGERRRR...!

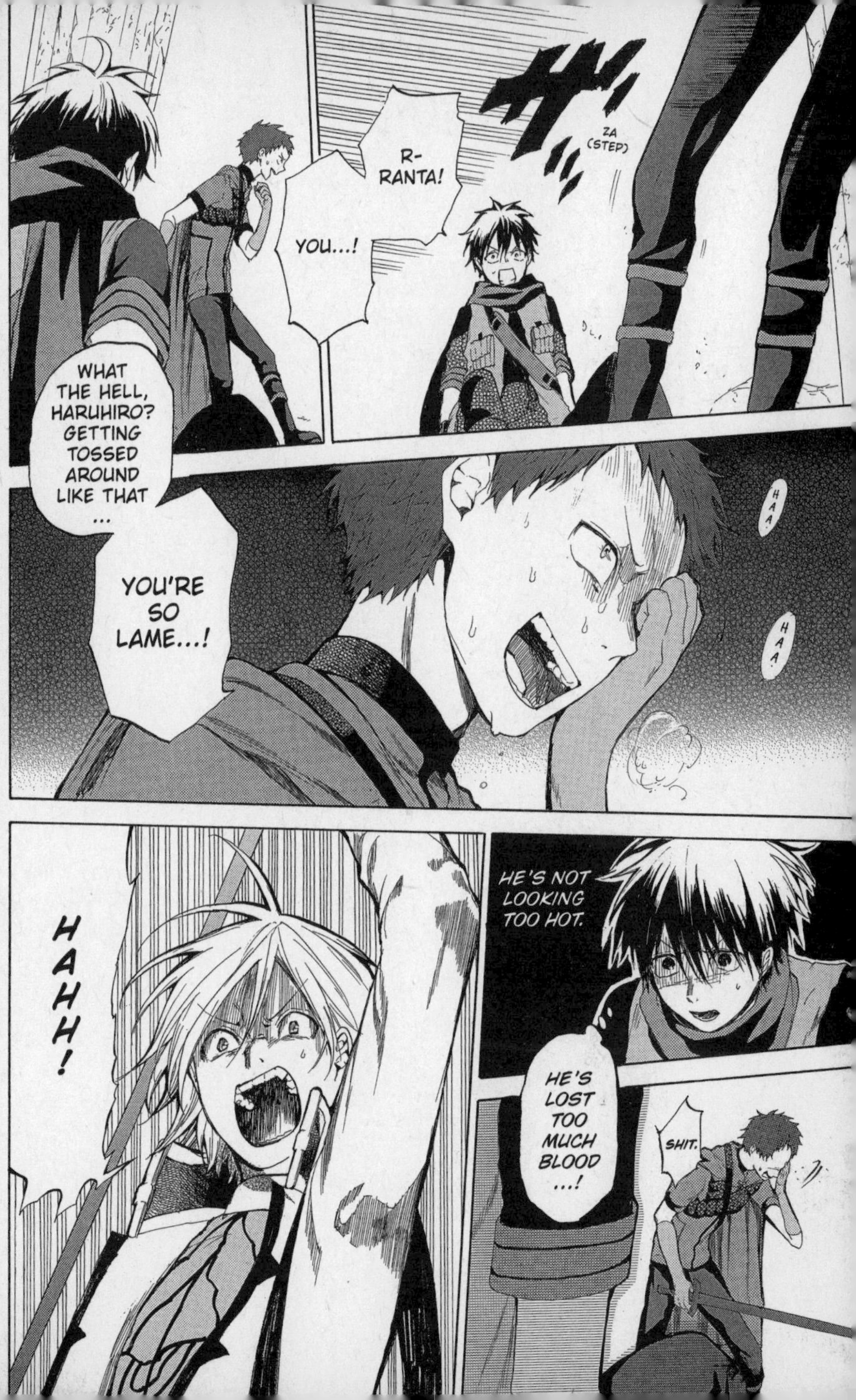
ZA (STEP)
R- RANTA!
YOU...!
WHAT THE HELL, HARUHIRO? GETTING TOSSED AROUND LIKE THAT ...
YOU'RE SO LAME...!
HAA
HAA
HE'S NOT LOOKING TOO HOT.
HE'S LOST TOO MUCH BLOOD ...!
SHIT.
HAHH!

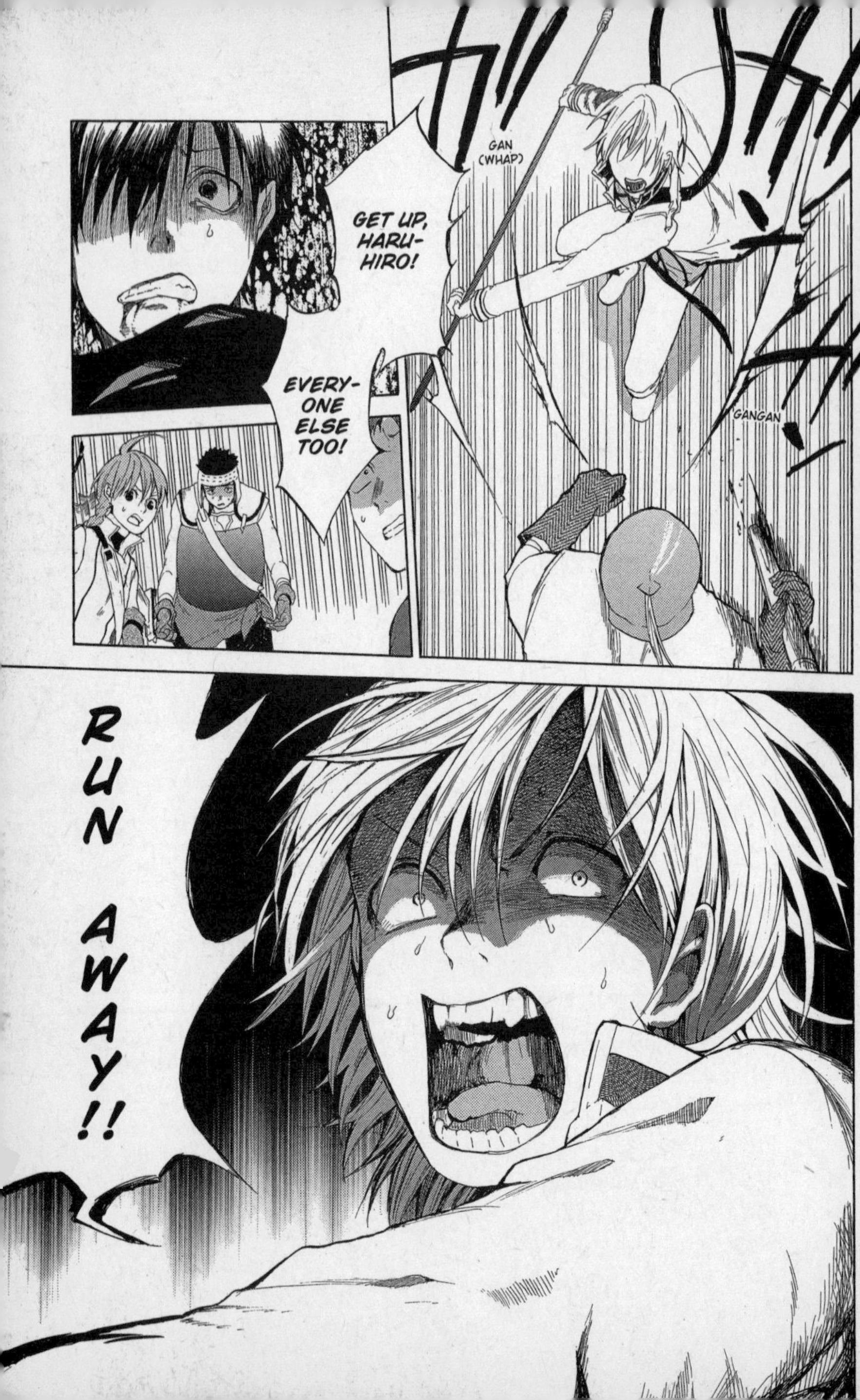
GAN (WHAP)
GET UP, HARUHIRO!
EVERYONE ELSE TOO!
GANGAN
RUN AWAY!!

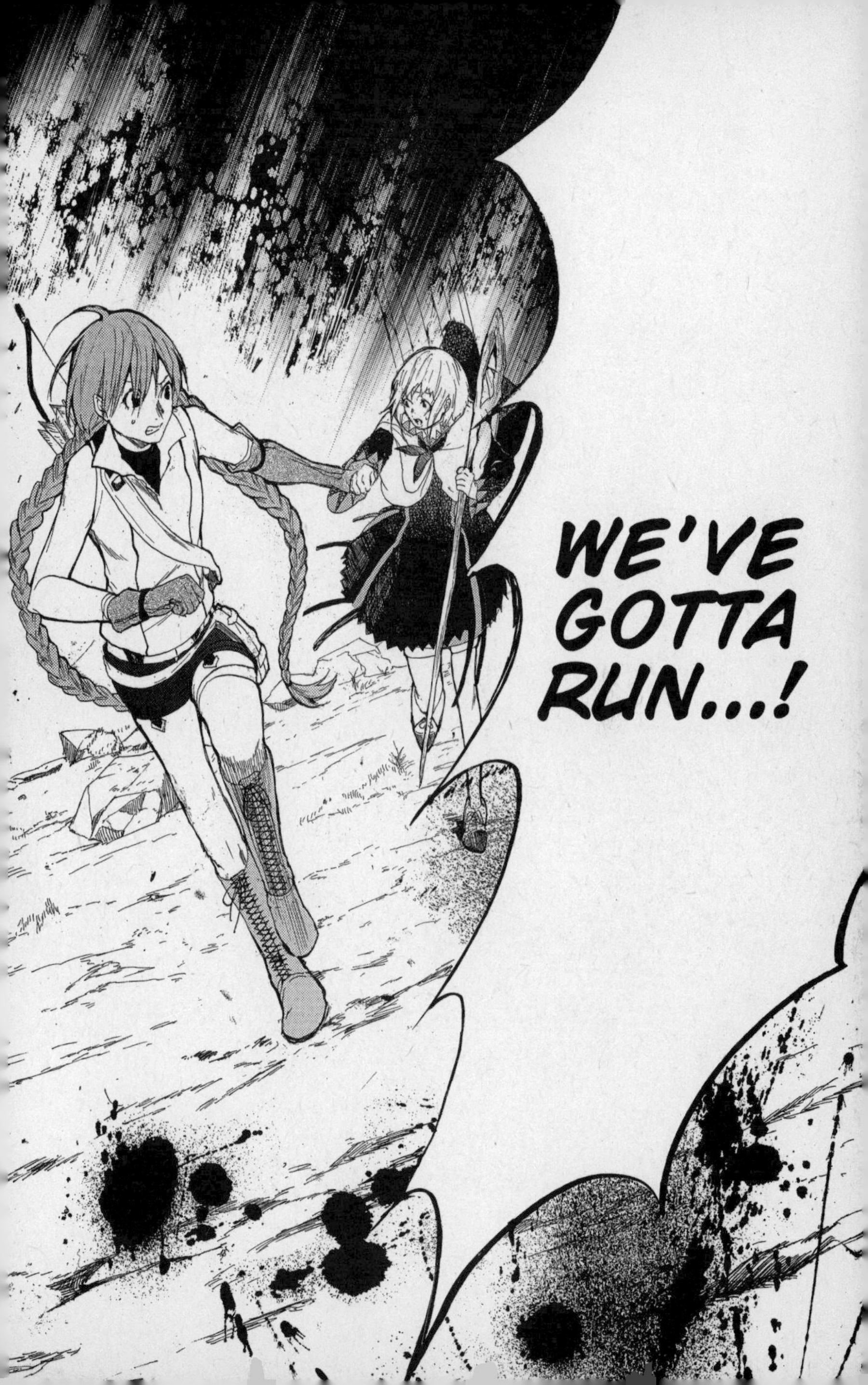
WE'VE GOTTA RUN...!

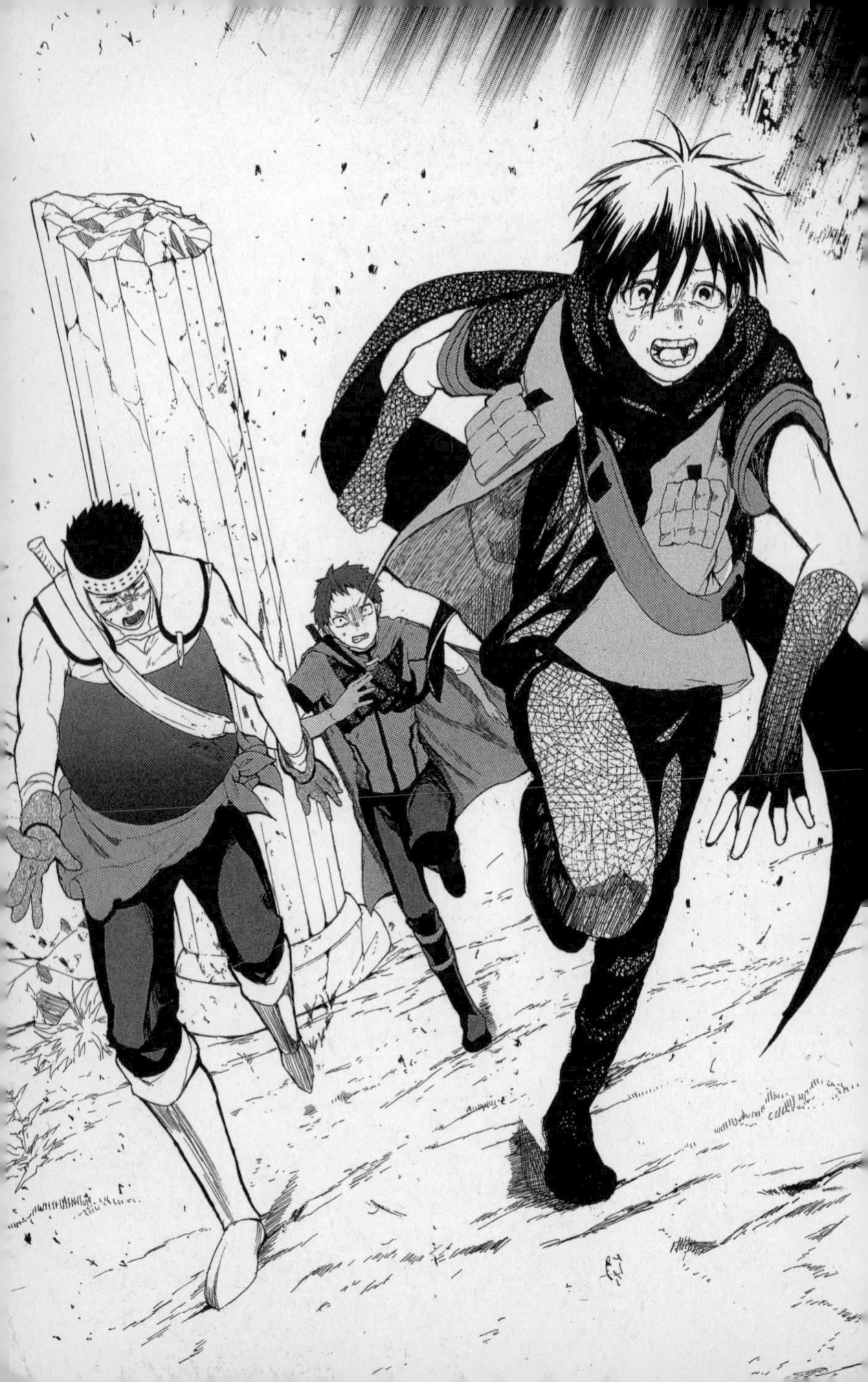

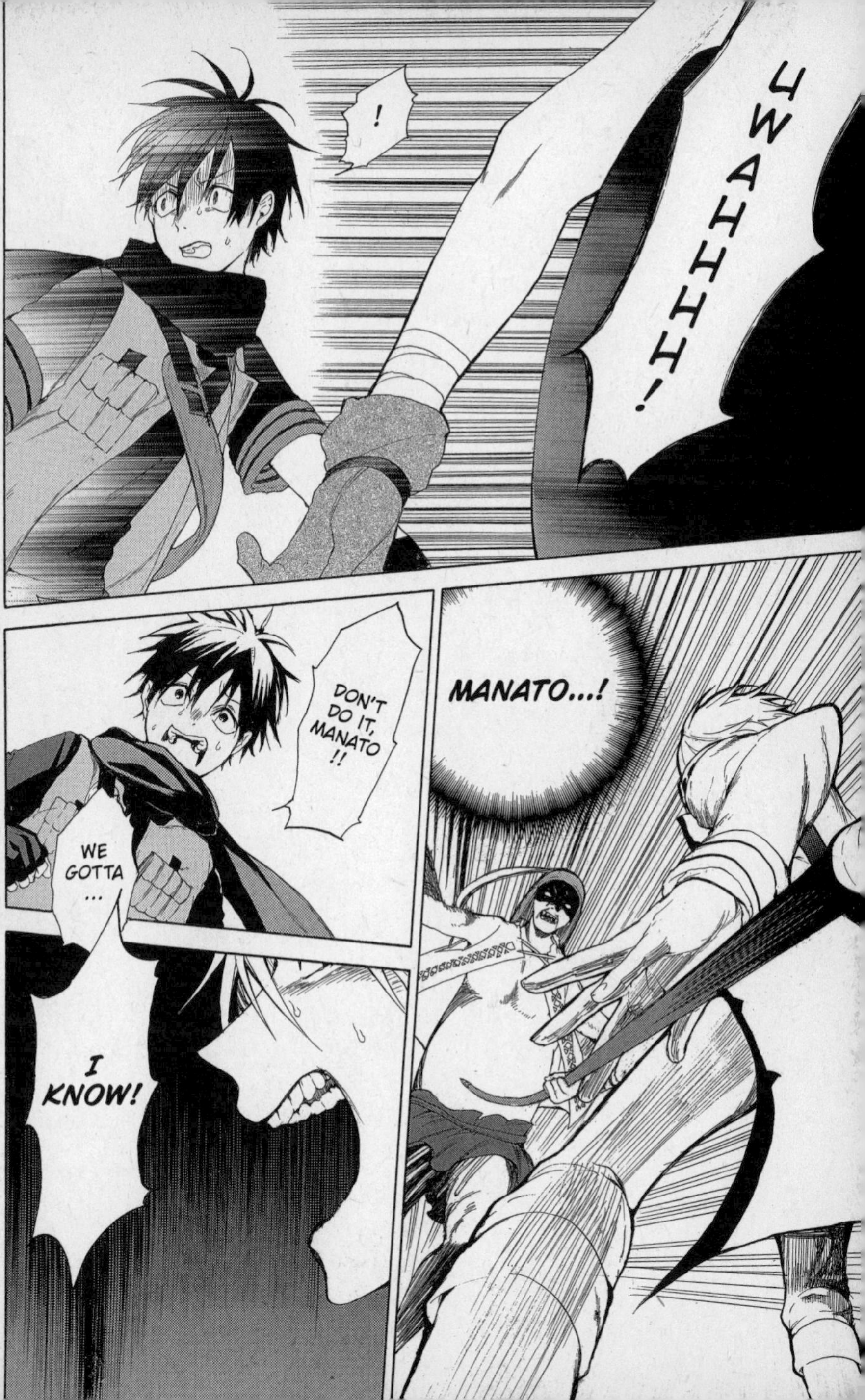
UWAHHHH!
!
MANATO...!
DON'T DO IT, MANATO!!
WE GOTTA ...
I KNOW!

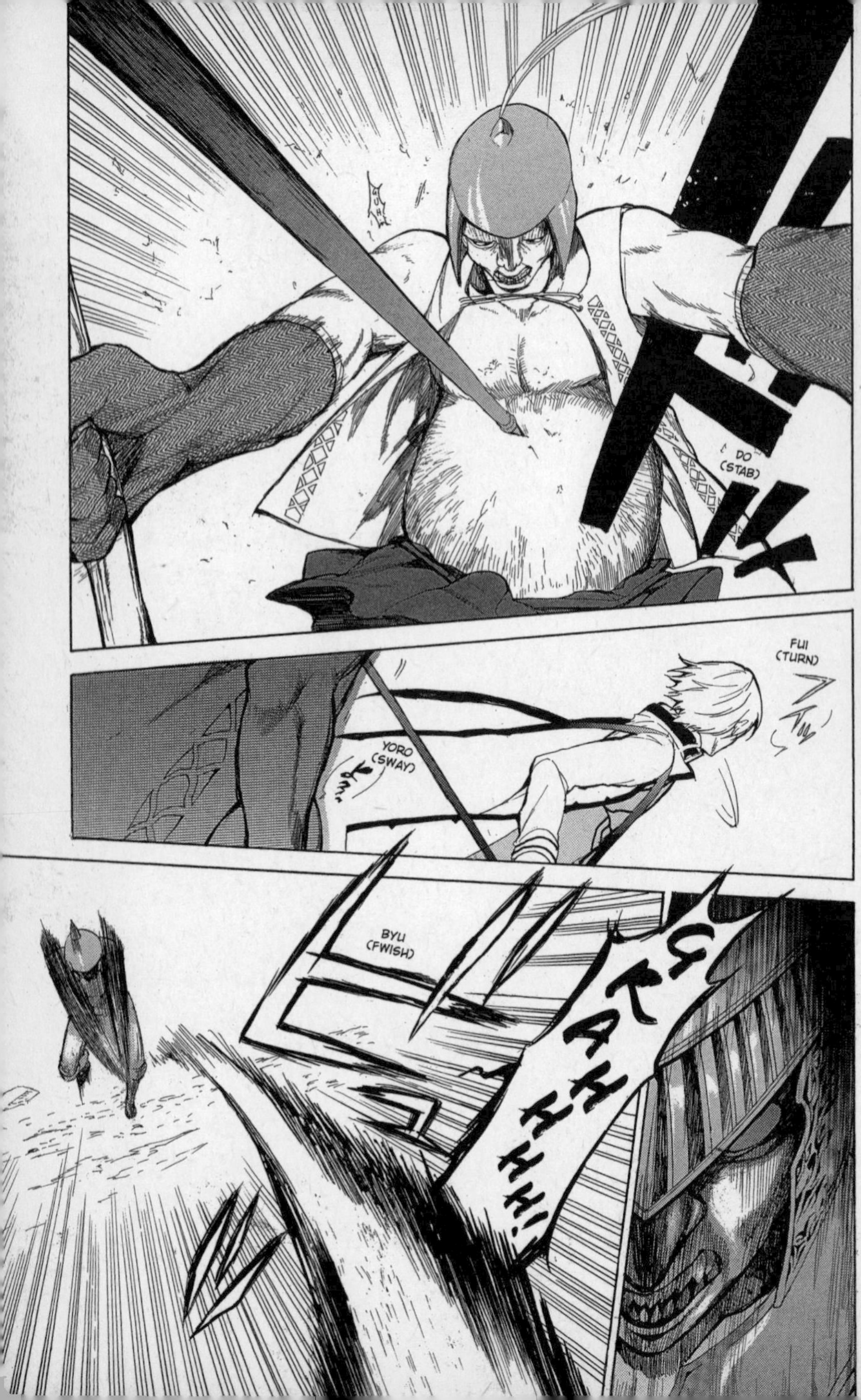
GUH
DO (STAB)
FUI (TURN)
YORO (SWAY)
BYU (FWISH)
GRAHHHHH!!

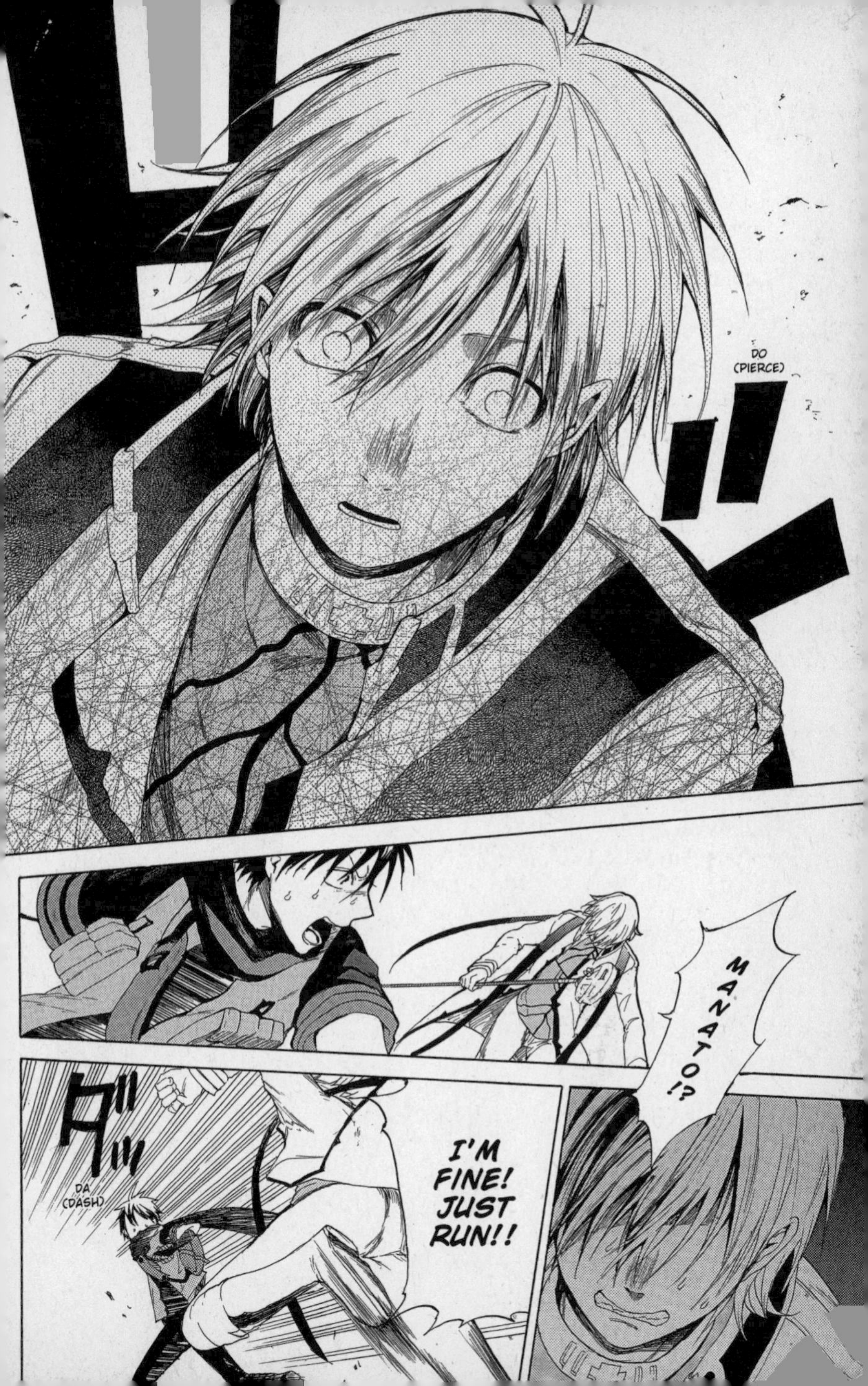
DO (PIERCE)
MANATO!?
I'M FINE! JUST RUN!!
DA (DASH)

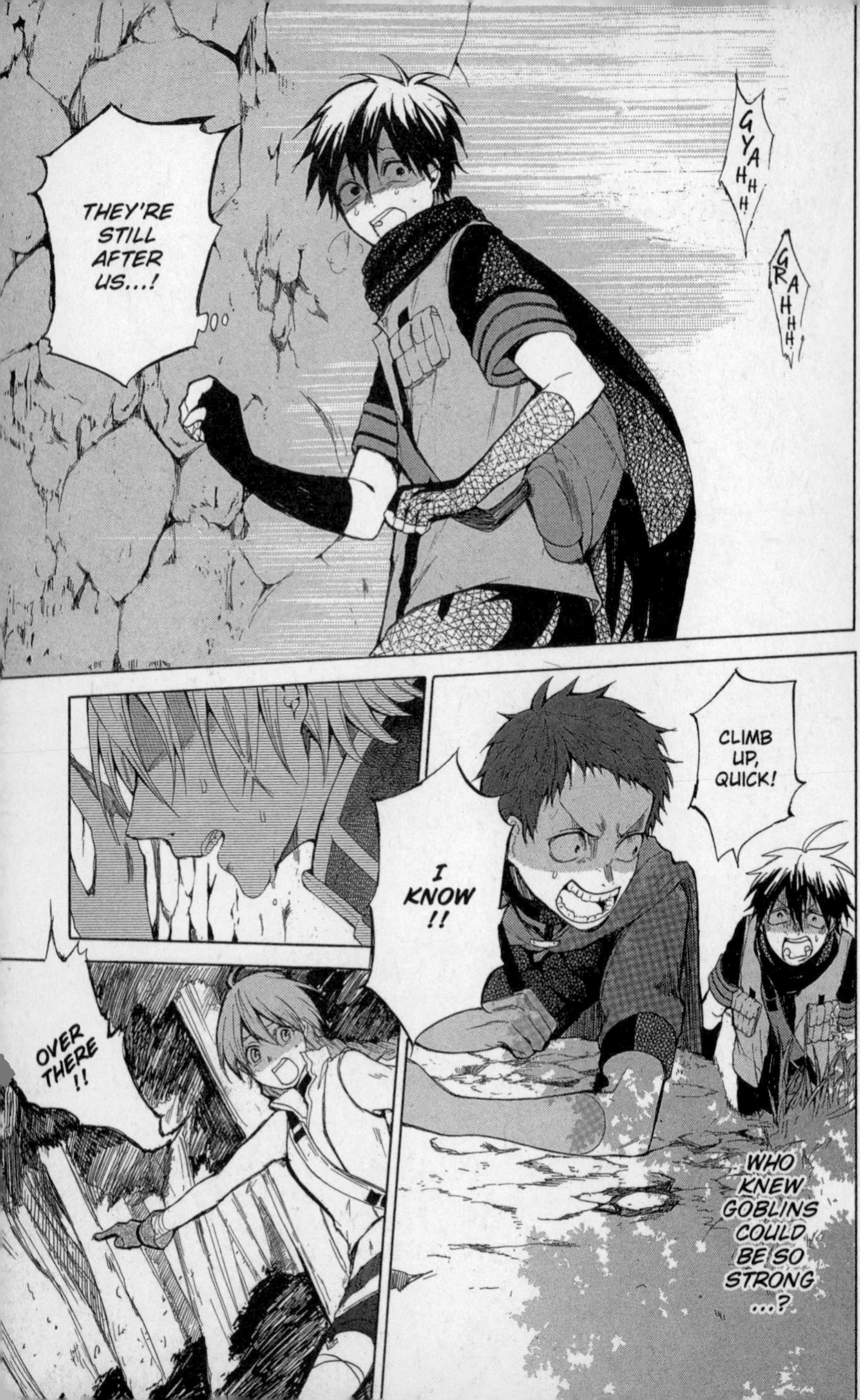
GYAHHH!
GRAHHH!
THEY'RE STILL AFTER US...!
CLIMB UP, QUICK!
I KNOW!!
OVER THERE!!
WHO KNEW GOBLINS COULD BE SO STRONG...?

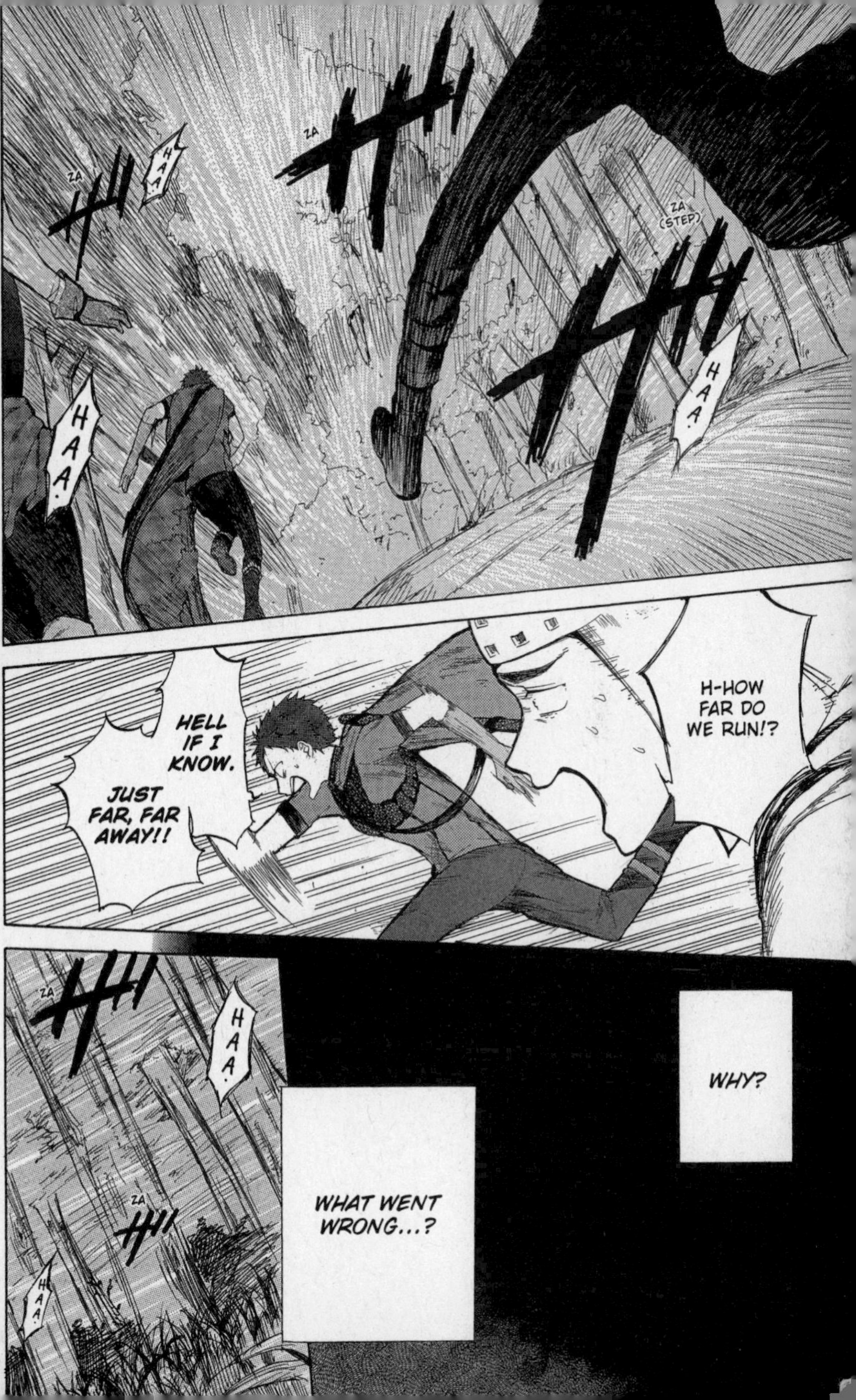
ZA (STEP)
HAA.
ZA
HAA.
ZA
HAA.
H-HOW FAR DO WE RUN!?
HELL IF I KNOW.
JUST FAR, FAR AWAY!!
WHY?
WHAT WENT WRONG...?
ZA
HAA.
ZA
HAA.

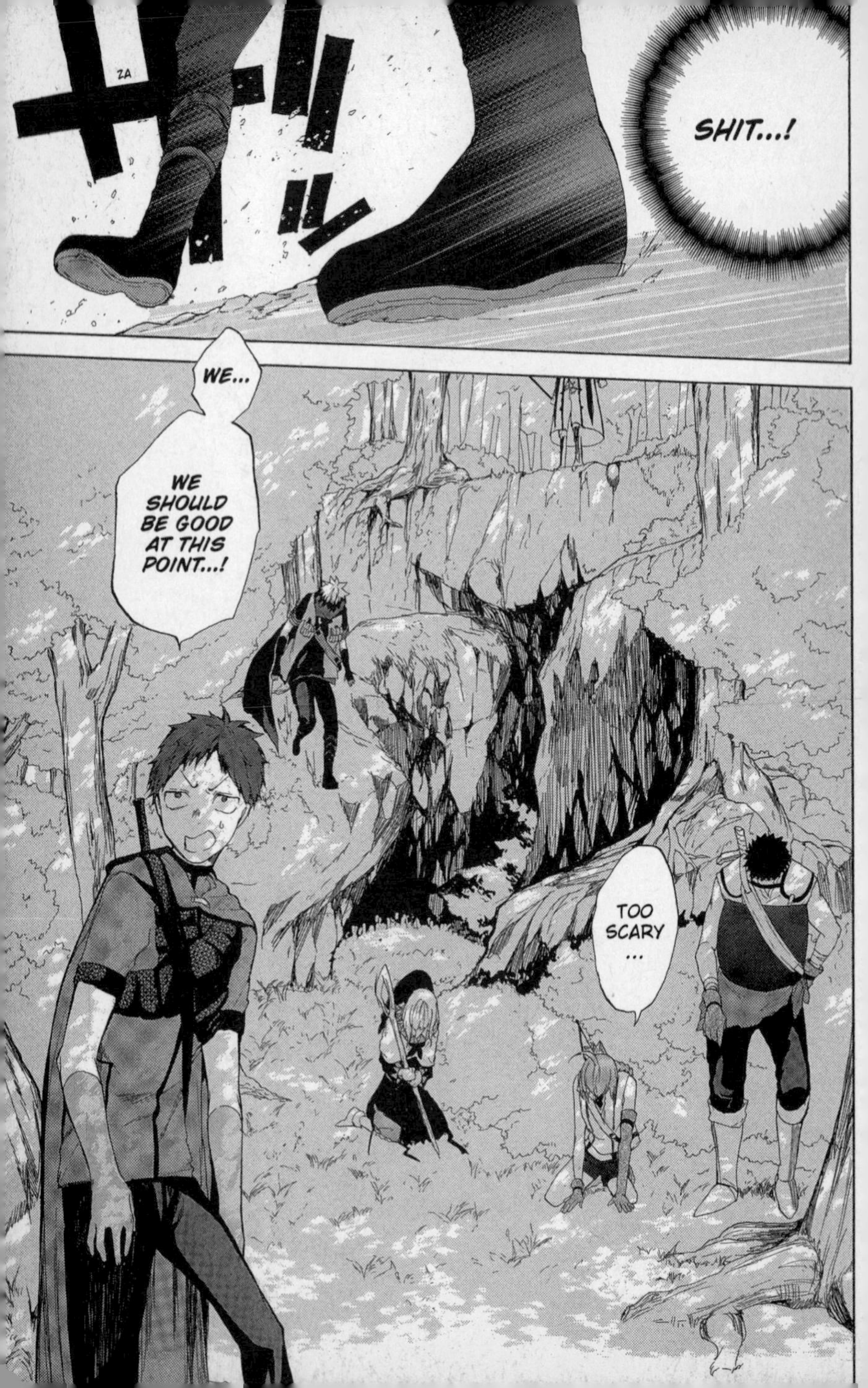
SHIT...!
ZA
WE...
WE SHOULD BE GOOD AT THIS POINT...!
TOO SCARY ...

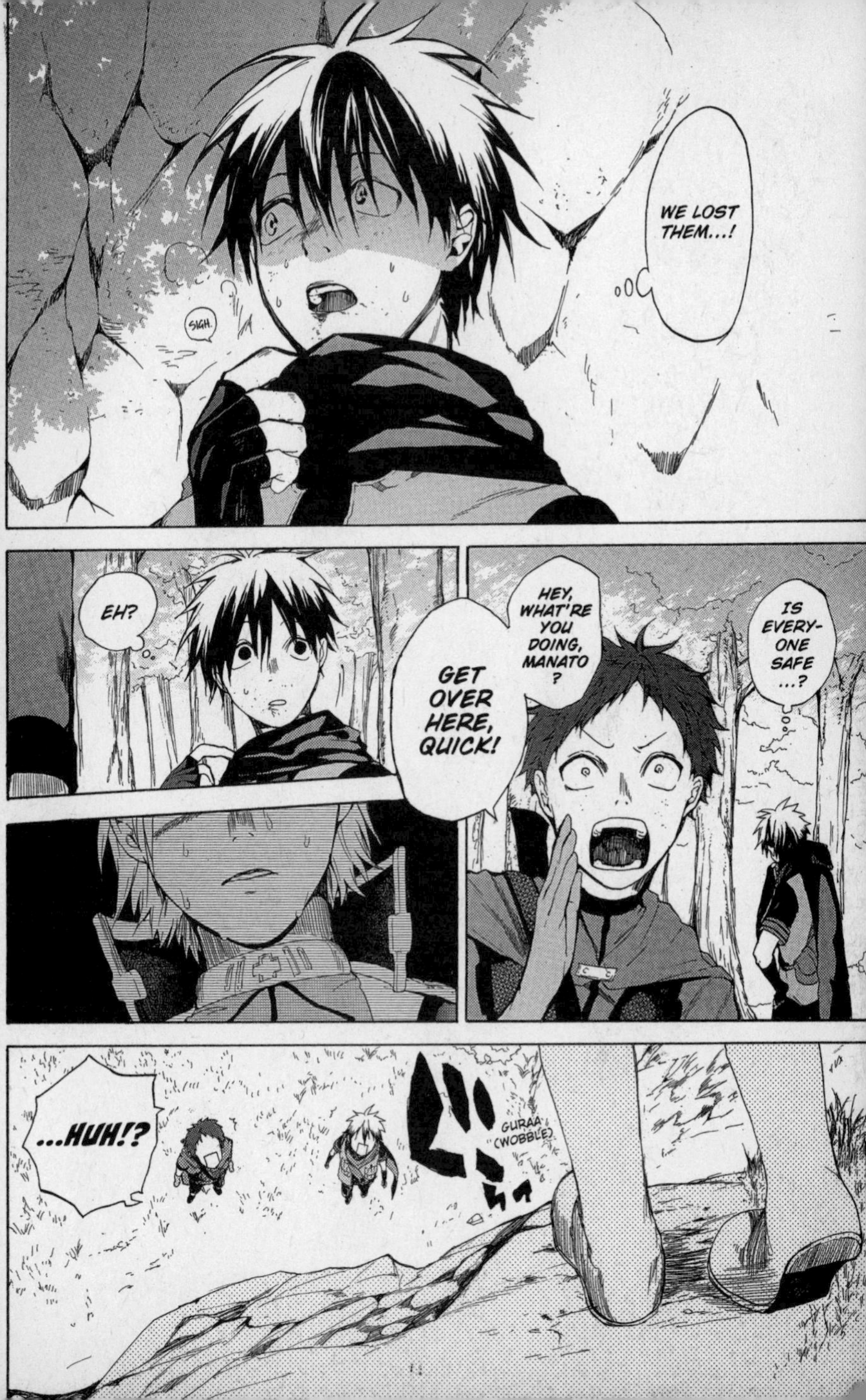
WE LOST THEM...!
SIGH.
IS EVERY-ONE SAFE...?
HEY, WHAT'RE YOU DOING, MANATO?
GET OVER HERE, QUICK!
EH?
GURAA (WOBBLE)
...HUH!?

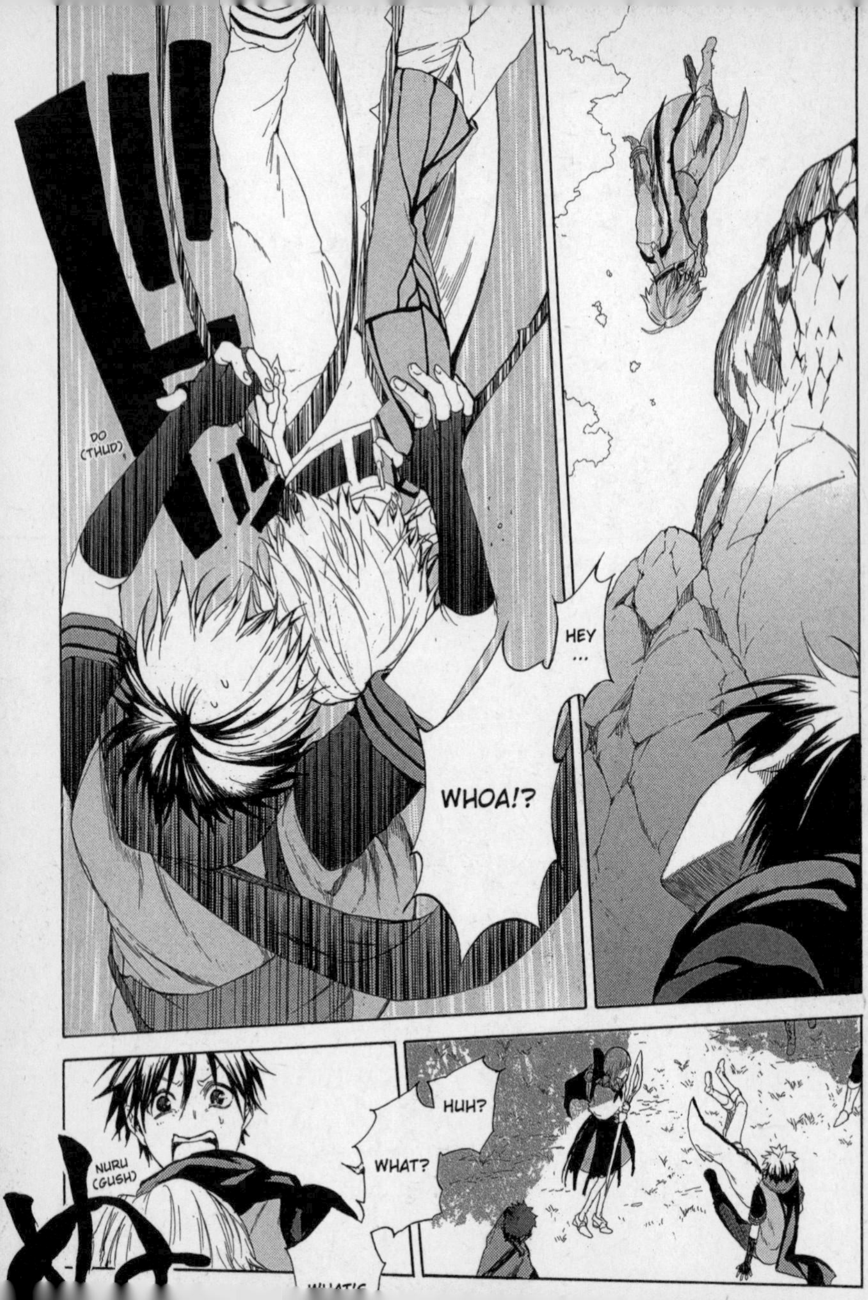
HEY ...
DO (THUD)
WHOA!?
HUH?
WHAT?
NURU (GUSH)

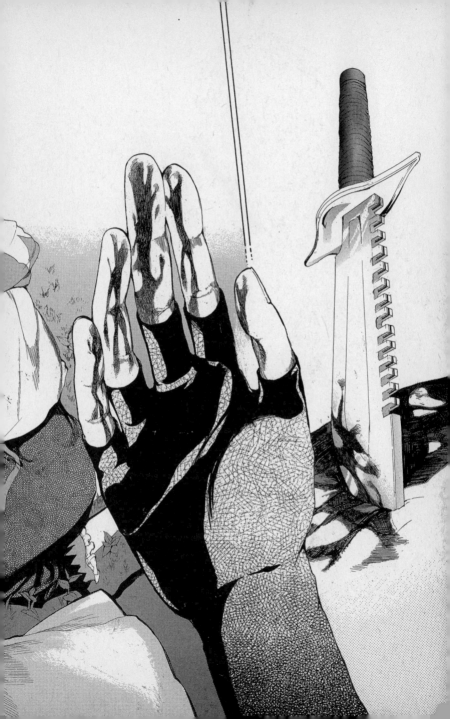

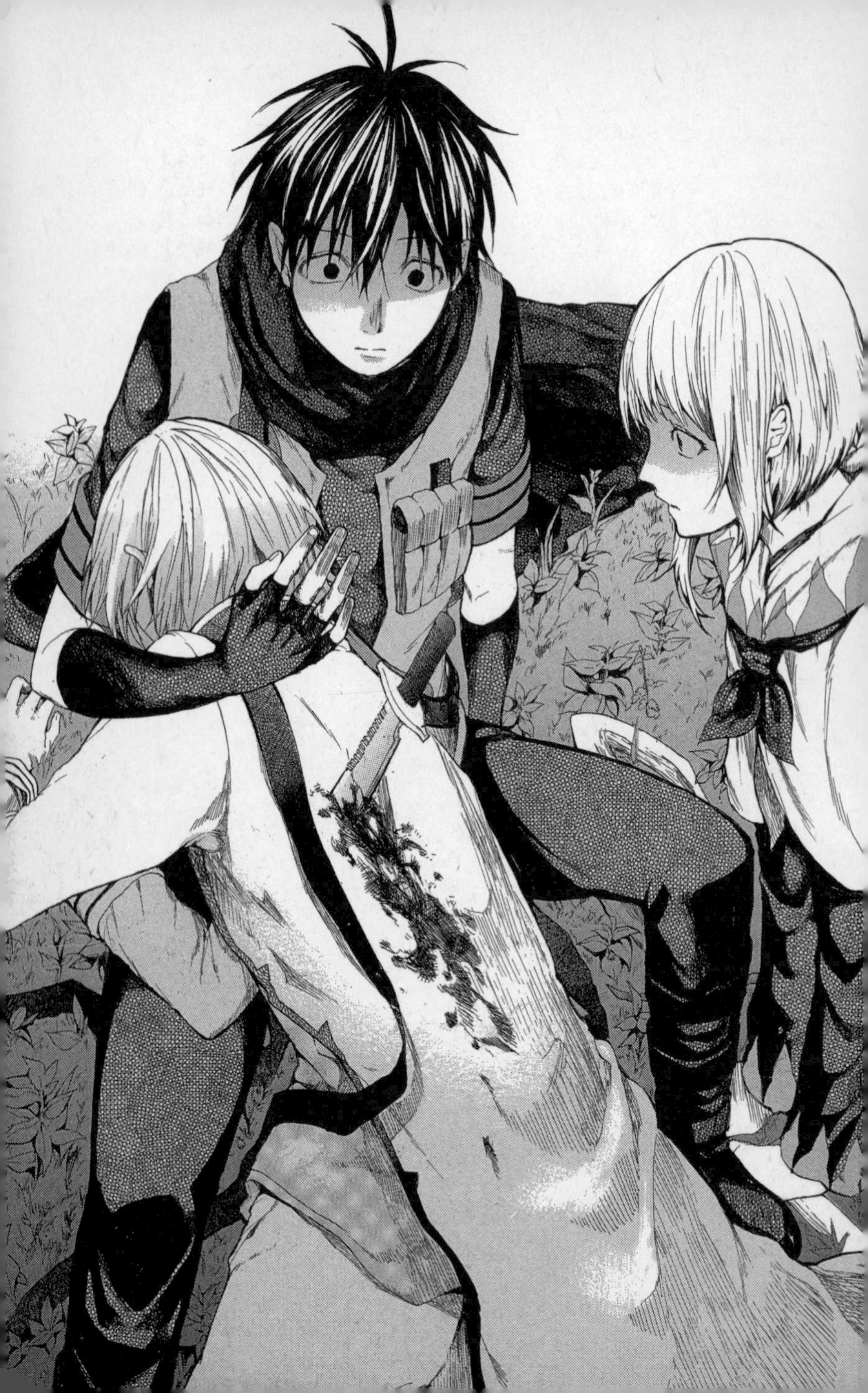

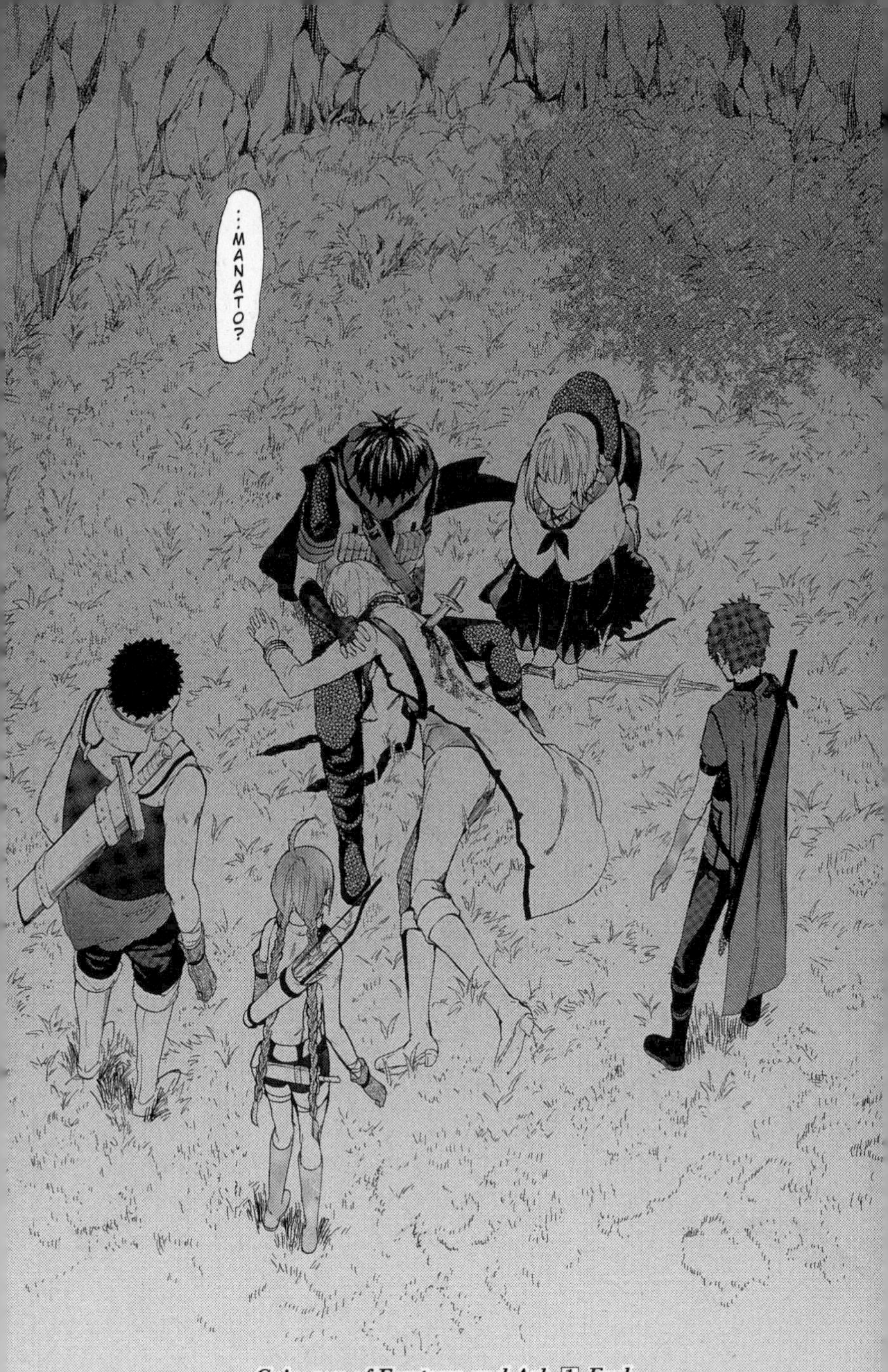
...MANATO?

Grimgar of Fantasy and Ash 1 *End*

HI THERE, I'M MUTSUMI OKUBASHI. AFTER READING THE ORIGINAL STORY AND DRILLING THE IMAGE INTO MY HEAD OF THE MUD-COVERED HARUHIRO AND FRIENDS GIVING ALL THEY HAD TO SURVIVE, I GOT TO DRAW THE MANGA VERSION. GIVEN THAT THIS IS MY FIRST TIME GETTING SERIALIZED, GETTING VOLUMES PUBLISHED, AND A WHOLE LOT OF OTHER "FIRSTS," I'M SO EXCITED TO KEEP DEPICTING THE GANG'S ADVENTURES! THANKS FOR YOUR SUPPORT!

-OKUBASHI

Thanks!

AO JYUMONJI

EIRI SHIRAI

MY SUPERVISOR, FATHER, MOTHER, AND FRIENDS

ASSISTANTS:
-OGAWA
-NOMOTO
-URYUU-SAN

OTHER SUPPORT FROM:
-MANABECCHI
-HISEKO
-SAKANISHI-CHAN

THANKS FOR READING, EVERYONE!

Grimgar of Fantasy and Ash

I

STORY BY
AO JYUMONJI

ILLUSTRATION BY
MUTSUMI OKUBASHI

ORIGINAL CHARACTER DESIGN BY
EIRI SHIRAI

TRANSLATION: CALEB COOK   LETTERING: PHIL CHRISTIE

HAI TO GENSOU NO GRIMGAR Volume 1
©2015 Ao Jyumonji/OVERLAP
© 2015 Mutsumi Okubashi / SQUARE ENIX CO., LTD.
First published in Japan in 2015 by SQUARE ENIX CO., LTD. English translation rights arranged with Square Enix Co., Ltd. and Yen Press, LLC through Tuttle-Mori Agency, Inc.

English translation © 2017 by SQUARE ENIX CO., LTD.

Yen Press
1290 Avenue of the Americas
New York, NY 10104

Visit us at yenpress.com
facebook.com/yenpress
twitter.com/yenpress
yenpress.tumblr.com
instagram.com/yenpress

First Yen Press Edition: June 2017

Yen Press is an imprint of Yen Press, LLC.
The Yen Press name and logo are trademarks of Yen Press, LLC.

The publisher is not responsible for websites (or their content) that are not owned by the publisher.

Library of Congress Control Number: 2017933038

ISBNs: 978-0-316-55856-3 (paperback)
978-0-316-55856-3 (ebook)

10 9 8 7 6 5 4 3 2 1

BVG

Printed in the United States of America